CALENDAR AND COMMUNITY

A History of the Jewish Calendar

Second Century BCE–*Tenth Century* CE

SACHA STERN

OXFORD
UNIVERSITY PRESS

OXFORD
UNIVERSITY PRESS

Great Clarendon Street, Oxford OX2 6DP

Oxford University Press is a department of the University of Oxford.
It furthers the University's objective of excellence in research, scholarship,
and education by publishing worldwide in

Oxford New York

Athens Auckland Bangkok Bogotá Buenos Aires Cape Town
Chennai Dar es Salaam Delhi Florence Hong Kong Istanbul Karachi
Kolkata Kuala Lumpur Madrid Melbourne Mexico City Mumbai Nairobi
Paris São Paulo Shanghai Singapore Taipei Tokyo Toronto Warsaw

with associated companies in Berlin Ibadan

Oxford is a registered trade mark of Oxford University Press
in the UK and in certain other countries

Published in the United States
by Oxford University Press Inc., New York

British Library Cataloguing in Publication Data

Data available

Library of Congress Cataloging-in-Publication Data

Data applied for

ISBN 0-19-827034-8

1 3 5 7 9 10 8 6 4 2

Typeset in Ehrhardt
by Atelier Fluxus Virus
http://www.fluxus-virus.com
Printed in Great Britain
on acid-free paper by
Biddles Ltd, Guildford and King's Lynn.

Preface

Calendar reckoning is not just a technical pursuit: it is fundamental to social interaction and communal life. The calendar provides an essential point of reference for interpersonal relations and time-bound communal activity. It determines how time is lived and utilized in the community, and sometimes shapes the community's distinctive identity. The calendar is also a way of conceptualizing the dimension of time, and hence, of 'making sense' of an important facet of human lived experience.

This study goes far beyond the technical question of 'how did the Jewish calendar work?' It is an attempt to identify the social and historical processes that led to the adoption or rejection of various calendar systems, and to show how calendars could affect relations between various Jewish and non-Jewish communities. The Jewish calendar—or more accurately, Jewish *calendars*—will thus be studied in the context of other, non-Jewish calendars, as well as in the wider context of Jewish (and non-Jewish) culture and communal life.

My contention, indeed, is that calendars are significant to social history. They are not just a technical tool for historians and epigraphists; nor are they merely an intellectual curiosity. Although, I would hope, this work will assist historians and epigraphists in their interpretation of early Jewish datings, this work should also be treated in its own right as a historical study of early Judaism and Jewish communities.

A few words about scope. By 'calendar' I do *not* mean, in this work, the list of annual festivals or of other annual occasions.[1] I shall restrict myself entirely to the calendar as *time measurement*: in particular, how months and years are reckoned. It is in this sense that the term 'calendar' will be used throughout this work.[2]

My period starts around the second century BCE, when the earliest sources on Jewish calendar reckoning first begin to appear. It ends in the

---

[1] This is why the early rabbinic work *Megillat Ta'anit* will barely be mentioned in this study.

[2] The question of how dates are recorded in ancient Jewish documents, inscriptions, and literary sources, is also outside the scope of this work. I shall also refrain from investigating how eras are reckoned; ancient eras are based on concepts of history and chronology which deserve a separate study in its own right.

early tenth century, with the calendrical schism between R. Saadya and Ben Meir. This dramatic event led to the finalization of the rabbinic calendar that is still in use today, and that has become standard throughout the Jewish world. Effectively, my period spans the entire history of the Jewish calendar, from its origins to its final form. Although it straddles Antiquity and the early Middle Ages, this period represents, as far as concerns the Jewish calendar, a coherent and unbroken historical continuum.

My main theme, or thesis, is that the Jewish calendar gradually evolved in this period from considerable diversity to normative unity. From the second century BCE to the first century CE, solar and lunar calendars are both attested in the sources; whereas from the first century CE the Jewish calendar becomes exclusively lunar. From this point until at least the sixth century CE the lunar calendar was reckoned by different communities in a wide variety of forms. But by the tenth century, at the end of our period, a *single* lunar calendar had taken shape, that of rabbinic Judaism. This rabbinic calendar may still have been challenged by the Karaites;[3] but in the course of time, it was to become universal and standard throughout world Jewry.

The evolution of the Jewish calendar reflects, in a sense, a wider historical pattern. To some extent, it epitomizes the gradual development of solidarity and *communitas* among the Jewish communities of late Antiquity and the early Middle Ages, and hence, the development of an increasingly united culture and religion.

My chapter division is thematic but also chronological. Ch. 1, 'Solar and Lunar Calendars', focuses on the period from the second century BCE to the end of the Roman Empire. I shall attempt to explain how and why the coexistence of solar and lunar calendars in the early part of this period gave way, from the first century CE onwards, to the predominance of the lunar calendar. Attention will be given to the fact that non-Jewish calendars, in the same period, appear to have evolved in the opposite direction. In the context of the Graeco-Roman world, I shall conclude, the lunar calendar became a distinctive marker of Jewish communal identity.

Ch. 2, 'The Intercalation' (i.e. the addition of a thirteeenth lunar month in the year), and Ch. 3, 'The New Moon', will deal with specific aspects of the Jewish lunar calendars that prevailed in the first century

---

[3] As well as by a number of marginal, sectarian groups loosely belonging to the Karaite movement: see al-Qirqisani, *The Book of Lights and Watch-Towers*, 1. 15–17 (Nemoy 1930: 388–90; Chiesa and Lockwood 1084: 149–51); al-Biruni (1879) 68.

CE and beyond. In these chapters I shall restrict myself to 'non-rabbinic' sources, which include Jewish literature and inscriptions, as well
as Classical and early Christian sources. Rabbinic sources will be left to
Chs. 4–5, because of their abundance; for this reason alone, the rabbinic
calendar deserves to be treated as a separate category. It is also appropriate to leave rabbinic sources to later chapters, because they extend
till the end of the period under study, whereas non-rabbinic sources do
not take us to much later than the sixth century. Non-rabbinic calendars
from the earlier period will also provide a useful context against which
the peculiarities of the rabbinic calendar will be better understood.

Evidence pertaining to non-rabbinic lunar calendars (Chs. 2–3), especially from the first century CE onwards, is extremely sporadic.
Nevertheless, some reliable inferences can be made. The conclusion that
will emerge from Chs. 2–3 is that calendars were reckoned very differently from one Jewish community to the next, so that festivals could
often be observed on totally different dates. Calendrical diversity existed not only in distant Diaspora communities, but also within Palestine
itself, such as in the Jewish community of Zoar. The historical implications of this finding are quite considerable. It suggests that as late as
the sixth century rabbinic authority in calendrical matters was yet to be
established outside the main rabbinic communities.

Ch. 4, 'The Rabbinic Calendar: Development and History', will
trace the development of the rabbinic calendar—so far as it can be
established—from Mishnaic origins to the fixed calendar of the late
Geonic period that is still in use today.

Chapter 5, 'Calendar and Community: The Emergence of the Normative Jewish Calendar', is the most interpretative of this study. It will
attempt to explain *why* the rabbinic calendar evolved the way it did.
I shall argue that the emergence of a standard, fixed calendar was not
the result of persecution or political crisis in the fourth century, as is
commonly believed, but rather of the complex relationship between the
Palestinian and Babylonian rabbinic communities in the Talmudic and
Geonic periods. It is in this chapter that the main thesis of my study
will receive its most explicit formulation.

I have striven in this work to be as comprehensive as I could be. Some
omissions, however, have been consciously and deliberately made. Nothing will be said, for instance, about the Samaritan calendar, for the good

reason that the earliest evidence available on Samaritan calendar reckoning belongs to the twelfth century or later.[4]

Another omission I have made is the Karaites, whose distinctive calendar might have deserved a whole chapter on its own. My decision not to include such a chapter in this book is largely due, again, to the nature of the evidence: there are few sources or documents on the Karaite calendar (or calendars) that date from before the tenth century. Although it cannot be doubted that the development of a standard rabbinic calendar system in the ninth century was in direct defiance of Karaite critique and opposition, and that the Karaite calendar must have been relevant, already in that period, to the development of the rabbinic calendar, little can be said about the calendars of the Karaites before the tenth to twelfth centuries, when calendar issues become dominant in Karaite–Rabbanite polemic.[5] I have taken the view, therefore, that a systematic study of the Karaite calendar would belong more appropriately to a book on Jewish calendars in these *later* centuries, and that it lies, therefore, outside my present scope. Nevertheless, a number of references will be made to Karaite calendars in various parts of my work, which should provide the reader with the essentials on this important topic.[6]

In his preface to *The Calendars of Ancient Egypt*, Richard Parker wrote: 'Calendars and chronology are not in themselves difficult subjects, but they are frequently made so by the assumption of their devotees that everyone understands always what they are talking about (Parker 1950: v).' I have tried hard to make this work accessible, and not to overburden it with technical detail. Detailed analyses have been laid out in the main text in smaller print. It should be possible for the reader to skip these passages if s/he so wishes.

Virtually all that has been published so far on the history of the rabbinic calendar is in Hebrew, and hence inaccessible to an English readership; many of these works, besides, are outdated and/or of limited academic value.[7] I have written this book with an English readership in

---

[4] See Robertson (1950), Akavia (1950), Powels (1977 and 1989). The only reference I have found belonging to our period is a statement by Socrates (5th c. CE) that the Samaritans always observe Passover after the spring equinox (*Hist. Eccl.* 5. 22; also in Sozomen, *Hist. Eccl.* 7. 18). See also *T. Pesaḥim* 1: 14 (p. 156).

[5] Karaite-Rabbanite calendrical polemics of the 10th–12th cc. have already been studied in some detail by Ankori (1959), an excellent study to which the reader will be frequently referred.

[6] See references in index.

[7] The most comprehensive works previously published on the history of the rabbinic calendar are Jaffe (1931) and Sar-Shalom (1984, esp. 17–30), both in Hebrew.

mind; wherever possible, reference has been made to primary and secondary sources in English translation.

Because of the complexity and scope of this study, the help of many teachers and colleagues has proved to be essential. Mention should be made of Jean Ajdler, Roger Bagnall, Sebastian Brock, Emma Dench, Isaiah Gafni, Mark Geller, Uwe Glessmer, Bernard Goldstein, Leofranc Holford-Strevens, Tuvia Kaatz, Michael Knibb, Tzvi Langermann, Tim Lim, Yannis Meimaris, Joseph Naveh, Judith Olszowy-Schlanger, Konstantinos Politis, Bezalel Porten, Joyce Reynolds, Brad Schaefer, Brent Shaw, Joseph Sievers, Emmanuel Silver, Colette Sirat, Shay Walter, Klaas Worp, and the library staff at the London School of Jewish Studies (I apologize for any omissions). Bernard Yallop checked all the astronomical data in the entire book. I am particularly grateful to Martin Goodman, who read parts of my work and invited me to deliver a number of papers on the calendar at his Oxford seminar. As ever, he has provided continuous encouragement throughout my work. I am also very grateful to Yaaqov Loewinger, an expert on the Jewish calendar, who also read some portions and has considerably sharpened my understanding of the calendar's astronomical and mathematical foundations. Finally, I am grateful to my wife Evadne, without whose support this work would have been inconceivable.

Readers may wonder why this book on the calendar, published in the year 2001, makes no reference to the so-called 'Millennium'. The answer is, of course, that this has nothing to do with the Jewish calendar. However, I have no doubt that the remarkable impact the 'Millennium' has had in the last few years on the Western world, not only in the religious sphere but also in cultural, social, and even political and economic terms, has focused my attention on the social and historical importance of time reckoning, calendar, and chronology. Somehow, it may have also influenced my understanding of Jewish calendar reckoning in Antiquity and the early medieval period.

S.S.

Contents

Abbreviations

AE	*L'Année épigraphique*
b.	ben/bar
B.	*Talmud Bavli* (Babylonian Talmud)
CIG	*Corpus Inscriptionum Graecarum*
CIL	*Corpus Inscriptionum Latinarum*
CIJ	J.-B. Frey, *Corpus Inscriptionum Judaicarum*, 2 vols. (Rome, 1938 and 1952)
CPJ	V. A. Tcherikover, A. Fuks, and M. Stern. *Corpus Papyrorum Judaicarum*, 3 vols. (Jerusalem and Cambridge, Mass., 1957–64).
DJD	Discoveries in the Judaean Desert, series ed. D. Barthélemy *et al.* (Oxford, 1956–)
HUCA	*Hebrew Union College Annual*
IEJ	*Israel Exploration Journal*
IGR	*Inscriptiones Graecae ad Res Romanas Pertinentes*, ed. R. Cagnat *et al.*
JHA	*Journal for the History of Astronomy*
JJS	*Journal of Jewish Studies*
JQR	*Jewish Quarterly Review*
JRS	*Journal of Roman Studies*
JSJ	*Journal for the Study of Judaism in the Persian, Hellenistic and Roman Period*
M.	*Mishnah*
n.v.	*non vidi*
PG	J.-P. Migne, *Patrum Graecorum Cursus Completus*
PL	J.-P. Migne, *Patrum Latinorum Cursus Completus*
QJRAS	*Quarterly Journal of the Royal Astronomical Society*
R.	Rabbi
REJ	*Revue des études juives*
RH	*Rosh ha-Shanah*
RQ	*Revue de Qumran*
SCI	*Scripta Classica Israelica*
SEG	*Supplementum Epigraphicum Graecum*

T.	*Tosefta*: followed by name of tractate, chapter, paragraph, and page number in *Tosefta*, ed. M. S. Zuckermandel (Pasewalk, 1880)
VT	*Vetus Testamentum*
Y.	*Talmud Yerushalmi* (Palestinian Talmud)
ZPE	*Zeitschrift für Papyrologie und Epigraphik*

I

Solar and lunar calendars

Solar and lunar calendars are both attested in early Jewish literature; but from the first century CE until this very day, the lunar calendar appears to have completely prevailed. The first section of this chapter will trace this apparent transition to an exclusively lunar calendar.

In the second section, an attempt will be made to explain why the Jews abandoned solar calendars around the first century CE. For this purpose, I shall assess the wider historical context in which this development occurred. Jewish calendar reckoning was sometimes influenced by other calendar systems, but sometimes strove to remain distinct. In the Roman period, I shall argue, the lunar calendar became to the Jews a marker of their distinctive communal identity.

The Jewish (and other similar) lunar calendars are usually referred to as 'lunisolar', because they keep up with the annual solar year by adding a 13th lunar month every two or three years; in this respect, these calendars comprise a solar element, which distinguishes them from purely lunar calendars such as the Muslim calendar. However, in this chapter and throughout this book I shall refer to the Jewish calendars as 'lunar', because their solar component is marginal by comparison with their mainly lunar nature. Truly lunisolar calendars, where the lunar and solar elements are more or less on a par, can only be found in Qumran and related sources (see below, sections 1.1.3–6, where the term 'lunisolar' is frequently used). Moreover, in the context of ancient Jewish calendars the term 'lunisolar' can often be a misnomer, because the addition of a 13th month is not always regulated by the cycle of the sun. As we shall see in Ch. 2, intercalation of a 13th month in the ancient Jewish lunar calendar was not regulated by the solar year (e.g. by the equinox) but instead by seasonal/agricultural criteria such as ʾaviv, and thus was only *indirectly* related to the solar year. It should also be noted, finally, that many ancient sources (e.g. rabbinic sources, as will be cited at the end of this chapter) consider the Jewish calendar to be based on the moon and hence only 'lunar'. For all these reasons, the term 'lunar' will be generally preferred.

1.1 FROM BIBLICAL ORIGINS TO THE END OF THE ROMAN PERIOD: THE RISE OF THE LUNAR CALENDAR

1.1.1 Biblical sources

Sources from before the beginning of our period are remarkably uninformative about the calendar. Although the dates of annual festivals and of historical events are frequently given in biblical sources, the Bible has no apparent interest in explaining how these dates were reckoned. We do not even know whether the calendar was based on solar years, on lunar months, or (in some way) on both. Gen. 1: 14 suggests that both the sun and the moon are to be used for reckoning festivals, days and years. Ps. 104: 19 is more ambiguous, and may imply that only the moon is used. These verses, however, are too brief and too vague to be treated as conclusive. Consequently, the calendar of Israel in the pre-exilic period remains, among scholars, an extremely controversial issue.

Various inferences have been made from the dates of the Flood, which according to the Masoretic, Samaritan, and most other texts of Gen. 7–8 began on the 17th of the second month and ended on the 27th of the same month of the next year, thus lasting one year and 10 days. As pointed out already in rabbinic sources, these 10 days may represent the difference between the solar and the lunar year.[1] This would suggest that the biblical calendar year was *lunar*, but that the Flood lasted the equivalent of one solar year.[2]

However, the reverse may be argued with regard to Num. 10: 11, according to which the Israelites left Sinai on the 20th of the 2nd month, having arrived there (according to Exod. 19: 1) in the previous year on the 1st of the third month. This means that they resided at Sinai for one year *less* approximately 10 days.[3] This would suggest that the biblical calendar year was *solar*, but that on this occasion the Israelites resided at Sinai for the equivalent of one lunar year.

That the calendar was lunar may be implicit in Jeroboam's calendrical reform, whereby Tabernacles were to be celebrated in the eighth month rather than on the seventh (1 Kgs. 12: 32–3). Reference to 'the *month* which he had devised of his own heart' (ibid., my emphasis) suggests perhaps that his reform had

---

[1] *Genesis* Rabbah 33: 7 (ed. Theodor–Albeck 313).

[2] See, with some reservations, Jaubert (1957*a*) 35 n.; Lim (1993) 125; Hendel (1995).

[3] See *Seder ʿOlam* 8; *Mekhilta de-R. Yishmael, Ba-Ḥodesh* 1 (ed. Horowitz–Rabin 206).

consisted in the insertion of an additional intercalated month, and hence, that
the calendar (before and after the reform) was lunar. Other interpretations of
Jeroboam's reform, however, are equally possible.[4]

It has long been argued that the Hebrew term for month, *hodesh*,
is itself an indication that the calendar was been lunar, since the notion of 'newness' implicit in the root *HDSh* can only refer to the new
moon. Likewise, the other Hebrew word for month, *yerah*, is derived
from *yareah*, which denotes the moon itself.[5]

This argument, however, is flawed, because even in a solar calendar
(such as the modern Gregorian calendar) the concept of the month, i.e.
a time unit of approximately 30 days, does not make sense unless we
posit that it must have originated, at some point, from the monthly cycle
of the moon. It is to be expected, therefore, that the term referring to
'month' would be related, in any language or in any calendrical context,
to the moon and to its cycle; cf. the 20-day month in Mesoamerican
calendars (Edmonson 1988: e.g. 221, 246). However, this has no bearing
on the calendar that is *currently* in use, nor does it imply that the month
employed in this calendar corresponds exactly, as it might have been
originally, with the lunar month. Thus the biblical usage of *hodesh* and
yerah does not preclude the existence of a purely solar calendar.

More detailed analysis of the biblical text and particularly of dates in
the Bible led Jaubert to formulate the hypothesis that the calendar of the
Bible was solar, and that it corresponded to the calendar of the book of
Jubilees (on which see below), with which it was in direct historical continuity.[6] Although this hypothesis has been endorsed by a large number
of scholars, others have convincingly refuted Jaubert's argument.[7]

1.1.2   The Hellenistic and Hasmonaean periods

It is only in the Hellenistic and Hasmonaean periods that Jewish sources
begin to set out explicitly how the calendar is reckoned. Some of these

---

[4] See e.g. Talmon (1986) 118–23.

[5] Abraham Ibn Ezra (12th c.), commentary on Lev. 25: 9; Ibn Ezra (1874) 8a and
(1839) 162–3. The argument has been recently reiterated by Schiffman (1994) 305,
and Beckwith (1996) 99 and 102.

[6] See especially Jaubert (1957*a*); also ead. (1953) and (1957*b*). She acknowledges,
however, that alongside the solar calendar of *Jubilees* that was used for datings and
for the dates of festivals, the new moons were also celebrated in the biblical period,
and would have followed a lunar reckoning (Jaubert 1957*a*: 156–7 and 35 n.).

[7] For refutations of Jaubert's hypothesis, see Baumgarten (1962); Wacholder and
Wacholder (1995); Beckwith (1996) 101–4.

sources describe the calendar in much detail: in particular, the books of *Enoch*, *Jubilees*, and calendrical texts from Qumran. These show a distinctive preference for solar calendars.

However, it should not be inferred from these sources that the calendar observed in practice by the Jews was solar. The polemical tone of *Jubilees* suggests, quite on the contrary, that many Jews did not follow its solar calendar, and preferred instead a calendar that was lunar. Further sources from this period confirm the existence of a lunar calendar. *Ben Sira*, a presumably Judaean work from the early second century BCE, considers that months and festivals are to be based entirely on the moon.[8] In Alexandria at the same period, to Aristobulus is attributed the comment that Passover, on the 14th of the month after evening, occurs at the full moon[9]—thus implying, necessarily, a lunar calendar. Finally the *Exagoge* of Ezekiel the tragedian—of which the date and provenance are admittedly unknown[10]—states that Passover occurred at the διχομη-νία, i.e. the full moon.[11] The term διχομηνία *could* have been used in the wider sense of 'middle of the month', whether of a solar or of a lunar calendar, but this is rather unlikely.[12] The normal usage of this term is 'full moon',[13] and this suggests, again, a lunar calendar.[14]

These sources, albeit sporadic, correct the impression we may otherwise have had that the solar calendars of *Enoch*, *Jubilees*, and Qumran were widely observed in this period. It is quite possible, in fact, that the calendar of *Jubilees* would only have been followed by marginal, sectarian groups.[15] But the safest conclusion is that both solar and lunar calendars were variously observed, in a relationship that remains somewhat unclear.

---

[8] Eccles. 43: 6–8; see also the Hebrew text (Ben Sira) of verse 50: 6, and the Greek text of verse 39: 12. See, however, Yadin (1965) 30. On the possible historical implications of the recensional variations of this text, see Glessmer (1999) 254–5.

[9] Ap. Eusebius, *Ecclesiastical History* 7: 32: 17–18. On the mid-2nd-c. BCE dating of Aristobulus, see Schürer (1973–87) iii. 579–87.

[10] Ibid. 563–6.

[11] See Jacobson (1983), text pp. 60–1, ll. 156–7, commentary pp. 131–2; also Charlesworth (1983–5) ii. 814.

[12] On the similar term *noumenia*, see section 1.1.10 below.

[13] Cf. e.g. Eccles. 39: 12.

[14] Collins (1991) infers further details about Ezekiel's calendar, but I am not convinced.

[15] See further below. On the likelihood that a Babylonian-type lunar calendar was observed in practice in the Hasmonaean period, see section 1.2.2 below.

This said, the calendrical texts from *Enoch*, *Jubilees*, and Qumran deserve to be examined in some detail, because of the wealth of information they supply. Modern scholars have already studied this material in depth; for reasons of scope, I shall refrain from excessive detail.[16]

1.1.3 Ethiopic *Enoch*

The relevant section of the Ethiopic *Enoch* (or *1 Enoch*), i.e. chs. 72–82, known sometimes as the *Book of Heavenly Lights* (or *Astronomic Enoch*, hence Milik's abbreviation 'Enastr') has been identified by Milik as the earliest stratum of *Enoch*, dating from the end of the third or beginning of the second century BCE, and constituting originally a separate work.[17] The main thrust of this work is astronomical rather than calendrical. It describes in detail the courses of the sun (72), of the moon (73, 78), and their relation to one another (74, 78).

Ch. 72 describes the sun's annual cycle, beginning from the vernal equinox and extending over a period of 12 months. Each month is 30 days long, except for the 3rd, 6th, 9th, and 12th, that have 31 days 'on account of the (sun's) sign' (72: 13, 19), an obscure phrase which appears to refer to the solstices and equinoxes which constitute the additional 31st days. Thus the year is exactly 364 days long (72: 32). Throughout this period the sun is described as entering and exiting various heavenly gates, each gate corresponding to a month.

Ch. 73, and again 78: 6–8, account for the phases of the moon. The surface of the moon is divided into 14 parts, which are successively lit and then, after full moon, successively darkened.

Solar and lunar years are then compared in ch. 74. Whereas the solar year, as above, is 364 days long (74: 12–13), in 3 lunar years there are 1062 days (i.e. 354 days per year), which leads to a discrepancy of 50 days in 5 years (i.e. 10 days per year) (74: 14).[18] However, the text contradicts itself in 74: 10–11, where the discrepancy is reckoned as 6 days per year, or 30 days every 5 years. This discrepancy of 6 days per year appears to assume a 360-day solar year, by ignoring the 4 additional days of the 364-day calendar.[19] The 360-day calendar appears again, indeed,

---

[16] For some bibliography, see references in Schürer (1973–87) i. 592 n. 15, i. 601 n. 33, iii. 313–14 n. 10; Glessmer (1999).

[17] Milik (1976), esp. p. 7; see also Schürer (1973–87) iii. 250–68, especially 254–6.

[18] Cf 79: 5: five days every half-year.

[19] The internal contradiction is further exacerbated, however, with a reference at the end of 74: 10 to the 364-day year.

in 75: 1–2 and 82: 4–6, where some (or all?) 'people' are blamed for not reckoning the 4 intercalary days of the year.

In spite of *Enoch*'s emphasis on the solar, 364-day calendar, lunar calendars are also briefly mentioned. In 78: 15–16, it is stated that lunar months consist of 29 and 30 days in alternation; hence, according to 79: 4, half a lunar year makes 177 days. Various lunisolar cycles are alluded to in 74: 13–16, where *Enoch* gives the comparative length of solar and lunar years over a period of 3, 5, and 8 years, and specifies the discrepancy between them. In referring to a 3-year period, the author probably has in mind the 3-year lunisolar cycle. This cycle consists of a lunar calendar (of 29- and 30-day months) that requires the intercalation of one 30-day month every 3 years.[20] By referring to an 8-year period, the author probably has in mind the 8-year lunisolar cycle, known from the Greek as an octaeteris. This cycle requires the intercalation of three 30-day months every 8 years.[21]

The Aramaic fragments of *Enoch* discovered at Qumran include passages unparalleled in the Ethiopic text, which present a systematic synchronization of solar and lunar calendars that conforms precisely to the 3-year cycle.[22] However, it remains unclear to me how, or on the basis of which criteria, these fragments were identified by Milik as belonging to an Aramaic *Enoch*, as opposed to other calendrical texts from Qumran that were not. Unlike the Aramaic fragments from Qumran that are identified with other parts of the book of *Enoch*, those from Milik's 4QEnastr corpus are very different from the Ethiopic text, and sometimes impossible to bring into relationship with it (Knibb 1978: ii. 11–13). I would not rule out the possibility, therefore, that the so-called *4QEnastr* texts, as well as the other Qumran calendrical texts (on which see below), are no more than *commentaries* or exegetical *expansions* of the original book of *Enoch*.

Charles interprets verse 78: 9 of Ethiopic *Enoch* as referring to the 76-year lunisolar cycle of Callippus (Greek astronomer, later fourth century BCE). This cycle would consist of an alternation of 29 and 30-day months, with one 28-day month every 76 years (Charles 1913: ii. 244).

This interpretation is rather unlikely, however, because it would entail the verse not making any mention, inexplicably, of the 30-day months of Callippus' cycle.[23] It would also be surprising for *Enoch* to refer to the octaeteris and then to Callippus' cycle, but not to the cycle of Meton (Greek astronomer, later fifth

---

[20] This intercalation assumes a lunar year of 354 days and a solar year of 364 days.

[21] Assuming a solar year of 365¼ days; see Charles (1913) ii. 241. As Charles rightly surmises, the 5 years are only mentioned for the sake of adding them to the 3 and obtaining 8. See also Milik (1976) 274–84, Neugebauer (1985) 400–1.

[22] 4QEnastr[a] = 4Q208 (Milik 1976: 273–84). For further details on this cycle, see section 1.1.6 below.

[23] As pointed out by Hartom (1967) i. 92 (note).

century) of 19 years, of which Callippus' cycle was only an improvement. Finally, it is actually unlikely that Callippus' cycle included a single 28-day month.[24]

Charles's interpretation is based on his own translation of this verse, according to which the lunar months are of 29 days or 'once' of 28 days. This translation is endorsed by Knibb (1978: ii. 183); but in a personal communication, Knibb advises me that the text of the older group of manuscripts (which he does not follow in his translation) in incoherent in this passage. This justifies the conjecture that the original meaning of verse 78: 9 may have been different. Neugebauer suggests, as an alternative interpretation of this verse, that the moon is *visible* for *either* 29 *or* 28 days.[25]

It must be stressed that elements of a lunar or lunisolar calendar are always only implicit in Ethiopic *Enoch*, and hence relatively unimportant. Preference is clearly given to the solar calendar. Thus *Enoch* states that the year is accurately completed only in conformity with the sun's cycle (74: 17).[26]

This said, it is unlikely that *Enoch*'s solar calendar was meant to be observed *in practice*. As a solar calendar, the 364-day year is actually impractical, because it falls behind the solar year, and hence the annual seasons, by approximately $1\frac{1}{4}$ days per year.

Milik has argued, accordingly, that the 364-day calendar of *Enoch* was only an *idealistic* model, never intended to be used in practice. All *Enoch* was concerned with was the construction of a simplified and ideal astronomical order; he had no interest in practical use or in scientific accuracy.[27] The idealistic nature of *Enoch*'s calendar finds confirmation, perhaps, in the repeated statement that Enoch's knowledge was revealed to him by the angel Uriel (in verses 72: 1, 74: 2, 75: 3–4, 79: 6, 80: 1, 82: 7), rather than obtained through empirical astronomical investigation.[28]

---

[24] The cycle of Callippus is described by the Greek astronomer Geminus, in *Elem. Astr.* 8: 50–60 (Aujac 1975: 56–8). See Ginzel (1911) ii. 409–19; Pedersen (1974) 127–8; Samuel (1972) 47–9; A. Jones (1997) 157–8.

[25] Neugebauer (1985) 408. A similar interpretation is suggested by the translation of E. Isaac in Charlesworth (1983–5) i. 57. See also Hartom (1967) i. 91–2; his Hebrew translation is not based, however, on the Ethiopic text.

[26] At least according to Charles's translation (1913: 54) and Neugebauer's (1985: 395). According to Knibb (1978) ii. 174, reference may also be made in this verse to the moon.

[27] Milik (1976) 14 and 277. For a similar, perhaps more distinctive idealization of lunar and solar cycles in the Palestinian Talmud (*Y. RH* 2: 4, 58a), see S. Stern (1996) 103–29.

[28] See Stone (1988) 161 and 164.

Albani (1994) and Glessmer (1996*a*) have argued that *Enoch* shares much in common with the Babylonian astronomical compendium MUL.APIN, which would have been used in Babylonia in this period as a simplified astronomical model for didactic or other theoretical applications. *Enoch*'s calendar may similarly have been used for purposes of theoretical astronomical study.

Neugebauer dismisses *Enoch* as an 'extremely primitive level of astronomy'—a view rightly rejected by Milik.[29] Stone's suggestion that *Enoch*'s calendar was a deliberate archaism is also, in my opinion, less likely.[30]

The approximate nature of *Enoch*'s figures should not be put down to 'primitiveness' or ignorance. It is unlikely that the author of *Enoch* was unaware of the $1\frac{1}{4}$-day discrepancy, which is empirically quite considerable.[31] *Enoch*'s apparent knowledge of the octaeteris (in 74: 13–16, see above) implies awareness of this discrepancy, inasmuch as the octaeteris assumes a solar year of $365\frac{1}{4}$ days. Some textual recensions of *Enoch* 80: 2–8 read that in the days of sinners the years shall be shortened, so that rain and vegetation will come late;[32] this also suggests awareness of a discrepancy between the human calendar and the actual seasons. According to most scholars, the calendar in question in these verses is the 364-day year (in relation to which rain and vegetation would have been delayed by $1\frac{1}{4}$ days per year).[33] Alternatively, however, the calendar in question may be the 360-day year, which *Enoch* attributes elsewhere to the sinners (82: 4, see above).

Whichever interpretation is favoured, the astronomical book of *Enoch* is unlikely to inform us, therefore, about actual calendrical practice. After all, the stated purpose of this book (in 72: 1) is to reveal the courses of the sun and moon, rather than to prescribe the observance of any specific calendar. Besides, the text of *Enoch* is historically problematic, as it appears to have been subject to a number of later interpolations which lead to textual inconsistencies (e.g. in 74: 10–14, see above).[34]

This does not prevent *Enoch* from constituting an important source for Jewish calendar reckoning in the Hellenistic period. This work, including its possible interpolations, suggests that a number of calendrical models were known and may have been used, some solar and some lunar

---

[29]   Milik (1976) 14 and 277, citing from a work of Neugebauer dated 1964 (*n.v.*); see also Neugebauer (1985) 387 ('primitive picture of the cosmic order') and 389 ('archaic primitiveness').

[30]   Stone (1988). According to Stone, deliberate archaism would also explain why the 19-year cycle is omitted in *Enoch* and contemporary Jewish sources.

[31]   *Pace* Beckwith (1970) 388–91.

[32]   See Charlesworth (1983–5) i. 58.

[33]   e.g. Beckwith himself (1970: 393); also Stone (1988) 165.

[34]   According to E. Isaac (Charlesworth 1983–5: i. 54 n. u), 74: 10–16 is a 'later fragmentary intrusion'.

(or lunisolar). *Enoch* also suggests that these calendars would normally have been set by mathematical calculation, rather than by empirical observation of new moons. But this is likely to reflect *Enoch*'s own interest in mathematical astronomy, rather than how contemporary Jews would have reckoned the calendar in practice.

For comparative purposes, it is worth noting that the cycles of intercalation designed by Greek astronomers such as Meton or Callippus, as well as the octaeteris, were apparently not observed in practice in any of the Greek cities of the Classical and Hellenistic period.[35]

1.1.4 Slavonic *Enoch*

Mention must also be made of the Slavonic *Enoch* (or *2 Enoch*, literarily distinct from Ethiopic *1 Enoch*: see Schürer 1973–87: iii. 746–50). It is commonly dated around the first century CE, and possibly of Egyptian authorship (ibid. 748–9). Date, place of origin, and authorship remain, however, extremely unclear; the historical significance of this work is thus difficult to gauge.

The solar calendar is clearly predominant in *2 Enoch*: indeed, solar months are given in 16: 2 in the context of accounting for the cycle of the moon! In 68: 1–3 mention is made of the Jewish months of Nisan and Siwan, and in 48: 2–3 of Siwan and Tevet; in the latter passage these months appear to be solar, as the summer and winter solstices are said to occur on the fixed dates of the 17th of these months. This passage, however, is problematic, for in the Jewish calendar there are seven months between Siwan and Tevet, whereas from summer to winter solstice there should only be six months.

In 73: 5 equivalence is made between *Iuars* (i.e. Iyyar) and the Egyptian month *Famenoth*, and in 73: 8 between Nisan and *Farmout*. This is problematic, as Phamenoth *precedes* Pharmouthi in the sequence of Egyptian months. This whole passage (ch. 73) is anyway of limited significance, as it is believed to be a later, Christian interpolation.[36]

The solar year length is given in verses 13: 3–4 and 48: 1 as 364 days.[37] The figure of 365¼ is found in some recensions of 14: 1, but this according to Andersen is evidently a later gloss.[38]

Various calendrical cycles are also referred to in this work: in 16: 8, the Metonic lunisolar cycle of 7 intercalations in 19 years (which is also in use in the present-day rabbinic calendar); in 15: 4, the 28-year solar cycle (which assumes a year length of 365¼ days, hence 28 years for the equinox to recur at the same time and on the same day of the week; also attested in the rabbinic calendar); and in 16: 5, the great cycle of 532 years (19 × 28 years; attested in Christian

---

[35] Samuel (1972) 54. The octaeteris may have been used at Athens in the Roman period, although the evidence is far from certain: see Follet (1976) 353–5, 359, 365–6.

[36] See F. A. Andersen in Charlesworth (1983–5) i. 212 n. a.

[37] See also 16: 2, 4, and Andersen ibid. 125 n. d, 130 n. f.

[38] Ibid. 125 n. c. The same applies to 16: 6, which implies the Julian leap year: see ibid. 125 n. d.

but not in rabbinic sources).[39] All these cycles, according to Andersen, are late interpolations.[40]

1.1.5 Jubilees

The book of Jubilees is dated to the second century BCE.[41] It uses the book of Enoch as a source (e.g. Jub. 4: 17–24), and apparently refers directly to the book of Heavenly Lights (4: 18, 21). Jubilees leans decisively in favour of a solar calendar ('the rule of the sun': 4: 21). In its account of the creation, it was the sun alone that was appointed to be 'a great sign ... for days and for Sabbaths and for months and for feasts and for years ...' (2: 9)—clearly a deliberate emendation of Gen. 1: 14.

According to Jubilees, the calendar consists of a 364-day year (6: 32), i.e. exactly 52 weeks (6: 30), which are divided into 4 periods of 13 weeks each (6: 29). The year is also divided into 12 months; the first day of the 1st, 4th, 7th, and 10th months are called 'days of remembrance' (6: 23),[42] and begin each of the 4 parts or seasons of the year (6: 23, 29); they were ordained by Noah as feasts (6: 24, 28).

Inasmuch as Jubilees appears to have heavily relied on the astronomical data of the book of Enoch, it is reasonable to assume that the 4 days of remembrance of Jubilees correspond to the additional 4 days referred to by Enoch (except that according to the latter they are reckoned as the 31st of every third month (3–6–9–12), rather than as the 1st of every subsequent month (4–7–10–1)), all other months being 30 days long only. Thus the verse in Jub. 5: 27 where 5 months are equated with 150 days could be dismissed as a mere approximation.

Further details have been inferred by Jaubert.[43] A year of 52 weeks exactly should always begin on the same day of the week, which can be firmly identified as Wednesday. Indeed, the harvest festival (i.e. Shavuᶜot) occurs in Jubilees in the 'middle of the 3rd month' (15: 1; 16: 3; 44: 4–5; this is also when the revelation at Mount Sinai occurred, 1: 1), i.e. on the 15th. This means that counting of the ᶜomer (sheaf) pentecontad would begin on the 26th of the 1st month. This is only possible if the biblical phrase 'after the Sabbath' (Lev. 23: 15–16), when the pentecontad begins, is taken to refer to the first Sunday after the last day of the festival of Unleavened Bread (21st of the 1st month),[44] and if the latter is taken to occur on a Wednesday. Consequently, the first day of the year, the

---

[39] Except for a possible reference to double this cycle in R. Eleazar ha-Qallir's סילוק לפרשת שקלים (אז ראית): see below, section 4.4.5.

[40] Andersen in Charlesworth (1983–5) i. 125 n. d.

[41] See Schürer (1973–87) iii. 308–18, 256.

[42] As in Charles's translation; 'days of appointed times' according to O. S. Wintermute's translation in Charlesworth (1983–5: i).

[43] Jaubert (1953, 1957a, b). For a summary, see Schürer (1973–87) i. 600–1.

[44] This interpretation of the biblical phrase might be compatible with that presented in the Mishnah as Boethusian: see below, n. 74.

festival of Unleavened Bread and Tabernacles always occur on a Wednesday, and the harvest festival always on a Sunday. This has been explicitly confirmed in Qumran sources where the calendar of *Jubilees* is used.

Jubilees differs from *Enoch*, however, in that its calendar is exclusively solar, and that this calendar is clearly intended to be observed *in practice*. Strict admonitions to observe the solar calendar appear in *Jubilees* 6: 31–8, with a warning that any deviation from this calendar would lead to the disruption of the years, new moons, and seasons (6: 33–4). The polemical, and perhaps even sectarian tone of this passage is couched in terms of the biblical distinction between Israel and the Gentiles: '. . . lest they forget the feasts of the covenant and walk according to the feasts of the Gentiles after their error and their ignorance' (6: 35). The passage goes on to attack 'those who will assuredly make observations of the moon— how it disturbs the seasons and comes in from year to year ten days too soon' (6: 36), which will lead them to the observance of festivals on the wrong dates (6: 37); this was due to take place after Moses' death, when the Israelites 'will not make the year 364 days only, and for this reason they will go wrong as to the new moons and seasons and Sabbaths and festivals' (6: 38; cf. 1: 14). Likewise, in 49: 7–8 and 14 *Jubilees* admonishes against adjourning Passover from day to day (i.e., perhaps, of the week, as opposed to the solar calendar, where the festival occurs always on the same day of the week) or from month to month (as in, perhaps, lunisolar cycles where an additional lunar month is periodically intercalated).

The polemic in these passages implies that at the time when *Jubilees* was written, the lunar calendar must have been widely used; adherents to the calendar of *Jubilees* may have been no more than marginal.[45] Mention of 'those who will assuredly make observations of the moon' (*Jubilees* 6: 36, Charles's translation) or 'examine the moon diligently' (Wintermute's translation in Charlesworth 1983–5: ii. 6) *may* indicate that the lunar calendar that was generally in use depended on monthly observations of the new moon.[46]

1.1.6 Qumran sources: the calendars

For a long time it was accepted among scholars that the Qumran sect followed a solar calendar similar to or identical with that of the

---

[45] See Stone (1988), Davies (1983).

[46] Alternatively, however, this verse may simply mean that the opponents of *Jubilees* would investigate the discrepancy between solar and lunar cycles.

book of *Jubilees*. This theory was first developed in detail by Jaubert (1953, 1957*a*, 1957*b*); it was then endorsed by Talmon (1958), and since then has often been presented as the scholarly consensus.[47] However, since the late 1980s this 'consensus' has been subject to some re-examination.[48] More attention has been given to the lunar calendars in Qumran sources. Moreover, the assumption that Qumran sources represent the views and practices of a single 'sect' has become increasingly untenable.[49]

A number of different calendars are represented, in fact, in sources from Qumran, and often in painstaking detail. What they have in common is not that they are either solar or lunar, but rather that they are all *schematic*. In this respect, Qumran calendrical sources are in direct continuity with the literary tradition of *Enoch* and *Jubilees*.[50] Qumran calendars can be grouped into two main categories: the 364-day calendar of *Jubilees*, and the 3-year (or 6-year) lunisolar cycle.

The calendar of *Jubilees* is described in detail in 4Q320–1 and 4Q325. It is prescribed as normative in the Damascus Rule and perhaps, by allusion, in the Community Rule. It is also assumed in the Temple Scroll (4Q325),[51] the Flood story (4Q252),[52] the Psalm Scroll (11QPs^{a}DavComp),[53] and the Sabbath Songs (4Q400).[54]

The Damascus Rule (CD 16,2–4) instructs that 'for the exact determination of their times to which Israel turns a blind eye, behold it is strictly defined in the *Book of the Divisions of the Times into their Jubilees and Weeks*'—no doubt the book of *Jubilees*.

The Community Rule appears to mention the 'days of remembrance' of the calendar of *Jubilees* (1QS 10,5) and its 4 seasons (10,6–8), in the context of the rules of conduct for the Master (משכיל). This passage, however, is extremely obscure.

According to the Psalm Scroll, David wrote 364 daily sacrificial songs, one for every day of the year, and 52 songs for every Sabbath—which corresponds to the calendar of *Jubilees*.

---

[47] e.g. Vermes (1994) 52–4 and in Schürer (1973–87) i. 599–601.

[48] See Baumgarten (1986, 1987), Beckwith (1992), Schiffman (1994) 304–5.

[49] For an updated assessment of Qumran calendrical literature, with select bibliography, see Glessmer (1999); S. Stern (2000*b*).

[50] Fragments of *Jubilees* have been discovered in large numbers at Qumran, suggesting interest in this work and some affinity with it. See Schürer (1973–87) iii. 309 n. 1; VanderKam (1992).

[51] Yadin (1983) i. 116–19; see also Baumgarten (1987).

[52] See Lim (1992, 1993).

[53] See Sanders (1965) 91–3.

[54] See Glessmer (1999) 255–9.

The 3-year (or 6-year) lunisolar cycle is represented in a number of texts from Qumran Cave 4, which all appear to refer to the same calendar.[55] Included in this body of texts are the Aramaic *Enoch* fragments published by Milik,[56] already referred to above. The 3-year cycle, in Qumran sources, consists of an alternation of 29-day and 30-day lunar months; there are 12 lunar months in the year, hence 354 days per year. Every 3 years an additional 30-day month is added, so as to keep up with the solar year. This additional month assumes a solar year length of 364 days, as according to the calendar of *Jubilees*, with which this cycle is often synchronized. At the end of each cycle, as in the calendar of *Jubilees*, the New Year recommences on the same day of the week, on Wednesday.[57]

A further reference to the lunar calendar has been identified in the 'Daily Prayers' text (4Q503), which lists the prayers to be recited each day of the month (Baillet 1982: 105–36). This text refers repeatedly to 'parts of light' and 'parts of darkness' (39 xiii 2; also 51–5 xiii 2 and 14; 76; 215; 218), which may be a reference to *Enoch*'s phases of the moon.[58] This would suggest that the month assumed in this text is *lunar*.[59]

The lunar phases described in 4QEnastr[b–c], and apparently followed by 4Q503, are integrated in 4Q317 into a *synchronic* calendar. This calendar, it may be presumed, combines the 364-day calendar with the lunar 3-year cycle, as is the case with other Qumran synchronic calendars (and presumably that of 4QEnastr[a]). There is nothing in the sources to suggest any other lunar calendar, at Qumran, than the 3-year cycle.

The beginning of the lunar month in the Qumran 3-year lunisolar calendar has been subject to intense controversy. In general terms, most scholars agree that the lunar month begins around the time of the new moon.[60] It is clear from 4QEnastr[b–c] and (perhaps) 4Q503 that the month begins and ends when the moon is dark, whereas at the middle of the month the moon is full. But the precise definition of the beginning of the month is far more debatable: whether it is the conjunction, or the first invisibility of the old moon, or the first visibility

---

[55] 4Q259 (= 4QS[e], see Milik 1976: 61–5), 4Q293, 4Q317–37.

[56] Especially 4QEnastr[a–c] = 4Q208–11, see Milik (1976) 273–84.

[57] See Milik (1976) 61–9, 274–84; Eisenman and Wise (1992) 109–19. For a full tabulation, see e.g. Wacholder and Wacholder (1995) 32–5.

[58] *Enoch* 73 and 78: 6–8 (see above), paralleled in 4QEnastr[b–c] = 4Q209–10.

[59] Baumgarten (1986). This interpretation is questioned, however, by Glessmer (1999: 252–4), on the grounds that the correspondence between the 'parts of light and darkness' and *Enoch*'s phases of the moon is far from explicit. Glessmer also refutes Baillet's suggestion (1982: 105–6) that some elements of this text imply the calendar of *Jubilees*.

[60] Beckwith (1992) 462–4; Wise (1994a) and (1994b) 222–32 (ch. 6); Talmon and Knohl (1995).

of the new moon (see further Ch. 3), cannot be inferred from 4QEnastr[b-c], not least because the figures in this text are occasionally inconsistent.[61]

Much of the discussion centres around the obscure term דוקה, which in 4Q321 occurs consistently on the 16th or 17th of each (lunar) month. Some interpret it as meaning 'observation'. If it refers to observation of the full moon, then the month would begin before the conjunction, as soon as the (old) moon becomes invisible.[62] In support of this theory, Wise (1994a: 119) argues that the listings in 4Q320 of the *last* day of each month suggest that the lunar calendar was also established on the basis of the observation of the final visibility of the old moon. This theory suggests that although the Qumran lunisolar calendar is based on a fixed, schematic cycle, regular observations of the moon would also have been carried out.

Talmon and Knohl interpret דוקה differently, as designating the time when the full moon begins to wane (literally, to 'thin'). They argue that דוקה in 4Q321 refers to the day *after* the full moon, whilst the last day of the lunar month in 4Q320[63] corresponds to the first invisibility of the old moon, thus implying that the month begins at the conjunction. Talmon and Knohl suggest (pp. 299–301) that this text polemicizes against the lunar calendar by emphasizing the days of waning and of darkness of the moon (whereas according to the lunar calendar itself, it is the full moons, i.e. the days of moonlight, that are emphasized and treated as festivals).

Some have argued, quite differently, that the term דוקה designates the new moon (the 'thin' moon), and hence, since דוקה occurs on the 16th or 17th of the month, that the lunar month of Qumran begins—*unlike* that of 4QEnastr[b-c]— with the full moon.[64] A parallel with this may be found in the little-known sect of the Magharians (on which see below, Ch. 3), which has been associated by some scholars with the Qumran sect.

1.1.7   Qumran sources and calendrical practice

Given this diversity of calendars, it may be wondered whether they were all intended to be used in practice. Schematic calendars excel in mathematical simplicity, but for this reason, they fail to comply with astronomical reality. Both the calendar of *Jubilees* and the 3-year lunisolar cycle assume an average solar year length of 364 days, which as we have seen, falls short of the real solar (tropical) year by approximately 1¼ days. There is no provision, in these calendars, for occasional

---

[61] *Pace* Wise (1994b) 229.

[62] So Wise (1994b) 229–30.

[63] According to Talmon and Knohl (1995: 297–8), reference to this last day can also be found in 4Q321.

[64] e.g. Wacholder and Wacholder (1995) 7–8 and 29–30; see bibliography cited in Wise (1994a) 100. This theory does not account for the listing of the last day of the months in 4Q320 (which in this theory would correspond to one day before the full moon).

adjustments or intercalations—in spite of various attempts, by modern scholars, to conjecture that there must have been.[65] Observance of these calendars over a protracted period would have caused the biblical festivals to occur in the wrong agricultural seasons, in blatant violation of Mosaic Law. This is unlikely to have been tolerated by any Jewish sect or community.

Likewise, the average length of the lunar month, which is assumed in the 3-year lunisolar cycle, is considerably too short. Every three years, the calendar month would fall behind the lunar month by approximately half a day. This discrepancy is smaller than the solar discrepancy of $1\frac{1}{4}$ days *per annum*, but arguably just as significant. This is because the phases of the moon are far more obvious to the casual observer than astronomical solstices and equinoxes. Whereas a discrepancy of one week between the calendar and the actual solar year can easily go unnoticed, a discrepancy of two days between the middle of the calendar month and the full moon is obvious to any inexperienced observer.

The length of the lunar (synodical) month is, in reality, over 44 minutes in excess of $29\frac{1}{2}$ days. Consequently, a lunar calendar cannot consist of a simple alternation of 29 and 30-day months. Approximately every 36 months an additional day must be inserted, and a further day every 360 months (which make up for the accumulation each month of 44 minutes). In the Qumran 3-year cycle, this requirement is partially met with the intercalation every 3 years of an extra-sequential 30-day month. However, this intercalation only provides an additional half-day to the cycle (i.e. the half-day remaining after deduction of $29\frac{1}{2}$ days for the actual lunar month).[66] Therefore, the 3-year lunar cycle of the Qumran calendar accumulates a discrepancy of approximately half a day every three years, and of an additional day every 360 months.

The calendars of Qumran sources could only have been used in practice if their users were not bothered by these discrepancies. Some scholars have entertained this possibility on the basis of a passage in *Enoch* 80: 2–8, which reads that in the days of sinners the years shall be shortened, so that rain and vegetation will come 'late'. This passage suggests a discrepancy between the calendar and the seasons; Enoch does not attribute this discrepancy to a fault in the calendar, but rather to human sin causing disruption of the seasons. Such a perspective could

---

[65] For a summary, see Beckwith (1970). For a more recent attempt, see Glessmer (1996*b*) and (1999) 262–8. Glessmer emphasizes that this attempt is only hypothetical, as it is not supported by any explicit statement in the text (1996*b*: 156–7).

[66] Beckwith (1992: 459) gives an erroneous account of this discrepancy, corrected in the later version (1996: 119).

have justified the observance of a calendar that was falling behind the moon and the seasons.[67]

This *Enoch* passage may have justified a moderate discrepancy; but whether it would have justified a *revolving* calendar, with festivals such as Passover occurring in all seasons of the year, remains perhaps to be established. To repeat, the observance of Passover in any other season than the spring would have been a blatant violation of Mosaic Law. Many scholars, therefore, would favour the view that if any of these calendars were ever adopted in practice, as suggested by the book of *Jubilees* and the Damascus Rule, they would have been abandoned early on, as soon as these discrepancies became excessive.[68] Alternatively, schematic calendars such as the calendar of *Jubilees* or the 3-year lunisolar cycle could have been used over a longer stretch of history, but only for short periods at a time. Discrepancies could have been rectified whenever necessary, on a purely *ad hoc* basis.

Most likely, perhaps, is that these schematic calendars served only as *idealistic* or *theoretical* models—much as has been argued in the context of *Enoch*'s calendars, with which Qumran calendars are evidently related.[69] Qumran calendars may also have been construed as relevant to some futuristic, ideal world order. This might be suggested from the synchronization, in 4Q320–1, of the lunisolar cycle with the cycle of priestly courses;[70] in the context of the Qumran community, the Temple-centred priestly courses would only have pertained to some eschatological ideal.

1.1.8   Qumran calendars and sectarianism

It has long been argued that the calendar observed at Qumran was sectarian, and hence that calendar was one of the main features of Qumran sectarianism.[71] This would provide a historical context for the coexistence of solar and lunar calendars in the period of Qumran literature (second century BCE to first century CE).

The evidence, however, is slim. There is a condemnation in the Hosea *pesher* (4Q166) of those that follow the festivals of the nations. There are also references in the *Damascus Rule* to the notion that those outside the

[67]   Beckwith (1970) 392–5; Wacholder and Wacholder (1995) 28–9 and 36–7.

[68]   Beckwith (1992) 461; Schiffman (1994) 304.

[69]   See my remarks above, section 1.1.3. Wise (1994*b*: 231) suggests that the measure of time, with the use of synchronistic calendars, may have been treated at Qumran as a religious act.

[70]   See, with full tabulations, Glessmer (1999) 241–3.

[71]   A view developed in particular by Talmon (1958).

remnant of the faithful have gone astray in the observance of Sabbaths and festivals (CD 3,13–15), and that members of the Covenant should observe the Sabbath, festivals, and the Day of Fast as according to the findings of the New Covenant (CD 6,18–19). However, these passages do not necessarily refer to the *dates* of the festivals: they may refer instead to their rituals and specific acts of worship.

In the Community Rule we find an explicit prohibition on bringing forward or postponing any of the festivals (1QS 1,13–15, and cf. 3,9–10), but this may simply mean that the calendar must be reckoned correctly— a statement which any Jew could have made in this period, without necessarily implying sectarian diversity.

The juxtaposition of the calendar of *Jubilees* with one version of the polemical text 4QMMT (4Q394) may be interpreted as an indication that the calendar was a sectarian issue; but Schiffman (1994: 305) has argued, on the contrary, that the absence of reference to the calendar in the main text of 4QMMT indicates that it was not central to Qumran sectarianism. Moreover, the occurrence of 4QMMT and of the calendar of *Jubilees* in the same manuscript (4Q394) does not necessarily mean that they constituted a single literary composition.

Finally, the Habakuk *pesher* (11: 2–8) speaks of the Wicked Priest's visit to the Teacher of Righteousness and to his followers on their Day of Atonement, in an attempt to disrupt their fast and day of rest. This story implies that they observed the Day of Atonement on different dates— a discrepancy which the Wicked Priest exploited to his own advantage. This is probably the closest we can get to evidence of calendar sectarianism;[72] but even here, there are alternative interpretations. Observance of a festival on different dates does not necessarily imply fundamentally different calendars. If the Teacher of Righteousness and the Wicked Priest were both observing, for instance, a calendar based on sightings of the new moon, then on this occasion they may simply have sighted the new moon on different days.[73]

---

[72] As assumed by Talmon (1951).

[73] A similar episode, involving two rabbis, is recorded in the Mishnah (*M. RH* 2: 9): they disagreed as to whether the new moon had been seen, and consequently as to when the Day of Atonement should be observed (as noted by Vermes 1987: 53). It should be noted that the stress in the Habakkuk *pesher* is not on the Wicked Priest's calendrical error, but rather on his violent treatment of the Teacher of Righteousness and his followers, and his deliberate disruption of their observances. The calendar is not, in this passage, the central polemical issue.

It is worth noting that external evidence of calendrical sectarianism among the Jews of this period is also remarkably slim. There are passages in the Mishnah regarding the Boethusians of the Second Temple period, but the argument is confined to the date of the ʿomer (sheaf) offering and of Shavuʿot (Pentecost), and does not appear to concern the rest of the calendar.[74] Apart from the Mishnah and the book of *Jubilees*, there is no explicit evidence of calendar sectarianism among the Jews of the Hasmonaean or of the early Roman periods.[75]

Thus the nature of the calendar observed in practice at Qumran, and whether it differed substantially from calendars observed by other Jews in the same period, is doubtful. It is certain, however, that Qumran sources developed a keen interest in schematic calendars, both solar and lunar, similar to those found in *Enoch* and *Jubilees*.

1.1.9 The first century CE and beyond: the end of the solar calendar

From the first century CE onwards, solar calendars disappear entirely from all Jewish sources. The Jewish calendar in Philo, Josephus, rabbinic, and Christian sources, as well as in documents and inscriptions, is only and exclusively lunar. This suggests that the lunar calendar had emerged, by the first century CE, as the only calendar in use among the Jews.

The historical significance of this change is quite considerable, and will be assessed in detail in the second section of this chapter. For now, it must be stressed that this change could be no more than the reflection of our sources: the absence of evidence does not *prove* that the solar calendar was no longer used by Jews at the end of the first century CE. Nevertheless, there are reasonable indications, as we shall see below, that calendar sectarianism had ceased by Josephus' period. It must also be acknowledged that at *some* stage, the solar calendar must have disappeared completely from Jewish tradition and practice, as no trace of it is ever found again in post-Qumranic Jewish sources.

---

[74] The 'Boethusians', we are told, did not agree to the reaping of the ʿomer taking place on the morrow of the first day of Passover (*M. Menaḥot* 10: 3); instead, they always observed the festival of ʿAtzeret (i.e. Shavuʿot)—and hence, by implication, the reaping of the ʿomer seven weeks earlier—on a Sunday (*M. Ḥagigah* 2: 4, without reference to Boethusians; *T. RH* 1: 15 (p. 210), with explicit reference to Boethusians), just as according to the calendar of the book of *Jubilees*. Needless to say, in both passages the Mishnah strongly rejects this practice. The Mishnah also suggests that the extent of this calendrical dispute was, in social terms, considerable.

[75] Josephus may be taken to suggest that there was *no* calendar sectarianism in his period: see below section 1.1.11.

The end of solar calendars and calendar sectarianism may well be tied up with the putative end, after 70 CE, of Jewish sectarianism and sects. That Sadducees, Essenes, Qumran, and other sectarian groups 'disappeared' after the great revolt and destruction of the Temple in 70 CE is an assumption that has been widely shared by Jewish historians.[76] Martin Goodman has pointed out, however, that the end of sectarianism is not logically connected with the Temple's destruction, and that there is no positive evidence that sects disappeared as early as the end of the first century CE.[77] But the end of the solar calendar—which as stated, must have occurred at *some* stage in the first century CE or later—does indicate that in some respects, Jewish practice was becoming less diverse.

The solar calendar makes a brief reappearance in late medieval Jewish sources, but only sporadically and attributed to obscure individuals or marginal, sectarian groups. Since they only emerge towards the end of the first millennium, they are unlikely to be in continuity with the Jewish solar calendars of the Hellenistic period.

Abraham Ibn Ezra (early–mid-twelfth century) polemicizes against an unknown work by 'Judah the Persian',[78] who appears to have contended that the biblical calendar was solar, and *may* also have advocated, at least implicitly, its adoption.[79] The identity of this Judah the Persian remains unclear, and although his views were endorsed by two much later writers, there is no evidence that any sectarian group ever adopted them in practice.[80]

According to the Karaite Judah Hadassi (mid-twelfth century), the Isunian sect (followers of Abu Isa, ?seventh century) observed a solar calendar 'just like the Sadducees'.[81] This apparently contradicts, however, the earlier Karaite al-Qirqisani (*c*.930 CE) who writes that he once asked Jacob b. Ephraim the Syrian[82] why Rabbanites associated and intermarried with the Isunians, to which Jacob replied: 'Because they do not disagree with us over the festivals'.[83]

---

[76] It has been recently reiterated by Cohen (1984).

[77] Goodman (1994). Archeological evidence for the destruction of the Qumran settlement in 68–70 CE (and hence, if a linkage is to be made, for the end of the 'Qumran sect') is very slim.

[78] Abraham Ibn Ezra, *Introduction to the Pentateuch* (in the section on the 'second way'), and commentary on Exod. 12: 2 and Lev. 25: 9; also Ibn Ezra (1874) 8a, and (1839) 162–3.

[79] See, however, Poznanski (1918) 214–15, with reservations on this point.

[80] Poznanski, ibid.; Mann (1931–5) ii. 471–2.

[81] Hadassi (1836) 41c, alphabet 97, letter *mem*.

[82] A disciple of R. Saadya Gaon, who is said to have written a commentary on the Palestinian Talmud: Pinsker (1860) ii. 14, citing Salmon's Arabic commentary on Ps. 140: 6.

[83] Al-Qirqisani, *The Book of Lights and Watch-Towers*, 1. 11. 2, as translated by Lockwood (Chiesa and Lockwood 1984: 144); cf. translation of Nemoy (1930) 382.

Poznanski interprets this as meaning that the Isunians did not reckon a different calendar from the Rabbanites.[84] But although al-Qirqisani is likely to be more reliable than Hadassi (see Poznanski), particularly as he appears to have had first-hand knowledge of the Isunian sect, this passage does not necessarily indicate that Isunian calendar reckoning was identical with the Rabbanite. Al-Qirqisani's reference in the same passage to Rabbanite festivals 'of their own invention' suggests indeed that the issue at stake was not calendar reckoning in general, but rather the Rabbanite Diaspora observance of a second festival day or the festival of Hanukkah, both of which the Karaites rejected but which the Isunians might have observed.

The observance of a 30-day month calendar by some Karaites is incorrectly inferred by Ankori from the *Midrash Leqah Tov*.[85] It is clear from the context of this passage that the reference is only to Anan's opinion that if the new moon is not visible, a 30-day month should be assumed.[86] Ankori also cites a passage of Benjamin al-Nahawendi;[87] but all al-Nahawendi states is that equinoxes and solstices must be reckoned according to a 30-day-month calendar, whereas he emphasizes in the same passage that festivals and other aspects of the calendar must be reckoned according to the moon, either by sightings of the new moon for Nisan and Tishre, or by alternating 29- and 30-day months for other months of the year. This, indeed, is corroborated by al-Qirqisani's account of al-Nahawendi's calendar.[88]

Another source does suggest, however, that some Karaites may have advocated a solar calendar. A text published by Ginzberg suggests that for reckoning the calendar, the sun should be followed rather than the moon, because the latter is not always visible and its cycle is irregular and unstable;[89] calendar months, therefore, should never be shorter than 30 days.[90] The identification of the author remains of course uncertain.

As to the 'Sadducees', mentioned by Hadassi as observing a solar calendar (see above), al-Qirqisani appears to concur with Hadassi by stating that the Sadducees reckoned 30-day months only.[91] This tradition may be related to the attribution of the same calendar, in a late medieval work, to the early

[84] Poznanski (1918) 211–12; similarly Ankori (1959) 274 n. 62.

[85] Tuviah b. Eliezer, *Midrash Leqah Tov* on Exod. 12: 2 (Buber 1884: ii. 28a): Ankori (1959) 273–5, but referring incorrectly to *Midrash Leqah Tov* on Lev. 23: 1 (Buber 1884: iii. 62b).

[86] Cited by Ankori himself (1959: 274).

[87] The passage is preserved in the 11th-c. commentary on the Pentateuch by Yeshua͑ b. Yehuda, published by Harkavy (1903) 176–8; Harkavy, however, misinterprets this passage (177 n. 6).

[88] Al-Qirqisani, *The Book of Lights and Watch-Towers*, 1. 14 (Nemoy 1930: 387; Chiesa and Lockwood 148).

[89] Ginzberg (1928–9) ii. 494–6, see MS, p. 1b, ll. 1–6.

[90] MS, p. 1a, ll. 21–3, as correctly interpreted by Ginzberg (1928–9) 494. The reading and interpretation suggested instead by Mann (1931–5: ii. 60 n. 111) are almost incomprehensible.

[91] Al-Qirqisani, *The Book of Lights and Watch-Towers*, 1. 6 (Nemoy 1930: 363; Chiesa and Lockwood 1984: 134).

Samaritan sect of Dositheans.[92] According to Abraham Ibn Ezra, however, the Sadducees followed a *lunar* calendar (commentary ad Lev. 25: 9). Wacholder (1983*a*: 154) accepts al-Qirqisani's report at face value (but attributes this calendar more specifically to the Boethusians). In my view, however, neither al-Qirqisani, Hadassi, nor Ibn Ezra, writing a millennium or more after the last known Sadducees, can be treated as historically reliable.

In the pages that follow, sources on the lunar calendar from the first century CE and beyond will only receive a superficial treatment, as a more thorough analysis is to follow in Chs. 2–3 (and, for rabbinic sources, in Chs. 4–5).

1.1.10 Philo of Alexandria

By contrast with works from the Hellenistic and Hasmonaean periods, sources from the Roman period are remarkably reticent about the Jewish calendar and the way it is reckoned. Nevertheless, a good deal of information can be inferred, not least from the writings of Philo. Philo discusses the Jewish calendar mainly in two passages of his works: *Quaestiones ad Exodum* 1, where he comments on the calendrical significance of Exod. 12: 2, and *Special Laws* 2. 10. 36 (39–222), where he discusses at length the biblical festivals of which the third is the *noumenia*, the new month.

In Philo's period, the Greek term *noumenia* would not necessarily have implied, in itself, a lunar calendar. Although it is usually translated as 'new moon', for the simple reason that Greek calendars, until the end of the Hellenistic period, were lunar (or nearly lunar), so that *noumenia* could be used in the astronomical sense of 'new moon', the plain and literal meaning of this term is actually 'new month', i.e. beginning of the month. Consequently, in the Roman period this term would also be used in the context of the Roman calendar, as meaning the beginning of the *solar* month, i.e. the *Kalendae*.[93] This may explain why Josephus finds it necessary to specify: '*noumenia* according to the moon'.[94]

---

[92] See Isser (1976) 76, 91–3.

[93] Plutarch, *Galba* 22 and *Romulus* 12; Dio, 60: 5: 3; also *P. Dura* no. 30, dated 232 CE. See Schürer (1973–87) i. 598.

[94] Νουμηνία κατὰ σελήνην: Josephus *Ant.* 4: 4: 6 (78); ibid. 7 (84). The same phrase is found in Thucydides (*Hist.* 2: 28), but probably in a different sense: i.e. the first day of the lunar month, as opposed to the first day of the calendar month (which in 5th-c. Greece did not always coincide): see Bowen and Goldstein (1994) 702–7. In *Special Laws* 2: 26 (140), Philo may be using this expression in the latter sense.

But Philo makes it abundantly clear that his *noumenia* is lunar. This is briefly (but explicitly) stated in *Special Laws* 2. 11 (41); the calendrical significance of the moon's monthly cycle is then given a full discussion in 2. 26 (140–2). The relevant passages will be analysed in detail in the next two chapters.

Mention should be made of the pentecontad calendar, consisting of an annual succession of seven 50-day periods (7 weeks and 1 day, the latter a festival, hence a 350-day year), which Philo implies was followed by the sect of Therapeutai.[95] This calendar, which also appears in the *Temple Scroll* (11Q19 xviii–xix, xxi) and implicitly in other Qumran texts (4Q327 fg. 1 ii), comprises a sequence of festivals that does not correspond to that of the Bible (except for Shavuʿot): e.g., in Qumran sources, the festivals of wine and of oil. The observance of the pentecontad calendar, however, would not necessarily have excluded observance in parallel of the biblical calendar (solar or lunar) and festivals.[96]

1.1.11 Josephus

In spite of the volume of his works, Josephus does not have much to tell us about the Jewish calendar: only, in a number of passages in *Antiquities*, that it is lunar.[97]

Josephus' reticence is odd, considering the attention he generally gives to sectarian divisions in Jewish Palestinian society. For as we have seen, the book of *Jubilees*, some Qumran sources, and some passages in the Mishnah suggest that the calendar could be an important sectarian issue. Yet in passages where Josephus describes, often at length, the practices and beliefs of the various Jewish 'parties', there is never any reference to calendrical disputes.[98] The same omission occurs in Philo's and Pliny's accounts of the Essenes[99] (in their case, however, the omission is less significant as their accounts of the Essenes are only incidental and hence not necessarily intended as comprehensive).

Josephus' omission suggests, perhaps, that by the first century CE the calendar was no longer a feature of Jewish sectarianism. The same lunar calendar, with little or no variation, may already have been observed.

---

[95] Philo, *Contemplative Life* 8 (65). On the possibly ancient origins of this calendar, see references in Schürer (1973–87) i. 600 n. 31.

[96] See Baumgarten (1987).

[97] *Ant.* 2. 15. 2 (318); 3. 10. 3 (240); 3. 10. 5 (248); 4. 4. 6 (78); 4. 4. 7 (84).

[98] See *Jewish War* 2. 8. 1–14 (108–66); *Ant.* 13. 5. 9 (171–3); 13. 10. 6 (297–8); 18. 1. 2–6 (11–25); *Vita* 2 (10–12).

[99] See references in Schürer (1973–87) ii. 560 nn. 13, 15.

1.1.12 Second to sixth centuries CE: literary sources

Literary sources from subsequent centuries confirm the impression that the Jewish calendar was now universally lunar. Of particular interest, besides rabbinic literature, is the evidence of non-Jewish, mainly Christian, sources. Most telling, perhaps, is the fact that the date of Easter, which was based on the date of the Jewish Passover, was reckoned by almost all Christians according to a lunar calendar—thus implying that the Jewish calendar itself was lunar.[100]

That the Jewish calendar is lunar is also explicit in the *Kerygma* attributed to the Apostle Peter, cited by Clement of Alexandria (*c*.200 CE), and in the anonymous *Epistola ad Diognetum*. Galen, in the mid or later second century, ascribes a lunar calendar to 'those in Palestine' and describes it in some detail.[101]

Not all non-Jewish sources, however, can be trusted to reflect the actual observances of contemporary Jews. Christian authors, in particular, would have been tempted to form assumptions about the Jews on the sole basis of a conjectured biblical past. In some cases it is evident that the author had no intention to refer to contemporary reality. A source often cited as evidence regarding the Jewish calendar in the Roman period is a quotation from Julius Africanus' *Chronography*, written at Emmaus in Palestine in the early third century.[102] Africanus refers to lunar years as 'Hebrew' (Ἑβραϊκά), and states that 'Greeks and Jews' (Ἕλληνες καὶ Ἰουδαῖοι) make three intercalations every eight years (the octaeteris). On this, the new Schürer comments that 'there is no reason to doubt this statement respecting his own time'.[103] However, it appears from the context of this passage that Africanus does not necessarily have his own time in mind. His point is only to justify his use of the octaeteris as a basis for his chronological computation of the period extending *from Nehemiah to Jesus*. His statement regarding Hebrews or Jews may just be relevant, therefore, to the calendars that would have been in use, in his view, in the late biblical period.

---

[100] On the date of Easter and its implications for the Jewish calendar, see below sections 2.4, 2.5, 2.6.1, 3.3.1, 3.4.1, 5.1.2, and 5.2.2. For Christians who did not observe the lunar calendar see Epiphanius, *Panarion* 50. 1. 6 with Holl and Dümmer (1980): 245 ad loc.

[101] Clement of Alexandria, *Stromateis* 6. 5 (41); *Epistola ad Diognetum* 4. 5 (anonymous, 2nd or 3rd c.); Galen, *In Hippocratis Epidemiarum Libros Commentarius* 1. 1 (ed. Kühn, xvii/1. 23); cited in M. Stern (1974–84) ii, no. 394.

[102] Julius Africanus, *Chronography*, book 5, ap. Eusebius, *Proof of the Gospel*, 8. 2 (390 d) (*PG* 22. 609 d–612a; Ferrar 1920 ii. 125).

[103] Schürer (1973–87) i. 592. The same assumption is made by Bickerman (1968) 30. Schürer considers Africanus' 'Greeks' to refer to the Syro-Macedonians (592 n. 14, and 595 n. 21); however, by the 3rd c. CE, they had long abandoned the lunar calendar in favour of a solar calendar. If Africanus is referring to his own time, he most probably means the Greeks of Greece, or specifically Athens. See sections 1.2.4 and 1.2.6 below.

Less problematic is the evidence of Galen: his reference, in the same passage, to calendar reckoning in 'the majority of *today*'s Greek cities',[104] suggests indeed that he is referring to contemporary reality. But even if he means to describe the Palestinian Jewish calendar of his own time, the source of his knowledge— observation, hearsay, or mere assumption—remains entirely unclear.

1.1.13 First to sixth centuries CE: inscriptions and documents

Epigraphic, papyrological, and other documentary evidence from outside Judaea has little to teach us about the Jewish calendar. Jewish inscriptions and documents in the Diaspora are nearly always dated according to non-Jewish calendars (e.g. Roman, Macedonian, Egyptian).[105] Jewish festivals are very rarely mentioned in the material that is extant.

Judaean documents, by contrast, are generally dated according to a Jewish calendar: for instance, the Judaean desert corpus from the period of the Bar-Kokhba revolt (131/2–5 CE).[106] Unfortunately, the documents in this corpus are also of limited use. Because they do not provide the days of the week or some other, non-Jewish dating system with which the Jewish dates could have been synchronized, we have no means of establishing exactly how their Jewish dates would have been reckoned. Judaean ostraka published by Yardeni (1990) supply full Jewish dates with days of the week; but since the era is never specified, and hence, the years are impossible to establish with certainty, these documents are again of limited use.

Judaean desert documents from the early second century (mainly from the Babatha archive) are slightly more informative, for reasons that will be explained below. Although they are dated according to Macedonian and Nabataean calendars, these documents suggest, as we shall see, that the Jewish calendar was not solar and hence, presumably, lunar.[107]

---

[104] Galen, *In Hippocratis Epidemiarum Libros Commentarius* 1. 1 (ed. Kühn, xvii/1. 21).

[105] For inscriptions, see *CIJ*; Horbury and Noy (1992); Noy (1993–5); Lüderitz (1983). For papyri (principally from Egypt), see *CPJ*; also Cotton, Cockle, and Millar (1995).

[106] Documents from Wadi Murabbaʿat are published in Benoit, Milik, and de Vaux (1961), referred to henceforth as *P. Mur.* (see nos. 22, 23, 24, 29, 30). Documents from Naḥal Ḥever were published initially by Yadin (1962) (see nos. 42, 44, 45, 46) and Broshi and Qimron (1989); they are now to be found in Cotton and Yardeni (1997).

[107] Section 1.2.5.

Against this general dearth of evidence, a few valuable exceptions stand out: two inscriptions from Berenike in Cyrenaica of the first century BCE or the first century CE, which refer explicitly to the festival of Tabernacles and to *noumeniai*, and which implicitly suggest, as I shall later argue, a *lunar* calendar;[108] and then much later sources, including an inscription from Catania of 383 CE where the phrase *luna octaba* most probably refers to the Jewish lunar calendar;[109] a marriage contract on papyrus in Aramaic from Antinoopolis, 417 CE, dated in full according to the Jewish lunar calendar;[110] and the fully dated tombstones of Zoar (south of the Dead Sea) from the fourth to sixth centuries.[111] These sources, which will be studied in detail in the next two chapters, confirm that from the first century CE onwards, the Jewish calendar was overwhelmingly lunar.

1.2 JEWISH AND NON-JEWISH CALENDARS

The purpose of this section is to investigate why solar calendars were abandoned by the Jews around the first century CE. This will be achieved by examining, in its broad historical context, the relationship between Jewish and non-Jewish calendars: how the Jewish calendar was influenced by other calendar systems, and how, sometimes, it may have striven to remain distinct.

1.2.1 The 'Jewish' calendar

The notion of 'Jewish calendar' has been taken for granted so far; it deserves, at this stage, to be defined. What makes a calendar 'Jewish' may be the fact that its users are mainly or exclusively Jews. This raises the question, however, of who would have qualified as 'Jews'. Thus it is difficult to define a calendar as 'Jewish' purely in terms of the ethnicity of its *users*.

Alternatively, a calendar can be defined as 'Jewish' in *functional* terms, inasmuch as it is used to determine the dates of Jewish festivals, fasts,

---

[108] *CIG* iii, nos.5361–2; *IGR* i, no. 1024; Roux and Roux (1949); *SEG* 16, no. 931; Reynolds (1977), nos. 17–18; Lüderitz (1983), nos. 70–1; Boffo (1994), no. 24, 204–16.

[109] *CIJ* i, no. 650; Noy (1993–5) i, no. 145; but see discussion in sections 3.3.2 and 3.3.4.

[110] Sirat *et al.* (1986); see below, section 3.3.3.

[111] For bibliography, see Naveh (1985) and below, section 2.6.3.

and other occasions. This definition may appear, at first sight, over-restrictive. However, there is a genuine case for arguing, at least in the context of Diaspora Jewry, that the observance of biblical and Jewish festivals and fasts would have been the primary and essential reason for maintaining a distinctive calendar.

The observance of festivals and new months, widely attested in Jewish communities of the Diaspora, would have necessitated some method for reckoning their dates. In some instances, a system for establishing the dates of specific festivals might have been sufficient: for instance, the date of Passover could have been defined as the first full moon in the spring. But the celebration of new months would have required a continuous calendar, running from month to month throughout the year.

Diaspora observance of new months and festivals is reasonably well attested in literary and epigraphic sources. It may be argued, indeed, that they were vital to any community wishing to identify itself as Jewish. Philo (in the *Special Laws*) describes and discusses at length the biblical festivals (including new months), their rituals and their meaning. In the absence of any statement to the contrary, we must assume that these festivals were observed by Jews in Alexandria. Of the festival of the first fruits (i.e. Shavuᶜot), at least, Philo says it is 'widely observed'.[112]

Epigraphic and papyrological evidence includes references to Tabernacles and new months in the Berenike inscriptions (see above and further below), Tabernacles again in a second-century-CE papyrus from Egypt,[113] and the festivals of Unleavened Bread and Pentecost (Shavuᶜot) in an inscription from Hierapolis in Phrygia.[114] There is also a possible reference to new months in an inscription from Alexandria, dated 3 CE.[115] The πόσεις referred to in *CPJ* i, no. 139 (Apollinopolis Magna, first century BCE) cannot be identified as Jewish festivals;[116] but the apparent reference to Passover in *CPJ* iii, no. 467 (second or third century CE) is perhaps more likely.

Additional evidence can be inferred from further literary sources. Horace's *tricesima sabbata* (in *Sat.* 1. 9. 69) probably refers to the celebration of the new month (i.e. the 'Sabbath of the thirtieth (day)');[117] this passage reflects, one assume, Jewish practices in the city of Rome. The decree of the people of Halicarnassus (in the 40s BCE) as cited by Josephus, *Ant.* 14. 23 (257–8), refers to the observance of Sabbaths and festivals by the Jews. Reference to the observance of festivals and new months is also found in Col. 2: 16, and may represent more

---

[112] Δημοτεληστάτη: *Special Laws* 1: 35 (183).

[113] Possibly Edfu: *CPJ* iii, no. 452a.

[114] *CIJ* ii, no. 777. The foregoing are listed in Schürer (1973–87) iii. 144–5, nn. 26, 28–9.

[115] Horbury and Noy (1992) no. 18.

[116] *Pace* A. Fuks in *CPJ* i, p. 255.

[117] As argued by M. Stern (1974–84) i. 326, and Schürer (1973–87) iii. 144–5. See Feldman (1989–90).

than a merely literary topos (cf. Isa. 1: 14). Trypho's entreaty to circumcise and keep the Sabbath, festivals, and new months, in Justin Martyr's *Dialogues* 8. 4, may also have some bearing on Diaspora Jewish practice (although Justin himself originated from Flavia Neapolis in Samaria). In the fourth century, John Chrysostom refers repeatedly to Jewish festivals observed in Antioch (in his homilies *Adversus Iudaeos*).[118]

The almost total absence of Jewish dates in the epigraphic and papyrological record from the Diaspora suggests that among Diaspora Jews, the Jewish calendar was otherwise seldom used. The use of Roman, Macedonian, and Egyptian calendars would have been dictated by the constraints of daily business and public life as well as by conventions inherent in the 'epigraphic habit'.[119] Thus the function of the Jewish calendar in the Diaspora would have been largely restricted to religious life.[120]

Nevertheless, the Jewish calendar must be distinguished from other, non-Jewish cultic calendars of the ancient world (such as the Egyptian cultic calendar, on which see below), in that it was not confined exclusively to religious use. In Palestine, the Jewish calendar was also used for secular purposes, as evident from Josephus, from the Judaean desert documents of the Bar-Kokhba period, and from the Zoar tombstone inscriptions.

Finally, whether the calendar of the Jews, in Judaea/Palestine or in the Diaspora, was always distinctively 'Jewish' remains to be established. In some cases, the Jews could have relied on non-Jewish calendars for the dates of their own festivals. This applies, in particular, to the pre-Roman period. In the Roman period, as we shall see, the existence of distinctive Jewish calendars—lunar rather than solar—becomes increasingly pronounced.

1.2.2 Persian, Seleucid and Hasmonaean periods

By the time the Romans arrived in the Near East in the first century BCE, the calendars in use in this region were almost entirely lunar.[121] This was the result of a succession of empires, Babylonian, Persian, and

---

[118] See references in Wilken (1983) 64.

[119] Phrase coined by MacMullen (1982).

[120] The earliest attested evidence of Jewish datings in the Diaspora is in the marriage contract of Antinoopolis (417 CE), and perhaps beforehand in the Catania inscription of 383 CE (see on the latter section 3.3.2). Otherwise, only non-Jewish datings are used. This usage is most distinctive in the dated documents and inscriptions of Ptolemaic and Roman Egypt (see references above, n. 105).

[121] See Samuel (1972), ch. 6, and especially p. 182 n. 1.

Macedonian, that for centuries had employed the lunar calendar for their official use. The Babylonians themselves had reckoned a lunar calendar since the earliest records.[122] This calendar was adopted by their imperial successors, the Persian Achaemenids, who disseminated it throughout their empire.[123] Thus the Babylonian calendar can be found as far as Elephantine, in the southern confines of Egypt, in official documents from the late fifth century BCE. Egypt was somewhat exceptional, in that it maintained its own civil calendar of 365-day years throughout Antiquity; in the Elephantine documents, Egyptian dates would often be cited alongside the Babylonian. Still, these documents reveal how far the Babylonian lunar calendar had spread.[124]

As the Macedonian calendar of the early Hellenistic rulers happened also to be lunar, it was soon assimilated with the Babylonian calendar, perhaps as early as in Alexander's lifetime.[125] Macedonian and Babylonian months were formally equated by the Seleucids not later than 245 BCE;[126] Macedonian names of months were used in Greek, and Babylonian names in Aramaic.[127] The Babylonian calendar was thus maintained in the Near East, and eventually outlived the disintegration of the Seleucid Empire. It became, indeed, the official calendar of the Parthian Empire,[128] of Nabataea (see below), and presumably of other kingdoms of the post-Seleucid era.

To assess the impact of the Babylonian calendar on the history of Jewish calendar reckoning, we must briefly return to the pre-exilic period. As we have mentioned at the beginning of this chapter, calendar reckoning in the early biblical period remains completely obscure; we do not even know whether the calendar of the early Israelites was solar or lunar. Calendrical evidence only begins to emerge, and in quite some detail, in literary sources from about the second century BCE; these suggest that among the Jews in this period, solar and lunar calendars may to some extent have coexisted.

---

[122] See Parker and Dubberstein (1956), Sachs and Hunger (1988–96).

[123] See Bickerman (1968) 24.

[124] Porten (1990); S. Stern (2000a); also Bickerman (1968) 25.

[125] Samuel (1972) 140–2.

[126] Samuel (1972) 139–41; also Bickerman (1968) 20.

[127] See e.g. Eshel and Kloner (1996). The text of 1 and 2 Maccabees, although written in Greek, uses *Babylonian* names of months (transliterated into Greek: see further below, section 1.2.4); but this may be a Hasmonaean expression of anti-Hellenic sentiment.

[128] Samuel (1972) 179–80, 187; Bickerman (1968) 25.

The origin of these competing solar and lunar calendars remains extremely unclear. It is not impossible that coexistence, in various forms, of solar and lunar calendars goes back to the pre-exilic, early biblical period. As a buffer zone between the kingdom of Egypt and the Mesopotamian empires, the kingdom of Israel may have been exposed to the conflicting influences of the Egyptian civil calendar, which was solar (or nearly solar, with its 365-day year), and of the Mesopotamian calendars, which were lunar.

Most scholars, however, appear to assume that only *one* calendar, either solar or lunar, could have been in use in ancient Israel. If the original Israelite calendar was lunar, then the introduction of a solar calendar in the Hellenistic period could be viewed as a marginal, sectarian innovation, perhaps under Egyptian influence, that was ultimately destined to be short-lived.[129] If, alternatively, the original Israelite calendar was solar, then the introduction of a lunar calendar in the post-exilic period was to have far-reaching consequences: eventually, indeed, this lunar calendar was to supersede, among the Jews, the original Israelite solar calendar.

According to the latter view, it is most probable that the lunar calendar was been adopted by the Jews under direct influence of the Babylonian calendar, which, as we have just described, was becoming the dominant calendar of the entire Near East.[130] But even if the original Israelite calendar was lunar, as according to the former view, the Babylonian calendar would also have exerted its influence upon it. Because the calendar in the Bible was ill defined, it would naturally have been prone to assimilation with the dominant Babylonian calendar.

Babylonian influence is evident, indeed, in the books of Zechariah and Esther, where equivalence is explicitly and consistently drawn between biblical (Israelite) numbered months and Babylonian lunar months.[131] This equivalence suggests that both calendars are identical. In Elephantine, likewise, the evidence suggests that the Jews used no other calendar but the Babylonian, even for the dates of Jewish or biblical festivals. The

---

[129] See Wacholder and Wacholder (1995).

[130] According to VanderKam (1981), the lunar calendar was only first adopted by the Jews under *Hellenistic* influence, in the period of Antiochus IV. However, this theory is convincingly refuted by Davies (1983: especially 82–3), chiefly on the basis of Zechariah and Esther (cited in next footnote below). The exclusive use of biblical, numbered months in some earlier post-exilic biblical works such as Haggai, Ezra, and Daniel does not necessarily lend support to VanderKam, for this usage can be dismissed as literary archaism.

[131] Zech. 1: 7, 7: 1; Esther 2: 16, 3: 7, 3: 13, 8: 12, 9: 1.

'Passover papyrus' certainly suggests that in 419 BCE Passover and Un-leavened Bread were observed in the *Babylonian* month of Nisan. This suggests that in the Persian period, the occurrence of Passover and other biblical festivals would no longer have depended on biblical *agricultural* criteria, such as *ʾaviv* (for Passover) or the harvest time (for Shavuʿot), but purely on the extraneous criteria of the Babylonian calendar.[132]

It may be assumed that the Babylonian calendar was also followed in Judaea in the Seleucid period, as well as of the Hasmonaean and Herodian periods, just as it was being followed in other kingdoms of the former Seleucid Empire. Indeed, Babylonian names of months are used in the books of Maccabees, where they are equated, again, with biblical numbered months.[133] Although the solar calendar appears to dominate in Jewish literature from this period, particularly in the works of *Enoch* and *Jubilees*, the evidence of *Maccabees* as well as the general historical context of the Hasmonaean period suggest in all likelihood that a Babylonian-type calendar would have been used in Judaea for public and official purposes, whereas the solar calendars would only have reflected sectarian or marginal views.[134]

Whether the Judaean calendar of the Hasmonaean period corresponded *exactly* to the Babylonian reckoning cannot be known. Hasmonaean rulers are more likely to have set their own calendar independently than to have relied on moon sightings and declarations of new moons that were being made in Babylonia, a region that was now part of a foreign kingdom. Still, the methods employed by the Hasmonaeans to determine lunar months were probably similar to those of the Babylonians.[135]

---

[132] The 'Passover papyrus': Cowley (1923) no. 21; Porten and Yardeni (1986) no. A4.1. See Porten (1990) and S. Stern (2000*a*). Note that this calendrical change was not irreversible: agricultural criteria are commonly used, in a later period, in rabbinic sources (see section 4.1.2).

[133] For references, albeit incomplete, see Schürer (1973–87) 18 and 588. The Babylonian origin of these names is obliquely acknowledged in 2 Macc. 15: 36, where the month of Adar is referred to as 'Syriac' (the alternative textual version, κυριακῇ, supplied in Swete (1899) 707, i.e. 'divine', is certainly erroneous, as it is completely without parallel; this reading is omitted entirely by Kappler and Hanhart (1959) 115).

[134] This impression is also conveyed by the book of *Jubilees* itself: see above, section 1.1.5.

[135] They may have been precursors of the procedure described in later rabbinic sources. See Wacholder and Weisberg (1971), who point out the similarity between Babylonian and rabbinic methods of determination of new moons, and argue that the rabbinic calendar of the Mishnah was originally borrowed from the Babylonian calendar and in direct continuity with it.

It is also questionable whether the Hasmonaeans made the same intercalations as in the Babylonian calendar, thus always celebrating Passover
in the *Babylonian* Nisan—as had been the practice in the Persian period
(e.g. at Elephantine). Datings from the Hasmonaean and early Roman
periods, that will be considered below in Chs. 2–3, suggest that Jewish
and Babylonian months regularly coincided. However, this evidence is
too sporadic to prove that the Babylonian calendar was *consistently* followed and used.[136] In this period, Babylonian intercalations were based
on a fixed cycle of 19 years;[137] this cycle is not attested in any Jewish
source prior to the institution of the fixed rabbinic calendar (fourth century CE), which *may* suggest that until then this cycle had never been
in use.

Avoidance of a 19-year cycle would not necessarily have been motivated by a de-
sire to be distinguished from the Babylonian calendar. This cycle may have been
considered unsuitable to the Jews for a number of other reasons. Firstly, the intercalation of a second month of Ululu (Elul) in the 17th year of the Babylonian
cycle[138] may not have been acceptable to the Jews, for whom the subsequent
month of Tishre had to correspond, every year, to the biblical 7th: if
an additional Elul were inserted, Tishre would have become the 8th month. To
overcome this problem, a different 19-year cycle, without intercalations of Ululu, would have been needed; but then the Jewish calendar would not have been
the same as the Babylonian.

Secondly, intercalation was governed in biblical law by the requirement that
Passover be celebrated in the season of ʾaviv. Because an agricultural criterion
of this kind was liable to some irregularity, it may not have lent itself to the
observance of a fixed and regular cycle.[139]

Nevertheless, it remains entirely possible—as the evidence indeed suggests—
that the Jews of the Hasmonaean and early Roman periods relied to a large
degree on the Babylonian cycle of intercalations.

---

[136] See especially section 2.3.5.

[137] The so-called 'Metonic' cycle, named after its Athenian inventor Meton
(later 5th c. BCE), was known independently to the Babylonians: see Parker and Dubberstein (1956) 1–9, Sachs and Hunger (1988–96) 14, Bickerman (1968) 23–4, also
Schürer (1973–87) i. 588–90. Evidence of the 19-year cycle in the Babylonian calendar goes back to the 5th c. BCE, and most scholars are now of the view that it was
instituted at the beginning of this century (Bowen and Goldstein 1988: especially 42
n. 17). Bowen and Goldstein suggest that the first cycle began in 498 BCE; according
to Hartner (1979) it was in 502 BCE; but this is all rather speculative.

[138] Parker and Dubberstein (1956) 1–9; Bickerman (1968) 24; Samuel (1972) 140.
This intercalation was regularized from 408 BCE (Parker and Dubberstein 1956: 6).

[139] See Bickerman (1968) 25–6. His statement that on this account the Jewish
calendar fell out of line with the Babylonian cycle is only based on much later rabbinic
evidence.

1.2.3   Ptolemaic and early Roman Egypt

In Ptolemaic Egypt, the situation was entirely different from that of the Seleucid Empire. For some millennia, the Egyptian civil calendar had been not lunar, but solar (or nearly solar, based on a 365-day year).[140] The Ptolemies themselves, at first, used a Macedonian lunar calendar.[141] But later in the third century, this calendar was neglected in favour of the Egyptian civil calendar, and thus fell into considerable disorder. By the beginning of the second century, the Ptolemaic calendar was completely restructured and assimilated with the Egyptian civil calendar.[142] Except for a possible short-lived restoration of the Macedonian calendar in 163–145 BCE,[143] the lunar calendar was hence completely and permanently abandoned.

By this time, coincidentally, Judaea was no longer under Ptolemaic rule (from 201/0 BCE). As a result, it can be said that throughout the Hellenistic period the rulers of Judaea, whether Ptolemaic or (after 201/0 BCE) Seleucid, employed official calendars that were lunar.

In Egypt itself, however, the Jews in Greek cities such as Alexandria would have been exposed, at the end of the third century, to a significant change. Whereas the Greeks of Alexandria, as well as the Ptolemaic rulers, had adopted the Egyptian civil calendar, the Jews of Egypt appear to have maintained a lunar calendar. This at least is suggested by Aristobulus, an Alexandrian Jew of the mid second century BCE, by Ezekiel the tragedian (date and location uncertain; see above, section 1.1), and eventually, in the first century CE, by Philo. It is just possible, therefore, that after the reform of the Macedonian calendar the Jews of Egypt were faced *for the first time* in their history with the responsibility of setting and reckoning their own, distinctive lunar calendar.

---

[140] See Parker (1950), especially 51–4; Depuydt (1997).

[141] Samuel (1962: 31–74 and 1972: 146) is of the view that this Macedonian calendar was based on a fixed 25-year cycle, which was in place at least as early as 280/79 BCE. See also Grzybek (1990) 135–41. Parker (1950: 26–9) assumed that this 25-year cycle was of Egyptian origin, and directly derived from the Egyptian cultic lunar calendar (on which see further below); Grzybek (1990: 52–60, 171–4) argues that it was of Macedonian origin. However, A. Jones (1997) has recently shown that the notion of a 25-year cycle Macedonian calendar is based on insufficient evidence: the Macedonian calendar in Egypt may have been based on some other cycle, or even on the empirical sighting of the new moon.

[142] Samuel (1962) 129–38 and (1972) 149–50; Bickerman (1968) 38–9. See e.g. *CPJ* i. no. 22 (dated 201 BCE), where Egyptian Epeiph and Macedonian Audnaios are equated.

[143] Bickerman (1968) 39–40.

Alongside the civil calendar, the Egyptians had reckoned a cultic lunar calendar that was based on a 25-year cycle, and that is attested as late as 190 CE. This lunar calendar, however, was restricted to priestly use and to the regulation of temple service.[144] The Jewish community would not have used it for their own festivals, because this calendar was tied to the civil, 365-day year calendar, and hence fell behind the solar year by approximately one day every 4 years (Parker 1950: 26). At this rate, the synchronism between biblical festivals and agricultural seasons would soon have been disrupted.

Moreover, in the Egyptian lunar calendar the month began on the day of invisibility of the old moon,[145] or sometimes on the day of the conjunction,[146] whereas Philo is quite emphatic, as we shall see, that the Jewish month begins at the first visibility of the new moon.

Furthermore, the Greek-speaking Jewish community is unlikely to have been exposed to the influence of an Egyptian priestly calendar that would only have been expressed in Egyptian language and writing.[147] The pagan associations of this calendar may also have been abhorrent to the Jews. It is to be assumed, therefore, that the Jewish calendar in later Ptolemaic Egypt was different and distinctive from any of the Egyptian calendars in use.

The exceptional circumstances of later Ptolemaic Egypt—which opposed it to the rest of the Hellenistic world, where the lunar, Babylonian calendar was consistently maintained—may explain why Philo expressed, more than any other Jewish writer of this period, the *distinctiveness* of the Jewish calendar:

But not all (peoples) treat the months and years alike, but some in one way and some in another. Some reckon by the sun, others by the moon. And because of this the initiators of the divine festivals have expressed divergent views about the beginnings of the year, setting divergent beginnings to the revolutions of the seasons suitable to the beginnings of the cycles. Wherefore (Scripture) has added, 'This month (shall be) to you the beginning', making clear a determined and distinct number of seasons, lest they follow the Egyptians, with whom they are mixed, and be seduced by the customs of the land in which they dwell (*Quaestiones ad Exodum* 1. 1, Marcus 1953: 4–5).

By 'Egyptians' he meant, no doubt, the Egyptians of his own day as much as those of the biblical narrative. The emphasis in this passage is

---

[144] See Parker (1950), especially 13–23, 26–9, 54; A. Jones (1997), with reservations about Parker's reconstructed 25-year cycle.

[145] Parker (1950) 13–23; Grzybek (1990) 140–1, 146–51.

[146] This may already have occurred in the late 3rd c. BCE (Parker 1950: 17), because of a slight discrepancy in the 25-year lunar cycle, causing the lunar calendar to fall behind the moon by one day every 500 years. The beginning of the Egyptian lunar month eventually coincided with the day of visibility of the new moon, but not before the mid 2nd c. CE (see Parker 1950: 16, also Samuel 1972: 145–6).

[147] In hieratic or demotic script: Parker (1950) 17–23.

mainly on when the year begins: according to Scripture it begins in the spring, whereas in the Alexandrian calendar the year began (from the beginning of the first century CE) on 29 August.[148] But Philo's reference in the same passage to solar and lunar reckonings is equally significant. Presumably, he had in mind the Egyptian civil calendar, which had become fully solar when it was changed to a 365¼ day calendar in conformity with Julius Caesar's calendar.[149] The Jewish calendar, by contrast, was lunar—as already emphasized by Philo elsewhere.[150]

This passage expresses, if only implicitly, the significance that a distinctive, lunar calendar must have had for the Jewish identity of the Alexandrian community. In some respects, it could be argued, the Jews of Egypt did not differ much from the Egyptian non-Jews: both used the civil Egyptian calendar in their daily life (as evident, in the case of the Jews, from papyri and inscriptions), and a lunar calendar for religious or cultic purposes. Presumably, Philo's point is only that the main calendar of the Egyptians was solar, and that this calendar was distinctly Egyptian, whereas the only identifiable Jewish calendar was lunar.

The distinctiveness of the Jewish calendar finds further expression in an inscription from Berenike in Cyrenaica, a former Ptolemaic possession where the Egyptian calendar was also in use. This inscription, put up by the local Jewish community Cyrenaica in the first century BCE or the first century CE, is dated both according to the Egyptian calendar (25 Phaophi) and according to the Jewish calendar, 'at the assembly of Tabernacles'.[151] If the Jews of Berenike had relied on the *Egyptian* calendar for the dates of their festivals, by treating Phaophi as equivalent to the biblical 7th month, then the festival of Tabernacles could not have coincided with the 25th of this month: for Tabernacles occur from the 15th to the 22nd of the 7th month. Evidently, therefore, the date of this festival was reckoned according to a different calendar, which as I shall later suggest, was most probably lunar.[152]

1.2.4   Josephus: calendars in early Roman Judaea

In the period when Philo was writing, Egypt was no longer the only part of the Eastern Mediterranean where the civil calendar was solar. Already in the late first century BCE, the cities of Asia Minor, Northern Syria,

---

[148] Bickerman (1968) 50; Samuel (1972) 177.
[149] Parker (1950) 70 n. 6 to introduction; Samuel (1972) 177 n. 1; Hagedorrn 1994.
[150] See above, section 1.1.10.
[151] *CIG* iii, no. 5361; *IGR* i, no. 1024; Roux and Roux (1949); Reynolds (1977) no. 17; Lüderitz (1983) no. 71; Boffo (1994) no. 24, 204–16. See citation below, in section 2.3.4.
[152] See section 3.2.3.

and the Phoenician coastline converted their Macedonian calendars into solar calendars. This was the direct result of the expansion of the Roman Empire, under which Greek cities were encouraged to conform, in various degrees, to the solar, Julian calendar. This conversion was presumably meant to facilitate, for official purposes, synchronization with the Julian calendar.[153]

The Jews of Judaea, however, appear to have resisted this trend and to have retained their lunar calendar. As we have seen, Josephus stresses in a number of places that the Jewish or biblical calendar was lunar. In this respect, the Jews were an exception within the Roman Near East, as we shall see further below.

In spite of this, Josephus does not refer to the Jewish lunar calendar as being particularly distinctive. Unlike Philo, who interprets Exod. 12: 2 as enshrining the distinctiveness of the Jewish calendar,[154] Josephus simply ignores the verse in the relevant passage of *Antiquities* and states, quite on the contrary, that Nisan is *equivalent* to the Macedonian Xanthikos and to the Egyptian Pharmuthi (2. 14. 6 (311)); only later does he bother to mention, as an afterthought, that Nisan is lunar (2. 15. 2 (318)). Even more surprising is the equivalence he draws between Macedonian and Jewish (or Babylonian) names of months, in these passages as well as throughout the *Antiquities*: if the Jewish calendar was lunar, whereas Macedonian calendars in this period were solar, they could never have been equated in this manner.

Macedonian names of months are consistently used throughout Josephus' works. Babylonian/Jewish names of months, by contrast, are completely absent in the *Jewish Wars*. They are mentioned in the *Antiquities*, but always together with their Macedonian equivalent (except in *Ant.* 11. 6. 2 (202): Adar).

The exact identity of Josephus' Macedonian dates has given rise to tremendous controversies (for a summary, see Schürer 1973–87: i. 596–9). In a few

---

[153] Samuel (1972) ch. 6, pp. 171–89; Bickerman (1968) 48–9. Although many of these new Macedonian calendars were modelled on the Julian calendar and closely resembled it, others were modelled on the Egyptian calendar, particularly in areas close to Egypt (e.g. Idumaea, Arabia, but also the city of Tyre): see Meimaris (1992) 35–45, 381–3. Meimaris is of the view that these new, Egyptian-type Macedonian calendars must have been introduced *before* the arrival of the Romans and the Julian calendar (ibid. 37). I see no reason, however, why such changes should have occurred spontaneously. It is more likely that solar calendars were adopted only after and as the result of the Roman conquest, but that the Egyptian model, being relatively similar to the Julian calendar, was favoured by communities that were closer to Egypt and hence more likely to have commercial or other dealings with it. See Grumel (1958) 172.

[154] In *Quaestiones ad Exodum* 1: 1, quoted above, section 1.2.3.

passages it has been shown that Josephus must be referring, as one would expect, to a contemporary Macedonian solar calendar: thus 3 Apellaios, which is given as the day of Vitellius' death (*Jewish War* 4. 2. 4 (654)), corresponds to the Macedonian calendar of Tyre (Schürer 1973–87: i. 597 n. 26). On the other hand, the regnal periods of the emperors Galba, Otho, and Vitellius are given by Josephus according to the Roman calendar (ibid., citing *Jewish War* 4. 9–11 (499–654)). This calendrical diversity has been correctly interpreted as the result of Josephus' use of a variety of sources (including Greek historical works and official Roman records). To quote Schürer (1973–87: i. 597, see pp. 597–9): 'A writer such as Josephus does not put himself to the trouble of converting dates, but gives them as they are transmitted'. There is no reason to assume, therefore, that Josephus would have restricted himself to a single calendar (such as the Tyrian calendar, as Niese and Schwartz contended).

Most confusing, however, is the equivalence drawn by Josephus in the *Antiquities* (but for some reason, not elsewhere) between Macedonian months and biblical numbered or Jewish/Babylonian months, in the following passages:

1. 3. 3 (80–1): 2nd month = Marsouanes/*Marheshwan* = Dios.
   1st month (by Moses' reckoning) = Nisan = Xanthikos.
2. 14. 6 (311): Nisan = Xanthikos = (Egyptian) Pharmuthi.
3. 8. 4 (201): Nisan = Xanthikos.
3. 10. 2 (239): 7th month = Hyperberetaios.
3. 10. 5 (248): Nisan = Xanthikos.
4. 4. 7 (84): Aba (ʾ*Av*) = Loos = (Athenian) Hekatombaion.
4. 8. 49 (327): Adar = Dystros.
8. 3. 1 (61): 2nd month = Iar = Artemisios.
8. 4. 1 (100): 7th month = Thisri = Hyperberetaios.
9. 4. 8 (109): 1st month = Nisan = Xanthikos.
11. 5. 4 (148): 9th month = Tebethos/*Tevet* (probably erroneous: should be *Kislew*) = Apellaios.
12. 5. 4 (248), 7. 6 (319): Khaseleu/*Kislew* = Apellaios.
12. 10. 5 (412): Adar = Dystros.

Josephus' equivalences cannot be dismissed as merely approximate. In most passages he clearly states that the *same* month is referred to by Jews and Macedonians under these different names; and more importantly, in all these passages the same *day* of the month is given for both the Jewish and the Macedonian month (except for the passages from book 8, above listed, where no day of the month is specified).

The same problem arises in other passages, from the *Antiquities* as well as the *Jewish War*, where Macedonian names of months are used on their own, but clearly designating biblical or Jewish months. This applies to the following cases:

(i) With reference to dates from the biblical narrative: *Ant.* 2. 15. 2 (318) Xanthikos; 4. 4. 6 (78) Xanthikos; *Jewish War* 6. 4. 5 (250) Loos.

(ii) With reference to dates of biblical or Jewish festivals, e.g. Passover on 14 Xanthikos: *Jewish War* 5. 3. 1 (99) and 5. 13. 7 (567) (cf. also *Ant.* 2. 14. 6 (311)).

(iii) Where parallels with rabbinic traditions can be made: e.g. *Jewish War* 6. 2. 1 (94) Panemos, cf. *M. Ta'anit* 4: 6 (on the interruption of the daily sacrifices during the siege of Jerusalem by Titus).[155]

In these passages, again, the implicit equivalence between Macedonian and Jewish months cannot be treated as approximate, inasmuch as a precise date is, in all cases, supplied and implicitly shared in common by both months.

To reiterate, Josephus' equivalences between Macedonian and Jewish months are problematic because in his period (and already by the early first century CE) all Macedonian calendars were solar, and hence totally incompatible with a lunar calendar. Yet there cannot be any doubt that in all the passages above quoted (and possibly also in others) the 'Macedonian' months referred to by Josephus as equivalent to biblical or Jewish months are *lunar*. Josephus says so explicitly, indeed, in a number of passages in *Antiquities*.[156]

I would suggest, therefore, two possible interpretations, which are not necessarily mutually exclusive. Firstly, Josephus' usage of Macedonian names for Jewish lunar months may be attributed to the simple fact that he is writing in Greek. These names may have served, to Josephus, as 'Greek' translations of the Babylonian names that were normally used, in Judaea, for the Jewish lunar months.[157]

Secondly, Josephus may be harking back to the lunar Macedonian calendar of the Hellenistic period, which under the Seleucids had been consistently equated with the Babylonian calendar.[158] In the first century CE, Josephus' period, this equivalence had become irrelevant, since the Macedonian calendar was now solar; but this might not have prevented Josephus from perpetuating the older calendrical tradition. Along with his contemporary Jewish readers, Josephus may have had difficulties in

---

[155] For another probable reference, see Schürer (1973–87) i. 596, no. 5; but other references supplied there by Schürer are, in my opinion, inconclusive. For a further case where a Macedonian name of month probably designates a Jewish month, see section 3.2.4.

[156] *Ant.* 2: 15,2 (318); 3: 10: 2–3 (239–240); 3: 10: 5 (248); and 4: 4: 6 (78) (all referred to above).

[157] I have mentioned above (n. 127) that 1 and 2 Maccabees, although written in Greek, use Babylonian names of months transliterated into Greek; but as suggested above, this may just be a Hasmonaean expression of anti-Hellenic nationalism, which Josephus would have had no reason to emulate.

[158] Except that in the Seleucid period, Nisan was equated with Artemisios, i.e. one month behind Josephus: see Bickerman (1968) 25; Samuel (1972) 143 and 179.

adjusting to a rapidly changing situation, where from a dominantly lunar calendar the non-Jews of the Roman East had suddenly switched, around the turn of the first century CE, to a solar calendar.

This may also explain Josephus' general unclarity with regard to Macedonian datings, which has given rise, as outlined above, to much scholarly controversy. The cities of Asia Minor and the Near East had each adapted their Macedonian calendars to the solar calendar in very different ways: some closely following the Julian calendar, others less so.[159] As a result, Macedonian calendars differed far more from each other in the first century than in the period when they were still lunar, and when the months would have begun, approximately, on the same days. Josephus' apparent failure to note this diversity and to specify, for each dating, *which* Macedonian calendar he was using, was symptomatic again, perhaps, of a failure to adjust to relatively recent upheavals in the Macedonian calendar in the first century CE.

Above all, Josephus' 'failure to adjust' would explain why unlike Philo—in whose time the Jewish lunar calendar had been distinctive from the Egyptian solar calendar for already over two centuries—Josephus does not perceive the Jewish, lunar calendar as particularly *distinctive* from that of the non-Jews. His assimilation of Macedonian and Jewish months, by then anachronistic, would have had the inevitable effect, whether intended or not, of *masking* the emerging distinctiveness of the Jewish lunar calendar.

1.2.5   Babatha's archive: the spread of the solar calendar

The rapid transformation of civil, non-Jewish calendars in the early Roman period was also to be felt, although in a completely different way, among the Jews of the province of Arabia. Before the creation of the Roman province in 106 CE, documents and inscriptions from the Nabataean kingdom are dated with exclusively Babylonian names of months.[160] The precise nature of the Nabataean calendar is impossible to reconstruct; however, it is reasonable to assume that it was lunar and essentially equivalent to the Babylonian calendar, and that this legacy from the Persian

---

[159]   See Samuel (1972) ch. 6; Meimaris (1992).

[160]   See e.g. inscriptions published by Healey (1993) (all from the 1st c. CE); also inscriptions in Negev (1971) (dated 17 CE; see footnotes for further references), Yadin (1962) 239 (= *P. Yad.* 1–3 in Yadin (1989), dated 22 Elul 94 CE, 3 Kislew 99 CE, and 2 Tevet 99 CE), and Starcky (1954) (dated 59 CE). The latter is a contract involving both Jews and Nabataeans.

period survived until the end of the Nabataean kingdom in 106 CE.[161] Bearing in mind the radical changes that occurred in Provincia Arabia soon after 106 CE, in terms not only of official language but also, more generally, of political and of legal structures,[162] it is in this period that a change of calendar is most likely to have taken place.

The Greek documents of the Babatha archive,[163] all from after 106 CE, are dated according to a completely new system. Most documents comprise a double date, Julian and Macedonian, the latter introduced with the standard formula: 'according to the compute of the province of Arabia' (*P. Yad.* 14–23, 27, 37). The correspondence between these two dating systems, almost always consistent, reveals beyond doubt that the Macedonian calendar of the province of Arabia was *solar*, and conformed already to the calendar of Arabia recorded a few centuries later in the *Hemerologia*.[164]

In the Aramaic and Nabataean documents, on the other hand, 'Babylonian' names of months are still in use.[165] But in one bilingual, Greek and Aramaic document, *P. Yad.* 27, Macedonian and 'Babylonian' names of months are correlated and hence implicitly equated: Panemos and Gorpiaios in the Greek section are rendered as Tammuz and (as reconstructed by the editors) Elul in the Aramaic. Furthermore, in one Greek document (a summons to the governor's court at Petra) Hyperberetaios is equated with *Thesrei* (i.e. Tishre: *P. Yad.* 14–15). These equivalences are the same as in Josephus; except that in Josephus they refer as we have seen to lunar months, whereas here the months are clearly solar, since they are synchronized in other documents with the Julian calendar.

---

[161] So Grumel (1958) 173; *pace* Meimaris (1992) 37 (see my remarks above, n. 153), and *pace* Cotton and Greenfield (1994) 214, nn. 19 and 24, who convert the Nabataean date of *P. Yad.* 3 (2 Tevet 99 CE) into Macedonian and Julian dates on the basis of the synchronization of the Roman Province of Arabia (which is evident in *P. Yad.* 27, on which see below), thus assuming that it was already in force before 106 CE.

[162] On which see Millar (1993) 407 and 414–18.

[163] Published by Yadin (1989), and referred to as *P. Yad.*

[164] On the *Hemerologia*, see Samuel (1972) 177.

[165] Thus *P. Yad.* 7 (= 'document vi' in Yadin 1962: 241–2), a deed of gift in Aramaic, dated 'according to the compute of this province' 24 Tammuz, year 15 (i.e. 120 CE). It was written in the district of Agaltain, in Zoar, a province of Arabia (see ibid. 242 and 251). An unpublished document dated 15 Shevat, year 25 'of the province' is, referred to in Beyer (1994) 192–3, no. 51. Babylonian/Nabataean names of months are also found in pagan Greek inscriptions as late as the 3rd c. CE: see Meimaris (1992) 169–70 (no. 30: ἀβ, from Avdat, dated 241 CE; first published by Negev (1978) 100–1, no. 10), and 172 (no. 40: Σιουάν, from Petra, dated 256 CE).

These equivalences, again, cannot be dismissed as merely approximate: because of the nature of these documents, their dates must have been precisely given. In *P. Yad.* 27, for instance, the three-month period from 1 Panemos to 30 Gorpiaios (in the Greek section) must have coincided *exactly* with the period from 1 Tammuz to 30 Elul, otherwise this document, confirming receipt of maintenance money for this period, would have been of little use to its holder. These documents prove, therefore, that the Babylonian names of months used by Aramaic- and Nabataean-speakers referred to *solar* months that were completely equivalent to the solar Macedonian months of the new Arabian province.[166]

But the pervasive use of civil, non-Jewish datings in these documents (Julian, solar Macedonian, and solar Babylonian) should not mislead us into believing that the Jews of Arabia had no distinctive calendar of their own. Fortunately for us, one of the documents—*P. Yad.* 18, a Jewish marriage contract—confirms that the Jews of Arabia could not have relied on the local, non-Jewish calendar for the dating of their festivals. It was written in Maoza on 5 April 128 CE, which corresponded, 'according to the compute of the province of Arabia', with 15 Xandikos. The Aramaic subscription is not dated. In Aramaic, however, the month of Xandikos would have been rendered as 'Nisan' (assuming consistency with *P. Yad.* 14–15 and 27); and yet a Jewish marriage contract could not have possibly been written on the *Jewish* 15 Nisan (at least this is most unlikely), for this is the first day of the festival of Unleavened Bread. It must be assumed, therefore, that besides the Aramaic/Nabataean/Macedonian *solar* calendar employed in all official documents, the Jews reckoned a separate, presumably lunar, calendar, for the dating of their festivals.

This assumption is all the more likely if we consider the close connections that existed between the Jews of Arabia and those of Idumaea and Judaea, particularly around the area of the Dead Sea.[167] For the dates of their festivals, the Jews of Arabia are likely to have ignored political boundaries and to have shared the same calendar as in Judaea, which as Josephus testifies, was lunar.

---

[166] Cf. the 'Babylonian' months of Heliopolis–Baalbek: Samuel (1972) 176.

[167] Babatha herself married a man from En Gedi, in the south of Judaea, and ended her days near that locality: see Yadin (1962) 247–8.

If this assumption is correct, the diversity of calendars in use in Arabia is bound to have led to considerable confusion. Errors in the synchronization of Julian and Macedonian calendars are not infrequent, indeed, in these documents.[168]

Most confusing, however, would have been that the same names (Nisan, etc.) were used for solar Nabataean and lunar Jewish months.[169] As a result, the Jews from Maoza near Zoar, just south of the Dead Sea, could use in the Aramaic sections of their official documents names of months that referred to a *solar*, Macedonian calendar, whereas not far from there, to the west of the Dead Sea in Idumaea and the Judaean Desert, the Jews were using the same names of months in their documents but referring instead, it would seem, to the Jewish, *lunar* calendar.[170]

Particularly uncertain, in this context, is the dating of *P. Mur.* 19, a divorce bill written at Masada in Judaea but dated to 1 Marḥeshwan year 6 in the era of Provincia Arabia (hence in 111 CE); and *P. Mur.* 20, a marriage contract involving perhaps a priestly family[171] dated to 7 Adar year 11 of Provincia Arabia (hence in 117 CE), but written this time in Haradona, an uncertain location that may have been only 5 km east of Jerusalem.[172] Were the 'Babylonian' months referred to in these documents lunar (as in Judaea, where the documents were written) or solar (as in Provincia Arabia, of which the era is used in the documents)? And why do the authors of these documents appear not to be troubled by this uncertainty?

To sum up, when the province of Arabia was created in 106 CE and, under the influence of the Roman Julian calendar, its calendar was adapted and made solar, the Jewish inhabitants of this region appear to have maintained their own, presumably lunar reckoning. Whereas until then, the Jews *could* have simply relied on the Nabataean lunar calendar,

---

[168] See *P. Yad.* 14–15; Sijpesteijn (1979) 240, on a document dated 124 CE; Lewis (1985–8), on a document dated 127 CE; Cotton (1995), on a document dated 129 CE; and for a most astonishing error, not from Arabia but from Judaea in the toparchy of Herodion, see *P. Mur.* 115 (dated 124 CE) and commentary by Benoit in Benoit, Milik, and De Vaux (1961) 250–1.

[169] This phenomenon was arguably not unique: as mentioned above, the solar Macedonian calendars of the Roman period employed the same names of months, but varied considerably from one city and/or region to the next.

[170] There is no reason to doubt that Judaean documents dated according to the years of the Bar-Kokhba revolt (the era of the 'liberation of Israel') and with 'Babylonian' months followed the Jewish lunar calendar: see *P. Mur.* 22, 23, 24, 29, 30; Yadin (1962), nos. 42, 44, 45, 46; Broshi and Qimron (1989).

[171] מן בני אלישיב: see comment by Benoit in Benoit, Milik, and De Vaux (1961) 112 (on l. 2).

[172] So according to Benoit, Milik, and De Vaux (1961) 111 on l. 1: Haradona is to be identified with Khirbet Harodon, and with Haror/Hadod? of *M. Yoma* 6: 8. See also Wasserstein (1989) 95 n. 5, who assumes that the dates in these documents were Jewish, as opposed to Cotton, Cockle, and Millar (1995) 228, who appear to assume that they were Arabian. On the use of the era of Arabia in adjacent territories see Cotton, Cockle, and Millar (1995) 228 n. 15.

it is possible that they were now faced for the first time—just as in the case of the Jews of Ptolemaic Egypt, three centuries earlier—with the responsibility of setting and reckoning their own, distinctive calendar. In this case, however, they would have simply looked across the border to Judaea, and followed the lunar calendar that was still operative in that region.

1.2.6   The Jewish calendar in the Roman Empire

In the first part of this chapter I suggested that the first century CE may have been a turning-point in the history of the Jewish calendar. It was certainly a turning-point in the history of *non-Jewish* calendars. As we have seen, the calendars of Asia, Egypt, and the Roman Near Eastern coastline underwent a radical transformation at the end of the first century BCE, when they effectively became, under the influence of the Julian calendar, solar.

The spread of solar calendars in the Near East was conterminous with the expansion of the Roman Empire in this region. The Mediterranean coastline, at the end of the first century BCE, was followed by Arabia in 106 CE. The solar calendar then spread further east towards the Euphrates: it was adopted at Dura-Europos at the turn of the third century, just as the city was being annexed into the Roman Empire.

A horoscope from Dura suggests that the lunar calendar persisted there as late as 176 CE (Samuel 1972: 142, 179–80, 187). However, this settlement had only recently come under Roman control, in the 160s, and it was only in the 190s that Dura was formally incorporated into the Roman imperial administrative structure (Millar (1993) 114–15, 131–3, 467). In this respect, therefore, the lunar horoscope of 176 belongs still to Parthian Dura. In the third century, by contrast, the calendar of Dura had become completely solar.[173]

The lunar calendar may have remained in official use at Palmyra in the Roman period—which would not be entirely surprising, given the interstitial position which this city occupied between the Roman and Parthian empires in social and economic as well as cultural terms (Millar 1993: 319–36). But whether Palmyra's calendar was lunar or solar remains completely unclear (Samuel 1972: 178–80).

The expansion of the Roman solar calendar, conterminous with that of the Roman Empire, is a process which also occurred in Italy in the late Republican period. Evidence suggests that local Italian calendars were gradually abandoned in this period in favour of the calendar of Rome. The Romanization of Italian calendars reached completion under Augustus, when the Julian calendar was massively diffused.[174]

---

[173] Welles, Fine, and Gilliam (1959) 10; see e.g. nos. 26 (227 CE) and 30 (232 CE).
[174] Crawford (1996) 426. I am grateful to Emma Dench for the reference.

This process—which Fergus Millar *could* have described in his *Roman Near East*—was so consistent that by the later second century CE, only decades after the death of Babatha, Galen could write that 'Romans, Macedonians, Asiatics, and many other nations' all followed a solar calendar.[175] In most parts of the Roman Empire, indeed, and certainly in all areas of high Jewish population (the Near East, Egypt, Asia Minor, and Rome and Italy) non-Jewish calendars had all become exclusively solar.

Bickerman (1968: 48) states that the cities of Ephesus and Miletus maintained their lunar calendar well into the Roman period; but all we actually know is that the old *names* of months were maintained.[176] An inscription from the territory of Sardis is quoted both by Bickerman and Samuel as evidence of a lunar calendar in use as late as 459 CE.[177] This, however, is a mistake. The inscription in question equates *V Kal. Mai.* (27 April) with 4 Desios (i.e. Daisios), which could *not* have been a lunar date (the new moon would have been visible at Sardis on 19 April 459 CE, so that 27 April would have coincided with approximately the 8th or 9th of a lunar month).[178] On the contrary, 27 April corresponded to 4 Daisios in the *solar* Macedonian calendar as reckoned at Sardis, where the first day of the month was called Sebaste and the second day the '1st' (see Samuel 1972: 133).

The only area of the Roman Empire where a civil lunar calendar is known to have survived was Athens, and perhaps, by extension, other parts of Greece.[179] In mainland Greece, however, evidence of Jewish inhabitants in the Roman period is extremely limited.[180] Possible evidence of a civil lunar calendar has also been found in an inscription from Odessus (now Varna) in Moesia Inferior, dated

[175] Galen, *In Hippocratis Epidemiarum Libros Commentarius* 1. 1 (ed. Kühn, xvii/1.24, cf pp. 21–2).

[176] See also Samuel (1972) 115, 123, 174–6, and 181–2, and Magie (1950), i. 480–1, ii. 1343 n. 40 (cited by both Bickerman and Samuel).

[177] *CIG* 3467 = *Inscr. Sardis* 18: see Samuel (1972) 132–3 and Bickerman (1968: 48).

[178] On the method I have employed to determine visibility of the new moon, see below sections 3.1.6–7.

[179] The evidence is collected and studied in detail by Follet (1976) 352–66. The best attestation of this calendar is in ephebic lists of gymnasiarchs and prytaneis from Athens of the 2nd–3rd cc. CE (ibid. 363–5). Further evidence can be adduced from literary sources, e.g. Censorinus, *De die natali liber*, 22. 5 (written in 238 CE), who attributes a lunar calendar not only to Athens but to 'most cities in Greece' (Follet 1976: 359), and similarly the letter of Julius Africanus above quoted (section 1.1.12, but see my remarks there). By 485 CE, the date of Proclus' death, the Athenian calendar appears to have become assimilated with the Julian calendar, as 17 Mounychion (the Attic month) is equated with 17 April (Follet 1976: 362, although it appears to me that in 485 CE a lunar month of Mounychion *could* have begun on 1 April, so that this evidence is not entirely conclusive). I am grateful to Rainer Thiel for referring me to Follet's work.

[180] See Schürer (1973–87) iii. 65–6.

to 215 CE, and equating 24 January with 7 Boedromion.[181] This equivalence is incompatible with all the known Macedonian solar calendars; it might be compatible, however, with a lunar calendar, as the new moon would have been visible at Odessus on the evening of 19 January 215 CE (probably not on the 18th). This would mean that the 7th of the month would have begun on the evening of 25 January, thus not quite the synchronism of this inscription. The discrepancy of one or two days could be explained as the result of error; alternatively, the lunar month could have begun somewhat before first visibility of the new moon. Be that as it may, there is again no evidence of Jewish population in this particular locality.[182]

A lunar calendar did survive in Egypt, but for purely cultic purposes.[183] The lunar month is also mentioned in a large number of Italian inscriptions with the formula *luna* + ordinal. This, however, does not reflect the existence of a lunar calendar; as I shall argue in Ch. 3, it is only a reference to the astronomical lunar month.[184]

The date of Easter was then the only element, in the Christian calendar, that was based on a lunar reckoning. Its derivation from the Jewish calendar, however, was explicitly acknowledged.[185] This, if anything, would have enhanced the perception that the lunar calendar was distinctively Jewish.

Thus in the context of the Roman Near East and of the Jewish populated areas of the Roman Empire, where all non-Jewish calendars happened to be solar, the survival of the Jewish lunar calendar would have stood out as remarkably exceptional—as Galen himself did not fail to indicate in the same passage.[186] This survival was perhaps no more than a reflection of Jewish conservatism.[187] But it is remarkable to note that whilst the non-Jewish calendars of the Roman Near East were switching from lunar to solar reckonings, the Jewish calendar was evolving, in the very same period, in the *opposite* direction: in the first

---

[181] Robert (1959) 210–11, cited perhaps over-confidently by Bickerman (1968: 48) as evidence of a lunar calendar.

[182] See Schürer (1973–87) iii. 72.

[183] See above, section 1.2.3. Cf the probably cultic lunar calendar, based on a 25-year cycle, that survived in Roman Gaul (Duval and Pinault 1986).

[184] Section 3.3.4.

[185] See below, sections 2.4, 2.5, 3.3.1, 3.4.1, and 5.1.2.

[186] Galen, *In Hippocratis Epidemiarium Libros Commentarius* 1. 1 (ed. Kühn, xvii/1. 23), where 'those in Palestine' means, in all likelihood, the Jews. See M. Stern (1974–84) ii, no. 394. It is surprising that Galen, writing in Alexandria, makes no reference to the Jews of Egypt. Perhaps what he means is that only in Palestine the Jews make use of the lunar calendar *in public life*, as is born out by the dating of events in Josephus' works, the dating of the Bar-Kokhba documents, etc.

[187] Similarly, the survival of the Athenian lunar calendar in Greece of the Roman period can be ascribed to cultural conservatism: see the remarks of Follet (1976) 355.

century CE, as we have seen, the Jews appear to have lost all interest in the solar calendar, so that only the lunar calendar prevailed.

This preference for a lunar calendar suggests perhaps a deliberate attempt, on the part of first-century Jews, to distinguish themselves from Roman culture and the increasingly expanding Graeco-Roman world. By contrast with the Persian, Seleucid, and Hasmonaean periods, when the adoption of the Babylonian calendar signified the Jews' integration into the dominant Near Eastern culture, in the Roman period the same lunar calendar (formerly Babylonian, now Jewish) became to the Jews a marker of cultural difference. However deliberate this may have been, it remains at least an undeniable fact that by the end of the first century CE, the lunar calendar had become to the Jews an indicator of their distinct identity.

The distinctiveness of the Jewish lunar calendar is noted in this and in subsequent centuries, if only briefly, by a number of Christian and other non-Jewish authors (such as Galen, whom I have just quoted). But surprisingly little is made of it in Jewish sources themselves. Philo, as we have seen, emphasized it at Alexandria, where calendrical distinctiveness would have gone back to the mid Ptolemaic period; but it is only implicit, at best, in sources such as Josephus. The distinctiveness of the Jewish calendar does find expression, however, in rabbinic sources, albeit in only one or two traditions:

Israel reckon by the moon and the nations by the sun ... and when the sun is eclipsed it is a bad omen for the nations since they reckon by the sun, and when the moon is eclipsed it is a bad omen for the enemies of Israel [euphemism] since they reckon by the moon.[188]

Esau reckons by the sun, which is large, Jacob reckons by the moon, which is small.[189]

These traditions are Palestinian; but the former is also recorded in the Babylonian Talmud.[190] In Babylonia, however, the situation would have been quite different: for the solar calendar had not spread beyond the borders of the Roman Empire. In the Parthian empire, the lunar Babylonian calendar was consistently maintained: evidence of its use at Babylon

---

[188] *Mekhilta de-R. Yishmael* 1 (ed. Horowitz–Rabin 7); *T. Sukkah* 2: 6 (p. 194).

[189] *Genesis Rabbah* 6: 3 (ed. Theodor–Albeck 42). Esau personifies, in rabbinic literature, the Roman Empire. 'Large' and 'small' refer in this passage to the difference in brightness between the two objects.

[190] *B. Sukkah* 29a. It is also found in later rabbinic sources, e.g. *Exodus Rabbah* 15: 27. See also *Song Rabbah* on S. of S. 5: 16.

and at Seleucia on the Tigris is available at least until the first century CE.[191] Although the Sasanians, from the early third century, adopted for official purposes a Persian/Zoroastrian calendar that was solar,[192] the traditional Babylonian calendar appears to have remained in use in Babylonia until the rise of Islam.[193]

In this context, the distinctiveness of the Jewish calendar would have been far less pronounced than in the Roman Empire.[194] The Jewish calendar was only to become distinctive in Babylonia after the arrival of the Muslims, who introduced a new lunar calendar—itself designed, no doubt, to enhance the identity of the new religion—which abolished a practice that had been characteristic of all Near Eastern and Hellenistic lunar calendars for well over two millennia: the intercalation.[195]

[191] Parker and Dubberstein (1956); Sachs and Hunger (1988–96); Samuel (1972) 179–80, 187.

[192] More precisely, a calendar based on a 365-day year, similarly to the Egyptian civil calendar: see Bickerman (1968) 43 and (1983), Hartner (1979).

[193] According to Bickerman (1983), the geographical distribution of Zoroastrian datings in this period appears to be restricted to Iran and regions to the north of it, as far as Cappadocia in the north-west; this does not include Mesopotamia or Babylonia.

[194] The rabbinic calendar in Babylonia would have differed from the non-Jewish Babylonian calendar inasmuch as it was set independently by the Palestinian rabbinic authorities: see Chs. 4–5.

[195] See the Koran, 9: 36–8. The practice of intercalation is attested in Babylonia as early as the third millennium BCE: Sachs and Hunger (1988–96) 14; Bickerman (1968) 22.

The intercalation

In the next two chapters, I shall examine specific aspects of the Jewish lunar calendars that prevailed in the first century CE and beyond, restricting myself to non-rabbinic sources, including Jewish literature, Jewish inscriptions, as well as early Christian sources. Rabbinic sources will be left to Chs. 4–5. For the sake of clarity, I shall examine separately the two essential features of lunar calendar reckoning: intercalation (Ch. 2), and the determination of new months (Ch. 3).

2.1 INTRODUCTION

2.1.1 The procedure of intercalation

An essential feature of Jewish and other ancient lunar calendars is the intercalation of an additional month (a 13th month) every second or third year. This intercalation is necessary in order to remain in line with the solar year. Twelve lunar months, indeed, amount to approximately $354\frac{1}{3}$ days (each month being on average slightly over $29\frac{1}{2}$ days), whereas the solar (tropical) year is just under $365\frac{1}{4}$ days; hence a discrepancy of almost 11 days. In order for the lunar year to keep up with the solar year, i.e. for lunar months to recur in or around the same seasons, this discrepancy must be compensated every three (and sometimes two) years with the intercalation of an additional lunar month. Because of this solar element, the Jewish calendar is sometimes called 'lunisolar'.

There are two ways of making intercalations. The first is purely *empirical*. An assessment is made every year—or at most, one or two years in advance—of the discrepancy that has accumulated between the lunar and the solar year. On that basis, the decision is taken whether to intercalate an additional month. In some cases, account is also taken of extraneous considerations, e.g. social, political or economic. The incidence of intercalated years is thus irregular and largely unpredictable.

A procedure of this kind is prescribed, for instance, in early rabbinic sources.

The second way is to rely entirely on a *fixed cycle*, i.e. a sequence of intercalary years that permanently repeats itself. The length of the cycle can vary (cycles commonly found are of 3, 8, 19, 25, or 30 years). Once this 'lunisolar' cycle is in place, it becomes self-perpetuating and no further decisions need to be made. The incidence of intercalated years is thus regular and predetermined *ad infinitum*.

The disadvantage of the first procedure is its unpredictable, irregular nature, and its dependence on an authoritative person or body of people who are responsible for deciding, every year, whether or not to intercalate. The disadvantage of the second procedure is its unavoidable inaccuracy. No cycle, indeed, achieves an accurate synchronization of lunar and solar years. The second procedure, unlike the first, makes no provision for occasional adjustments or corrections.

2.1.2 The 'limits' of lunisolar synchronization

Intercalation assumes as a premiss that every lunar month must coincide, at least approximately, with a specific season in the solar year: for instance, in the Jewish calendar the first month (Nisan) must coincide with the spring (as can be inferred from the term אביב, *'aviv*, in biblical sources: cf. Exod. 12: 2, 13: 4). On the basis of a precise definition of 'spring', it may be possible to identify the precise boundaries or limits within which the first lunar month is allowed to occur. The present-day rabbinic calendar, for instance, follows the 'rule of the equinox', that Passover cannot occur before the calendrical vernal equinox.[1]

Limits of this kind, if precisely defined, can be used as the main criterion for empirical intercalation. They also form the theoretical basis of cyclical intercalation. But in practice, once a cycle is running, these limits no longer need to be referred to (except, perhaps, for the purpose of verifying, from time to time, the accuracy of this cycle).

In our study of intercalation in Jewish calendars, therefore, the two following questions will be considered:

(i) was intercalation irregular, and hence presumably empirical, or was it regular, and hence presumably cyclical?

(ii) what were the limits, within the solar or seasonal cycle, for the occurrence of various lunar months?

---

[1] For a more accurate definition, see Loewinger (1986) and below, section 4.2.2.

2.1.3   The evidence

Except for rabbinic sources, Jewish sources in this period say virtually nothing about the procedure of intercalation. The evidence of datings is also too sporadic to be informative: without continuous calendrical records for any given locality or community, it is difficult to establish, for instance, whether intercalations were made irregularly or cyclically. Christian sources are generally more informative on the question of intercalation in the Jewish calendar; but their reliability in reporting contemporary Jewish practice can sometimes be difficult to ascertain.

The synchronization of Jewish lunar calendars with the solar year, which is evident in all our sources and documents, leaves at least no room for doubt that intercalation was universally carried out. On the question of procedure of intercalation, it is likely that both empirical intercalation and fixed cycles were used at various times by various Jewish communities and groups. But evidence of cyclical intercalation does not go much beyond the books of *Enoch* and Qumran materials, which have already been surveyed in the previous chapter.

On the question of the 'limits' of lunisolar synchronization, e.g. those within which the month of Nisan was to occur, our sources tend to be more informative. More attention will be devoted to this question, therefore, than to the procedure of intercalation. It is clear that there was no universal agreement on these 'limits'. The main point that will emerge from this chapter, indeed, is the *diversity* of calendrical practice that appears to have existed among the Jewish communities of late Antiquity.

2.2   THE EARLY PERIOD: *ENOCH*, QUMRAN, AND OTHER SOURCES

2.2.1   Lunisolar cycles

As we have seen in Ch. 1, a distinctive characteristic of sources from the Hellenistic to Herodian periods, particularly in *Enoch* and Qumran literature, is their interest in fixed calendrical schemes. A number of lunisolar cycles are alluded to in Ethiopic *Enoch* (74: 13–16): the triennial cycle, which consists in intercalating one 30-day month every three years; and the octaeteris or 8-year cycle, which consists in intercalating 3 months over a period of 8 years. As I have argued (section 1.1.3), it is doubtful whether these cycles were observed in practice.

Qumran calendrical sources present a detailed lunisolar calendar that rigorously conforms to the 3-year cycle (or to its double: see section 1.1.6). Whether or not this calendar would have been used in practice remains completely uncertain (see section 1.1.7).

Thus it is unclear whether in practice intercalations were empirical or cyclical in this early period.[2]

2.2.2 The rule of the equinox

As to the 'limits' within which Passover would have occurred, evidence may be drawn from the work of Aristobulus of Alexandria (mid second century BCE)[3]. Fragments of his work are cited by Anatolius bishop of Laodicea (Syria), whose treatise on the date of Easter, written in the 270s CE, is itself preserved in fragmentary form in Eusebius' *Ecclesiastical History*. There, Aristobulus and later Jewish authorities are credited with the 'rule of the equinox', which is that Passover should always occur on or after the vernal equinox:

And this [i.e. the rule of the equinox] is not our own reckoning, but it was known to the Jews long ago even before Christ and it was carefully observed by them. One can learn it from what is said by Philo, Josephus, (and) Musaeus, and not only by these, but also by both of the Agathobuli, who are still more ancient and are surnamed the teachers. One can learn it also from what is said by the excellent Aristobulus ... When these (writers) explain questions concerning the Exodus, they say that it is necessary that all alike sacrifice the Passover after the vernal equinox, in the middle of the first month; and this occurs when the sun passes through the first sector of the solar, or as some of them call (it), the zodiacal cycle (Anatolius ap. Eusebius, *Ecclesiastical History*, 7. 32. 16–17).[4]

Not all the authorities mentioned by Anatolius are extant: nothing is known, indeed, of the Agathobuli, and the attribution of another work, equally unknown, to a Musaeus may well be pseudepigraphic.[5] It is impossible to comment, therefore, on the reliability of Anatolius' interpretation of their works.

---

[2] On whether the Babylonian 19-year cycle was used by the Jews in this period, see above, section 1.2.2, and below, section 2.3.5.

[3] Schürer (1973–87) iii. 579–87.

[4] This fragment of Anatolius' *Canons on the Passover* was published separately by Denis (1970) 227–8; my translation is from Charlesworth (1983–5) ii. 837.

[5] Charlesworth (1983–5) ii. 837, note b.

But Anatolius' attribution of the rule of the equinox to Philo and Josephus, whose works we are well acquainted with, is actually debatable, as I shall argue below (sections 2.3.1–2). This may cast doubt on Anatolius' interpretation of the other sources he cites, not least of Aristobulus. It should be noted that the attribution of this rule to ancient Jewish authorities suited the needs of Anatolius, whose whole purpose was to justify the adoption of this rule for his own computation of the date of Easter. We are entitled, therefore, to question the impartiality of his interpretation.

To compound this problem, the only fragment of Aristobulus on the date of Passover which we possess comes from Anatolius himself. This passage is consecutive to the one quoted above:

And Aristobulus adds that on the feast of Passover of necessity not only the sun will be passing through an equinoctial sector, but the moon also. For, since there are two equinoctial sectors, the vernal and the autumnal, and since they are diametrically opposite one another, and since the day of Passover was assigned to the fourteenth of the month in the evening, the moon will stand in the positions opposite and over against the sun, just as one can see (it) at the seasons of full moon. (So) the one, the sun, will be in the sector of the vernal equinox, and the other, the moon, of necessity will be in (the sector of) the autumnal (equinox) (Anatolius ap. Eusebius, *Ecclesiastical History*, 7. 32. 17–18).

The status of this passage is problematic in many respects. Firstly, it is unclear how much of it is a citation from Aristobulus. Although it is possible that the whole passage is Aristobulus', it is equally conceivable that only the first sentence is his, the rest ('For, since there are two equinoctial . . .') being Anatolius' comment on it. Secondly, it is unclear whether the citation is verbatim, or only a paraphrase.

Nevertheless, it can hardly be doubted that Aristobulus stated, in one form or another, that at the time of Passover the sun is in an 'equinoctial sector' ($\dot{\iota}\sigma\eta\mu\epsilon\rho\iota\nu\dot{o}\nu$ $\tau\mu\hat{\eta}\mu\alpha$). The meaning of this phrase, which Rufinus translates as *aequinoctii pars* or simply as *aequinoctium* (the equinox),[6] is obviously critical. The equinox—when day and night are of equal length—is astronomically defined as the point in time when the sun crosses the celestial equator. The point of crossing (where the equator and the ecliptic intersect) can hardly be referred to as a 'sector' (or segment: $\tau\mu\hat{\eta}\mu\alpha$). Besides, Aristobulus cannot possibly mean that the full moon always occurs on the same day as the equinox. A possible interpretation of 'equinoctial sector' could be, therefore, a sector in the sun's

---

[6] Also in Denis (1970) 227–8.

trajectory (the ecliptic) that *straddles* the celestial equator; which in calendrical terms would correspond to a period *before and after* the equinox.

Anatolius, however, interprets this phrase as referring to the first sector (δωδεκατημόριον) of the solar year or ('as some of them call it') the
zodiacal cycle; as he explains, the solar year consists of twelve such sectors which correspond to twelve months, the first of which begins at the
vernal equinox (ap. Eusebius, *Ecclesiastical History*, 7. 32. 15–17).[7] This
implies that Passover always occurs *after* the equinox, within the first of
the twelve parts of the solar year.

Anatolius' interpretation is sufficiently plausible not to warrant excessive scepticism. As Anatolius adds, moreover, 'many other matters have
been discussed by (Aristobulus) . . . in which he attempts to show that
the festival of Passover and of Unleavened Bread must be observed after the equinox' (ibid. 7: 32: 19). The relevant passages of Aristobulus
are unfortunately not quoted, as Anatolius considers it inappropriate to
engage in matters 'from which the veil of the Mosaic law has been re-
moved' (ibid.); nevertheless, we may give him the benefit of the doubt
and assume that in other passages, Aristobulus states more explicitly that
Passover comes after the equinox.

This passage of Aristobulus is the earliest attestation of what was later
to be known as the 'rule of the equinox'. This rule has no apparent basis,
indeed, in biblical sources.

Synchronization of the festivals with the solar year is implicit in the Bible, but
only in relation to *agricultural* seasons: Shavuʿot occurs at the time of the wheat
harvest (Exod. 23: 16, 34: 22; Deut. 16: 9–10), and Tabernacles at the time of
the ingathering of the crop (Exod. 23: 16, Lev. 23: 33–44, Deut. 16: 13). The
first month, when Passover occurs, is called חדש האביב ('the month of *ʾaviv*':
Exod. 13: 4, 23: 15, 34: 18; Deut. 16: 1), an apparent reference to the ripeness
of the barley crop (see Exod. 9: 31); the Septuagint renders this as μὴν τῶν νέων,
'the month of the new (crop)'.

In Exod. 34: 22, the festival of Tabernacles is associated with the phrase
תקופת השנה. Rabbinic sources interpret this phrase as meaning the (autumnal)
equinox,[8] but this is unlikely to have been its original meaning.[9] The most literal

---

[7] This scheme finds a parallel in *1Enoch*'s account of the solar year. According to
1Enoch 72, the sun rises from and sets in a total of 12 'gates', 6 in the east and 6 in
the west, of which, both in the east and in the west, 3 gates are on either side of the
equator. In the 1st (solar) month the sun rises from the 4th gate (72: 6); this month
begins therefore at the vernal equinox.

[8] See section 4.1.2.

[9] In Ps. 19: 7 the term תקופה may mean, perhaps, 'solstice', i.e. the time when
the sun reaches the 'extremities' (קצות) of the sky (the northernmost point of its
trajectory in the summer, and the southernmost point in the winter).

translation of תקופה (*tequfah*) is 'turn of the year'. Onkelos takes this to mean the 'end' of the (agricultural) year, as suggested indeed by the parallelism with Exod. 23: 16. The Septuagint renders it as the 'middle of the year'.

None of these verses, however, suggest the use of the equinox as a criterion for the synchronization of the festivals with the seasonal cycle.

Aristobulus' rule of the equinox is more likely to have originated, therefore, from outside the Bible. It reflects an interest in astronomy which may have been fostered by the cultural environment of Ptolemaic Alexandria; the passage cited by Anatolius certainly shows awareness of astronomical theory. This raises the possibility that Aristobulus' concept of when Passover occurs may be no more than *theoretical*.

In practice, indeed, it remains possible that the Jews of Alexandria did not concern themselves with anything but *ʾaviv*, the biblical injunction that Passover occur when the new crops are ripe. If so, the rule of the equinox may not have been adopted by the Jews till much later, possibly not before the fourth century CE.[10]

2.3   THE FIRST CENTURY: PHILO, JOSEPHUS, AND EPIGRAPHIC SOURCES

Anatolius is probably right with regard to Aristobulus, but his attribution of the rule of the equinox to Philo and Josephus, in the passage above quoted, is less certain. As we shall see, the statements of Philo and Josephus regarding the 'boundaries' of the date of Passover remain somewhat unclear.

2.3.1   Philo of Alexandria

The connection between the first month (in which Passover occurs) and the vernal equinox is frequently stated in the works of Philo. This implies, as with Aristobulus, an interest in astronomical concepts which biblical sources do not display. But unlike Aristobulus, Philo fails to define precisely how the first month and the equinox are related.

Philo's most extensive discussion of this topic is in the *Quaestiones*; and yet all he states there is that '(Scripture) thinks it is proper to reckon the cycle of months from the vernal equinox', and that the vernal equinox must be reckoned as 'the beginning of the cycle of months' (*Quaestiones ad Exodum* 1, on Exod. 12: 2). These statements

---

[10] In the rabbinic calendar: see section 4.2.2.

are obviously approximate, as a lunar month—which Philo assumes else-where[11]—cannot always begin on the day of the equinox. It is unclear, therefore, whether Philo means that the equinox should always occur *on or after* the beginning of the first month, or *on or before* it, or possibly either before or after, but within certain defined limits.

Similar statements are found elsewhere in Philo's works. In *Special Laws* 2. 28 (150–4), the first month is said to occur at the time of the vernal equinox, but again without clarification. In the *Life of Moses* 2. 41 (222) the first month is obscurely referred to as the 'beginning' of the vernal equinox, which suggests, rather oddly, that the vernal equinox is a *period* rather than a point in time. Philo may have in mind the period when the sun is in some 'equinoctial sector', as in the Aristobulus fragment.[12]

But other passages in Philo imply, rather inconsistently, that the equinox is connected not with the *beginning* of the first month, but rather with the *middle* of it. Elsewhere in *Special Laws*, for instance, Philo states that the festival of Unleavened Bread, on the 15th of the 1st month, oc-curs 'at the first season, by which is meant the spring season and vernal equinox'; and later in this passage, that the festival of Tabernacles, on the 15th of the 7th month, occurs at the autumnal equinox.[13] In the context of a lunar calendar these statements are actually incompatible, as six lunar months are considerably shorter than the period from vernal to autumnal equinox; again, they must be taken as mere approximations.

Thus Anatolius' attribution to Philo of the rule of the equinox is pos-sible but not really substantiated by the sources. There is certainly a connection, in Philo's works, between the festivals and the equinoxes; but this connection does not take the shape of a clear or consistent rule. Philo's ambiguity may be itself significant: in his own mind, the limits of the first lunar month may not have been clearly defined.

It is also interesting to note that Philo has nothing to say about inter-calation, even though intercalation is implicit from the synchronization of his lunar calendar with the equinox and the solar year.

2.3.2 Josephus

Josephus is even less informative than Philo. All we can find is a passage in *Antiquities* 3. 10. 5 (248), where Josephus states that 14 Nisan, when

[11] See section 1.1.10.

[12] See also *Special Laws* 2. 28 (153), as plausibly emended in Colson (1937) 398.

[13] *Special Laws* 1. 35 (181) and (186); see also ibid. 2. 33 (204) (Tabernacles), and *Decalogue* 161 (Unleavened Bread and Tabernacles).

Passover is celebrated, occurs when the sun is in the zodiac sign of Aries. The beginning of Aries was (and still is) the traditional astronomical designation of the vernal equinox.[14] It is perhaps on the strength of this passage, therefore, that Anatolius attributed to Josephus the rule that Passover always occurs after the equinox.

Confirmation of this rule may also be inferred from the equivalence that is drawn in one passage between the Jewish month Nisan and the Egyptian month Pharmuthi (*Antiquities* 2. 14. 6 (311)). In Josephus' period, Pharmuthi began on 27 March in the Julian calendar,[15] thus only a few days after the equinox.[16] Inasmuch as Nisan is lunar and Pharmuthi solar, the equivalence Josephus draws between these months can only be approximate.[17] Nevertheless, it does suggest that Passover, in the middle of Nisan, generally occurred in Pharmuthi, which is after the vernal equinox.[18]

Whether these passages warrant Anatolius' inference of a 'rule' of the equinox remains, however, unclear. Josephus may simply be reporting that Passover *usually* occurs in Aries or in Pharmuthi, after the equinox, but without this constituting a formal calendrical *rule*.

To clarify whether or not the rule of the equinox was formally observed in Josephus' period, further evidence pertaining to the first century CE needs to be considered.

2.3.3 Passover in Jerusalem, 37 CE

A passage in Josephus suggests that before the destruction of the Temple in 70 CE, Passover could be celebrated in Jerusalem relatively late.

[14] See e.g. Geminus, *Elem. Astr.* 1. 8; Vitruvius, *De Architectura* 9. 3. 1–2; Ptolemy, *Tetrabiblos* 1.10 (Robbins 1940: 58–61); Philo, *Life of Moses* 2. 24 (124); Anatolius ap. Eusebius, *Ecclesiastical History* 7. 32. 17 (cited above); al-Biruni (1879: 55, 60–1; see also p. 141, where he writes, similarly to Josephus, that Passover occurs when the sun is in Aries; and cf p. 63); Maimonides, *Laws of Sanctification of the Moon*, 9: 3. See further Loewinger (1986) 45–6 (n. 3).

[15] Samuel (1972) 177.

[16] The vernal equinox occurred in this period around 23 March, although it was *deemed* to occur, in the Julian calendar, on the 25th: see below, n. 142.

[17] Pharmuthi may be taken to represent in this passage the 'limits' within which Passover occurs; however, it would be unreasonable to expect an Egyptian month to correspond exactly to Jewish calendrical parameters.

[18] Less informative is the frequent equivalence in Josephus' *Antiquities* of Nisan with the Macedonian month Xanthikos, for as I have argued in section 1.2.4, the Macedonian months referred to in this context are most likely lunar.

According to *Antiquities* 18. 5. 3 (122–4), news of the death of the emperor Tiberius in 37 CE reached Vitellius, then governor of Syria, when
he was on the fourth day of his visit to Jerusalem for an ancestral Jewish festival. Josephus' precision (the 'fourth' day) suggests he is using
an accurate source. This festival was apparently Passover, as we shall
presently see.

The date of Tiberius' death is well known to us from classical Roman
sources: it was 16 March 37 CE.[19] The official report of his death at
Misenum would not have reached the city of Rome before the 18th.[20]
By estimating how long it would then have taken for the news to reach
Vitellius in Jerusalem, we may infer when approximately the festival of
Passover occurred.

Since Passover occurs around the time of the full moon, only two options can be considered, in this context, for the year 37 CE: 21 March
or 19 April. Assuming Vitellius arrived in Jerusalem, together with
Herod Antipas, at the latest on 14 Nisan (as they were coming, according
to Josephus, to offer a sacrifice to God on the occasion of the festival,
a clear reference to the Passover sacrifice of 14 Nisan), the fourth day
of his visit would have been at the latest either 24 March or 22 April
respectively.

However, 24 March must be discarded, because news of Tiberius'
death could not have reached Jerusalem from Rome in six days. Travel
by sea (at this time of the year) or by land would have taken a number of
weeks. Moreover, couriers are likely to have made their way in the first
instance to Antioch, where they would have expected to find Vitellius;
the additional journey to Jerusalem would thus have caused further delay. It is most plausible, therefore, that news of Tiberius' death would
have taken just over a month to reach Jerusalem: Passover, in that year,
would have been celebrated in Jerusalem on 19 April.

Travel by sea at this time of the year was considered still uncertain.[21] A record
journey from Puteoli to Alexandria (which is shorter than from Rome to the
Judaean coast) took, in the best season and best conditions, nine days;[22] but this
would not have been possible in the month of March.

---

[19] Tacitus, *Annals* 6. 50; Suetonius, *Life of Tiberius* 73. 1. See Seager (1972) 245.
[20] This can be inferred from Josephus, *Ant.* 18. 6. 10 (224–34). See Barrett
(1989) 50–1.
[21] According to Vegetius, *De Re Militari* 4. 39, navigation is still *incerta et discri-
mini propior* between 10/11 March and 26/7 May. See Casson (1971) 270.
[22] Casson (1971) 282–3, citing Pliny, *Natural History* 19. 3–4.

Travel by land was slower. For government couriers, Ramsey estimates an average of 50 Roman miles per day under normal conditions,[23] but this is based on a misinterpretation.[24] Wellesley estimates a maximum of 125 Roman miles per day, but this would only have been achieved in cases of exceptional emergency.[25]

For the sake of comparison it is worth noting that news of the accession of Galba in Rome took almost a month to reach Alexandria (by sea, from 9 June to 6 July 68 CE), even though it was the summer. News of the accession of Pertinax took over two months for the same journey in the winter (from 1 January to 3 March 193 CE, either by sea or by land).[26]

Preference for 19 April over 21 March can be explained in terms of the rule of the equinox: the vernal equinox occurred in this period around 23 March, before which, according to this rule, the celebration of Passover would have been precluded. However, the relatively late occurrence of Passover in 37 CE does not necessarily *prove* that such a rule was in existence, as we shall further elaborate below.

Another passage in Josephus, often quoted in this context, must be dismissed as inconclusive. In the *Jewish War*, Josephus describes a portent that occurred before the beginning of the war on 8 Xanthikos, 'at the time when the people were assembling for the Feast of Unleavened Bread'.[27] According to E. Schwartz (1905: 144), 'Xanthikos' in this context cannot designate a Jewish lunar month, since the Feast of Unleavened Bread only begins on 15 Nisan; the people would not have assembled for the festival one week earlier. It follows, in Schwartz's view, that '8 Xanthikos' is a Macedonian dating, which would have corresponded in 66 CE—the year that is evidently referred to in this passage—with 15 Nisan. Assuming, furthermore, that the Macedonian calendar used by Josephus was always that of Tyre,[28] Schwartz concludes that in 66 CE 15 Nisan would have occurred on 25 April, more than one month after the vernal equinox.

The date of 25 April is, however, untenable, because the full moon—with which Passover should have approximately coincided—occurred in that year on 28 April—as Schwartz himself indicates but yet, remarkably, ignores.[29] On

---

[23] Ramsey (1925) 68–9; followed by Casson (1974) 188.

[24] The misinterpretation is of a text of Procopius, *Anecdota* 30. 3, mistranslated by Ramsey (1925) 60; for the correct translation, evident by comparison with *Anecdota* 30. 10, see Loeb edn., p. 347.

[25] Wellesley (1967) 27, based on Tacitus, *Histories* 1.18.1.

[26] As pointed out by Ramsey (1925) 69.

[27] *Jewish War* 6. 5. 3 (290), as translated by Thackeray (Loeb edn., 1928).

[28] Schwartz based his assumption—which itself is highly questionable—entirely on a single passage in Josephus, *Jewish War* 4: 2: 4 (654); see discussion in section 1.2.4. In the Macedonian calendar of Tyre, 8 Xanthikos always corresponded to 25 April.

[29] According to Schwartz himself (1905: 144). In actual fact, if the calendar was based on sightings of the new moon, 15 Nisan would not have occurred before 30 April (for the sources of my astronomical data, see Ch. 3).

his own evidence, his dating of Passover for 66 CE must be rejected as completely implausible.

The correct interpretation of this passage in Josephus is provided by Safrai (1965a: 123–4 and 160 n. 1), who demonstrates that it was quite normal for the people to assemble in Jerusalem one week before the festival, in order to have time to undergo the required purification rituals. Therefore '8 Xanthikos' means 8 Nisan; it does not correspond to any solar Macedonian dating.[30]

2.3.4   The Berenike inscription

Turning to the Diaspora, we may now examine the inscription from Berenike (Cyrenaica), commonly dated to 24 CE, that refers to the festival of Tabernacles.[31] This inscription has been partly discussed in Ch. 1. Its calendrical significance has been widely noted, but to my knowledge no definitive conclusion about its date has ever been reached.

The inscription records a decision by the Jewish community of Berenike to grant regular honours to a Roman benefactor. It begins with an Egyptian date, as was normal in Cyrenaica (being a former possession of the Ptolemaic kingdom); but this date is immediately followed by a Jewish dating:

['Έ]τους νε', Φαῶφ κε', ἐπὶ συλλόγου τῆς σκηνοπηγίας, ἐπὶ ἀρχόντων Κλεάν-δρου. . .

55th year, 25 Phaoph<i>, at the assembly of Tabernacles, under the archons Kleandros etc. . .[32]

According to the date of the inscription, therefore, the assembly of Tabernacles would have coincided with 25 Phaophi.[33]

What is meant by 'assembly of Tabernacles' is unfortunately unclear. The festival of Tabernacles lasts, in fact, seven days: from the 15th to

---

[30] Niese (1894: 551, in apparatus on l. 9) also rejects, in this passage, the Tyrian dating, and concludes that Josephus must be using here the 'more ancient Jewish reckoning' (what he means by this is not very clear).

[31] CIG iii, no. 5361; IGR i, no. 1024; Roux and Roux (1949); Reynolds (1977), no. 17; Lüderitz (1983) no. 71; Boffo (1994), 204–16, no. 24.

[32] Roux and Roux's translation (1949) of σύλλογος as 'fête' is somewhat less accurate. Boffo (1994: 216) suggests, 'in occasione dell'assemblea per la Festa dei tabernacoli', and Lüderitz (1983: 152), 'bei der Versammlung des Laubhüttenfestes'.

[33] The reference to the 'assembly of Tabernacles' is clearly part of the date of the inscription. There is no reason to treat it as part of the narrative (which would then refer to some other time). The text that follows, indeed, is a list of the current archons, standard in the dating of all public inscriptions; this indicates that the narrative of the inscription has not yet begun in this passage.

the 21st day of the 7th month.[34] Some scholars are of the opinion that 'assembly of Tabernacles' refers in fact to the '8th day', which follows immediately the festival of Tabernacles and is called in the Bible עצרת, *ʿAtzeret* (literally, 'assembly'):[35] in other words, the 22nd of the 7th month.[36] This, however, is problematic, as in biblical sources the '8th day' is clearly distinct from the festival of Tabernacles.[37] It is safer, perhaps, to consider any of these eight days (including Tabernacles and *ʿAtzeret*) as equally possible.

The Egyptian date needs also some clarification. From the beginning of the first century CE period, when the Egyptian calendar was permanently synchronized with the Julian calendar, 25 Phaophi corresponded in most years to 22 October.[38] But before the reform of the Egyptian calendar, account must be taken of the fact that the Egyptian year was only 365 days long, hence a discrepancy with the Julian calendar of one day every 4 years; 25 Phaophi would then have coincided with a later date in October.[39] It is critical to establish, therefore, the exact year of this inscription.

The meaning of '55th year' is unfortunately unclear, and has been subject to much controversy. Reference in the inscription to the activities of a Roman official indicates that it was erected some time after 96 BCE, i.e. after the end of the Cyrenaican kingdom, and in the early Roman period. Inasmuch as the phrase '55th year' refers ostensibly to some era, and as the only era that is known to have been used in Roman Cyrenaica is the Actian era (from the battle of Actium, which was fought on 2 September 31 BCE), the most natural interpretation of the 55th year is that it refers to the year beginning on 29 August 24 CE.[40]

Various alternatives, however, have been suggested. Reynolds, in particular, believes that an era beginning from 95 BCE was also in use in Cyrenaica; which would yield for our inscription the earlier year of 41

---

[34] Lev. 23: 34, 40–2; Num. 29: 12; Deut. 16: 13–15; Neh. 8: 18.

[35] Lev. 23: 36; Num. 29: 35; Neh. 8: 18.

[36] Baldwin Bowsky (1987) 503; Boffo (1994) 210 n. 12.

[37] Baldwin Bowsky's arguments are not particularly convincing. Note, as she herself points out (1987: 503–4), that *ʿatzeret* is rendered in the Septuagint, Philo and the Church fathers as ἐξόδιον, and not as σύλλογος.

[38] In years preceding a Julian leap year, 25 Phaophi corresponded to 23 October.

[39] Parker (1950) 70 n. 6 to introduction; Samuel (1972) 177 n. 1. For conversion tables, see Skeat (1954).

[40] Perl (1971) 369, ad p. 322 n. 2. So Lüderitz (1983) 153; and not 25 CE, as stated by Roux and Roux (1949) 294, which less plausibly requires the Actian era to have begun almost one full year *after* the battle of Actium.

BCE, on a date corresponding to 26[41] October. In Reynolds's final opinion this date is less likely than 24 CE, because one of the archons listed
in the inscription holds the Roman citizenship. The option of 41 BCE, as
well as others, is more firmly dismissed by Laronde (1987: 466), on the
grounds that there is no evidence to substantiate it.[42] In Laronde's view,
it is historically unlikely that an era other than the Actium era would
have been used in Cyrenaica.[43]

On calendrical grounds, however, 24 CE must also be rejected, because 22 October in that year coincided with the *beginning* of the lunar
month (the new moon would have been visible at Berenike on that
very evening), whereas Tabernacles begin on the 15th day of the lunar
month.[44]

The year 41 BCE, on the other hand, is eminently suited to the dating
of this inscription. In that year and month, the new moon would have
been visible for the first time on 11 October in the evening; 26 October (or 25 Phaophi) would thus have corresponded to the first day of
the festival of Tabernacles. In this light, the dating of 41 BCE deserves
serious consideration.

If 26 October 41 BCE is accepted as the date of this inscription, and
identified as the first day of Tabernacles, the festival of Tabernacles
would have occurred remarkably late. Indeed, it would have been observed much later than the rule of the equinox demanded. Passover

[41] So Skeat (1954); and not the 24th, as erroneously converted in Reynolds
(1977) 244–5.

[42] See also Boffo (1994) 206 and 210 n. 12. The only inscription quoted by
Reynolds (1977) as evidence of an era from 95 BCE is no. 3; however, the dating
of the latter is itself contentious, and more likely, according to Laronde, to follow the
era of Actium.

[43] Following the view that the 'assembly of Tabernacles' must have been the 22nd
of the lunar month, Baldwin Bowsky (1987: 504–6) works out that the only years
when this lunar date coincided with 25 Phaophi were 13 BCE and 7 CE; favouring
the former as the year of the inscription, she infers the existence of an era from 67
BCE, the year of the Pirate Wars. This approach is excessively speculative, and rests
on assumptions about the date of the 'assembly of Tabernacles' and about how the
lunar calendar would have been reckoned (on which see further Ch. 3, especially
section 3.2.3) that are completely unwarranted. See Boffo (1994) 210 n. 12.

[44] Lunar months began almost universally, in Jewish and non-Jewish calendars,
around the new moon; there is no reason to assume that the calendar at Berenike
was different. I shall argue in section 3.2.3 that the reference to *noumenia* in the same
inscription suggests that the month began when the new moon was first sighted. On
the method I have employed to determine when new moons would have been visible,
see sections 3.1.6–7. The dating of 25 CE (see above, n. 40) is similarly impossible,
since 22 Oct. 25 CE coincided with the *c*.11th day of the lunar month.

would have occurred, in the same year, on 29 April, well over a month after the vernal equinox. Within the terms of the rule of the equinox, however, Passover should have been observed in the previous month, on 31 March. This suggests that the late occurrence of Tabernacles in Berenike was not due to the 'rule of the equinox', but rather to entirely different factors, as we shall now discuss below.

2.3.5 Conclusion

Evidence of a rule of the equinox in this period is scant. Although it is attributed by Anatolius to first-century figures such as Philo and Josephus, this rule is not explicitly enunciated in any of their works. Philo is inconsistent regarding the relationship between Passover and the equinox. Josephus' comment that Passover occurs when the sun is in Aries does not necessarily imply a formal or well-defined calendrical rule.

The events of 37 CE, as told by Josephus, and the Berenike inscription, suggest that festivals in the first century BCE to the first century CE were celebrated late. Further evidence that will be considered in the next chapter lends support to this conclusion.[45] This does not imply, however, that the rule of the equinox was in observance. On the contrary, the date of Tabernacles in the Berenike inscription is so late that it cannot be explained in terms of the observance of this rule. The lateness of festivals in the first century BCE to first century CE must be attributed, therefore, to other factors.

It is possible that intercalation in the Jewish calendar was based entirely, in this period, on the Babylonian system of intercalations. The dates which we have examined in this section conform, indeed, to the dates of the Babylonian calendar. Thus Nisanu in the Babylonian calendar began in 37 CE on 6 April,[46] and Tashritu began in 41 BCE on 12 October, exactly as Nisan and Tishre would have done in the Jewish calendar according to the evidence from Josephus and the Berenike inscription that we have considered.[47] Adherence to the Babylonian system

---

[45] Sections 3.2.1 and 3.2.4.

[46] Parker and Dubberstein (1956) 46. The given date of '6 April' means that the Babylonian month began the evening before. Note, however, that the days of the month in Parker and Dubberstein (1956) were based on outdated astronomical data, and thus were only intended as approximations (as acknowledged ibid. 25). The *names* of months, on the other hand, were based on cuneiform and other evidence that is completely secure: thus it is certain that Nisanu began *on or around* 6 April.

[47] Parker and Dubberstein (1956) 44 (41 BCE) and 46 (37 CE). Likewise in 130 BCE, Nisanu began on 11 April (ibid. 42) which corresponds to the most likely date of the

of intercalations may have been a tradition stretching back to the Persian period, as attested at least in the Passover papyrus from Elephantine of the late fifth century BCE.[48] However, it seems strange that as late as the first century CE, Roman Judaea and (even further) Berenike were still under the sphere of Babylonian calendrical influence.

E. Schwartz has suggested that in the period of the Temple, Passover was celebrated late so as to enable pilgrims to reach Jerusalem on time for the festival.[49] This suggestion not only is plausible in its own right, but also finds support in a rabbinic tradition that the year would be especially intercalated to allow the pilgrims already on their way to reach Jerusalem for the festival.[50]

If correct, this suggestion would explain why in subsequent centuries, after the destruction of the Temple in 70 CE, the observance of Passover appears to have receded to earlier dates in the solar year, as we shall now see.

2.4 THE SECOND AND THIRD CENTURIES

For subsequent centuries we become almost entirely dependent on non-Jewish sources—a familiar pattern in the Jewish history of this period. Non-Jewish sources can often be mistaken or unreliable, but this is not a reason to discard them entirely. Indeed, the question of whether ancient sources reflect historical reality applies just as well, albeit perhaps to a lesser extent, to Jewish sources such as Philo and rabbinic literature.

Jewish Nisan, as implicit from a dating in Josephus (see below, section 3.2.1); and in 66 CE, Tashritu began on 10 October (ibid. 47), which tallies again with the most likely Jewish date (below, section 3.2.4). In general terms, the Babylonian Nisanu always began after the vernal equinox, thus relatively late. The limits of 1 Nisanu in the Hellenistic and early Parthian periods are approximately 25 March–23 April (ibid. 3, 38–46).

[48] See section 1.2.2.

[49] E. Schwartz (1905) 148–50. Like many other scholars, Schwartz follows Anatolius and attributes the rule of the equinox to Philo and Josephus; but he considers this rule to have been only theoretical in the 1st c. CE. Schwartz's argument is built on the assumption that Passover was celebrated in 66 CE on 25 April (i.e. over one month later than the equinox). This is actually incorrect, as I have shown above (section 2.3.3); nevertheless, his argument remains plausible on the basis of the other evidence I have considered.

[50] *T. Sanhedrin* 2: 12 (p. 417); *Y. Sanhedrin* 1: 2 (18d); *B. Sanhedrin* 11a.

Particular caution must be exercised, however, in the case of Christian sources, because of a tendency on their part to draw assumptions about Jewish practice that were not based on contemporary reality, but rather on a conjectured biblical past. Some sources will be discarded entirely for this reason: Julius Africanus and Epiphanius, as we shall see below. Other Christian sources are considerably more reliable; in particular, those pertaining to the fourth-century controversies on the date of Easter, which frequently refer to the dates of the Jewish Passover. Fourth century sources will be examined in the following section (2.5).

For the second and third centuries, evidence relating to intercalation in the Jewish calendar is at best sporadic. There is a brief but important passage in Galen (mid or later second century), already mentioned in Ch. 1. Galen reports that 'those in Palestine'—in all likelihood, the Jews—follow a lunar calendar in which, unlike solar calendars, the equinox does not occur on a fixed date. In this context he writes:

Those who reckon the months in this manner are forced to make an intercalation as soon as the remnant of the previous years has accumulated into the period of one month. And it is written in the works of Hipparchus as well of other astronomers when additional months must be intercalated.[51]

Significant in this passage is Galen's reluctance to attribute to the Jews a definite cycle of intercalations: he refers the reader, instead, to Greek astronomical handbooks. This may reflect his own ignorance of Jewish practice; for as M. Stern (1974–84: ii. 309) writes, 'the references to the Jews by Galen do not necessitate the assumption of a solid knowledge of Judaism . . . while Galen expressly testifies to his sojourn in Palestine . . . he does not mention Jews in this connection'. But alternatively, it may be taken to indicate that the Jews in Palestine did *not* have a regular cycle of intercalations. They may have intercalated the year by rule of thumb: i.e., as described by Galen in this passage, whenever the discrepancy between the solar and the lunar years had so accumulated that the insertion of an extra month was needed. This would correspond to the empirical procedure that is known from rabbinic sources on Palestinian Jewish practice in the same period.[52]

Other sources relating to intercalation in the second and third centuries must be completely dismissed. Mention has already been made of a much-quoted passage

[51] Galen, *In Hippocratis Epidemiarum Libros Commentarius* 1. 1 (ed. Kühn, xvii/1. 24; my translation), partially cited in M. Stern (1974–87) ii, no. 394, pp. 327–8.
[52] See section 4.1.2.

from Julius Africanus (third century, Emmaus, Palestine), in which the Greeks and the Jews are credited with the 8-year cycle of intercalations (or octaeteris).[53] As I have shown in Ch. 1, this passage does not refer to Africanus' own period. Africanus' sole purpose is to justify his use of the octaeteris as the basis for his calculation of the period extending from Nehemiah to Jesus. In this respect, the octaeteris may be no more than an exegetical assumption; it does not even reflect, necessarily, a historical tradition about Jewish intercalation in the Second Temple period. Africanus' statement is also in itself ambiguous: that the Jews make three intercalations in eight years does not necessarily entail a consistent and regular cycle, but perhaps only an average that can be assumed when calculating a long period of years (such as from Nehemiah to Jesus). It would be incorrect, therefore, to treat this passage as evidence that the Jews actually used, at any stage in history, the octaeteris.[54]

For similar reasons, I would dismiss the evidence that has been cited by modern scholars from Epiphanius' *Panarion*.[55] It was written somewhat later, in the late fourth century, and refers back to the first century CE; I shall discuss it here because my reasons for dismissing it are similar to those applying to Africanus.

In his discussion on the date of Passover at the time of the crucifixion, Epiphanius attributes to the Jews of this period a fixed calendar based on an 85-year cycle. This cycle consists of a regular alternation of 29-day and 30-day months, with one extra day every 3 years (hence 28 extra days for the whole 85-year cycle). Every 14 years 5 intercalations are made, hence 30 intercalations in 84 years; in the 85th year of the cycle, a 31st intercalation is made. Epiphanius argues, however, that this calendar was inaccurate, and that Jesus knew the exact reckoning; which would explain why he appears to have celebrated Passover earlier than the other Jews.[56]

However, the evidence we have surveyed above (in section 2.3) does not corroborate the existence, among first-century Jews, of such a sophisticated cycle. Further evidence will confirm in the next chapter that the calendar in the first century was set empirically, without conforming to any fixed or calculated cycle. Epiphanius' concern in this passage is chiefly to resolve an exegetical problem (Jesus' date of Passover); his solution may be treated, therefore, as conjecture rather than as putative historical fact. Epiphanius' unreliability in historical and chronological matters is, in any case, notorious. As in the case of Africanus, I would be inclined to ignore this source as evidence of first-century Jewish practice.

[53] See ch. 1 n. 102.
[54] *Pace* Bickerman (1968) 30 and Schürer (1973–87) i. 592.
[55] See Bornstein (1924) 326–7.
[56] Epiphanius, *Panarion* 51. 26. 5–27. 3; in translation, Williams (1994) 58–9. The exact reckoning, according to Epiphanius, that Jesus knew consisted not of 28 extra days for the 85-year cycle, but only 24 days—or according to another textual version, 21 days—and 3 double hours. It is difficult to understand, however, how this would have accounted for Jesus' date of Passover; Epiphanius' text is somewhat obscure. The text should perhaps read '26 days', which would constitute a more accurate reckoning.

Mention must also be made of al-Biruni, a much later Arabic author from about 1000 CE, according to whom the Arabs borrowed from the Jews, 200 years before Islam, a 24-year cycle of 9 intercalations.[57] This cycle is equivalent, as far as intercalations are concerned, to three times the octaeteris. The octaeteris itself is also mentioned by al-Biruni as one of the cycles that the Jews considered (he means, apparently, when they instituted the fixed rabbinic calendar), alongside the 19-year cycle and various multiples thereof.[58] All this implies, however, is that the octaeteris was *known* to the Jews of the late Roman period, but not necessarily that it was used by them in practice.

Thus although the second and third centuries remain obscure, we may accept Galen's intimation that in this period, no regular cycle of intercalation was used.

2.5 THE FOURTH CENTURY: PASSOVER AND THE CHRISTIAN EASTER

The fourth century opens up a corpus of evidence of considerable importance to the history of the Jewish calendar: the Christian sources on the date of Easter.

The date of Easter became the object of intense controversy in the second half of the second century, and then again, following an apparent lull, during the fourth century and later. Little is known about the second-century controversies; but sources from the fourth century abound. One of the main issues was whether the Christian Easter should be observed at the same time as the Jewish Passover. Frequent reference, in Christian Paschal sources from this period, to the dates of the Jewish Passover provides us with much information about the Jewish calendar that would have been in use.

The nature and history of this important Christian controversy is interesting in its own right. I shall return to it in detail in Ch. 5, with the suggestion that the development of Christian calendar reckoning in this period may have exerted some influence on the development of the Jewish, rabbinic calendar. In this chapter, however, I shall ignore the broader significance of this controversy and restrict myself to direct references, in these sources, to contemporary Jewish calendrical practice.

[57] Al-Biruni (1879) 13–14, 73. This tradition is also cited in later Muslim sources, e.g. Maqrizi, cited in Bornstein (1924) 316. Two hundred years before Islam takes us to the early 5th c. CE, but I am willing to treat this figure as only an approximation.

[58] Al-Biruni (1879) 63.

2.5.1 The rule of the equinox in the fourth century

A consensus emerges in Christian sources, from the beginning of the fourth century, that the Jews in this period ignored the rule of the equinox and frequently celebrated Passover on the preceding full moon.

This notion is actually already implicit in the Canons of Anatolius, written at Laodicea (Syria) in the 270s CE. As I have mentioned (section 2.2), Anatolius himself was among the first Christians to advocate the rule of the equinox. This rule he ascribed to the Jews of earlier Antiquity:

Those [Christians] that place the first month in it [i.e. in the 12th segment of the zodiac, that precedes the equinox] and that fix the 14th of the month [i.e. Passover] by it, commit, as we think, no little and no common blunder. For this [i.e. the rule of the equinox] is not our own reckoning, but it was known to the Jews long ago even before Christ and it was carefully observed by them. One can learn it from what is said by Philo, Josephus, (and) Musaeus, and not only by these, but also by both of the Agathobuli, who are still more ancient and are surnamed the teachers. One can learn it also from what is said by the excellent Aristobulus, who was enrolled among the seventy who translated the sacred and divine Scriptures of the Hebrews for Ptolemy Philadelphus and his father . . .[59]

His avoidance of any reference to contemporary Jewish practice, and his insistence, instead, on ascribing the rule of the equinox to the 'Jews long ago even before Christ', to first-century authors such as Philo and Josephus, to the 'still more ancient' Agathobuli, and finally to Aristobulus of the early Ptolemaic period, suggests implicitly that the Jews of his day did not subscribe to this rule.

It is not till the early fourth century, however, that we find explicit statements in Christian sources that contemporary Jews ignored the rule of the equinox and celebrated Passover, 'in error', one month too early. The emphasis, there, has significantly shifted. Whereas Anatolius' main purpose was to legitimize the rule of the equinox by invoking the authority of Jewish sages of old, subsequent sources emphasize the error of contemporary Jews as a polemical argument against those Christians who observed Easter at the same time as the Jews.

The earliest source for us to consider is a letter on the date of Easter attributed to Peter, bishop of Alexandria in the first decade of the fourth

---

[59] Anatolius, *Canons on the Passover*, ap. Eusebius, *Ecclesiastical History*, 7. 32. 15–16, partially cited by Denis (1970) 227–8; translation from Charlesworth (1983–5) ii. 837.

century, addressed to an unknown Tricentius.[60] Both correspondents agreed, it seems, that 'the men (i.e. the Jews) of the present day now celebrate it (Passover) before the equinox'.[61] But Tricentius appears to have argued that Easter should be observed at the same time as the Jewish Passover, even if the latter was erroneous, because the crucifixion occurred at no other time but when the Jews were celebrating this festival.[62] Peter responded that the Jews had only reckoned in error since the destruction of the Temple, but that in the days of Jesus, the rule of the equinox was still observed; it was the date of Passover as reckoned in Jesus' period that Christians should follow.

I shall return to this letter, and to its historical implications, in further detail below. For now, it is sufficient to note that the Jews whom Peter and Tricentius encountered in Alexandria (and perhaps, further afield) celebrated Passover before the equinox. I would treat this source as reliable precisely because of its polemical character: Tricentius' reference to Jewish practice as a justification of his early observance of Easter had to be based on some historical reality, otherwise his argument would have lost all its force and credibility.

The next group of sources for us to consider relates to the Council of Nicaea of 325 CE, of which one of the main items on the agenda was the date of Easter. The decisions that were taken at this Council have been preserved in letters sent by Constantine to the Syrian and Palestinian absentees at the Council, that are cited in Eusebius' *Life of Constantine* and hence by early Byzantine church historians (Barnes 1981: 217). In his account, Eusebius states that before the Council of Nicaea,

another most virulent disorder had existed, and long afflicted the Church; I mean the difference respecting the salutary feast of Easter. For while one party asserted that the Jewish custom should be adhered to, the other affirmed that the exact recurrence of the period should be observed, without following the authority of those who were in error, and strangers to gospel grace (*Vita Constantini* 3. 5).

[60] This letter, preserved in the preface of the *Chronicon Paschale*, was published separately by Migne, *PG* 18. 512 b–520 b, following Galland, *Ex Chron. Pasch.* (Venice, 1729), which itself follows Du Cange's first edition of the *Chronikon Paschale* (Paris, 1688), and on which was based the English translation by Hawkins (1869: 325–32). However, a better edition of this text, based on MS Vat. gr. 1941, was published by Dindorf (1832) and followed by Migne, *PG* 92. 73 b–c.

[61] *PG* 18. 516 a, and *PG* 92. 73 b; Hawkins (1869) 326; Dindorf (1832) 7.

[62] As interpreted by E. Schwartz (1905) 109. According to Grumel (1960: 172), Tricentius advocated the observance of Easter on a fixed date of the Julian calendar; this interpretation appears, however, to be groundless, and may be based on an erroneous textual reading to which I shall return below.

The decision of the Council, on this issue, is reported in one of Constantine's letters as follows:

It was resolved by the united judgement of all present that this feast ought to be kept by all and in every place on one and the same day... And first of all, it appeared an unworthy thing that in the celebration of this most holy feast we should follow the practice of the Jews... (ibid. 3. 18).

Thus it was resolved at Nicaea that the Jewish custom should no longer be adhered to, and that instead, a 'single rule' (ibid., end) should be followed for the date of Easter. The nature of this rule—and hence, by contrast, the nature of the Jewish custom—is not explicitly stated in this letter, nor in any other contemporary source. Daunoy (1925) surmises, in fact, that no rule was ever formulated at Nicaea, for the simple reason that the churches would have been excessively divided on this matter.[63] For political reasons, it was safer for Constantine to avoid too much explicitness. Rather than risking a heated debate on calendrical rules and cycles, it was safer to agree that Christians would be united in not following the custom of the Jews.

In adopting this course, the Council of Nicaea was aiming in particular at the Christian churches of the East, whose custom, especially in Syria, had long been to observe Easter at the same time as the Jews.[64] This custom had been formally laid down in the *Didascalia*, written in the first half of the third century in Northern Syria,[65] as follows: 'start when your brothers who are of the people (the Jews) make Pascha' (5. 17. 1), 'when that people make Pascha, you fast, and complete your vigils in the middle of their azymes' (5. 20. 10).[66] It is no surprise, therefore, that Eusebius reports that the 'bishops of the East' defended their old custom at Nicaea and disagreed on the date of Easter; eventually, however, they yielded to majority opinion.[67] Long after the Council of Nicaea, Christians in

---

[63] On the varieties of Christian Easter cycles in the 3rd and 4th cc., see briefly section 5.1.2.

[64] See E. Schwartz (1905) 104–21.

[65] But perhaps elsewhere in the Roman Near East: see M. Metzger (1985) i. 16. For a general introduction, see Simon (1986) 311–15.

[66] See also the parallel text cited by Epiphanius, *Panarion* 70. 10. 2 (Williams 1994: 412).

[67] Eusebius, *On the Date of Easter*, 8 (*PG* 24. 701); id., *Vita Constantini* 3. 19. See also Athanasius, *De Synodis*, 5 (*PG* 26. 688 b–c), and id., *Ep. ad Afros Episcopos*, 2 (*PG* 26. 1032 c); Daunoy (1925) 425–7, citing further passages from Socrates and Sozomen.

the East continued observing Easter according to their custom,[68] thus meeting with consistent opposition from their own, pro-Nicene Church leaders. The Council of Antioch, in 341 CE, condemned in its first Canon those who observed Easter with the Jews (Turner 1913: 215); the same stance was adopted two years later by the Eastern bishops at the Council of Sardica (see below).

Observing Easter with the Jews entailed that it would frequently occur before the equinox. This is evident from a document from the Council of Sardica (that we shall examine in detail below), but becomes even more explicit in later fourth-century sources. Thus the *Apostolic Constitutions*, a revised, post-Nicene version of the *Didascalia* written in Syria around 380 CE (M. Metzger 1985: 55–60) now ruled explicitly that instead of following the Jews, the date of Easter should be reckoned in accordance with the rule of the equinox (5. 17. 1–3); it also cited as the 7th Apostolic Canon that 'if a bishop, priest or deacon celebrates the holy day of Easter before the vernal equinox with the Jews, he shall be deposed' (8. 47). Evidence that many Christians did in fact follow the Jews and observe Easter before the equinox can be found in John Chrysostom's third homily against Judaizing Christians, written and delivered at Antioch in 387 CE, in which he upheld the Council of Nicaea and attacked those Christians who were about to follow the Jews and observe Easter one month too early.[69] The same issue was raised in the same year in other regions: for instance, an anonymous homily from Anatolia stresses the error of the Jews who transgress their own law as laid down by Philo, Josephus, and other Hebrew sages, and often observe Passover before the equinox.[70] In the 360s, the Novatians of Bithynia and Phrygia are said to have begun following the Jews and observing

[68] In Persian Mesopotamia in c.344 CE, Aphraates writes that Jews and Christians differ in that the former celebrate Passover on the 14th, whereas to the latter the great day of the Passion is Friday the 15th (i.e. the day corresponding to the original Friday the 15th when the crucifixion took place, which was observed in the Nestorian and Jacobite calendars on a Friday rather than on the 15th of the lunar month: see Grumel 1958: 338 and 341); the Jews, moreover, keep 7 days of Unleavened Bread after Passover, whereas the Christians observe Unleavened Bread as a festival of the Saviour (Aphraates, *Demonstration* 12, in Parisot 1894: 521 and Pierre 1989: 578). This implies that both celebrate at around the same time, at least in the same month (as *per* the ancient Eastern custom), and that they only differ as to the specific day in the week (Thornton 1989*a*: 408 n. 27). For a slightly different interpretation, see Simon (1986) 319–20.

[69] John Chrysostom, *Adversus Iudaeos*, *PG* 48. 861–72; Harkins (1979).

[70] *PG* 59. 747 ff.; Floëri and Nautin (1957) 117–25.

Easter before the equinox.[71] In the same period, Epiphanius attributes this practice to the heresy of the Audians (in Scythia?), and in this context explains at length the error of the Jews who celebrate Passover before the equinox.[72]

All these sources demonstrate that throughout the fourth century, the Jews often observed Passover before the equinox, in areas as diverse as Egypt, Syria, Anatolia, and Western Asia Minor.

It is worth noting that observance of Passover before the equinox would also have been possible according to contemporary (or slightly earlier) rabbinic sources. A Tannaitic tradition rules that the year should not be intercalated (and thus Passover postponed by one month) because of the equinox alone:

על שלשה סימנין מעברין את השנה: על האביב, ועל פירות האילן, ועל התקופה. על שנים מעברין, ועל אחד אין מעברין.

The year may be intercalated on three grounds: *ʾaviv* (the ripeness of the crops), (the ripeness of) fruits of trees, and the equinox. On two of these grounds it should be intercalated, but not on one of them (alone).[73]

This passage implies that if both crops and fruits were sufficiently ripe, no intercalation would be made, even if this meant Passover occurring before the equinox. This may have happened quite frequently.[74] The rule of the equinox was eventually adopted by the rabbinic calendar, perhaps already in the fourth century, as we shall see in Ch. 4. But it is likely that at the beginning of the century, Palestinian rabbis still celebrated Passover in some years before the equinox,[75] just it was practised by other, contemporary Jewish communities elsewhere.

2.5.2 From the first century to the fourth: a radical change

The observance of Passover before the equinox, widespread in the fourth century, contrasts with our findings for the first century, when Passover appears to have occurred considerably later, sometimes over a month

---

[71] Socrates, *Hist. Eccl.* 4. 28, 5. 21–2 (*PG* 67, esp. 540, 624 b, 630 b); Sozomen, *Hist. Eccl.* 7. 18 (*PG* 67. 1469 b–c); see also Floëri and Nautin (1957) 118.

[72] *Panarion* 70, esp. 9–13 (Williams 1994: 410–16).

[73] *T. Sanhedrin* 2: 2 (p. 416); see parallels in *Y. Sanhedrin* 1: 2 (18d) and *B. Sanhedrin* 11b. For a fuller discussion of this passage, which is only partially quoted here, see section 4.1.2.

[74] So according to Beckwith (1996) 284–6.

[75] See Bornstein (1924) 322–3.

after the equinox. This suggests, in Jewish calendrical practice, a rather radical change.

The theory that the Jewish calendar changed in this manner is of course not new. It lies at the forefront of the argument of Peter of Alexandria, which I have outlined above: namely, that in the times of Jesus the Jews observed the rule of the equinox, but that following the destruction of the Temple they 'fell into error' and began observing Passover at the wrong time. A similar idea is also implicit, as we have seen, in the *Canons* of Anatolius. Modern scholars such as Grumel have accepted this account at face value;[76] as we have seen, the evidence would appear to vindicate it.

This change, however, remains to be explained. I have suggested above (section 2.3.5), following Schwartz, that the late observance of Passover before the destruction of the Temple (in 70 CE) may have been to enable pilgrims to reach Jerusalem in good time. If this is correct, it would follow that after the destruction of the Temple and the cessation of pilgrimage to Jerusalem, the postponement of Passover would no longer have been necessary. Passover could then have been celebrated as soon as the conditions required for *'aviv*, however defined, were considered to be met; which might often have been before the equinox.[77]

I have also suggested that the late observance of Passover until the first century CE may have been due to Babylonian influence. If so, it is likely that as the Roman Empire established itself in the Near East in the course of the first and second centuries CE, the influence of the Babylonian calendar over the Jews of the Roman Empire gradually waned.

Thus we may endorse the view of Peter of Alexandria that a change in Jewish calendar reckoning occurred after 70 CE, but for entirely different reasons. This change was not the result of error, but simply an adjustment to changing historical circumstances. This would explain why, by the beginning of the fourth century, the celebration of Passover before the equinox had become widespread throughout the Jewish world.

[76] Grumel (1960) 163–4; except that he assumes the change to have occurred, for some reason, around the turn of the 3rd c. Most problematic is his suggestion that at that time a new calendrical computation was *formally instituted*: besides the fact that no record of this event is found, if only implicitly, in any of the Jewish sources, it is clear that in this period the Jews lacked the institutional framework for issuing a single, authoritative decision for all the communities in the Roman Empire.

[77] See above, n. 74.

2.5.3 The 'limits' of Passover: Peter of Alexandria and the Sardica document

Two important fourth-century documents that I shall now examine indicate the 'limits' within which the pre-equinoctial, Jewish Passover of this period would have occurred. The first is the letter of Peter of Alexandria, already discussed above. In the following passage, Peter apparently cites from Tricentius' letter to him:

Εἴτε οὖν σφαλλόμενοι Ἰουδαῖοι κατὰ τὸν σεληνιακὸν δρόμον ποτὲ μὲν τῷ Φαμενὼθ ἄγουσι τὸ ἑαυτῶν πάσχα, εἴτε κατὰ τὸν ἐμβόλιμον μῆνα κατὰ τριετίαν τῷ Φαρμοῦθι, οὐδὲν ἡμῖν διαφέρει· πρόκειται γὰρ ἡμῖν οὐδὲν ἕτερον ἢ τὴν ἀνάμνησιν τοῦ πάθους αὐτοῦ ποιεῖσθαι καὶ (lacuna) κατὰ τοῦτον τὸν καιρόν, ὡς οἱ ἀπ' ἀρχῆς αὐτόπται παραδεδώκασι πρὶν Αἰγυπτίους πιστεῦσαι.

Οὐ γὰρ νῦν πρῶτον ἐπιτηροῦντες τὸν σεληνιακὸν δρόμον ἄγουσιν αὐτὸ ἐξ ἀνάγκης δὶς μὲν τῷ Φαμενώθ, ἅπαξ δὲ κατὰ τριετίαν τῷ Φαρμοῦθι· ἀπ' ἀρχῆς γὰρ καὶ πρὸ τῆς Χριστοῦ παρουσίας πάντοτε οὕτως ποιήσαντες φαίνονται.

Whether the Jews erroneously sometimes celebrate their Passover according to the course of the moon in the month Phamenoth, or according to the intercalary month every third year in the month Pharmuthi makes no difference to us: our only concern is to commemorate his passion and ... at this time, as the original eyewitnesses have recorded for us before the Egyptians received the faith.

For now is not the first time that by observing the course of the moon, they celebrate it, by necessity, twice in Phamenoth and once every third year in Pharmuthi; for it is from the beginning, even before the advent of Christ, that they have plainly always done so.[78]

Although nothing is known about Tricentius, it is reasonable to assume that he resided, like Peter, in Alexandria (hence his use of Egyptian names of months). Thus E. Schwartz (1905: 126–7) assumes that this passage refers specifically to the Alexandrian Jewish calendar of the early fourth century.

---

[78] Text of Dindorf (1832: 7), cited in E. Schwartz (1905: 109) and followed by Grumel (1960: 163–4), with my translation of the main parts of this passage. In the second paragraph, Dindorf reads δὶς ('twice'), following the Vatican MS (where the actual reading is δεισ). This reading is evidently correct, and tallies indeed with the first paragraph. The first edition of the *Chronicon Paschale* reads instead ισ (16); this reading, followed by PG 18. 516 b, the Latin translation in Dindorf ibid., and the English translation in Hawkins (1869: 327), not only is ungrammatical (one would need Φαμενὼθ τῷ ις), but also suggests that in every first and second year Passover always occurred on 16 Phamenoth, which is clearly nonsensical. In the second paragraph, Grumel renders the first clause in the negative ('by *not* observing etc.'), but it is clear that the negative particle οὐ pertains to νῦν ('not now', which I have rendered as 'now is not'), in opposition with the final clause ('from the beginning').

The interpretation of this passage presents, however, a problem: for if the Jewish calendar is lunar and observes the course of the moon—as is explicit, fortuitously, in this same passage—the sequence of two Passovers in Phamenoth and one in Pharmuthi could not repeat itself indefinitely. In order to maintain synchronization with the Egyptian solar calendar, intercalation (and occurrence of Passover one month later, in Pharmuthi) would often be necessary after an interval of only one year. One-year intervals are standard, indeed, in cycles of intercalation such as the octaeteris or the 19-year cycle.

Table 2.1. Passovers twice in Phamenoth and once in Pharmuthi.

	Common year	Common year	Intercalary year
Year 1			11 Pharmuthi
Years 2–4	30 Phamenoth	19 Phamenoth	8 Pharmuthi
Years 5–7	27 Phamenoth	16 Phamenoth	5 Pharmuthi
Years 8–10	24 Phamenoth	13 Phamenoth	2 Pharmuthi
Years 11–12	21 Phamenoth	10 Phamenoth	

This is evident from Table 2.1, which presents a sequence of hypothetical Passovers that would regularly occur two years in Phamenoth then the third year in Pharmuthi. For convenience, I am assuming in this table that the lunar year falls 11 days behind the Egyptian calendar every year, and that intercalated months are 30 days long.[79] The next Passover in the sequence (year 13), which would have to be in an intercalated year, would occur on 29 Phamenoth—thus yielding *three* Passovers in Phamenoth in succession (years 11–13).

In order to maintain lunisolar synchronization (where Passover could occur again, as in the first year, on 11 Pharmuthi), more frequent intercalations would be needed, e.g. in the year following 21 Phamenoth (of year 11). An intercalation in year 12 would lead to the occurrence of Passover in Pharmuthi, after only *one* year's interval. In any event, therefore, the sequence 2 Phamenoth–1 Pharmuthi would eventually be broken.

As a result, perhaps, of this observation, Schwartz appears to treat the phrase 'twice in Phamenoth and once every third year in Pharmuthi' not as a regular sequence but rather as an average proportion of occurrences: i.e. that Passover occurs twice more often in Phamenoth than it does in Pharmuthi. On this basis, he infers that Passover could occur on the last 19 days of Phamenoth and the first 11 days of Pharmuthi, hence

[79] This is sufficiently accurate for our purposes. A system of this kind would lead to a discrepancy from the lunar months of only one day in 18 years. For an illustration, see section 3.3.1.

between 12 Phamenoth (8 March) and 11 Pharmuthi (6 April). Assuming these were the 'limits' for the occurrence of Passover, the equinox would then have lied almost exactly in the middle of this period.[80]

Schwartz's inference, however, is too rigid. Tricentius' statement is clearly no more than an approximate generalization; the proportion of 2 : 1 need not be taken as absolutely precise.

Grumel prefers to ignore Schwartz's limits, and proposes instead, somewhat arbitrarily, that in the Jewish Alexandrian calendar the earliest possible 1 Nisan would have coincided with 1 Phamenoth. This yields, for Passover, the limits of 14 Phamenoth (10 March) to 13 Pharmuthi (8 April).[81] If these limits are correct, the majority of Passovers would have occurred after the equinox.[82] Peter does intimate that in most cases the Jewish Passover occurred *before* the equinox, but this may be dismissed as polemical exaggeration.

Grumel's limits, however, are no less hypothetical than those of Schwartz. This passage cannot serve as evidence of the *precise* limits of Passover. The vagueness of Tricentius' statement suggests, indeed, that precise limits for the occurrence of Passover were either unknown to him, or simply did not exist. Besides, it is unclear whether Tricentius is referring to some firm calendrical rule, or simply to average practice. Nevertheless, his statement can be treated as a reliable indication of the *approximate* range of dates within which Passover, in early fourth-century Alexandria or Egypt, was likely to occur.

Let us turn, now, to one of the most remarkable documents pertaining to the Jewish calendar in the fourth century, first discovered by Schwartz and published in his article of 1905.[83] It was drafted at the time of the

---

[80] E. Schwartz (1905) 127. I am not sure why Schwartz assumes that Passover would occur on the last 19 days of Phamenoth and the first 11 days of Pharmuthi, rather than on the last 20 and first 10 days (hence a proportion of exactly 2 to 1) respectively.

[81] Grumel (1960) 166. According to Grumel the latest limit is actually 11 Pharmuthi, because for some reason he assumes that the octaeteris would have been used.

[82] The equinox was reckoned by 4th-c. Alexandrians as 21 March: Grumel (1960) 164.

[83] E. Schwartz (1905: 122–3); reprinted by Turner (1939: 641–3), Bornstein (1924: 320–1, with Hebrew translation), and Grumel (1958: 41). This document is part of MS Verona, Biblioteca Capitolare LX (58), fos. 79ᵛ–80ᵛ, a collection of materials compiled by Theodosius the Deacon (otherwise unknown) dating from about 700 CE. A facsimile of it is appended to Schwartz's article. The text will be cited in full in the next chapter, where I shall discuss textual and calendrical issues in further detail.

Council of Sardica, in the winter of 343 CE,[84] by a dissident faction of Eastern bishops. In it, they proposed a 30-year cycle for the computation of the date of Easter that would conform with the rule of the equinox and the Council of Nicaea.[85] This cycle is laid out in the document for the years 328 to 357 CE (30 years). For each year, the Julian date of the 14th of the first lunar month is given, on the basis of which the date of Easter could have been worked out.

What is remarkable about this document is that alongside its 30-year cycle, which is presented as the Christian reckoning (*quo numero facimus nos Christiani*), a list of the dates of the Jewish Passover is supplied (*quibus supputationibus faciunt Iudei pascha*). This list only extends to the first 16 years, from 328 to 343 CE. Many of the Jewish Passovers, as by now might be expected, occur before the vernal equinox; indeed, this is what distinguishes them from the Christian cycle. But the most conspicuous feature of the Passover dates is that they all occur, according to this document, in the (Julian) month of March.

These Jewish Passover dates must be considered reliable on a number of accounts. They were listed in this document for the explicit purpose of demonstrating that the Eastern bishops were committed to the rule of the equinox and the decisions of the Council of Nicaea, and would not observe Easter at the same time as the Jews; their 30-year cycle differed, indeed, from the Jewish dates.[86] The polemical credibility of this argument would have depended on the authenticity of these Jewish dates; they are unlikely, therefore, to have been merely invented or forged.

It is also significant that the Jewish dates in this document do not extend beyond 343 CE, the year when the document was written. It seems that the authors of this document were cautious not to predict when the Jews would celebrate Passover in future years, and to record only those dates of Passover which were known to have actually occurred. Eastern bishops were quite capable of knowing when, in recent years, the Jewish Passover had been observed. Since the custom of many Eastern Christians was still to observe Easter at the same time as the Jews, the authors

[84] Or according to E. Schwartz (1905), in the winter of 342 CE; see Hess (1958) 63–7, 140–4.

[85] The rule of the equinox is not explicitly mentioned in the document, but it is hard to imagine this cycle being designed without the rule of the equinox as one of its given premisses.

[86] Grumel (1958) 43–4. If the Jewish Passover occurs towards the end of March, after the vernal equinox, then the Christian date in this document is identical with it (e.g. in year 2, 30 March). Otherwise, the Christian date occurs 30 days later, in April.

of this document—who were obviously interested in the question of the date of Easter—could easily have kept reliable records of when the Jews in their region had celebrated Passover in the last 16 years.

In these 16 years, the dates of Passover range between 2 March (in the 10th year) and the 30th of March (2nd year). This suggests that the 'limits' of Passover were conterminous with the month of March. E. Schwartz (1905: 123–6) surmises, quite plausibly, that to the Jews of this document, the observance of Passover in March would have been a *rule*. The decision whether or not to intercalate would have depended entirely on this rule: intercalation was made whenever it was needed for Passover to occur within the month of March.

Given the distinctiveness of the Jewish lunar calendar in the Roman Empire, dependence on March, a month of the Julian calendar, may seem at first sight surprising. The Julian calendar, however, would have provided the Jews with a convenient guideline for the synchronization of their lunar calendar with the solar year. The 'rule of March' was simple and convenient, and perhaps most natural for Jewish communities to adopt.

An allusion to this rule may be implicit in an obscure passage of Socrates' *Ecclesiastical History*, in which he describes the difference of opinion among Eastern Christians regarding the date of Easter. Some, he writes, followed the Jews even when they were in error; whilst others observed Easter after the equinox, saying it should always be kept when the sun was in Aries, in the month of Xanthikos (according to the Antiochene calendar) or of April (according to the Roman calendar).[87] This statement is inconsistent, because April/Xanthikos is not equivalent to the period when the sun is in Aries: Aries begins at the vernal equinox,[88] thus in the month of March. But Socrates' misleading emphasis on April/Xanthikos *may* be intended to express the fact that those who followed the Jews, by contrast, always observed Easter in March. The Jews they were following, on this assumption, would have observed the 'rule of March'.[89]

Various attempts have been made by modern scholars to infer from the Sardica document the existence of a Jewish cycle of intercalations. These attempts fail, however, to convince. Bornstein (1924: 319) writes, in a perhaps

---

[87] Socrates, *Hist. Eccl.* 5: 22 (*PG* 67: 629A): οἱ δὲ μετ' ἰσημερίαν ἐπετέλουν, τὸ συνεορτάζειν Ἰουδαίοις ἐκτρεπόμενοι· φάσκοντες ἀεὶ τοῦ ἡλίου ἐν Κριῷ ὄντος καθήκειν τὸ Πάσχα ἐπιτελεῖν, τῷ Ξανθικῷ μὲν κατὰ Ἀντιοχέας μηνί, Ἀπριλλίῳ δὲ κατὰ Ῥωμαίους. The Macedonian calendar of Antioch was identical with the Julian calendar, except for the names of its months and the beginning of the year in Hyperberetaios/October: see Samuel (1972) 174–7.

[88] See above, section 2.3.2.

[89] Socrates' reference, in this passage, to the Antiochene calendar may also lend support to my interpretation; as I shall argue below, it is the Jews of Antioch who are most likely to have observed the rule of March.

uncharacteristically superficial manner, that the document implies a Jewish 30-year cycle. This is clearly incorrect: the 30-year cycle is ascribed in this
document specifically to the Christians, without any indication that it was borrowed, in some form or other, from the Jews.[90]

More elaborate, but equally disconcerting, is Grumel's (1958: 42–3) attempt
to infer from this document a Jewish 19-year cycle of intercalations. Grumel
notes that the dates for the first 14 years of the (Christian) 30-year cycle
correspond exactly with those of the last 14 years of the (Christian) Alexandrian 19-year cycle. The Jewish dates in our document, for the first 14 years,
also correspond with the Alexandrian cycle, except that the rule of the equinox
is not followed, and hence Passover often occurs one month earlier. By some
inexplicable extrapolation, Grumel infers from this that the Jews must have followed a 19-year cycle similar to the Alexandrian.

This inference, which Grumel reiterates elsewhere (1960: 173–4), is completely unfounded. Firstly, the apparent similarity of the Jewish 16-year sequence
with the Alexandrian cycle is largely the result of Schwartz's considerable textual
emendations, which have the effect, whether deliberate or not, of *artificially* reconciling the Jewish dates with the Alexandrian cycle. The validity of Schwartz's
emendations will be discussed in detail in Ch. 3.[91]

Secondly, and more fundamentally, it is *a priori* impossible to reconstruct
a 19-year cycle on the basis of a list of only 16 years. By a similar extrapolation,
Grumel could just as well have inferred that the Jews followed a 30-year cycle,
or indeed, any other cycle (e.g. a 25-year cycle; but a 24-year cycle, or any other
multiple of the octaeteris, is less likely because of the sequence from year 2 to
year 11 of four intercalary years at regular intervals of three years).

In the absence of a repeated pattern within these 16 years, there cannot be
conclusive evidence of any cycle at all. The fact that the sequence of dates in
these 16 years is compatible with a section of the Alexandrian cycle could easily
be coincidental. The dates and intercalations in these years could just as well
have been empirically set, from year to year, without deliberate resort to any
fixed cycle.

It is more likely, in fact, that no fixed cycle was used, inasmuch as it was the
'rule of March' that regulated the intercalation. The decision whether or not

[90] Other comments of Bornstein on this document are also erroneous. According to him the authors of this document were Quartodecimans (on which see below,
section 5.1.2); but this is contradicted by the respect shown in the document to the
Council of Nicaea. Bornstein promises in this article (1924) to return elsewhere, in
further detail, to the Sardica document; at this stage in his research, he had clearly not
studied it in depth. It is interesting to note that two of the most seminal monographs
of the 20th c. on the Jewish calendar were published by Bornstein and Schwartz only
one year apart from each other (1904 and 1905 respectively); and yet they do not appear to have ever become well acquainted with each other's work.

[91] It should be noted that Schwartz himself does not attribute to the Jews a fixed
cycle. On Schwartz's textual emendations of specific dates, see section 3.3.1. All that
concerns us in this chapter is the fact the Jewish dates occur in March; this is not
affected, in any way, by Schwartz's emendations.

to intercalate could have been made quite simply, from year to year, depending on whether Passover would not otherwise occur in the month of March; in
this context, use of a fixed cycle would have been more cumbersome and quite
unnecessary.

An empirical procedure of this kind is implicit in the anonymous Paschal
homily of 387 CE, which describes the Jewish practice of intercalation as follows:
'If the 14th of the moon occurs before the first month . . . they add an intercalary
month of 30 days' (Floëri and Nautin 1957: 117, ll. 1–11). By 'first month' the
author means, as explained in the same passage (and also at p. 119, l. 3), the
first *solar* month according to the erroneous reckoning of the Jews, which begins
some time *before* the equinox. He may be referring, more specifically, to a given
month in some other calendar, such as the month of March. At all events, this
passage conveys the impression that the procedure of intercalation was purely
empirical, and did not follow a standard cycle.

The Jews of the Sardica document can be tentatively identified as
those of Antioch (E. Schwartz 1905: 123–6). We know from John
Chrysostom's third homily *Against the Jews*, dated 387 CE, that the Jews
of Antioch observed Passover before the equinox (as many did elsewhere:
see above). More specifically, Schwartz argues that the dissident faction that redacted the Sardica document was led by Antiochene bishops,
whose information about the Jews was most likely to have come from
their own city. Moreover, unlike a number of other civil calendars, that
of Antioch was identical with the Julian calendar;[92] a Jewish community
that used the month of March as the criterion for intercalation is likely
to have been in a city where the Julian calendar was in civil use.

The choice at Antioch of the month of Dystros (March) as the Passover month
may appear surprising, as it was the following month, Xanthikos, that was normally associated (and sometimes equated) with Nisan.[93] The equivalence of
Nisan with Xanthikos is attested in Josephus' *Antiquities*, in the Babatha documents from the province of Arabia, and in dated inscriptions from Palmyra.[94]
It is also assumed in the Christian Syriac calendar.

E. Schwartz (1905: 126) suggests that Dystros was chosen because this was
the month when the equinox occurs. This is to assume, however, that the equinox
would have been treated as calendrically significant; which, in the absence of the
rule of the equinox, is by no means certain.

Alternatively, it is possible that the biblical requirement of ʾaviv or (as in the
Septuagint) τὰ νέα was considered to be fulfilled as early as in Dystros. It is

[92] See above, n. 87. The Antiochene equivalent of March was Dystros.

[93] At least from the 1st c. CE. In the Hellenistic period, Nisan was generally
equated with Artemisios (the month following Xanthikos): see Bickerman (1968) 20;
Samuel (1972) 142–3, 179.

[94] Josephus, Babatha: see above, sections 1.2.4–5. Palmyra: see Samuel (1972) 178–
9; also *CIJ* 820.

conceivable that the term חדש האביב ('month of *'aviv'*) or μὴν τῶν νέων was interpreted not as the lunar month of Nisan, but as a *solar* month, within which 14 Nisan was to occur; this solar month could well have been identified with Dystros.

In Alexandria, by contrast, the Julian calendar had never been in use; it would not have been practical, therefore, for Alexandrian Jews to use a Julian month as a criterion for intercalation. This would explain why the 'limits' of Passover, in the letter of Peter of Alexandria, were expressed in terms of Egyptian months ('twice in Phamenoth, once in Pharmuthi'), and hence differed considerably from the Sardica document 'limits' of the month of March.[95]

The result of this was that the Jews of Alexandria did not follow the same calendar as the Jews of the Sardica document (or Antioch). In some years, they would have observed Passover one month apart. This indicates how the Jewish calendar could vary significantly from one community to the next. Variety was partly due to the influence of local, non-Jewish calendars: this was the case, at least, at Antioch, where the date of Passover was regulated by the Julian month of March. We may assume that in other cities, for instance in Asia Minor, where the months of the local Macedonian calendar were not conterminous with those of the Julian calendar,[96] the Jews would have adopted different 'limits' for Passover; which would imply further diversity still.

E. Schwartz has attempted to infer the limits of Passover in Jewish communities of Asia Minor from the *Martyrdom of Polycarp* (8. 1; 21), which states that Polycarp was martyred at Smyrna on 23 February[97] on the 'great Sabbath' (Σάββατον μέγα). The year of this martyrdom has been subject to much debate, which need not detain us here: opinions range from about 150 to 177 CE. According to the *Martyrdom of Pionus* (2: 1 and 3: 6), moreover, Pionus was arrested and martyred some time in the mid third century on the same date.

Assuming that the 'great Sabbath' was the Sabbath preceding the Jewish Passover, E. Schwartz (1905: 127–30) infers that in Asia Minor Passover was observed by the Jews extremely early in the year. He attributes this to the early occurrence of Xanthikos in the Asian calendar (21 February–23 March).

This interpretation must be rejected on a number of counts:

---

[95] E. Schwartz (1905) 126–7. The phrase 'twice in Phamenoth, once in Pharmuthi', even if flexibly interpreted, can hardly refer to the month of March, which in the Egyptian calendar corresponded to 5 Phamenoth–5 Pharmuthi.

[96] See Samuel (1972) 174–8.

[97] So according to the Moscow MS, generally considered more authoritative; others read March or April. See Camelot (1951) 239, 270.

(i) As Bowersock points out, in the context of a Christian text the term 'great Sabbath' could refer to any Sunday,[98] or alternatively to the day before the *Christian* Easter.[99] There is no indication in this passage that it refers to any aspect of the Jewish calendar.

(ii) The term 'great Sabbath' echoes John 19: 31, where the Sabbath following the crucifixion is called a 'great day'. We may consider, therefore, that the 'great Sabbath' of Polycarp's martyrdom is not intended as a real, historical dating, but rather as a literary topos implying parallelism between the crucifixion of Christ and the martyrdom of this saint.[100]

(iii) The Jewish designation of the Sabbath preceding Passover as the 'great Sabbath' (שבת הגדול) does not appear in Jewish sources before the tenth or eleventh century.[101] The passage in John 19: 31 is not relevant as it refers to the Sabbath *following* Passover.[102] Thus there is no reason to identify the 'great Sabbath' of Polycarp's martyrdom with any particular date in the Jewish calendar.[103]

2.5.4   Calendrical diversity: evidence from the Council of Nicaea

In his report of the decisions of the Council of Nicaea in 325 CE, Constantine made no explicit mention of the Jews' observance of Passover before the equinox. He did mention, however, that they observed Passover on an erroneous date, as follows:

---

[98] Bowersock (1995) 82, citing Epiphanius, *De Exp. Fid.* 24 (*PG* 42. 829c–d); see also *Panarion* 8. 6. This expression, however, may be idiosyncratic to Epiphanius. Sunday conflicts with the narrative of the *Martyrdom of Polycarp*, in which the 'great Sabbath' (8. 1) follows directly on the Friday of Polycarp's arrest (7. 1), and with the casual equation of Great Sabbath and Sabbath. I am grateful to Leofranc Holford-Strevens for his remarks.

[99] Ibid. 83, citing John Chrysostom, *Hom. in Ps.* 145. 2 (*PG* 5. 525d). Further options are also possible, but this lies beyond my scope.

[100] Buschmann (1994) 20. Against this argument, however, see Lieu (1997) 70–2.

[101] See Tabory (1995) 127–8 n. 186, and remarks thereon by Oppenheimer (1996) 226.

[102] Besides, in this source the adjective 'great' does not qualify 'Sabbath' but 'day'. See Beckwith (1996) 294.

[103] For various other suggestions, see Lieu (1997) 70–9. Lieu favours the view that the 'great Sabbath' means here Passover itself, or the first day of Unleavened Bread, following the rabbinic interpretation of 'Sabbath' in Lev. 23: 11, 15–16 (ibid. 73–4). This, however, is hardly more convincing. Even if the writer intended Passover itself, the association of Polycarp's martyrdom with Passover is likely to be a literary topos rather than a factual date.

Ἐκεῖθεν τοίνυν κἂν τούτῳ τῷ μέρει τὴν ἀλήθειαν οὐχ ὁρῶσιν, ὡς ἀεὶ[104] κατὰ τὸ πλεῖστον αὐτοὺς πλανωμένους, ἀντὶ τῆς προσκούσης ἐπανορθώσεως, ἐν τῷ αὐτῷ ἔτει δεύτερον τὸ Πάσχα ἐπιτελεῖν. τίνος οὖν χάριν τούτοις ἑπόμεθα, οἳ δεινὴν πλάνην νοσεῖν ὡμολόγηνται; δεύτερον γὰρ τὸ Πάσχα ἐν ἑνὶ ἐνιαυτῷ οὐκ ἂν ποιεῖν ποτε ἀνεξοίμεθα.

Hence it is that on this point also they do not see the truth, so that, always getting most things wrong, instead of (making) the appropriate adjustment they celebrate Passover twice in the same year. Why then should we follow those who confess to being sick in grievous error? Surely we shall never consent to keep this feast a second time in the same year.[105]

The notion that the Jews celebrate Passover twice in the same year demands to be explained. Modern scholars have generally followed the explanation provided by Epiphanius (late fourth century).[106] It is based on the assumption that the year runs from one vernal equinox to the next. Accordingly, if the Jews celebrate one Passover after the equinox and the next Passover (12 lunar months later) before the next equinox, both Passovers will have occurred within the same year (i.e. at the beginning and at the end of the equinoctial year). To cite Epiphanius' interpretation:

For if we always celebrate on the Jewish date, we shall sometimes celebrate after the equinox, as they often do, and we too; and again, we shall sometimes celebrate before the equinox, as they do when they celebrate alone [i.e. not with the mainstream Christians]. Therefore if we celebrate then too, we may keep two Easters in one year, one after the equinox and one before it [i.e. before the following equinox]; but the next year we shall not keep any Easter at all, and the whole will turn out to be error instead of truth. For the year will not be over before the day of the equinox; and the cycle of the course (of the sun), which God has given men, is not complete unless the equinox has past (*Panarion* 70. 11. 5–6, Williams 1994: 414).

There are, however, objections to this interpretation. Firstly, it is unlikely that Constantine (or whoever authored his statement) would have assumed that the year began at the vernal equinox. In *calendrical* terms, it

---

[104] So according to the Moscow MS of the *Vita Constantini*, which is generally considered reliable, and so in all MSS of Socrates, *Hist. Eccl.* 1. 9. 37 (*PG* 67. 92A; Hansen 1995: 35) and Theodoret, *Hist. Eccl.* 1. 8 (*PG* 82. 933C; Parmentier and Scheidweiler 1954: 44, on 1. 10. 5), who cite Constantine's letter. According to Heikel (1902: i. 85), most manuscripts of the *Vita Constantini* read δή or δεῖ; however, this reading is likely to have been an error: see Winkelmann (1975) 91.

[105] Eusebius, *Vita Constantini* 3. 18.

[106] Duchesne (1880) 18–21; C. W. Jones (1943) 20; Grumel (1960) 169.

certainly did not: the solar calendars in use in the Roman Empire did not begin the year at the equinox. Constantine could not have had in mind the Hebrew biblical calendar of which the first month is Nisan,[107] for, as a lunar month, Nisan does not necessarily commence at the equinox; moreover, it was precisely the occurrence of Nisan that was being debated. Epiphanius appears to suggest, at the end of the passage quoted, that Constantine had in mind an *astronomical* solar year that began from the vernal equinox.[108] Astronomical erudition, however, does not fit the context of Constantine's letter, particularly as the equinox is not even mentioned.

The Julian calendar began the year on 1 January; the Egyptian civil calendar on 29 August; all the Macedonian calendars, in Asia Minor as well as in Syria, began the year in the autumn (except for Lycia, where the year began in January, following the Julian calendar, and Attica, where the year began in July). The only calendar in the Roman Empire that began the year on the vernal equinox (more precisely, on 22 March) was that of the Province of Arabia.[109] Constantine could hardly have been referring to the latter.[110]

My second objection to Epiphanius' interpretation is that it implies, as a corollary, that in some (equinoctial) years the Jews would not observe Passover at all. As Epiphanius explicitly states, if the Jews celebrate Passover before the first equinox and then, in the following year, after the next equinox, then in the period from first to second equinox Passover will never have been celebrated. Constantine's letter, however, does not refer to this possibility, which is surprising if we consider that not observing Passover at all would surely have been worse than observing it twice in the same year.

A different interpretation of Constantine's statement is suggested by Beckwith (1996: 69). According to Beckwith, the Jews in the Diaspora would have kept Passover twice every year, because of their uncertainty as to whether the year had been intercalated by the Palestinian rabbinic court, and hence on which full moon, whether before or after the

---

[107] A suggestion of C. W. Jones (1943) 20.

[108] Evidence of such a notion can be found, for instance, in *1 Enoch* 72: 6.

[109] On all the above, see Grumel (1958) 166–75. On Arabia, see also MacAdam (1986) 34, who attributes the Arabian new year to Arabia's cultural affinity with Babylonia, where the year began in the spring; this, the author adds, 'also broadens the scope of the term "Arab"' (for the Babylonian calendar, see Sachs and Hunger 1988–96: 14).

[110] Beckwith (1996: 69 n. 36) cites the *Apostolic Constitutions* 5. 13 as evidence of a year beginning in Syria around the vernal equinox; but all this source actually does is to count April as the first month of the year.

equinox, Passover was to have been celebrated. Such a practice would have resembled the rabbinic Diaspora observance of two consecutive days for each festival, which resulted from the uncertainty surrounding the date of the new moon (as described in rabbinic sources, and to be discussed in Chs. 4–5).

Beckwith's interpretation would certainly eliminate the objections I have raised against Epiphanius, but it must be discarded on two grounds. Firstly, this suggested Diaspora observance of two Passovers is completely hypothetical, and has no historical or other evidence to substantiate it. The biblical provision for a second Passover (in rabbinic sources, פסח שני), which was observed by individuals who had 'missed' the sacrifice at its appointed time (Num. 9: 9–14), does not lend support to Beckwith's hypothesis.

Secondly, Beckwith assumes the dependence of Diaspora communities on the calendrical decisions of the Palestinian rabbinic court. This assumption is based on contemporary rabbinic sources,[111] but these reflect rabbinic wishful thinking rather than historical reality. All the evidence suggests, in fact, that Diaspora communities took charge of their own calendar, without ever referring to Palestinian calendrical authority. The communities of Antioch and in Alexandria, as we have seen, chose their own 'limits' of Passover and ran their calendar accordingly. The calendrical independence of Diaspora communities will be confirmed below and in the next chapter.[112] Diaspora Jews had no reason, therefore, to be 'uncertain' about their dates of Passover; there was no need, for any community, to celebrate it twice in every year.

The correct interpretation of Constantine's letter, in my view, follows precisely from this point. By stating that the Jews 'celebrate Passover twice in the same year', he simply meant that different Jewish communities observed the festival at different times, and hence, that the Jews *as a whole* could be seen to observe it, every year, on two occasions.

The context of the council of Nicaea makes this interpretation all the more plausible. One of the stated purposes of the council of Nicaea— indeed, its main purpose—was to achieve the unity of the Church. This is why the date of Easter, together with the Arian heresy, constituted the main items on its agenda.[113] The unity of the Church is also one of the

[111] See below, section 5.3.1.

[112] On the non-observance of a second festival day in Diaspora communities, see in particular the evidence from Josephus in section 3.2.1.

[113] See Barnes (1981) 217; Daunoy (1925) 425; Zernov (1933) 32.

main themes of Constantine's letter on the date of Easter.[114] By referring to divisions among the Jewish people and their inability to keep Passover on the same date, Constantine would have been drawing an intended contrast between the Jews and the Church, that would be united, from now on, in its observance of Easter.

A number of later fourth-century sources, contemporary with Epiphanius, appear not to have connected the notion of celebrating Passover twice in a year with the rule of the equinox. This indicates, perhaps, that Epiphanius' interpretation of Constantine's statement was not shared by all. Some sources, indeed, may have understood Constantine's statement in the way I am suggesting.

The *Apostolic Constitutions* state in one passage that Easter should be observed after the equinox so as not to observe it 'twice in the year'; the rule of the equinox is repeated further on, again, after an admonition against following the Jews 'who are in error'.[115] But another passage suggests that the concept of observing Passover twice in a year was not intrinsically connected, as according to Epiphanius, to the rule of equinox: 'Reckon precisely until the 21st of the moon [i.e. lunar month]; otherwise, the 14th of the moon might occur in some other week, and in error, we might celebrate Pascha, in ignorance, twice in the year, or we might celebrate the resurrection of our Lord Jesus Christ on some other day than Sunday' (5: 17: 3).

Easter (or 'Pascha') was observed, according to the *Apostolic Constitutions*, on the first Sunday following the 14th day of the moon (lunar month). It could not occur later, therefore, than the 21st of the moon. This passage appears to be saying that failure to reckon precisely in this manner would cause Easter (referred to here, somewhat inaccurately, as '14th of the moon') to be observed on the Sunday of some other week, i.e. later than the 21st, or on some other day than Sunday. The implication of such an error would be the celebration of Pascha 'twice in a year'.

In this context, the error of 'twice in a year' has nothing to do with the equinox. It is associated with the celebration of Pascha *too late* in the wrong *week*, rather than, as according to Epiphanius, *too early* and in the wrong *month*. This passage is only compatible, therefore, with my interpretation of Constantine's letter. All the *Apostolic Constitutions* means is that if errors are made in the reckoning of Easter, different communities will celebrate Easter at different times, and hence Easter will have been celebrated 'twice in the year'.

Evidence can also be adduced from the anonymous Anatolian homily of 387 CE. Although this homily criticizes the Jews for not obeying the rule of the equinox,[116] it does not mention at any point that this leads to their observance of Passover twice in the same year. This omission is significant, because the whole purpose of this homily is to explain and justify the rule of the equinox. If the

---

[114] See *Vita Constantini* 3. 18–19 *passim*.

[115] *Apostolic Constitutions* 5. 17. 1 and 5. 17. 3. The equinox is given there as 22 Dystros (i.e. March, in the Antiochene calendar). In the St Petersburg MS, however, the phrase 'after the equinox' in 5. 17. 1 is entirely omitted (M. Metzger 1985: ii. 266).

[116] Floëri and Nautin (1957) 121–5 (paras. 12–16).

author of the homily had understood Constantine's statement in the same way as Epiphanius, surely the danger of observing Easter twice in the same year should have constituted an important argument in favour of the rule of the equinox. His omission of this argument suggests, albeit *e silentio*, that Constantine's letter may have been understood differently, perhaps in the same way as I have proposed.

Thus Constantine's letter can be taken as further confirmation of the diversity that existed, in the early fourth century, between the calendars of various Jewish communities, particularly regarding the Passover month and hence, the intercalation.

2.6 THE FOURTH TO SIXTH CENTURIES: THE PERSISTENCE OF DIVERSITY

From the fourth to the sixth centuries, evidence regarding the intercalation becomes rather sporadic. But the impression conveyed is that the situation remained largely unchanged. In this period, there is still no evidence of fixed cycles of intercalation. The rule of the equinox appears to have remained ignored in most Jewish communities—in spite of its possible adoption in fourth-century rabbinic circles.[117] We may thus question the extent of rabbinic influence on Jewish communities, even in this late period.

2.6.1 Justinian's decree

Let us begin with evidence pertaining to the date of Easter. This obscure passage in Procopius' *Anecdota* (or *Secret History*) has often been quoted by historians as an example of Justinian's maltreatment of the Jews, but to my knowledge, has never been properly interpreted or understood:[118]

Yet these constant and daily tamperings with the laws of the Romans were not the only harm he did, but the Emperor also took pains to abolish the laws which the Hebrews honour. If it ever happened, for instance, that the year in its recurring rounds brought on the Feast of Passover before the festival of the Christians, he would not allow the Jews to celebrate this at the proper time not to make any offering to God at that feast nor to perform any of the rites customary among them. And many of them used to be brought to trial as having tasted the flesh

---

[117] See section 4.2.2.

[118] See e.g. Juster (1914) i. 282–3, 356–7. Juster's suggestion that on another occasion Justinian postponed the date of Easter by one week (which he did not) so that it should not coincide with the Jewish Passover is a complete misinterpretation of his sources.

of lambs at this time by those who were in a position of authority, and these punished them by heavy fines, arraigning them for violation of the laws of the State (*Anecdota* 28. 16–19, Loeb translation).

Justinian's persecution is often viewed as an expression of Christian prejudice against Passover, which was to become commonplace in medieval Europe. However, it is unclear why the Jews were prohibited, in this instance, from celebrating Passover only if it occurred before Easter. Moreover, it is difficult to make sense of the phrase, '*if it ever happened* that the year in its recurring rounds brought on the Feast of Passover before the festival of the Christians': for Easter was observed on the first Sunday following the full moon, so that Passover (14 Nisan) would *normally* occur before it.[119]

What Justinian's decree appears to have meant, I would suggest, was that the Jews were allowed to celebrate Passover in the same month as Easter, but not in the preceding month (this would be the meaning of 'before Easter'), which is to say, in the month preceding the vernal equinox.

The reasons behind such a decree—which Procopius himself may not have fully understood—are to be sought in the context of the Christian Paschal controversies of the later Roman period. As we have seen, a number of dissenters from the council of Nicaea, in the East but also in parts of Asia Minor, perpetuated the custom of observing Easter at the same time as the Jewish Passover (i.e. even before the equinox). The Novatians, in particular, adopted this custom in Bithynia and Phrygia in the second half of the fourth century;[120] in the sixth century, under Justinian, this heresy was still in existence in some areas of the Byzantine Empire. The tradition of observing Easter 'with the Jews' is also likely to have survived in parts of the East until Justinian's period.

Justinian may have reasoned that if the Jews were forced to observe Passover in the same month as the Orthodox, Nicene Easter, i.e. after

---

[119] Easter may have occasionally occurred one month earlier than Passover, i.e. on the Sunday following the *earlier* full moon, but only under the following two conditions: firstly, that the Jews observed the rule of the equinox—for which there is no positive evidence—and secondly, that the Jews assumed a different equinox from that of the Christian Church. If the Jewish equinox was *later* than according to Christian reckoning, then Passover could have been postponed, on occasion, to the following month. Even then, a postponement of this kind would only have been rare, as the discrepancy between the Jewish and Christian equinoxes could not have been great; whereas Procopius appears to imply, quite on the contrary, that it was the occurrence of Passover *before* Easter that was less frequent.

[120] See above, section 2.5.1.

the equinox, the Novatians and other heretics who followed the Jews would soon lose their distinctiveness, because they would be observing Easter at the same time as the other Christians; and hence, their heresy would naturally die. If this interpretation is correct, it would mean that Justinian's persecution was not anti-Jewish *per se*, but rather an indirect, political measure designed at eliminating anti-Nicene heresies.

More important to us, this decree would suggest that as late as the sixth century, Jews were still widely observing Passover before the equinox, as we have seen was the case in the fourth century.

Whether Justinian was successful in imposing the rule of the equinox upon the Jews is a tantalizing question which must remain unanswered. The rule of the equinox was also promoted by the rabbis, perhaps as early as the fourth century CE, and yet their success appears to have been also limited. However, the eventual acceptance of this rule in the Jewish calendar is more likely to have been the result of ever increasing rabbinic influence on Diaspora communities in the course of the early medieval period, than the result of a rather eccentric decree of Justinian that was perhaps ineffective and only short-lived.

2.6.2 The *ketubah* of Antinoopolis

A Jewish document of utmost importance for the study of the calendar in the late Roman period is the marriage contract (*ketubah*) from Antinoopolis in Egypt, dating from 417 CE (Sirat *et al.*). The precise date of this document involves detailed analysis that pertains, above all, to the problem of the beginning of the lunar month. This analysis will be left, therefore, to the next chapter (section 3.3.3). My conclusions, however, are also relevant to the question of the intercalation; they are presented here in summary. According to the *ketubah* of Antinoopolis, the month of Kislew in 417 CE began on 26 October. This means that the preceding Nisan (in 417 CE) began on 4 March. Passover, 14 Nisan, thus occurred in that year on 17 March, which means that the rule of the equinox was not observed.[121]

2.6.3 The Zoar inscriptions

Among the most important archaeological discoveries for the study of the calendar in this period are the Jewish tombstone inscriptions from

---

[121] The vernal equinox occurred that year on 19 March, in the early evening. Contemporary reckonings of the equinox, however, were all *later* than 19 or 20 March: see next section below.

the site of Zoar (Es-Safi, Jordan), at the mouth of the river Zared, south of the Dead Sea. These inscriptions are unusual in that their dates, exclusively Jewish, are recorded in detail and with much precision.

The first inscription was discovered and published in 1925 (Cowley 1925), and two others in 1943 (Ben-Zvi 1943; Sukenik 1945). It was not until 1985 that a further inscription was published by Naveh (1985), followed in 1987 by a fifth inscription (Naveh 1987); further inscriptions were then published by him in 1995, bringing them to a total of twelve inscriptions (Naveh 1995). Since then, many more tombstones from Zoar have come to light. Four of these have been published by myself (S. Stern 1999), and two by Naveh (1999); but a dossier of about 325 photographs of unpublished Zoar tombstones has now been assembled and recorded by Konstantinos Politis, of which about 10% are Jewish and in Aramaic, and the rest are Christian and in Greek. Yannis Meimaris, in association with Sebastian Brock, is currently working on their publication.[122]

Because they are so precisely dated, the Jewish inscriptions from Zoar provide a unique opportunity to reconstruct the calendar that would have been in use in that community. One of the most important questions this will raise is whether or not this southern Palestinian community conformed to the calendar that can be inferred from contemporary rabbinic sources. My conclusions in this chapter are restricted to calendrical matters pertaining to intercalation; further aspects of the Zoar calendar will be discussed in the next chapter.

Jewish inscriptions from Zoar are all dated to the year 'from the destruction of the Temple', an era that is also attested elsewhere.[123] In

---

[122] I am grateful to Konstantinos Politis for showing me, in advance of publication, the dossier that is deposited at the Medieval and Later Antiquities Department of the British Museum. The site of Zoar has not been systematically excavated; most of the tombstones collected by Politis were discovered on the site by local peasants (see Politis 1998). Some tombstones, particularly Aramaic-Jewish, have been circulating on the international market of antiquities and are difficult to trace; their provenance from Zoar, however, is generally confirmed. All the tombstones are made of local sandstone, similar in size (30–40 cm long, 25–35 cm wide), and bear similar inscriptions; they date from the 4th–6th cc. CE. The correlation Aramaic–Jewish and Greek–Christian is almost completely consistent.

[123] This era is unique in that it is probably the only distinctively Jewish era to have been used in late Antiquity and the early Middle Ages. It is attested for instance in the *ketubah* of Antinoopolis (see section 3.3.3); at Kefar Nevuraya, a synagogue lintel inscription dated 494 from the destruction (Naveh 1978 no. 13, pp. 31–3); at Baalbek, in a 9th-c. funerary inscription published by Naveh together with the Zoar inscriptions (Naveh 1995: 493); in funerary inscriptions from 9th-c. Venosa in southern

addition, except for some earlier inscriptions, they are dated according to the year of the Sabbatical cycle. The synchronization of Sabbatical cycle and era of destruction of the Temple is generally, but not always, consistent.

Unfortunately, the first and only three inscriptions that were known from 1943 to the mid 1980s happened to be inconsistent. Numerous attempts were made by archaeologists and calendar experts to reconcile their datings, often with most ingenious emendations.[124] But once Naveh assembled his corpus of twelve inscriptions, a consistent pattern became immediately apparent; this pattern has since been confirmed by the more recently discovered inscriptions. All previous theories, therefore, can be swept away as irrelevant and obsolete.[125]

Naveh found that the majority of inscriptions assume the era of destruction to have begun, in year 1, in the first year of a Sabbatical cycle; thus years from the destruction that coincide with a Sabbatical year (year 7 of the cycle) are always multiples of 7. The minority that deviate from this scheme do so only by one year, either positively or negatively (Naveh 1995: 495). These deviations, I have argued elsewhere, are most likely the result of error (see Table 2.2).

Following earlier scholars, Naveh has suggested that the year from the destruction began on 9 Av, the anniversary of the destruction of the Temple, thus slightly earlier than the Sabbatical year that began on 1 Tishre; this would explain the one-year discrepancies in some of the tombstones that are dated to the intervening month of Elul (i.e. the '−1' discrepancies in N10 = Z315, S14 = Z177, and N3). As I have argued elsewhere, however, a year beginning on 9 Av is unattested in Jewish sources; moreover, it does not account for the '−1' discrepancies in Z254 and S15 = Z308, nor for the '+1' discrepancies in other inscriptions. It is just as plausible, therefore, that years from the destruction were in fact conterminous with Sabbatical cycle years and ran from 1 Tishre, and that discrepancies were generally the result of error (S. Stern 1999). In any event, the question of whether some of the '−1' discrepancies were erroneous or (as *per* Naveh) deliberate does not affect the dating of the inscriptions, nor our conclusions in this present work.

Italy (Cassuto 1945*b*); and even later, in Cairo Geniza documents dated 976 (T.–S. A42.1) and 998 (T.–S. E3.75[1–8]) from the destruction, and in MS Vat. Ebr.31[1], dated 1005 from the destruction. See also Bornstein (1921*a*) 324–38 and Friedman (1980) i. 104–6.

[124] To mention but a selection: Cassuto (1945*a*), Akavia (1945), Wacholder (1973) 180–4, and Assis (1978). For more extensive bibliography, see Naveh (1985).

[125] They will be ignored, therefore, in the following discussion. Sukenik's reading of '300' instead of '346' in inscription N2 has been proved wrong, for instance, by comparison with N12 (Naveh 1995: 113).

Table 2.2. The Zoar inscriptions: years and months.

Inscription[a]	Era of destruction year	Sabbatical cycle year	Era of destruction year (corrected)[b]	Month
N6 = Z253	282	—		—
Z293	286	—		—
Z134	288	—		—
N18 = Z292	290	3		Kislew
Z99	3(03)	2		Adar 1
Z138	303	2		Iyyar
S13 = Z307	305	—		Adar
Z254	318	2	317 (−1)	Tevet
N7	323	1		Iyyar
Z158	326	—		—
N9	338	2		Shevat
N2	346	3		Shevat
N12	346	3		Adar 1
N5	35(7)[c]	7		Nisan
Z144	3(6)1	4		Tevet
N10 = Z315	362	4	361 (−1)	Elul
N1	364	1	365 (+1)	Marḥeshwan
N4	386	1		Tevet
S14 = Z177	398	5	397 (−1)	Elul
N11	398	6		Kislew
Z88	399	7		Tevet
S15 = Z308	400	7	399 (−1)	Nisan
Z312	402	3		Siwan
S16 = Z306	406	1	407 (+1)	Marḥeshwan
Z149	407	2	408 (+1)	Kislew
Z101	4(08)	—		—
N17 = Z323	433	6		Nisan
N3	435	7	434 (−1)	Elul

[a] N = Naveh (1995), (1999); S = Stern (1999); Z = Zoar, unpublished dossier of K. D. Politis. N1–3 are the three inscriptions originally discovered (1925 and 1943). S inscriptions are numbered S13–16, in sequence with the numeration of Naveh (1995). Inscriptions are listed in chronological order. I have omitted fragmentary inscriptions where essential elements of the date are missing (e.g. N8). As I suspect further inscriptions may be discovered and published in the near future, this list must be treated as provisional.

[b] Corrections required to obtain a consistent synchronism between era of destruction and Sabbatical cycle years.

[c] In a personal communication Joseph Naveh has confirmed to me that this reading is virtually certain.

Wherever a discrepancy occurs, I have assumed that it is the year from the destruction, rather than the Sabbatical cycle year, that should be corrected.[126] Errors are unlikely to have been made in the Sabbatical years, because the Sabbatical cycle, and particularly the Sabbatical (7th) year, would have considerably affected the agricultural and commercial life of the Jews of Zoar.[127] The era from the destruction, by contrast, would have been of little practical consequence to them.[128] It is most unlikely, therefore, that in inscriptions N1, N3, S15 and S16, year 1 of the cycle was erroneously substituted for year 7 (the Sabbatical year) or vice versa. However, we cannot exclude the possibility that in inscriptions dated to the *middle* of the Sabbatical cycle, such as Z254, N10, S14, it was the Sabbatical cycle year that was wrongly entered. This will not affect, however, our conclusions in this present chapter.

For the purposes of our analysis, we now need to convert the years of these inscriptions into years of our era (CE). As stated above, it is evident from the synchronization of the majority of the inscriptions that year 1 from the destruction corresponded to the first year of a Sabbatical cycle. Most scholars have assumed that the Sabbatical cycle was reckoned in the ancient world the same as it is today.[129] Whether this assumption is always justified remains to be addressed; but evidence from the later Roman period suggests that by then, the present-day cycle would already have been in force. The *ketubah* of Antinoopolis of 417 CE, in particular, provides firm evidence of this.[130]

According to this accepted cycle, 69/70 CE would have been regarded as the 1st year of a Sabbatical cycle; according to Zoar reckoning, therefore, this would have been the first year of the era from the destruction (the Temple was actually destroyed in the summer of 70 CE). To convert Zoar years from the destruction to years of our era (CE), 68/9 years must therefore be added.

---

[126] The same assumption is implicit in Naveh's table (1995: 494).

[127] According to *T. Shevi'it* 4: 11 (p. 66) and parallels, as well as the Rehov inscription (see e.g. Levine 1981: 146–53), the river Zared marks the eastern boundary of the land of Israel (for purposes of Sabbatical-year laws, etc.). This entails that the Sabbatical-year laws would have been applicable at Zoar (I am grateful to Philip Alexander for this observation).

[128] As argued by Akavia (1951/2) 126–8.

[129] For the generally accepted computation of Sabbatical years, see Zuckermann (1866); Bornstein (1921c) 243–52; and more recently, Grabbe (1991).

[130] Sirat *et al.* (1986) 25–7; see discussion below, section 3.3.3. This computation is then firmly attested in the *Baraita de-Shemuel*, dated 776 CE (see S. Stern 1996), and in documentary evidence from the end of the 1st millennium CE (Friedman 1980 i. 102–3).

In the absence of decisive evidence, it is hard to prove that before the fifth century CE, the same Sabbatical cycle would have been in use. Wacholder (1973) has argued, consequently, that the Sabbatical year was reckoned in Antiquity one year *later* than it is today. However, his evidence is contentious, and is largely confined to the first century CE. Wacholder himself acknowledges that in the final analysis his argument depends entirely on a single piece of evidence, *P. Mur.* 18, which is dated to the second year of Nero (which we know was 55/6 CE); this year is apparently equated in the document with the Sabbatical year.[131] His interpretation of *P. Mur.* 18, however, is itself debatable and uncertain. Firstly, the meaning of its reference to the Sabbatical year is unclear, as it is not part of the dating at the beginning of the document. Secondly, the second regnal year of Nero may have begun, according to the Jewish computation, in Nisan of 55 CE, which would still have been, according to the traditional computation, a Sabbatical year.[132] Finally, it is unwise to build an entire argument on a single piece of evidence, as the possibility of scribal error must always be taken into account.

Wacholder's theory is also problematic in that it implies that at some stage in late Antiquity, the computation of Sabbatical years was changed and brought back by one year, thus becoming the computation that is in use today. No explanation is provided as to how or why such a radical change should have been made.

For argument's sake, I shall also take account of Wacholder's cycle: according to Wacholder's computation, 69/70 years must be added to Zoar years from the destruction (to convert them into years CE), as his Sabbatical cycle runs one year later. However, it will become evident from my analysis of Zoar inscriptions, both in this chapter and in the next, that the Jews of fourth- to sixth-century Zoar are far more likely to have followed the generally accepted Sabbatical cycle.

Most relevant to us, at present, are the inscriptions that indicate intercalated years. Z99 and N12 are dated to the 'first Adar', which implies an intercalation; whilst N11 and Z101 state explicitly that the year was intercalated.[133] The dates of these inscriptions are listed in Table 2.3, and

---

[131] To cite, from Wacholder (1983*b*: 132–3): '1Macc. 5: 48 and 53, the allusions in Josephus, and *S. ʿolam* 30 contain enough ambiguity to prevent the construction of secure charts ... But only Mur. 18 ... (i.e.) the newly-found contract at Murabbaʿat makes all studies that follow the calendar of Zuckermann and Schürer obsolete'. See also Wacholder (1973) 169–71.

[132] Nero became emperor on 13 October 54 CE, but this would not normally have been reckoned as the starting-date of his regnal years (*pace* Benoit, Milik, and de Vaux 1961: 103). See Bickerman (1968) 66, Meimaris (1992) 357–80. For rabbinic evidence of regnal years beginning in Nisan, see *M. RH* 1: 1, *Y. RH* 1: 1 (56b), *B. RH* 2a–b.

[133] It must be emphasized that in other inscriptions, where reference is *not* made to intercalated years, we cannot assume that their year was plain. Note, for instance, that N2 is dated to the same year as N12, but without reference to intercalation; the same applies to Z99 and Z138.

Table 2.3. The Zoar inscriptions: intercalated years.

Inscription	Era of destruction year	Sabbatical cycle year	Year CE
Z99	3(03)[a]	2	371/2
N12	346	3	414/5
N11	398	6	466/7
Z101	4(08)	/	476/7 (?)

[a] The reading תלת ('three') is most likely on epigraphic grounds, but תלתין ('thirty', hence the year 330) cannot be entirely excluded. The latter is perhaps less likely because it would entail a one-year discrepancy with the Sabbatical cycle year.

converted into years CE according to the computation explained above. These dates are unlikely to be erroneous, because the synchronization of years from the destruction with Sabbatical years is consistent in all cases (except for Z101, where the Sabbatical cycle year is not extant). The explicit references in the inscriptions to 'first Adar' or to the intercalated year are also unlikely to be mistakes.[134]

N11 is dated to 3 Kislew, a few months before the occurrence of the intercalated month (the second Adar). This advance indication that the year would be intercalated does not necessarily indicate, however, that a fixed cycle was in use, or even that the decision to intercalate was taken in advance. All that is provided, indeed, is the *date of death* of the deceased; the inscription itself may have been written many months later, after the intercalation of the year had occurred.

More significant are the intervals between these intercalated years. On the basis of these intervals, we can establish that the 8-year cycle (octaeteris) was definitely *not* used, at least not continuously throughout this period. From 303 (Z99) to 398 (N11) the interval is 95 years, whereas after 12 cycles of 8 years, the interval between two intercalated years should have been 96 years. Moreover, from 346 (N12) to 398 the interval is 52 years, which amounts to 6 cycles of 8 years (= 48 years) and 4 years; whereas in the octaeteris, intercalated years are never 4 years apart.[135]

---

[134] The year of Z99, as indicated in my note to Table 2.3, may be read as 330 instead of 303. Although 330 is less likely, allowance will be made for this uncertainty. The overall conclusions, however, will not be affected.

[135] Also from 303 to 408 (Z101) the interval is 105 years, whereas after 13 cycles of 8 years, the interval should have been 104 years. The datings of Z99 and Z101, however, are somewhat uncertain.

Other cycles, such as the 19-year cycle, may be possibly eliminated on the basis of S13 (= Z307). This inscription is dated to the month of Adar, without specification; presumably its year was common, otherwise 'first' or 'second' Adar would have been specified (as it is in Z99 and N12). The year of this inscription—assuming it is not erroneous—is 305 from the destruction, two years after the intercalated year of 303 (Z99). The following year (306), therefore, must presumably have been intercalated, since in any lunisolar calendar intercalation must been made at least every three years. If we add 306 to our chart, we obtain a sequence of intercalated years that is incompatible both with the 19-year cycle[136] and with the 25-year cycle.[137] These cycles could thus not have been used, at least not continuously throughout this period.

Although other cycles (e.g. of 30 years) cannot be excluded, and although the evidence I have adduced above is not absolute, it is probably most plausible to conclude that intercalation was irregularly and empirically carried out, without any fixed cycle being used.

Firmer evidence can be drawn regarding the rule of the equinox. The inscriptions suggest, indeed, that this rule was not observed. Inscription N11 is dated 398 from destruction, which we have identified as 466/7 CE. In that year, the day of Passover (14 Nisan) could only have occurred $c.5$ April.[138] No alternatives are really plausible, because one lunar month earlier, on 6 March, would be too early (well before the equinox), and 5 May would be excessively late. Now since the year

---

[136] The sequence 303–306–346–398–408 can be reduced, by removing all multiples of 19, to the sequence of 18–2–4–18–9; each of these numbers representing the position of intercalated years in a hypothetical 19-year cycle. From year 2 to year 9 (inclusive) of such a cycle, there would be a period of 8 years comprising 4 intercalations (2, 4, 9, and an additional intercalation, necessarily, between 4 and 9), which is excessive in any lunisolar cycle. The existence of such a cycle is therefore implausible. This argument depends entirely, however, on the reliability of the dating of Z99 (i.e. 303) and Z101 (i.e. 408).

[137] In actual fact, the 25-year cycle can be discarded without resort to either S13 or Z101. The sequence 303–346–398 (see chart in main text) can be reduced, by removing all multiples of 25, to the sequence of 3–21–23; each of these numbers representing the position of intercalated years in a hypothetical 25-year cycle. From year 21 to the following year 3 (inclusive) of such a cycle, there would be a period of 8 years comprising 4 intercalations (21, 23, 3, and an additional intercalation, necessarily, between 23 and 3), which again is excessive in any lunisolar cycle. This argument still depends, however, on the reliability of the dating of Z99 (i.e. 303).

[138] The new moon would have been first visible on 22 March in the evening. Note, however, that this date of Passover is only approximate, because in the majority of cases the month began at Zoar slightly earlier, as will be shown in the next chapter, section 3.4.2. Account will be taken of this below.

of N11 was intercalated, Passover of the *previous* year (465/6 CE) must have occurred 13 lunar months earlier, which works out as 17 March.[139] The vernal equinox, however, occurred in that year on the afternoon (i.e. towards the end) of 19 March.

At first sight this difference is slight, and could be explained either by redefining the rule of the equinox so that the equinox could have occurred as late as 16 Nisan, on the day of the offering of the ʿomer (sheaf),[140] or by assuming that a discrepancy of two or three days from the equinox was only an unintentional error. But on further examination, this discrepancy would have been far more significant.

Firstly, I have assumed that the new month began at the first visibility of the new moon. But as we shall see in the next chapter, in the majority of cases from Zoar the new month would have begun *earlier*, between conjunction and visibility of the new moon. Passover is likely, therefore, to have occurred in 466 CE on the 16th of the month, even further apart from the equinox.

Secondly, and more importantly, it is highly unlikely that the Jews of Zoar referred to the astronomical true equinox, which occurred, as stated, on 19 March. Instead, they would have referred to the equinox that was assumed by various calendars, Jewish or non-Jewish, in the same period. The Easter cycle of the Alexandrian Church assumed, from the beginning of the fourth century, an equinox on 21 March (Grumel 1960: 164, 171); in Syria of the later fourth century, the *Apostolic Constitutions* assumed an equinox on 22 March;[141] whilst contemporary rabbinic sources, following a similar tradition as in the Julian calendar, assumed 25/6 March.[142] If so, the breach of the rule of the equinox, at Zoar, would have been considerable.

The Jews of Zoar could not have failed, moreover, to realize that they were in breach of this rule. The proportion of tombstones discovered at Zoar indicates that the Jews lived in the midst of a predominantly

---

[139] The new moon would have been visible at Zoar on 3 March in the evening; but see previous note.

[140] As the rule of the equinox is indeed defined in some rabbinic sources: see section 4.2.2.

[141] *Apostolic Constitutions* 5. 17. 3, mentioned above, n. 115. This equinox date went back to Anatolius in the late 3rd c.: Grumel (1958) 31–2; Strobel (1984) 152.

[142] For the tradition that all equinoxes and solstices occurred on *VIII Kal.* (24/25th of the month) of the Julian calendar, see Columella, *On Agriculture* 9. 14. 11–12 and Pliny, *Natural History* 18: 221, 246, 256, 264, 311. The same is implicit in rabbinic sources, B. ʿAvodah Zarah 8a and Y. ʿAvodah Zarah 39c; see S. Stern (1996) 105–6, and below, section 5.4.2.

Christian community. The Christians at Zoar are likely to have followed the rule of the equinox, as did most Christians in the fourth century and beyond.[143] If so, in 466 CE they would have observed Easter one month later than the local Jews, in the second half of April.[144] The date of Easter must have enhanced the awareness, both of Christians and of Jews, that the local Jewish Passover did not conform to this rule.

The evidence is not restricted to N11. Inscription Z99 yields a similar result: in the year preceding this inscription, 371 CE, the day of Passover would have occurred on 18 March (assuming it followed first visibility of the new moon, on 4 March in the evening), whilst the true vernal equinox occurred in that year on the afternoon of 20 March.[145] If the equinox was reckoned as later, the rule of the equinox would clearly have been breached. The Christians, besides, would have observed Easter one month later.

N12, on the other hand, does not provide further information in this respect. Passover would have occurred, in its year, on 10 or 11 April. In the year preceding this inscription, 414 CE, Passover would have occurred on 21 March.

If the year of S13 (373/4 CE) was *not* intercalated, as argued above, then Passover would have occurred even earlier than inferred above, on 15 March 374 CE (first visibility of new moon 1 March in the evening; the equinox was on the morning of the 20th). It is unlikely, indeed, to have occurred in the next lunar month, for then Passover of the *previous* year (in 373 CE), 12 lunar months earlier, would have occurred very late, around 25 April; this is well over 5 weeks later than the date of Passover inferred from N11 (17 March), and is therefore unlikely. S13 suggests, therefore, that Passover of 374 CE may have been observed as early as 15 March.

Thus the limits of Passover may have been around 15 March (S13)–10 April (N12).

If we assume, for argument's sake, Wacholder's Sabbatical cycle, then all our dates must move forwards by one year. The calculations above, relating to the rule of the equinox, must then be altered. However, this would not affect our main conclusion, that the rule of the equinox was breached.

The year of N12, for instance, would become 415–16 CE. In 416 CE, Passover would have occurred on the 30th of March (one lunar month later, on 29 April, is less plausible as it is well over 5 weeks after the equinox—see below). If so,

---

[143] The custom of observing Easter 'with the Jews' is attested further north in Syria (e.g. at Antioch) and in Mesopotamia, but not in Palestine (see above, section 2.5.1). In the absence of evidence to the contrary, we may thus assume—though not without some reservations—that Palestinian Christians followed the normative Easter cycles (Alexandrian or Anatolian) in conformity to the Council of Nicaea.

[144] This applied whether they followed the Alexandrian or the Anatolian cycles. Similarly in 387 CE, Passover, according to those cycles, would have occurred on 19 March whilst Easter was postponed to (Sunday) 25 April (see references above, section 2.5.1, and below section 3.4.1).

[145] This inference depends, however, on the reliability of the dating of Z99 (i.e. 303).

Passover of the *previous* year, 13 lunar months earlier, would have coincided with 12 March, in clear breach of the rule of the equinox.

The year of N11, moreover, would become 467/8 CE. In 468 CE, Passover would have occurred on 25 March (one lunar month later, on 23 April, is less plausible as it is 6 weeks after the Passover date inferred from N12—see below). If so, Passover of the *previous* year, 13 lunar months earlier, would have coincided with 7 March, thus in further and more pronounced breach of the rule of the equinox.

The alternative but less plausible option is that Passover of N12 occurred on 29 April, and Passover of N11 on 23 April, with Passover of the previous year occurring on 5 April. This would mean that most Passovers occurred in April, often more than a month after the equinox, and hence often one month after the Christian Easter—a rather unlikely occurrence. I would prefer, therefore, to conclude that the limits of Passover according to Wacholder's cycle would have been around 7–30 March.

Although the early date of 7 March cannot be dismissed as impossible—as we have seen, the Jews of fourth-century Antioch would have celebrated Passover as early as the beginning of March—it is perhaps less likely than the later dates which I have inferred as limits of Passover according to the generally accepted Sabbatical cycle. Wacholder's cycle, in the context of Zoar, is therefore less likely.

2.6.4 Conclusion

The evidence of the *ketubah* of Antinoopolis, the Zoar inscriptions, and Justinian's decree reveals that as late as the fifth and sixth centuries, the rule of the equinox was generally not observed.

The historical implications of this finding are quite considerable, because contemporary or earlier rabbinic sources suggest that the rabbis promoted the rule of the equinox as early as the fourth century CE.[146] If the rabbis themselves observed this rule, their calendar would have been at variance with that of the Jews of Zoar (and Antinoopolis, and presumably elsewhere). In practical terms, this would have meant that in 371 CE, 374 CE, 466 CE, and presumably also in other years, the Jews of Zoar celebrated Passover one month earlier than in the Palestinian rabbinic communities. The Zoar calendar differed in further ways, indeed, from the rabbinic calendar, as will be seen in the next chapter.

This challenges the common assumption that by the later Roman period, the rabbis and rabbinic Judaism had become a dominant force in Jewish Palestinian society. What is particularly unique about Zoar, indeed, is its proximity to the main centres of rabbinic activity in Judaea and Galilee. There is no reason to treat the Zoar community as exceptional or 'sectarian'. Their ability to ignore the authority of their rabbinic

---

[146] See Bornstein (1924) 322–3, citing *B. RH* 21a, and below, section 4.2.2.

neighbours and celebrate the festivals on different dates has much to teach us about the extent of rabbinic authority in Palestine in one of the most important formative periods of rabbinic Judaism.

In Galilee itself, by contrast, there may be evidence that the rule of the equinox was observed. The mosaic floor of the Sepphoris synagogue (late Roman, early Byzantine period) comprises a Zodiac wheel in which the month of Iyyar is inscribed in the sign of Taurus, Tishre in the sign of Libra, etc., implying that Nisan would have corresponded to the sign of Aries.[147] This indicates, perhaps, an assumption that Nisan would mostly occur after the equinox.[148]

But the general conclusion that emerges is that calendrical diversity persisted, among various Jewish communities, till at least the sixth century CE. In this period, the rule of the equinox was far from universally observed. The persistence of calendrical diversity in the late Roman period will find further confirmation in the following chapter.

---

[147] The sign of Aries is in the section of the mosaic that has not been preserved. See illustrations in Nagy *et al.* (1996) 135–7.

[148] See above, section 2.3.2.

3

The new moon

3.1 INTRODUCTION

3.1.1 The 'new moon': some definitions

In many lunar calendars, the beginning of the month can be affected by extraneous, i.e. non-lunar, factors. These factors may be political, as in ancient Greek calendars,[1] or religious, as in the rabbinic calendar.[2] Nevertheless, the monthly cycle of the moon remains the most essential criterion of any calendar that is defined as 'lunar'.

In almost all ancient lunar calendars, the month begins around the time of the new moon. Precisely when this is, however, varies considerably from one calendar to the next.[3] The most common definition of the 'new moon' is when the new crescent becomes visible for the first time. This occurs invariably in the evening, not long after sunset, and close to the point on the horizon where the sun has set. The first day of the month will generally begin, therefore, on that *evening*. This is the case, for instance, in the Babylonian calendar.[4]

In other calendars, the lunar month begins at an earlier time: when the old moon ceases to be visible. Since the old moon is visible for the last time in the morning, shortly before sunrise, and close to the point on the horizon where the sun will rise, the first day of the new month

---

[1] Because the new month, in ancient Greek calendars, depended on the arbitrary decisions of city magistrates, considerable variation from one city to the next could regularly arise. See Aristoxenus (late 4th c. BCE), *Harmonica* 2. 37 (Macran 1902: 192): '... the 10th of the month at Corinth is the 5th at Athens and the 8th somewhere else'; Plutarch, *Life of Aristides*, 19. 8–9 (330–1); and generally, Samuel (1972).

[2] In the rabbinic calendar, religious considerations prohibit the month of Tishre from beginning on certain days of the week (the rule of לא אד"ו): see section 4.4.3.

[3] For general, but not comprehensive introductions, see Bickerman (1968) 16–21; Samuel (1972) 1–15 (note however that his diagrams on pp. 9–10 are incorrect); Parker (1950) 4–7. For more detailed astronomical studies, see references cited in nn. below.

[4] Parker and Dubberstein (1956); Sachs and Hunger (1988–96).

will generally begin on the first *morning* when the old moon is no longer visible. This is the case, for instance, in the Egyptian cultic calendar.[5]

In some calendars, finally, the 'new moon' is given a more 'scientific' definition: it is the moment of the conjunction; this is the case, for instance, in the Chinese calendar. 'Conjunction' is the moment when the moon, along its orbit, passes between the sun and the earth. At this point, the moon is at minimal illumination; to the naked eye, it is completely invisible. In such calendars, the month will generally begin at some point (e.g. morning or evening) of the day when conjunction occurs.[6]

The time interval between conjunction and first visibility of the new moon is quite considerable, and hence calendrically significant. Because of its small size and its proximity to the sun, the moon sliver is not visible to the naked eye immediately before or after the conjunction. The new crescent only becomes visible after it has reached a certain size (which is a function of its age and of other factors), and after it has become sufficiently distant from the sun.

In addition, the new moon is only visible at a specific time of the day: between sunset and moonset. At this stage of the moon's orbit, the interval between sunset and moonset is often not more than a half an hour. It is only in this short period of time, when the sun is 'isolated' from the moon and deep enough below the horizon, that the sky becomes sufficiently dark for the thin moon crescent to become visible against its background.

As a result, the time interval between conjunction and first evening of visibility is often as long as one day (24 hours); it ranges, however, at Mediterranean latitudes between a minimum of about 15 hours and a maximum of well over two days.[7] This variation depends on earthly co-ordinates and the relative positions of sun and moon at sunset. First sighting of the new moon can also be further delayed, sometimes considerably, by weather conditions.

Thus in any lunar calendar, it makes a significant difference, typically of two calendar days,[8] whether the month begins at the conjunction or at the first sighting of the new moon.[9]

---

[5] Parker (1950) 13–23; Grzybek (1990) 140–1, 146–51.

[6] I am grateful to Yaaqov Loewinger for his assistance in wording this paragraph.

[7] See Loewinger (1994) 477 and n. 14; idem (1996*a*) 73–5, citing Schaefer; Ajdler (1996) 206–9.

[8] For an illustration, see Table 3.1 in section 3.3.1 below.

[9] The same time interval applies, in reverse, to last visibility of the old moon. But first *invisibility* of the old moon (one day after the last visibility of the old moon), upon

3.1.2 Calculation and observation

Precise definition of the concept of 'new moon' is important not only for *when* the lunar month begins, as explained above, but also for *how* the beginning of the month is determined. For the conjunction cannot be determined in the same way as the new crescent is first sighted. Because the moon is invisible at the time of the conjunction (except in cases of solar eclipses), the conjunction cannot be empirically sighted or observed; it has to be determined, therefore, through a calculation.

By convention, the ('true') conjunction has always been calculated by ancient[10] and modern[11] astronomers as the moment when moon and sun are at the same (geocentric) ecliptic longitude. This calculation can only be made on the basis of a good astronomical lunar theory, supported by precise observations of the courses of the sun and of the moon. It is a complex procedure which must be repeated each month, because the synodical cycle of the moon (i.e. the full cycle of the moon's phases from one conjunction to the next; otherwise known as 'lunation') is variable and irregular: it varies between approximately 29 days 6½ hours and 29 days 20 hours.[12] To calculate the true conjunction of each month is not, therefore, an easy or practical way of reckoning the calendar.

This is why, for calendrical purposes, the calculation and use of a *mean* conjunction, rather than of the true conjunction, tends to be preferred. The mean conjunction can be simply calculated on the basis of the mean lunation and of one standard epoch (reference point). The mean lunation can be established, once and for all, by averaging out the lunations that have occurred between two solar or lunar eclipses (i.e. two observable conjunctions or oppositions):[13] it is slightly over 29½ days. By a similar method, but using a greater number of eclipses, the time of a mean conjunction can be determined; this mean conjunction can then be used as epoch. Knowledge of the mean lunation and this epoch is sufficient for the calculation of any subsequent mean conjunction. The establishment of such a system requires some expertise; but once in place, it becomes a simple calculation that is relatively easy to implement.

which some calendars are based, can often coincide with the day of the conjunction. The difference between these two, therefore, is not always calendrically significant.

[10] Ptolemy: see Pedersen (1974) 94, 220–5. Maimonides: see Loewinger (1994) 484 and (1996a) 50.

[11] See Meeus (1991) 319–24, 378.

[12] Meeus (1991) 324; Ajdler (1996) 701.

[13] 'Opposition' is the moment of full moon. See Pedersen (1974) 161–4.

By contrast, it is most arduous to calculate the first visibility of the new moon—i.e. to predict when the new crescent will first be capable of being sighted. This demands not only accurate knowledge of the courses of the sun and of the moon, but also an accurate astronomical theory of the criteria required for the moon to become visible—which even modern astronomers have not yet successfully established (more on this below). Furthermore, this calculation would only indicate whether *astronomical* conditions for visibility of the new moon will be fulfilled; but whether the new crescent will actually be sighted depends largely on weather conditions, which are impossible for anyone to calculate or to predict.[14] This is why the most natural and most practical way of establishing the appearance of the new crescent is not through calculation, but simply through empirical sighting.

Thus calendars based on first visibility of the new moon (or equally, on first invisibility of the old moon) are generally established through observation; whereas calendars based on the conjunction are generally determined by calculation.

These two calendars differ in other important ways. A calendar based on calculation is regular and can be set well in advance; it can also be shared uniformly, by a wide range of people and communities. An empirical calendar, based on observation, is totally irregular and unpredictable; it will also be set at different times from one community to the next. The empirical calendar, indeed, depends on a procedure of lunar observations which may be carried out with different degrees of regularity or accuracy; moreover, visibility of the new moon varies considerably from place to place, depending on geographical co-ordinates (mainly latitude and longitude) and local weather conditions.

For the study of any lunar calendar, therefore, it is critical to determine whether it was calculated and based on the conjunction, or empirical and based on the observation of the new (or old) moon.

3.1.3   The Jewish lunar calendar

The purpose of this chapter is to establish how Jewish lunar calendars, and particularly their new moons, were reckoned. By now it should be clear that this question is not merely technical. It concerns not only the times when new months began, but also the procedures involved, and as

---

[14] The same difficulties apply, obviously, to predicting first invisibility of the old moon.

I have just suggested, the extent to which the same calendar could have been reckoned by different and separate communities.

It is well known that the rabbinic calendar was originally based on the appearance of the new moon, which involved a procedure of observation (as described in detail in *M. RH*); and that later, it was replaced with a calculated calendar, based on the mean conjunction (or *molad*). The history of the rabbinic calendar will be left to the next chapter. In this chapter, I shall examine the evidence of non-rabbinic sources.

The evidence, as in previous chapters, is generally scarce. Nevertheless, early Jewish lunar calendars will be found to have been based, in general, on the appearance of the new crescent. This was also the practice of the Babylonians and (later) the Seleucids, whose calendars, as outlined above in Ch. 1, became dominant in the Near East by the end of the first millennium BCE, and whose influence on the Jewish calendar has been noted there.

The Babylonians carried out regular and systematic observations of the positions of the moon and other celestial bodies, that were meticulously recorded in astronomical diaries (Sachs and Hunger 1988–96). When observations, for whatever reason, had not been made, calculated predictions were recorded instead.[15] Observation, however, formed the basis of their calendar; the new moon began, as a rule, in the evening when the crescent was first sighted.[16]

The Macedonian calendar, and indeed Greek calendars in general, are also likely to have been based on sightings of the new moon.[17] As we have seen in Ch. 1, the Macedonian calendar was almost immediately assimilated to the Babylonian calendar in the Seleucid period.

[15] For instance, predictions would be made of the time interval between sunset and moonset on the first day of the month: Sachs and Hunger (1988–96) i. 21. Solstices and equinoxes were calculated, at least from 322 BCE, on the basis of the 19-year cycle of intercalations (ibid. 26, citing Neugebauer). See further Fatoohi, Stephenson, and Al-Dargazelli (1999).

[16] This does not rule out the possibility, however, that calculation of the visibility of the new moon may at some stage have replaced its actual sighting. See Parker and Dubberstein (1956) 1–4; Sachs and Hunger (1988–96) 13; Neugebauer (1955) i. 41–3; also Wacholder and Weisberg (1971) 227–42.

[17] Samuel (1972) 57, 141; Follet (1976) 354; but this is an assumption rather than a proven fact. The ability of Strepsiades, in Aristophanes, *Clouds* 1131–4, to count down the days to the end of the month without uncertainty whether it would be full or defective, suggests that in 5th-c. BCE Athens a schematic alternation of full and defective months could be generally assumed (courtesy of Leofranc Holford-Strevens). See Plutarch, *Life of Solon*, 25. 3 (cited below, n. 55), and other sources cited below in section 3.2.2. Evidence from the date of Alexander's death remains ambiguous; see most recently Grzybek (1990) 15–16, 29–35, and 52–60, and critical comments by A. Jones (1997) 164.

The Egyptian cultic calendar, by contrast, began the month at the morning of first invisibility of the old moon. Parker has shown, however, that because of a discrepancy in the 25-year lunar cycle that was in use in the Ptolemaic and Roman periods, the beginning of the month gradually shifted towards conjunction (with which it began to coincide in the second century BCE) and eventually towards visibility of the new moon (with which it coincided by the mid-second century CE).[18]

But sighting of the new moon was not necessarily the basis of all early Jewish calendars. The lunar months of Qumran calendars *may* have begun at other times, e.g. at the conjunction or at invisibility of the old moon.[19] In the later Roman period, a number of sources suggest that the conjunction was increasingly preferred. We will have to consider whether this represents a general trend in Jewish lunar calendars, and whether this trend reflects a similar development in the rabbinic calendar, which is known to have shifted from empirical observation to a fixed calendrical calculation.

3.1.4   The Magharians

As stated at the beginning of this chapter, in almost all ancient lunar calendars the month began around the time of the new moon. The only Jewish calendar known to have begun the month at the time of the full moon is that of the Magharians. The Magharians are a little-known sect, first mentioned by the Karaite al-Qirqisani (*c*.930 CE) and then by al-Biruni (*c*.1000 CE). Al-Qirqisani places this sect, chronologically, between the Sadducees and Jesus;[20] and this apparently corroborates a statement by Shahrastani (early twelfth century) who dates them 400 years before Areios, thus also about the first century BCE. In view of this corroboration, Harkavy treats this dating as reliable;[21] but this is to ignore that both authors are drawing on the same source, namely the work (not extant) of Daud b. Marwan al-Muqammis (late ninth to early tenth century);[22] they

---

[18]   Parker (1950) 16–17; see also Samuel (1972) 145–6; and see above, sections 1.2.2–3.

[19]   See discussion in section 1.1.6.

[20]   Al-Qirqisani, *The Book of Lights and Watch-Towers*, 1. 2. 8 (Nemoy 1930: 326–7, Chiesa and Lockwood 1984: 102). References by al-Qirqisani, ibid. 1. 7 (Nemoy 1930: 363–4, Chiesa and Lockwood 1984: 134–5) to Magharians and Sadducees in juxtaposition suggest that both sects were similar.

[21]   Harkavy (1984) 58, who identifies the Magharians with the Essenes or the Therapeutai (p. 59), and rejects, not without justification, Graetz's view that the Magharians were followers of the early 9th-c. Karaite Nahawendi (p. 78, and p. 90 n. 124).

[22]   On whom see al-Qirqisani, *The Book of Lights and Watch-Towers*, 1. 8. 5 (Nemoy 1930: 366, Chiesa and Lockwood 1984: 137), and Harkavy (1984) 62–4 and 85 n. 52. Al-Qirqisani's dependence, in this context, on al-Muqammis, is, however, only

cannot be treated, therefore, as corroborating each other. Poznanski (1905: 20–3) sees no reason why the Magharians could not have been a later sect, for instance of the seventh or eighth century. It should be noted, however, that al-Qirqisani reports that in his day the Magharian sect was already extinct.[23]

Both al-Qirqisani and al-Biruni mention that the Magharians began their month at the full moon. According to al-Qirqisani, this is because the Magharians believed that when it was created, the moon was perfect and full.[24]

Al-Biruni's account of the Magharian calendar is garbled and incomprehensible. Citing al-Warrak (d. 909 CE) as his source, he states that the Magharians' new year's day occurs at the full moon on a Wednesday, and that this is the starting point for days, months, and the cycle of the festivals.[25] As we know, however, it is impossible for the new year full moon to occur every year on the same day of the week.[26] Al-Biruni may mean that the *original* full moon of the 4th day of creation (i.e. Wednesday), and perhaps all subsequent new year full moons that happen to occur on Wednesdays (which would occur on average every 7 years), serve to the Magharians as *epochs* for the calculation of subsequent days, full moons, and festivals, within cycles of (on average) 7 years. This would mean that the calendar of the Magharians was reckoned by calculation rather than by observation.[27]

Some scholars have identified the Magharians with the Qumran sect, and argued that the lunisolar calendar of Qumran sources started at the full moon;[28] others reject this as unlikely.[29]

implicit (*The Book of Lights and Watch-Towers*, 1. 7, Nemoy 1930: 363–4, Chiesa and Lockwood 1984: 134–5).

[23] *The Book of Lights and Watch-Towers* 1. 18 (Nemoy 1930: 391, Chiesa and Lockwood 1984: 152).

[24] *The Book of Lights and Watch-Towers* 7: 5–6. See also ibid. 1: 7; unfortunately Nemoy (1930: 363) mistranslates this passage as reading 'new moon' (instead of 'full moon'), and this error is repeated by Chiesa and Lockwood (1984: 134) and Wacholder (1983a: 149). The error is noted, however, by de Vaux (1950) 421 and n. 4, and by Glessmer (1999) 222–3. The correct translation was already supplied by Poznanski (1905) 14–15. See also Golb (1960) 348–50, with further 11th-c. sources referring apparently to the same sect; Beckwith (1992) 463. That the Magharians reckon from the full moon is also reported in the mid 12th c. by Judah Hadassi (1836) 41b, alphabet, 97 letter *tet*; as his source he cites Daud b. Marwan al Muqammiṣ (ibid., alphabet 98, letter *resh*).

[25] Al-Biruni (1879) 278. For different translations see Di Lella (1962) 252; de Vaux (1950) 423.

[26] For this reason Golb (1960: 349) rejects al-Biruni's account as unreliable. See also Fossum (1987) 313: 'we may thus feel justified to conclude that Wednesday as well as the full moon had some calendric significance for the Magharians, but that Biruni or Warraq has garbled his information'.

[27] For other suggestions see Beckwith (1992) 464–6.

[28] See section 1.1.6.

[29] Di Lella (1962) 248–54. Golb (1960) and Beckwith (1992) view the Magharians as a separate sect.

3.1.5 The evidence of Jewish dates

I shall now explain the methodology I shall follow, in this chapter and elsewhere in this book, to establish whether calendars were based on the conjunction, or rather on the appearance of the new moon.

In most cases, my evidence will consist of Jewish lunar dates that can be found in (non-rabbinic) literary sources, documents, and inscriptions. These dates will indicate when the beginning of the month occurred. If the beginning of the month coincided, consistently, with the conjunction, we may infer that the calendar was based on calculation or on some fixed cycle; if the beginning of the month coincided with the time of appearance of the new crescent, we may infer that it was based on lunar observation. If no consistent pattern is found—e.g. in the Zoar inscriptions, where the beginning of new months is erratic and does not consistently correspond to either the conjunction, the new moon, or any other stage in the lunar month—the possibility of error, or alternatively, of non-lunar extraneous factors, should also be considered.

The use of Jewish dates as evidence for the beginning of the month depends on our ability, firstly, to identify these dates, and secondly, to establish when in that period the conjunction or visibility of the new moon occurred.

Let us begin with the identification of dates. A Jewish date is only informative if it can be identified in relation to some other point of reference: typically, another known calendar. For instance, the Catania inscription of 383 CE is dated according to both the Jewish and the Roman (Julian) calendars. Our firm knowledge of the Julian calendar will enable us to identify, in relation to it, the Jewish date of this inscription, and hence when the Jewish month would have begun. The same procedure will be applied to the document from the Council of Sardica.

Double datings of this kind, however, are unfortunately rare. The Judaean desert documents from before and during the Bar-Kokhba revolt, for instance, are all meticulously dated, but only according to the Jewish calendar.[30] Consequently, they do not tell us anything about how their calendar was reckoned.

Another point of reference in relation to which a Jewish date can be identified is the day of the week. For instance, a passage of Josephus informs us that Shavuᶜot in 130 BCE occurred on Sunday. This is sufficient to establish whether the beginning of the month coincided with the conjunction or with some other moment in the moon's orbit. The

---

[30] See section 1.1.13.

same procedure will be applied to the *ketubah* of Antinoopolis and to the Zoar inscriptions.

In following this procedure I am making the assumption that the 7-day week was reckoned by the Jews of Antiquity in the same way as it is today. This is not always possible to prove. Firm evidence that the week was reckoned as it is today can only be found in sources from the second or third century onwards, when days of the week are first attested in Greek, Roman, and Christian sources and inscriptions in conjunction with identifiable Julian dates.[31] But in the absence of evidence to the contrary, it is likely that the week was always reckoned by the Jews in the same way, from the earliest period until the present day. Indeed, we do not find any reference in any ancient source, whether Jewish, Christian, or other, to any dispute or division about the reckoning of Sabbath and the days of the week.[32] The week appears to have transcended, quite remarkably, calendrical sectarianism and/or diversity.

---

[31] The earliest source is Vettius Valens (early 2nd c. CE) in *Anthologiarum Libri* 1. 9 (ed. Pingree), who provides a method for calculating the day of the week on the basis of the Julian date which tallies with our present-day reckoning. According to Worp (1991), there is a sufficient level of agreement between the dates of documentary sources from late Antiquity and our 7-day week to warrant the view that throughout the Graeco-Roman world, the 7-day week was reckoned in the same way as it is today; he argues that non-matches, although in a sizeable minority, are likely to be the result of error. Among the earlier relevant inscriptions are *CIL* 3: 1051, dated Thursday, 23 May 205 CE from Apulum (Alba Iulia) in Dacia; and *AE* 1941: 77 (= *AE* 1980: 60), dated Saturday, 20 Nov. 202 CE (from Rome), which tally with our present-day reckoning. *CIL* iv. 4182 (from Pompeii) is dated Sunday, 6 Feb. 60 CE, which should have been, according to our reckoning, a Wednesday (see Deman 1974: 273); but there is a strong possibility that this dating is erroneous. On the introduction of the 7-day week in Roman calendar reckoning, see Ginzel (1911) ii. 177 and Brind'Amour (1983) 256–68. Dio Cassius reports that in his time (the early 3rd c.), the 7-day week was treated by 'all peoples, even the Romans' as an ancestral tradition, even though its use may actually have been quite recent (37. 18. 2). Days of the week are particularly frequent in late Roman Latin Christian inscriptions, and generally tally with today's reckoning: see index in Diehl (1961) 311–12; for an early example, see Diehl (1927) 193, no. 3391: Friday, 5 Nov. 269 CE. Days of the week are also frequently mentioned in Christian works on the date of Easter (see e.g. citations in E. Schwartz 1905 chs. 2–5, pp. 29–104); thus the cycle of Hippolytus begins on the 14th of the lunar month coinciding with Saturday, 13 Apr. 222 CE.

[32] The only exception I can think of is a reference in the *Chronicle* of Michael the Syrian (12th c.) to an Ananite sect in Babylonia in 825 CE that profaned the Sabbath and observed Wednesday instead (Gil 1992: 496–7). The reliability of this report, however, is doubtful, as it is not corroborated in any other source (e.g. in al-Qirqisani's accounts of the Ananites in *The Book of Lights and Watch-Towers*, 1. 13 (Nemoy 1930: 383–6; Chiesa and Lockwood 1984: 145–7).

3.1.6 Astronomical data

As stated above, the ability to determine when Jewish months would have begun depends not only on identifiable Jewish dates, but also on the knowledge of when the conjunction or first visibility of the new moon would have occurred. Current astronomical knowledge makes it possible to establish this with a reasonable degree of accuracy. In the last few decades, there has been a renewed interest among professional and amateur astronomers in the problem of the visibility of the new moon. The development of information technology has also facilitated the creation of a number of computer programmes that are at once reliable and easy to use.

The programme I have mainly used in the course of my work is *Ḥazon Shamayim*, by Eytan Tzikoni. This programme calculates the times and dates of lunar conjunctions and oppositions, and of equinoxes and solstices, in both the Julian/Gregorian and the Jewish (rabbinic) calendars; it also provides detailed astronomical information regarding the positions of the sun and the moon, for any given location and any given period. Although all times are supplied with the greatest degree of precision (i.e. down to minutes and seconds), I have refrained in this work from citing *precise* figures, partly not to overburden the reader, and partly because these precise figures carry a certain measure of approximation and are thus likely to be corrected as astronomical knowledge improves.[33]

---

[33] Particularly problematic in this context is delta t (Δt). Delta t is the difference between terrestrial dynamical time (TT), an ideal atomic timescale used by astronomers since 1984 for the calculation of all geocentric ephemerides (i.e. positions of celestial objects from the theoretical perspective of the centre of the Earth), and universal time (UT), a timescale based on the rotation of the earth on its axis and used as standard in daily life (Δt = TT − UT; earlier or alternative versions of TT include ET, TDT, and DT). Because UT is dependent on the rotation of the earth, it is subject to variation; therefore, it does not share the ideal characteristics of TT. Since the rotation of the earth has always been used as the common basis for the measurement of time, only UT is relevant for the determination of times in earlier historical periods. The time of ephemerides in earlier historical periods (calculated in TT) must therefore be converted from TT to UT (see Meeus 1991: 71–5). For instance, in the early 4th c. CE Δt is thought to have been close to 2 hours; this means that the time of an astronomical event of this period, calculated in TT, would actually have occurred, in UT, two hours earlier. The rotation of the earth (and hence UT) is known to be slowing down (partly as a result of tidal friction from the pull of the moon), but at an irregular and somewhat unpredictable pace. As a result, the value of Δt for ancient periods remains rather speculative. Astronomers derive it from ancient records of solar and lunar eclipses from ancient Babylon, ancient and medieval China, medieval Europe, and the Muslim Arab world (Stephenson and Morrison 1995, Stephenson 1997, Steele and Stephenson 1997). Besides Δt, for

In order to verify the reliability of *Ḥazon Shamayim*, I have checked its results against those of another astronomical programme, *Ephemeris Tool* (by Manfred Dings). The differences between them have turned out to be minimal,[34] and generally insignificant in the context of this study.

The most important feature of *Ḥazon Shamayim* is that it calculates, for any given location and any given period, the evening on which the new moon would have been first visible (and likewise, *mutatis mutandis*, the morning on which the old moon would have been invisible). This calculation is based on two alternative astronomical criteria of visibility of the new moon: the modern Indian criterion, and Maimonides'. In the context of this study, both criteria have been taken into consideration.[35] Whenever the results were borderline, I have treated visibility as doubtful.[36]

the position of the moon, account must be taken of changes in the value of the tidal term (Bernard Yallop, pers. comm.). Furthermore, adjustments must be made to UT to take account of the equation of time (the difference between mean and true time: see Meeus 1991: 171). Because of the uncertainties surrounding these and other astronomical questions (especially in the area of lunar theory: see references cited above in this n.), our conclusions in this work cannot be treated as absolutely definitive.

[34] Differences between *Ḥazon Shamayim* and *Ephemeris Tool* partly reflect the fact that they use different Δt formulae: the Morrison and Stephenson formula (1982), and the Stephenson and Houlden formula (1986) respectively (both formulae cited in Meeus 1991: 73). I am grateful to Tuvia Kaatz for shedding light on this matter. In the context of this study, the difference between the two formulae (approximately 15 minutes in the 5th c. CE, but only about 3 minutes in the 5th c. BCE) has generally been insignificant. For a more recent formula, see Steele and Stephenson (1997: 122–4).

[35] Loewinger (1994: 491; 1996a: 60–1 and 74–5) has found that Maimonides' is a reliable criterion of *non-visibility* in the Mediterranean region, which means that if it returns a verdict that the new moon was not visible, there is no need to search any further. He suggests, indeed, that this was never intended as a criterion of visibility of the new moon, but rather as a one of its *non-visibility*: Maimonides' purpose was only to establish a method of identifying false witnesses (or false sightings) of the new moon, as required by *M. RH* 2: 6–8 (Loewinger 1994: 495; 1996a: 57–9, 74). For *visibility* of the new moon, however, modern criteria such as the Indian must be preferred. Other modern criteria may be slightly more reliable than the Indian, but these variations are only slight. See also Doggett and Schaefer (1994) 402.

[36] Another programme worthy of mention is *MoonC*, by Monzur Ahmed. This programme provides a wide range of modern visibility criteria, as well as global charts that give a clear idea of where lunar visibility would have been only borderline. Unfortunately this programme has been of limited use in this study, as it does not stretch back to earlier than 500 CE.

3.1.7 Visibility and sighting of the new moon

It must be clearly stressed that in spite of their reliability *per se*, programmes that calculate the visibility of the new moon do not indicate with certainty when lunar months would have begun. The reason for this is threefold:

(i) *Visibility criteria.* The astronomical criterion of visibility is yet to be conclusively defined. Existing models, both ancient and modern, are based on a combination of empirical experience and mathematical inference, but should be treated as guidelines rather than as 'laws' or rules. 'Moonwatches' organized by Schaefer have shown that in some cases, the moon was sighted even though criteria of visibility were not met.[37]

(ii) *Weather.* The criteria used by these programmes are only astronomical. Visibility of the new moon can be severely delayed, however, by the weather. In an attempt to take account of this important factor, Schaefer has formulated an algorithm that includes atmospheric conditions for any location at any time of the year.[38] The algorithm has not been fully published, nor is it available in the form of a computer program. But even with this algorithm, it remains impossible to predict or 'postdict' whether *specific* meteorological conditions, such as cloud formation, would have obstructed visibility of the moon at any particular time and location.

For our purposes, it may be assumed that in a Mediterranean climate, cloud formation is more likely during the winter months. On the other hand, after it has rained, the air is usually much clearer, making it easier to see the crescent. In the winter months, moreover, weather conditions may be compensated by astronomical factors which tend to make the interval between conjunction and lunar visibility relatively shorter.[39]

(iii) *Human observation.* Lunar calendars that begin the month with the appearance of the new moon are not based on calculated predictions of its visibility, but rather on actual sightings of it (as I have explained above). This human factor must be taken into consideration. On the first evening of visibility, the new crescent is only visible for a short period of time (typically, half an hour or less) and relatively low on the horizon

---

[37] Doggett and Schaefer (1994); Schaefer (1996). See also Loewinger (1995; 1996*a*: 65–73, esp. 73).

[38] Schaefer (1987; 1988). For a brief summary see Loewinger (1994) 493; (1996*a*) 64.

[39] Ajdler (1996) 696–7. This demands further investigation.

(Loewinger 1994: 476–9). Even if it is visible, therefore, it will not be sighted by anyone unless a deliberate and sometimes painstaking watch is undertaken. Babylonian and rabbinic sources suggest that watches of this kind were carried out on a monthly basis. We cannot assume, however, that this was always and everywhere the case. Sightings of the new moon in other Jewish communities may have been more sporadic, which would have delayed the beginning of their months by one day.

Lunar months could also begin one day too early, if the new moon had been falsely sighted. The potential for false sightings has become evident in the course of Schaefer's moonwatches, to quote:

... a significant fraction of observers will claim to have sighted the crescent even when it is impossible (e.g., when the Moon is below the horizon). Honest observers may make honest mistakes, for there are many objects in the sky (e.g., wisps of cloud or aircraft illuminated by the Sun) that can be mistaken for a crescent. Furthermore, the power of an observer's imagination (particularly that of an inexperienced observer) is undoubtedly a significant factor in false sightings (Doggett and Schaefer 1994: 398) ... If a 100 observers look for the crescent, roughly 15 will mistakenly (yet honestly) claim to see the moon. Therefore, lunar months based on a few positive sightings from a large number of observers will invariably and mistakenly start early (ibid. 402).

Consequently, the authors conclude that 'historical dates recorded on lunar calendars undoubtedly are affected by this bias' (p. 398).

The extent to which statistical data drawn from modern-day moonwatches are relevant to earlier historical periods remains, however, to be established. In pre-modern societies, people may have been more experienced at observing the skies. Moreover, the Babylonian calendar was based not merely on sightings but also on detailed calculations, which presumably eliminated, to a large extent, the incidence of false sightings. The same would apply to the early rabbinic calendar, where detailed interrogation of the witnesses was carried out in order to detect false sightings.[40] Nevertheless, the possibility of false sightings, in the light of this research, must be given serious consideration even in the context of the ancient world.

Thus although the computer programs I have used provide an accurate astronomical assessment of the visibility of the new moon, they do not necessarily indicate when the new moons would have been sighted, and hence when lunar months, in any given calendar, would have begun.

---

[40] *M. RH* 2: 5–8. See Wacholder and Weisberg (1971); Ajdler (1996) 388–93.

3.1.8   The conjunction

Calendars based on the conjunction are considerably more reliable and predictable. Because they are usually based, as explained above, on calculations, they are not prone to the irregularity or uncertainty of calendars based on sightings of the new moon.

For reasons explained above, I shall assume that these calendars would have followed the mean (rather than the true) conjunction. To obtain the date and time of the mean conjunction for any given month, I shall rely entirely, in this work, on the calculation of the *molad* (literally 'birth', i.e. conjunction) used in the present-day rabbinic calendar (see section 4.4.1). This method is not only highly convenient, but also sufficiently accurate for my purposes.

The *molad* is nowadays about 2 hours behind the astronomically accurate mean conjunction, if we assume that it is based on Jerusalem Mean Time.[41] This 2-hour discrepancy is currently increasing at a rate of 10 minutes per 100 years (UT), but this rate of increase has not always been the same.[42] On this basis, *molad* and accurate mean conjunction are thought to have coincided around the fourth century CE (Loewinger 1996*b*: 75). Thus for the period we are dealing with (second century BCE–tenth century CE), the *molad* represents a reasonable approximation—within a maximum margin of error of one hour—of the mean conjunction.[43]

It is important to note, however, that it is not always possible to know whether the mean conjunction would have been calculated, in all calendars, to the same degree of accuracy. Therefore, in borderline cases (where the *molad* is close to the beginning or end of the day) I shall treat the result as doubtful.

I shall generally assume that in calendars based on the conjunction the day unit (24-hour period) would have begun in the evening, just as in calendars based on sighting of the new moon.[44]

[41]   i.e. 2 hours and 21 minutes ahead of Universal Time (UT). See Loewinger (1994) 477 n. 12; Ajdler (1996) 177–8; and at length, Loewinger (1996*b*).

[42]   It is a non-linear function of time because of Δt and variations in the mean lunation. See Loewinger (1996*b*) 75.

[43]   Adjustments to the time of the *molad* may also be necessary to take account of the equation of time (see above, n. 33), though this never exceeds 20 minutes.

[44]   This is a working assumption about which one cannot always be certain, even in the context of calendars based on sighting of the new moon. See the remarks of Grzybek (1990: 142 n. 64), who argues elsewhere (ibid. 142–6)—although not convincingly—that the day unit in the Macedonian calendar began at sunrise. In the context of Jewish calendars, however, it is reasonable to assume that the day unit always began in the evening, as is implicit in biblical law: see Exod. 12: 18 and Lev. 23: 32.

3.1.9 Non-lunar factors

Finally, it is important to repeat that in all the sources we will be considering, the possibility of error, or alternatively, of non-lunar extraneous factors, should never be ruled out.[45] Little is known, unfortunately, of the political, religious, or other factors which may have influenced the determination of new months in non-rabbinic communities. We do not even know, for any given community, who would have been in charge of setting the Jewish calendar. Before drawing any firm conclusion, therefore, considerable caution must be exercised.

3.2 THE EARLY PERIOD: THE SIGHTING OF THE NEW MOON

From the Hasmonaean period to the third century CE, non-rabbinic sources suggest that most Jewish lunar calendars were based on the appearance and sighting of the new moon. But it must be emphasized that evidence, in this context, can never be more than sporadic.

3.2.1 John Hyrcanus and Josephus

In 130 BCE, John Hyrcanus was engaged in a campaign against the Parthians with Antiochus VII Sidetes, in the area of the river Lycus (the Great Zab, beyond the Tigris, in Adiabene). Nicolaus of Damascus, cited by Josephus, reports that Antiochus remained stationed for two days by the river Lycus at the request of John Hyrcanus, because of some ancestral festival during which it was forbidden for the Jews to march out. Josephus explains that Pentecost (Shavuʿot) occurred after the Sabbath, and that it would have been forbidden to travel on the Sabbath or on the festival.[46]

Josephus' identification of the 'ancestral festival' (in Nicolaus' passage) as Pentecost would have been based either on some independent historical source, or on the reasonable assumption that since Antiochus was in the middle of his campaign, a midsummer festival could only have been Pentecost. But Josephus' knowledge that Pentecost occurred

---

[45] See above, section 3.1.1.

[46] *Ant.* 13. 8. 4 (250–2); cited in M. Stern (1974–84) i. 239–40, no. 88. For the year of this event (130 BCE), see ibid. 240 n., and Pucci (1981). See also Schürer (1973–87) i. 206–7. I am grateful to Joseph Sievers for drawing my attention to this passage.

that year on a Sunday (hence two consecutive days during which the Jews could not travel) cannot have been inferred from Nicolaus' passage alone, because this passage could just as well have implied that Pentecost occurred on Friday. It appears, therefore, that Josephus obtained his information from some independent source.

Josephus clearly does not mean that Pentecost *always* occurs on Sunday, as in the calendar of *Jubilees* and (according to the Mishnah) of the Boethusians (see sections 1.1.5 and 1.1.8). His use of the aorist tense (ἐνέστη) is a clear indication that the occurrence of Pentecost on Sunday was a single event, not a regular occurrence. John Hyrcanus is unlikely, besides, to have followed a sectarian calendar (on the sectarian nature of the calendar of *Jubilees*, see section 1.1.5). In Josephus' narrative, moreover, this event appears to pre-date Hyrcanus' 'conversion' to the Sadducean party (*Ant.* 13: 10: 5–6 (288–96)); and that the Sadducees observed Pentecost on Sunday is anyway unproven (see Jaubert 1957*a*: 55).

Josephus' account is not necessarily reliable or correct; but if it is, it would imply a calendar based on the sighting of the new moon. We may assume that Pentecost occurred on the 50th day after the first day of Passover, as in the mainstream Jewish calendar.[47] In 130 BCE, therefore, 1 Nisan would have occurred on a Sabbath. Two reasonable options for the new moon of Nisan 130 BCE must be considered: either a date in mid-March, or a date in mid-April. If the former, we may establish with the help of our computer programs that the mean conjunction would have occurred on Wednesday, 11 March, in the morning hours; whereas the new moon would have first been visible on Thursday evening, the 12th.[48] Neither tallies with Josephus' dating, unless we posit that for some reason the new moon was not actually sighted till the next evening, on Friday the 13th—thus yielding 1 Nisan on a Sabbath.

More likely, therefore, is that Nisan began in 130 BCE in mid-April. The conjunction would have occurred on Thursday, 9 April in the afternoon or evening, which again does not tally with Josephus' dating. But the new moon would have been visible on Friday evening, 10 April,

[47] Besides rabbinic sources, see the Septuagint rendering of Lev. 23: 11 (cited in Schürer 1973–87: iii. 312); Philo, *Special Laws* 2. 29 (162) and 30 (176); and above all Josephus himself, in *Ant.* 3. 10. 5 (250) and 6 (252).

[48] The Julian calendar was not in existence in this period, but it is extrapolated backwards, as is conventional among astronomers. Wherever I cite a Julian date, I assume, according to convention, a 24-hour period that begins and ends at midnight. Thus 'Thursday evening the 12th of March' is equivalent, in the Jewish calendar, to the evening of *Friday*. The data supplied here are valid for the geographical co-ordinates of both Jerusalem (where John Hyrcanus' calendar was presumably set) and Babylon (which may have determined the lunar calendar of Adiabene).

thus yielding 1 Nisan on a Sabbath. This late occurrence of Nisan (and hence of Passover) is compatible with the evidence we have considered for this period in Ch. 2.

According to both options (mid-March or mid-April), however, it is evident that the calendar could only have been based on sightings of the new moon.

No attention is given in this passage to the Diaspora observance of two festival days. Had Hyrcanus observed two days of Pentecost, the occurrence of the first day of Pentecost on a Sunday would have caused him and Antiochus a total delay of three days. It may be argued that because he was coming from Jerusalem, Hyrcanus was not bound by local Diaspora customs. The point I wish to make, however, concerns not Hyrcanus but rather Josephus himself. Josephus' gloss on Nicolaus' report suggests that Hyrcanus' delay of two days could *only* be explained as the result the consecutive occurrence of the Sabbath and a festival. Josephus does not appear to consider the possibility that Antiochus' delay may have been caused by Hyrcanus' observance, in the middle of the week, of two festival days.

Josephus' assumption in this passage is significant, but comes as no surprise: for the Diaspora observance of two festival days is nowhere mentioned in any of Josephus' works,[49] nor indeed in any non-rabbinic ancient Jewish source (including, for instance, Philo). This suggests that the Diaspora custom of two festival days was *specific* to rabbinic Judaism, and was totally unknown outside it.

The reason for this is clear. As we shall later see, the rabbinic concept of two Diaspora festival days was predicated on the assumption that Diaspora communities had to follow the calendar that was set by the Palestinian rabbinic court. Since they could not obtain the Palestinian dates in time for the festivals, two days had to be observed in doubt (see section 5.3.1). In practice, however, few communities are likely to have observed this custom. Diaspora communities, as we have already seen, were not dependent on the Palestinian rabbinic calendar; they reckoned their own calendar independently and in their own specific ways.[50] In

---

[49] Josephus himself must have been well aware of Diaspora customs, as he had been living in Rome for about two decades at the time when the *Antiquities* were written.

[50] This has become evident in Ch. 2 (see section 2.5.4), and will further be confirmed below. The only known exception to this was the Babylonian rabbinic community, which accepted the calendrical authority of the Palestinian rabbis and hence observed two festival days: see section 5.3.2.

this context, Diaspora Jews had no reason to be 'uncertain' about the dates of festivals. To Jews such as Philo or Josephus, the observance of two festival days would have been completely unnecessary.

The only non-rabbinic source that has been suggested as evidence of Diaspora observance of two festival days is a first-century BCE papyrus from Apollinopolis Magna, edited by Alexander Fuks in *CPJ* i. 254–5, no. 139. This document is a list of contributions to a Jewish dining-club; it mentions a third feast (πόσις) on the '15th', and a fourth feast on the '16th'. Fuks suggests (p. 255) that this refers to a communal Passover feast that occurred, in the Diaspora, on 15 and 16 Nisan (two consecutive days). This suggestion must be firmly discarded, for the following reasons:

(i) Although some members of the club appear to have been Jewish, there is nothing to indicate that these πόσεις, i.e. 'drinking parties', were 'festivals', nor indeed that they were 'Jewish'.

(ii) Reference to 16 Nisan as a festival in its own right (the '4th feast'), distinct from that of the 15th (the '3rd feast'), does not agree with the rabbinic concept of two Diaspora festival days, according to which the two days are observed out of doubt regarding the date of a *single* festival.

(iii) Passover is never reckoned as the '3rd' festival, either in the Bible or in Philo.[51]

3.2.2 Philo of Alexandria

If evidence on the Jewish calendar in early Roman Egypt is anywhere to be found, it is in Philo's *Special Laws*.[52] From a number of passages it is evident that according to Philo, the lunar month begins not at the conjunction, but at the first appearance of the new moon.

In his introduction, Philo lists the new month (*noumenia*) as the third of the ten festivals recorded in the Law. Philo describes it as follows:

Τρίτη δ᾽ ἡ μετὰ σύνοδον τὴν κατὰ σελήνην νέαν νουμηνία.

The third is the new month (*noumenia*), which is after the conjunction (*synodos*) according to the new moon.[53]

The critical point in this passage is that the *noumenia* occurs *after* the conjunction, and not at the same time. The usage of the term *synodos* for

---

[51] In Philo, *Special Laws* 2: 11 (41), it is listed as the 4th festival.

[52] The Sabbath, new months and festivals are given full treatment in the *Special Laws*, 2. 10–36 (39–222).

[53] *Special Laws* 2. 11 (41). Colson (1937) translates: 'the new moon which follows the conjunction of the moon with the sun'. This is less accurate, but still a reasonable literary rendition.

astronomical 'conjunction' is well attested not only in ancient astronomical sources (e.g. in Ptolemy's *Almagest*),[54] but also in other branches of literature, where it is also distinguished from the first day of the month (the *noumenia*).[55] The phrase 'conjunction according to the new moon' in this passage is awkward, therefore, and may be the result of some textual error.

The time of the *noumenia* receives clarification later on, where Philo gives reasons why it is treated as a festival:

Τὴν δ' ἐν ἑορταῖς ἔλαχε τάξιν νουμηνία διὰ πολλά. πρῶτον μὲν ὅτι ἀρχὴ μηνός, ἀρχὴ δὲ καὶ ἀριθμοῦ καὶ χρόνου τίμιον.

ἔπειτα δὲ ὅτι κατ' αὐτὴν οὐδὲν ἀφώτιστον ἐν οὐρανῷ· συνόδῳ μὲν γὰρ ὑποδραμούσης ἥλιον σελήνης τὸ πρὸς γῆν μέρος ἐζόφωται, νουμηνίᾳ δὲ πέφυκεν ἀναλάμπειν.

τρίτον δὲ ὅτι τῷ ἐλάττονι καὶ ἀσθενεστέρῳ κατ' ἐκεῖνον τὸν χρόνον τὸ κρεῖττον καὶ δυνατώτερον ὠφελείας ἀναγκαίας μεταδίδωσι· νουμηνίᾳ γὰρ ἄρχεται φωτίζειν αἰσθητῷ φέγγει σελήνην ὁ ἥλιος, ἡ δὲ τὸ ἴδιον κάλλος ἀναφαίνει τοῖς ὁρῶσι.

The new month holds its place among the festivals for many reasons. First, because it is the beginning of the month, and the beginning in number and in time is worthy of honour. Secondly, because at that time, nothing in the sky is without light; for at the conjunction, when the moon runs under the sun,[56] its side facing the earth is darkened; but at the new month, it begins to shine. Thirdly, because at that time, the stronger and more powerful supplies necessary help to the smaller and weaker: for at the new month the sun begins to illuminate the moon with the light which is perceived, and the moon reveals its own beauty to those who see it (*Special Laws* 2. 26 (140–1)).

From both the second and the third reasons it is absolutely clear that the *noumenia*, which marks the beginning of the calendrical month (as explicit in the first reason), occurs not at the conjunction, when the moon is completely hidden (see second reason), but only when the new moon begins to shine and becomes visible to the observer (second and third reasons).

---

[54] See also Geminus, *Elem. Astr.* 8–9.

[55] e.g. Plutarch, *Romulus* 12 (at the foundation of Rome, the *synodos*, on the last day of the month, was a solar eclipse); and id., *Solon* 25. 3 (Solon ordained that the day of the *synodos* should be reckoned as 'old and new', and only the next day as the *noumenia*).

[56] This is how the conjunction was understood by Hellenistic astronomers. See Vitruvius, *De Architectura* 9. 2. 3–4 (Loeb edn. 228–31), citing Aristarchus; Geminus, *Elem. Astr.* 9. 6, 10, 10. 1 (Aujac 1975: 59, 60, 61, but with reference to solar eclipses).

The definition of the term *noumenia*, the first day of the lunar month, as the time when the new moon is first sighted, is not original to Philo but common in Hellenistic and Roman literature;[57] it goes back, presumably, to the Greek lunar calendars of the Classical and Hellenistic periods. It is unlikely, however, that Philo is merely drawing on a literary topos. If the Jewish calendar was reckoned differently, Philo would have had no reason not to mention it.

Other passages in Philo appear at first sight to contradict this point. Just before the passage above, Philo states that 'the lunar new month is the time from one conjunction to the next, which students of astronomy have accurately calculated',[58] thus apparently implying that the month begins at the conjunction. The sentence is itself inconsistent, because the time from one conjunction to the next is actually the 'month', not, as stated here by Philo, the 'new month' (*noumenia*).[59] In any event, what Philo has in mind is clearly not the *beginning* of the month, but rather its *length*. Now the mean length of the lunar synodical cycle is astronomically defined as the interval from one mean conjunction to the next; it cannot be defined with reference to the visibility of the new moon. This explains why it is the conjunction that is referred to in this passage.[60]

For similar reasons, Philo describes elsewhere the four phases of the moon as running from one conjunction to the next (*Spec. Laws* 1. 35 (178)). In astronomical terms, indeed, the first phase of the moon begins at the conjunction; this is not to be confused with the commencement of the calendrical month.[61]

Following the passage above quoted, Philo states as a fourth reason for the festival of the new month: '. . .the moon traverses the zodiac in a shorter fixed period than any other heavenly body: for it accomplishes that revolution in the span of a single month. Therefore the conclusion of its circuit, when the moon ends its course at the starting point where it began, is honoured by the law as a festival day . . .' (2. 26 (142)). The moon's revolution across the zodiac, known as the sidereal cycle, takes just over 27 days and is thus shorter than the synodical cycle (from one conjunction to the next) by approximately two days and five hours. It is an astronomical notion that is not known to have been used as the basis of any lunar calendar month. Besides, Philo clearly states, as we have seen above, that the length of the month corresponds to the *synodical* cycle. Clearly, this passage cannot be taken literally. Philo is using homiletical licence to provide a further rationale for the festival of the new month.

In a number of passages Philo states that the 15th of a lunar month corresponds to the full moon: e.g. the 15th of the seventh month (first day of

---

[57] See Geminus, *Elem. Astr.* 8. 11–14 (Aujac 1975: 49–50), citing Aratus; ibid. 9. 16, 10. 6 (pp. 61, 62); Pliny, *Natural History* 18. 321–5.

[58] On this translation of μαθηματικῶν, see Colson (1937: 408–9); also Pedersen (1974) 26–30.

[59] As pointed out by Colson (1937: 390–1 n. 2), who proposes on these grounds a textual emendation.

[60] A similar phrase is found in Geminus, *Elem. Astr.* 8. 1, 9. 16 (Aujac 1975: 47, 61): 'the moon is the time from one conjunction (*synodos*) to the next'.

[61] Cf. Vitruvius, *De Architectura* 9. 2. 1–4 (Loeb edn. 226–31), citing Berosus and Aristarchus.

Tabernacles), or the 15th of the first month (first day of festival of Unleavened Bread).[62] Similarly the festival of Passover, which occurs on the 14th of the first month (*Special Laws* 2. 11 (41)), was celebrated when the moon was '*about* to be full' (*Life of Moses* 2: 41 (224)). In a lunar calendar based on the conjunction, i.e. where the conjunction occurs on the 1st of the month, the full moon should occur approximately 14¾ days later, i.e. (in 3 out of 4 cases) on the 16th, and in all cases, the full moon is only *visible* on the night of the 16th. If the lunar calendar is based on appearance of the new moon, the full moon should generally occur nearer to the 14th. These passages, however, are of little significance to us as they are only meant as gross approximations.

Although it is clear, from the passage above quoted, that in Philo's Jewish calendar the month began when the new moon was first apparent, Philo does not explain how in practice his calendar would have been set. He does not specify whether the new moon was actually *sighted*, and whether any authority, in Alexandria or elsewhere, was formally in charge of declaring the beginning of the months. There is certainly no suggestion, in Philo's writings, that the dates of the new months were 'imported' from Judaea or from a Judaean rabbinic court. Rabbinic sources confirm themselves, indeed, that calendrical information was generally not transmitted from the Palestinian rabbinic authorities to the communities of Egypt (see section 5.3.2).

In the absence of evidence to the contrary, we may thus conclude that in Philo's Alexandria, the sighting of the new moon and the determination of calendar dates would have been carried out entirely at a local level. It is likely that an authoritative body within the Jewish community conducted this procedure and made the appropriate calendrical decisions.

If Jewish communities such as in Alexandria were able to set their own calendar on the basis of their own sightings of the new moon, this would have led to tremendous calendrical diversity. As we have seen, visibility of the new moon would have varied considerably from place to place because of different geographical co-ordinates, weather conditions, and human observational accuracy. As a result, different Jewish communities are likely to have observed the festivals at slightly different times. This would reinforce our conclusions of the previous chapter, that Jewish calendar reckoning in Antiquity was characterized by its diversity.

---

[62] *Special Laws* 1. 35 (189), 2. 33 (210) (Tabernacles), ibid. 2. 28 (155) (Unleavened Bread).

3.2.3 The Berenike inscriptions

A peculiar phrase that occurs in two inscriptions from Berenike (Cyrenaica), one of which has been examined in the previous chapter,[63] may confirm what has been found in Philo's works.

Each of these inscriptions records a decision by the Jewish community of Berenike to honour a Roman[64] official, by crowning him with an olive wreath and hair band at every *synodos* and *noumenia* (καθ' ἑκάστην σύνοδον καὶ νουμηνίαν). This is translated by Roux and Roux (1949: 285, 287) as: 'à chaque assemblée et nouménie',[65] as indeed the most common meaning of *synodos* is 'assembly'.[66] However, this term has also the specific connotation of 'religious society' or of a religious society's festive meetings,[67] and this is possibly what is meant in this inscription.[68] It is even possible that in juxtaposition with *noumenia*, the term *synodos* refers, in these inscriptions, to the annual Jewish festivals.[69]

I should like to suggest, however, that the term *synodos*, where other Greek terms for 'assembly' or 'festival' could equally have been used (e.g. σύλλογος, which is used, with reference to the festival of Tabernacles, at the beginning of one of these inscriptions),[70] would not have been chosen at random. As we have seen in connection with Philo, *synodos* and *noumenia* are well attested in an astronomical context as meaning 'conjunction' and '(appearance of) new moon'. The juxtaposition of these terms in the Berenike inscriptions may thus have had the function, if only *stylistic*, of a rather sophisticated astronomical *double entendre*.

If this interpretation is correct, it would confirm, firstly, that the Jews of Berenike associated their new months with the moon, and hence, that

---

[63] CIG iii, nos.5361–2; IGR i, no. 1024; Roux and Roux (1949); *SEG* 16, no. 931; Reynolds (1977), nos. 17–18; Lüderitz (1983), nos. 70–1; Boffo (1994) 204–16, no. 24.

[64] That the official was Roman only appears explicitly in the fully dated inscription, *CIG* iii, no. 5361; *IGR* i, no. 1024; Reynolds (1977), no. 17; Lüderitz (1983), no. 71; Boffo (1994).

[65] Likewise Lüderitz (1983) 150 and 153: 'bei jeder Zusammenkunft und (an jedem) Neumond'; and Boffo (1994) 216: 'a ogni riunione e a ogni luna nuova'.

[66] Thus it is used by Josephus always and exclusively in this sense: see in particular *Antiquities* 14. 23 (257–8).

[67] For Jewish sources, see *CPJ* i. no. 138, ll. 4, 8, 16, and Horbury and Noy (1992) 44, no. 26; both texts belong to the late 1st cent. BCE.

[68] Schürer (1973–87) i. 90.

[69] Baldwin Bowsky (1987: 495) translates *synodos* as 'Sabbath', but this is perhaps less likely. The inscriptions imply, incidentally, that the new month (*noumenia*) at Berenike was the occasion of a public celebration.

[70] Cited in section 2.3.4.

they employed a specifically lunar calendar.[71] Secondly, and more importantly, this astronomical *double entendre* would imply, from its usage of the term *noumenia*, a correspondence between the festival of the new month and the first appearance of the new moon. On this basis, it may be possible to infer that the Jewish new month in Berenike did not occur at the conjunction, but only when the new moon was first sighted—just as according to Philo's calendar.

Again, no details are available as to the calendrical procedure that would have been carried out. In the absence of evidence to the contrary, we must assume that the Jews of Berenike determined the new months independently, on the basis of their own sightings of the new moon.

The uncertainty of the year of the fully dated Berenike inscription[72] makes it impossible to draw reliable conclusions from its dating. However, if the option of 26 October 41 BCE is correct,[73] then a calendar based on sighting of the new moon is perhaps most likely. This date, indeed, corresponds exactly with the first day of Tabernacles, the 15th day of the lunar month, if one assumes that the month begins at the first visibility of the new moon. The phrase 'at the assembly of Tabernacles', at the beginning of the inscription, is likely to refer to the first day of the festival, which the Bible appears to accord prime importance.[74] In a calendar based on the conjunction, by contrast, 26 October 41 BCE would have coincided with the 4th day of the festival, the 18th of the lunar month.

3.2.4 Cestius' assault on Jerusalem, 66 CE

A passage in Josephus (*Jewish War* 2. 19. 2–4 (517–28)) regarding the Roman assault on Jerusalem in 66 CE may furnish additional evidence that the calendar, in this period, was based on sightings of the new moon. Cestius' initial engagement with the people of Jerusalem is said to have taken place at the time of the festival of Tabernacles, on a Sabbath (517). After a period of 7 days had elapsed,[75] Josephus gives the date as 30 Hyperberetaios (528).

Niese (1894: 250) assumes, as in most other places, that this date is according to the Tyrian calendar, and thus corresponds to 17 November 66 CE. This, however, is impossible, because 7 days earlier, 10 November 66 CE, would not have been a Saturday but a Monday. Moreover, Monday, 10 November could not have been anywhere near the festival of Tabernacles, since the 15th of the lunar month would only have occurred *c*.22 November 66 CE.

---

[71] In section 1.2.3, it has already been established that they could not have used the Egyptian civil calendar for the dates of Jewish festivals.

[72] See above, n. 64. On the year of the inscription, see in detail section 2.3.4.

[73] This is the option I have favoured, on calendrical grounds, in section 2.3.4.

[74] The prohibition of work and the ritual of palm-taking are restricted, according to *Leviticus* 23: 35 and 39–40, to the first day of the festival.

[75] Consisting of 3 days (522) and another 3 days, followed by a fourth (528).

If, alternatively, Josephus' date is Jewish (as I have argued would have been the normal case: see section 1.2.4), and corresponds to 30 Tishre, then assuming a calendar based on visibility of the new moon, this 30 Tishre would have occurred on 9 October 66 CE. Seven days earlier, 2 October, would have been a Thursday, which again is incompatible with Josephus' Sabbath. If the calendar was based on the conjunction, 7 days before 30 Tishre would have been earlier in the week, again not on a Sabbath.

However, we may assume that Tabernacles was celebrated that year one month later—for as we have seen in Ch. 2, festivals during the Temple period were celebrated relatively late. Assuming a calendar based on visibility of the new moon, 30 Tishre would then have occurred on 8 November 66 CE,[76] and 7 days earlier, 1 November, would have been a Sabbath—exactly as according to Josephus' narrative.[77]

Cestius' assault would thus have commenced on the Sabbath, 23 Tishre (1 November 66 CE), consecutive upon the last day of the festival on 22 Tishre.[78]

If this reconstruction is correct, it would confirm a number of points that have been raised in this and previous chapters:

   (i) Josephus' Macedonian names of months generally designate Jewish lunar months.
   (ii) Festivals were celebrated relatively late during the Temple period.
   (iii) The Jewish calendar was based on visibility of the new moon.

[76] In actual fact, the next new moon would already have been visible on 7 Nov. 66 CE in the evening, which means that the outgoing month (Hyperberetaios/Tishre) should only have been 29 days long, and the day referred to by Josephus as '30 Hyperberetaios' (i.e. 8 Nov.) should actually have been 1 Dios. However, there are many reasons why the beginning of Dios/Marḥeshwan might have been postponed to the next day: poor visibility due to November atmospheric conditions, or alternatively, disruption of the calendrical procedure because Jerusalem was under siege. It should be noted that Josephus' date τριακὰs Ὑπερβερεταίου μηνόs may mean not specifically the 30th day of Hyperberetaios, but the last day of the month, whether the 29th or the 30th, as was common usage in Greek. But if he is referring to the 29th (i.e. Friday, 7 Nov.), his chronology would be impossible to reconcile with this lunar month (ending 7 Nov.), just as it cannot be reconciled with the previous month.

[77] Obviously 30 Tishre was also a Sabbath. It is significant that Cestius waited for the next Sabbath to launch his second offensive (see Schürer 1973–87: ii. 474 and n. 60). The plausibility that he assaulted Jerusalem on both occasions on a Sabbath lends support to the accuracy of Josephus' datings in this passage.

[78] Strictly speaking, the festival of Tabernacles was already over. But because Sabbath was consecutive to it, it is perhaps reasonable for Josephus to refer to the Jews as 'abandoning the festival' to resist Cestius' assault (517). On the possibility of Tishre festivals occurring in this period on Friday, see below, section 4.2.2. On the subsequent interval between 30 Hyperberetaios (528) and 8 Dios (555), see (Schürer 1973–87) i. 599 n. 29.

3.2.5 Second-century sources

One other source confirms that in the earlier period, the Jewish month would have been based on sightings of the new moon. In a Christian sermon attributed to the apostle Peter, but first cited in the late second century by Clement of Alexandria, the following statement is made about the Jews:

And when the moon is not visible, they do not celebrate the so-called first Sabbath, nor do they celebrate the *neomenia*, nor the (festival of) Unleavened Bread, nor the Feast, nor the Great Day.[79]

The meaning of 'first Sabbath', 'Feast', and 'Great Day' is not entirely clear, but it is clearly assumed that the Jewish calendar depended on the first appearance of the new moon.[80]

The same is implicit, although more ambiguously, in the similarly anonymous *Letter to Diognetus*, apparently from around the same period,[81] which says of the Jews: 'They observe the months and the days by sitting in watch (παρεδρεύοντας) for the stars and moon . . .'.[82] This statement, however, may be figurative and not to be taken literally. The exact meaning of παρεδρεύοντας is also somewhat unclear.[83]

Still in the same period (mid second century CE), Galen ascribes to 'those in Palestine'—in all likelihood, the Jews[84]—a lunar calendar consisting of 29- and 30-day months: 'According to the reckoning of those in Palestine, the twelve months amount to a number of 354 days. For, because the interval from the conjunction of it (moon) with sun until the next conjunction takes up, in addition to the 29 days, another extra half(-day), because of this they split the two months, which make up 59 days, into two unequal parts, making one of them of 39 (read: 30) days, and the other of 29.'[85] At first sight, this passage implies a *fixed* calendar, where 29- and 30-day months follow each other in alternation. Such a calendar could not have been based on sightings of the new moon. The beginning of months may have coincided, instead, with the day of the conjunction (this, however, is not to be inferred from Galen's reference in this passage

---

[79] *Kerygma of Peter*, ap. Clement of Alexandria, *Stromateis* 6. 5 (41) (*PG* 9: 261 a). The 'Feast' is possibly Tabernacles (see M. Stern (1974–84) i. 560), and the 'Great Day' the Day of Atonement. See, however, D. Schwartz (1997) 110.

[80] On this and the next source, see Thornton (1989*b*). His inferences from other passages are difficult to accept.

[81] It 'probably dates from the 2nd, or perhaps the 3rd, cent.' (Cross and Livingstone 1997: 483).

[82] *Letter to Diognetus* 4: 5 (*PG* 2: 1173A); Lake (1913) ii. 359.

[83] Lake translates: 'Their attention to the stars and moon for the observance of months and days'.

[84] See Ch. 1 n. 186.

[85] See Ch. 1 n. 101.

to the conjunction, which is only mentioned in the context of the lunation or length of the lunar month).[86]

Attention must be given, however, to the broader context of this passage. Galen's concern in this passage is only to show that in a lunar calendar, where the year is 11 days shorter than the solar year, the equinox does not occur on a fixed date. It is possible, therefore, that the purpose of this passage is only to present the *average* length of the lunar month, and hence, of the lunar 12-month year, rather than to describe the actual workings of the Palestinian calendar. Moreover, there is no clear indication in this passage that in the Palestinian calendar the alternation of 29- and 30-day months (inherent in *any* lunar calendar) must be *regular* or *fixed*. The evidence of this passage is therefore inconclusive.

3.3   THE LATER PERIOD: THE DAY OF THE CONJUNCTION

From the fourth century, as we have seen in Ch. 2, evidence regarding the Jewish calendar becomes much more extensive. Our findings for this later period will be of considerable importance. A number of sources will suggest, indeed, that the Jewish month no longer began at the sighting of the new moon, but rather at the conjunction. Whether this reflects a radical change in Jewish calendar reckoning, or only diversity of practice between various Jewish communities, will have to be duly considered.

First I shall examine fourth-century Christian Paschal sources, then Jewish documents and inscriptions.

3.3.1   The Sardica document

General aspects of this document have been discussed in Ch. 2. It was redacted at the Council of Sardica, in the winter of 343 CE, by a dissident faction of bishops from the East. The document lists the dates of the Jewish Passover from 328 to 343 CE, following the reckoning, it would seem, of the Jews of Antioch. The most conspicuous feature of this document, already discussed in Ch. 2, is that all the Jewish Passovers occur in the (Julian) month of March. In this chapter, I shall examine the dates of these Passovers in greater detail, with a view of establishing when exactly the Jewish lunar month began.

A question which arises from the outset is whether the information conveyed in this document should be considered reliable. In Ch. 2 (section 2.5.3), I have argued that the occurrence of all the Passovers in

---

[86]   See my remarks on Philo, *Special Laws* 2. 26 (140), in section 3.2.2 (near n. 60).

March is reliable on a number of counts. To rehearse: the Jewish dates were listed in this document for the explicit purpose of demonstrating that the Eastern bishops, being committed to the rule of the equinox and the decisions of the Council of Nicaea, would not observe Easter at the same time as the Jews. The polemical credibility of this argument would have depended on the authenticity of these Jewish dates; they are unlikely, therefore, to have been merely invented or forged.

Moreover, the fact that the Jewish dates in this document do not go beyond 343 CE (whereas the 30-year Christian cycle, in parallel, continues for another 14 years) must be considered significant: this was the year, indeed, when the Council of Sardica took place. It seems that the authors of this document were cautious not to predict when the Jews would celebrate Passover in future years, and to record only those dates of Passover which were known to have actually occurred. They appear to have paid attention, therefore, to actual Jewish practice.

However, if their main purpose, as stated, was only to contrast their 30-year cycle with the Jewish dates, we may wonder how *accurately* the Jewish dates would have been entered. The main point, indeed, was only to show that they occurred in March. Even if, as I have argued in Ch. 2 (section 2.5.3), the authors of this document were able and likely to have kept records of when the Jews in their region had celebrated Passover in the last 16 years, the dates entered in the Sardica document might have been only approximate.

According to Grumel (1958: 43–4) and E. Schwartz (1905: 123), the Christian 30-year cycle was constructed, either partially (Grumel) or wholly (Schwartz), on the basis of the Jewish Passover dates. Schwartz suggests that the whole purpose of the Eastern bishops was to strike a compromise between the Council of Nicaea and the local Eastern custom of 'following the Jews'; this was achieved by observing Easter[87] on the same day as the Jews, unless it occurred before the equinox, in which case Easter would be postponed to the next month, 30 days after the Jewish date. If, as argued by Schwartz and Grumel, the Christian cycle was based on Jewish dates, its authors are unlikely to have relied on dates that were approximate or inaccurate. Thus either theory would suggest that the dates recorded in this document are fully reliable and accurate.

Unfortunately, the theories of Schwartz and Grumel remain unsubstantiated. They appear to have relied on an interpretation of the text that is unlikely. The introductory text of this document reads:[88] 'Conputatur autem primus [primus] annus triginta annorum scriptorum in comp<u>tationibus in quibus faciunt Iudei phascha a prima indictione...', which they understood to mean: 'The first

---

[87] More precisely, the 14th of the lunar month; Easter would be observed on the following Sunday.

[88] See full text below.

year of the 30 years written (below, i.e. the Christian cycle) is reckoned *in accordance with* the computations in accordance with which the Jews make Passover, from the first indiction (328 CE) . . .'. However, the translation of *in* as 'in accordance with' is rather unlikely.[89] The correct translation of this passage is probably: 'The first year of the 30 years written (below) in the tables [lit. 'computations'] of the *Jewish* Passovers is reckoned from the first indiction'. Thus this sentence is only referring to the Jewish dates; it does not imply that the Christian dates were based, in any way, on the latter.[90]

Another problem is the *textual* reliability of this document. All that has been preserved is a Latin translation, in a codex dating from about 700 CE (Telfer 1943: 181–2). Many of its dates are internally inconsistent as well as calendrically impossible; they are clearly wrong, and most probably the result of inaccurate transmission. The problematic dates were emended by E. Schwartz in his first publication of the document in 1905, and his emendations have been accepted by others in all subsequent publications.[91]

For practical convenience, I reproduce below the whole text as edited by E. Schwartz (1905: 122–3).[92] Original manuscript readings are indicated in square brackets (sometimes with the abbreviation *MS*), and emendations in pointed brackets. Common Era (CE) years (from 328 onwards) in square brackets are also the editor's addition, as well as some editorial comments (e.g. *sic*).

De pascha autem scribsimus uobis XXX annos, quoniam XXX annos fecit dominus noster in carne super terram, pascha autem facta est XXX anno XXV die Martii mensis. conputatur autem primus primus [*sic*] annus triginta annorum scriptorum in comp<u>tationibus in quibus faciunt Iudei phascha [*sic*] a prima indictione que facta est sub Constantino [328], quo tempore conueni<t> magna synodus in ciuitate Nicaea, cum diu quaererent episcopi de phascha ut computetur. prima indictio [indici *MS*] a primo anno conputationis, et prima indictio inputata post quintam decimam est XVI anno positus in conputatione annorum pasche. a primo anno conputatur numerus iste usque ad XXX annum qui est

---

[89] The Latin word *in* is generally not attested in this sense, although it could be argued that in this document it is an unsatisfactory translation of the Greek ἐν, which can be used in this sense (so according to Bailly 1903: 665, entry 7, citing Thucydides 1. 77, 7. 11, etc.), and which probably would have appeared in the original Greek text.

[90] So in Bornstein's Hebrew translation (1924: 320). I am grateful to Leofranc Holford-Strevens for his comments.

[91] See above, Ch. 2 n. 83.

[92] A facsimile of the document is appended at the end of his 1905 article; it appears to have been faithfully transcribed.

primus mensis Aprilis. possiti [*sic*] autem sunt distinctiones numeri Iudeorum nobis sic:

Quibus supputationibus faciunt Iudei pascha:		Quo numero facimus nos Christiani:	
[328] I an(nus)	XI Mar.	I an.	X Ap.
[329] II an.	XXX Mar.	II an.	XXX Mar. [Ap. *MS*]
[330] III an.	XVIIII Mar.	III an.	XVI<II> Ap. [Mar. *MS*]
[331] IIII an.	[X]VIII Mar.	IIII an.	VI<I> Ap.
[332] V an.	XXVII [XXIII *MS*] Mar.	V an.	<X>XVI<I> Mar.
[333] VI an.	XVI Mar.	VI an.	XV Ap.
[334] VII an.	V Mar.	VII an.	IIII Ap.
[335] VIII an.	XXIIII Mar.	VIII an.	XXIIII Mar.
[336] VIIII an.	XIII [XVI *MS*] Mar.	VIIII an.	XI<I> Ap.
[337] X an.	II Mar.	X an.	<I> Ap.
[338] XI an.	XXI Mar.	XI an.	XXI Mar. [Ap. *MS*]
[339] XII an.	X Mar.	XII an.	VIIII Ap. [Mar. *MS*]
[340] XIII an.	XXV<IIII> Mar.	XIII an.	XXVIIII Mar. [Ap. *MS*]
[341] XIIII an.	XVIII[I] Mar.	XIIII an.	XVI<I> Ap. [Mar. *MS*]
[342] XV an.	V<II> Mar.	XV an.	VI Ap.
[343] XVI an.	[X]XXVI Mar.	XVI an.	<X>XVI Mar. [Ap. *MS*]
et reliqui XIIII anni.			
[344]		XVII an.	XIIII Ap. [Mar. *MS*]
[345]		XVIII an.	[X]III Ap.
[346]		XVIIII an.	XXIII Mar. [Ap. *MS*]
[347]		XX an.	XI Ap. [Mar. *MS*]
[348]		XXI an.	XXX<I> Mar. [Ap. *MS*]
[349]		XXII an.	XVIIII Ap. [Mar. *MS*]
[350]		XXIII an.	VIII Ap.
[351]		<X>XIIII an.	XXVIII Mar. [Ap. *MS*]
[352]		<X>XV an.	XVI[I] Ap. [Mar. *MS*]
[353]		XXVI an.	V Ap.
[354]		XXVII an.	XXV Mar. [Ap. *MS*]
[355]		XXVIII an.	XIII Ap. [Mar. *MS*]
[356]		XXVIIII an.	II Ap.
[357]		XXX an.	XXII Mar. [Ap. *MS*]

Although Schwartz's emendations have been endorsed, as stated, by all subsequent scholars, they should not be accepted at face value: many of them are based on assumptions that are actually far from certain.

In spite of his claim (1905: 123), Schwartz did not base his emendations on what would have been the most likely scribal errors. For instance, the Jewish date for the year 340, if a scribal error, would have been more plausibly emended from

XXV to XXX than to XXV(IIII) (Schwartz's emendation). But as Schwartz (ibid.) points out, errors in the numerals may have originated in the Greek original, or in the course of its translation into Latin. Thus even if it is likely, as in the Jewish date for 336, that V was substituted for II (as implied by Schwartz's emendation), it would not be appropriate to rely entirely on conjectures of this kind.

Schwartz's emendations rely almost entirely, instead, on calendrical considerations. For instance, confusion appears to have occurred, in the Christian dates, between the months of March and April. Clearly, 30 April (manuscript reading for 329) and 9 March (for 339) are mutually exclusive, since all dates in the cycle should have occurred within a maximum period of one month. Schwartz resolves this problem with the simple suggestion that in many cases, the sequence March–April was erroneously inverted into April–March.[93] This solution implies that the authors of this cycle assumed as equinox 21 March, as according to the Alexandrian reckoning.[94]

A greater problem, which affects Jewish and Christian dates alike, is presented by the numerals. It can be taken for granted that these dates pertain to a lunar calendar; Passover and its Christian equivalent (referred to in other Christian sources as the '14th of the moon') should thus occur around the time of the full moon. On that basis, dates such as XXIII March for 332 (the Jewish date) or XVI March for the same year (the Christian date) can be dismissed, *a priori*, as impossible, as neither would have coincided, even approximately, with the full moon. These dates require, therefore, to be emended.

Schwartz's emendations of individual dates are based on two additional assumptions that are actually far from certain. Firstly, he assumes that Jewish and Christian dates would have been either identical, or—if the Jewish date occurred before the equinox—exactly 30 days apart. This is because he considers, as stated above, that the Christian cycle was constructed entirely on the basis of the Jewish dates. But as we have seen, Schwartz's assumption is challenged by Grumel's theory that the Jewish calendar was only used for determining the *initial* date of the 30-year cycle; in his view, subsequent Jewish dates would have been inconsequential to the Christian cycle.

Secondly, Schwartz assumes that Jewish as well as Christian dates must have succeeded each other, from year to year, at regular intervals of either −11 days (in an ordinary year) or +19 days (in an intercalary year) with reference to the dates of the Julian calendar. Regular intervals of this kind would be likely in the context of a fixed cycle, such as in the Christian cycle of this document. But that regular intervals would have applied to the *Jewish* dates is inconsistent with Schwartz's own theory (1905: 124, and see below) that the Jewish dates were based on empirical sightings of the full moon. If the Jewish calendar was empirical, Passover dates would not have succeeded each other with such regularity.

---

[93] As aptly explained by Bornstein (1924) 320–1. The years in question are 329–30; 338–39; 340–1; 343–4; 346–7; 348–9; 351–2; and 354–5. This suggestion would not apply, however, in the case of 357.

[94] Grumel (1960) 164, 171. For other reckonings of the date of the equinox, see section 2.6.3.

Thus although Schwartz's emendations have been endorsed by all subsequent scholars, including Grumel, they are based on assumptions that are often inconsistent with either Schwartz's or Grumel's own theories. This does not mean that these emendations must be rejected; they must be treated, however, with great caution.

In view of the textual uncertainties that affect this document, I shall adopt a cautious approach and ignore, in first instance, all dates in the manuscript that are clearly erroneous. These dates of Passover can be assumed erroneous inasmuch as they widely diverge from the time of occurrence of the full moon. Since we cannot be certain as to how to correct them, these dates cannot serve as evidence for our analysis of the Jewish calendar. I shall restrict myself therefore to dates in the manuscript that are *not necessarily* in need in correction, and hence that are (presumably) textually reliable.

I shall also ignore the evidence of the Christian dates. This is because it remains unclear, as stated above, to what extent the Christian cycle was modelled on the Jewish dates. Its relevance to the Jewish dates is therefore unclear.

The purpose of Table 3.1 is to establish, on the basis of the reliable Jewish dates in the manuscript and of astronomical data, when the Jewish lunar month is most likely to have begun. The Jewish 'Pascha' referred to in this document is taken to mean, as in all Christian sources,[95] the 14th day of the lunar month, when the Passover sacrifice (if applicable) would have been prepared.[96] The results of this table are plain: the majority of Passover dates suggest a calendar compatible with the *conjunction*.

Other options, as indicated in the table, must be completely discarded. E. Schwartz (1905: 124) argued that the date of the Jewish Passover would have been determined empirically, as the day in March when the full moon was sighted;[97] however, it is evident from our table that Passover occurred invariably one or two days beforehand (except for only

---

[95] Also in Philo, *Special Laws* 2. 11 (41). Rabbinic sources, however, tend to confuse Passover (*Pesah*) with the first day of Unleavened Bread, or even with the entire festival (15–21 Nisan): see *Y. Halah* 2: 1 (58b) (cf. *T. Sotah* 11: 2, p. 314), *B. RH* 13a (see *Tosafot* ad loc., s.v. דאקריבו), *B. Kiddushin* 37b–38a.

[96] Note that the subsequent evening, when the Passover sacrifice would have been eaten, would have been treated in the Julian calendar as part of the same day (at least until midnight), even though it was reckoned in the Jewish lunar calendar as the beginning of the 15th.

[97] This explains, in his view, why the dates of Passover for after 343 CE could not be predicted.

Table 3.1. The Sardica document: dates of the Jewish Passover
and the lunar month.

Year CE	Date in MS[a]	Full moon (day and hour)	Mean conjunction[b]	14th of lunar month[c]		
				from first invisibility	from conjunction[d]	from first visibility
328	11	12 (16h.)	27/2 (3h.)	**10**	**11**	13
329	30	31 (15h.)	17/3 (1h.)	29	**30**	1 April
330	19	21 (7h.)	6/3 (10h.)	18	**19**	21
331	(18)	10 (23h.)	23/2 (18h.)	7	8–9	10
332	(23)	28 (23h.)	13/3 (16h.)	25	26(–27)	28
333	16	18 (7h.)	3/3 (1h.)	15	**16**	17
334	5	7 (9h.)	20/2 (10h.)	**5**	**5**	7
335	24	26 (1h.)	11/3 (7h.)	**24**	**24**	26
336	(16)	14 (4h.)	28/2 (16h.)	13	12(–13)	15
337	2	3 (14h.)	17/2 (1h.)	**2**	**2**	4
338	21	22 (14h.)	7/3 (22h.)	**21**	**21**	23
339	10	12 (7h.)	25/2 (7h.)	**10**	**10**	12
340	(25)	30 (8h.)	15/3 (5h.)	27	28	30
341	19	19 (21h.)	4/3 (13h.)	17	17	**19**
342	(5)	9 (3h.)	21/2 (22h.)	6	7	8
343	(36)	27 (20h.)	12/3 (20h.)	25	(25–)26	27–28[e]

[a] In brackets are dates in the manuscript that are clearly erroneous.

[b] Merely for reference. Times are based on the *molad*, and only gross approximations; for precise values of the *molad*, see Bornstein (1924) 320–1. Times are given here in modern hours, from midnight to midnight.

[c] The Jewish 'Pascha' referred to in the Sardica document is taken to mean, as in all Christian sources, the 14th day of the lunar month (see main text). In the Jewish calendar, the 14th of the month would have normally begun in the previous evening.

[d] Assuming that the first day of the month was the 24-hour period, from one evening to the next, within which the mean conjunction was calculated to have occurred. If the molad occurred near the beginning of the evening, I have treated the result as doubtful by indicating the alternative possibility in brackets.

[e] Visibility of the new moon on 13/3 is uncertain, hence two possible dates.

Note: All dates are in March, except for the mean conjunction where February or March are specified. All coincidences with the manuscript dates are highlighted in bold.

one case, year 341).[98] A calendar based on sightings of the new moon is also incompatible with the document's Passover dates (except, again, for year 341). A calendar based on first invisibility of the old moon is preferable, but still only compatible in 5 out of 10 cases (ignoring manuscript dates that are clearly erroneous).

The conjunction, by contrast, is compatible with the document's Passover dates in 9 out of 10 cases. The only exception (the date of year 341), as it happens, is emended by Schwartz to read '18'; if we emended it instead to '17', consistent compatibility with the conjunction would be achieved. Compatibility with the conjunction does not necessarily mean, however, that the calendar was reckoned by calculating the conjunction. It may have been reckoned by following a fixed cycle or scheme. In such a case, coincidence with the conjunction would not necessarily have applied in all cases, and Schwartz's emendations would be quite reasonable.

Table 3.2. The Sardica document: erroneous dates emended.

Year	Manuscript	Emended by conjunction	Schwartz's emendation
331	XVIII	VIII or VIIII	VIII
332	XXIII	XXVI or XXVII	XXVII
336	XVI	XII or XIII	XIII
340	XXV	XXVIII	XXVIIII
342	V	VII	VII
343	XXXVI	XXV or XXVI	XXVI

Note: In many of these cases the conjunction occurred near the beginning of the evening (see Table 3.1). Consequently, two alternative emendations must be considered.

The clearly erroneous dates—which I have until now ignored—could also be emended in such a way as to be compatible with the conjunction. In some cases, again, these emendations would differ from Schwartz's. See Table 3.2.

Conjectural emendations, however, are probably best avoided. It is sufficient to conclude, on the strength of the dates in the manuscript that are presumably not erroneous, that the Jewish calendar in this document appears to have been based compatible with the conjunction, and thus not empirical but based on a calculation.

The inability of the document's authors to predict future dates of the Jewish Passover (for after 343 CE) may have been due to the fact that they would not have known exactly how this calculation was made.

---

[98] The same is evident from the dates and times of the full moons supplied by Schwartz himself (1905: 126). Again, his argumentation is strangely inconsistent.

The question of how this calendar was calculated or reckoned is, indeed, of interest. On the basis of Schwartz's emended text, Grumel (1958: 42–3) puts forward the theory that the Jews of this document reckoned a 19-year cycle similar to the Christian, Alexandrian cycle of Easter. In Ch. 2 (section 2.5.3), I have rejected this theory on the grounds that a 19-year cycle cannot be inferred from a record of only 16 years. In addition, the dates of Passover are unlikely to have repeated themselves every 19 years, because this would easily have been discovered by the Eastern bishops (provided, as I assume, that they kept annual records of the dates of the Jewish Passover). Knowledge of such a cycle would have enabled them, without difficulty, to predict the dates of Passover after 343 CE.

If we are to surmise how the Jewish calendar of this document was calculated and reckoned, it is perhaps more likely that the dates of Passover were made to succeed each other at regular intervals of −11 days (in a common year) and +19 days (in an intercalary year), relative to the dates of the Julian calendar. This is certainly born out from Schwartz's emendations; but even without his emendations—which, as stated above, cannot be accepted at face value—we find that intervals between the 'non-erroneous' years consistently follow this scheme (these are the intervals between years 328–30, 333–5, and 337–9; see Table 3.1).

This scheme, however, would have been slightly inaccurate: it would have led to a discrepancy with the lunar months of approximately one day every 18 years.[99] To correct this error, we may surmise that in some years an interval of −12 (or +18) days would have been substituted.[100] If this correction was made irregularly and on a purely *ad hoc* basis, this would explain why the bishops were unable to predict with certainty the dates of Passover for after 343 CE.

But in spite of its attractions, the suggestion that the Jews followed a −11/+19 scheme (with occasional *ad hoc* corrections) remains no more than hypothetical.

To conclude, the Sardica document suggests, to the extent that its dates are reliable and accurate, that the Jewish calendar of early fourth-century CE Antioch was compatible with the conjunction, and thus presumably calculated.

3.3.2   The Catania inscription

Later in the century, in 383 CE, a Jew in Catania (Sicily), Aurelius Samuel, erected a marble plaque in memory of his wife with a precise

---

[99] This explains why towards the end of the 16 listed years, if we follow Schwartz's emendations in conformity with the −11/+19 scheme, the date of Passover would have occurred in 341 on 18 March, one day later than according to the conjunction. Grumel (1958: 44) refers to this discrepancy as one day in every 30-year cycle, but this is imprecise.

[100] In the Alexandrian 19-year cycle, the error was corrected with a −12 day interval at the end of every cycle (the *saltus lunae*): see e.g. Grumel, ibid.

record of the date of her death, in the Julian as well as in the lunar calendar. The relevant section of the inscription reads as follows:

... fatum complebit XII Kal(endas) Novebres, diae Veneris, luna octaba, Merobaudes iterum et Satornino consulibus ...[101]

...(she) completed her allotted life on 21 October, a Friday, on the 8th day of the lunar month, when Merobaudes for the second time and Saturninus were consuls ...

The date as it stands is problematic, because in the consular year referred to, which corresponds to 383 CE, 21 October was not a Friday but a Saturday. This discrepancy could not have resulted from a different reckoning of the days of the week: by the later fourth century, evidence confirms that the 7-day week was standard throughout the Roman world (see section 3.1.5). We must assume, instead, that the date was incorrectly entered. Inasmuch as a Jew would not have mistaken Friday for a Sabbath, it is the day of the month that is most probably erroneous. The inscription should therefore have read: *XIII Kal.*, i.e. 20 October.[102]

Besides this Julian date, a lunar date is also provided: *luna octaba*. The meaning of this phrase is undoubtedly the '8th day of the lunar month', as originally proposed by Libertini.[103] The usage of *luna* (in the ablative) together with an ordinal is well attested, in this sense, in

---

[101] *CIJ* i. no. 650 = Noy (1993–5) i. no. 145, ll. 4–7. For a previous attempt to ascertain the calendrical significance of this inscription, see Wasserstein (1991/2).

[102] Noy (1993–5) i. 190; Worp (1991) 224.

[103] Libertini was the first publisher of the inscription; he is cited by J. B. Frey in *CIJ* i. 467, who also translates *luna octaba* as 'le huitième jour de la lune'.

early Latin inscriptions.[104] It is also attested in contemporary inscriptions, mainly Christian,[105] and in texts relating to the computation of the date of Easter.[106]

Noy (1993–5: i. 190) translates *luna octaba* as 'in the eighth month', on the grounds that 20 October 383 CE would have occurred in the Biblical eighth month (Marḥeshwan). This interpretation must be dismissed. Besides the fact that biblical numbered months are hardly attested in Jewish sources after Qumran, it is highly unlikely that the meaning of *luna octaba* in the Catania inscription would have differed from its well attested general usage.

Since lunar datings of this kind, alongside Julian dates (and sometimes the days of the week), are well attested in contemporary non-Jewish inscriptions, we may question whether *luna octaba* in this inscription is a specifically 'Jewish' dating. It could have been borrowed directly, by Aurelius Samuel, from a non-Jewish source. Indeed, the very idea of inscribing a detailed date of death is likely to have been borrowed from the

---

[104] e.g. *CIL* 1(2): 2511 (= *AE* 1922: 91; *AE* 1963: 35; *AE* 1983: 394): *luna III* (67 BCE, Feretium, Etruria). *CIL* 4: 4182 (= *AE* 1897: 24): *luna XVI* (6 Feb. 60 CE, Pompeii). *AE* 1982: 808 (3rd-c. Pannonia, dedication to Mithras). *CIL* 3: 1051: *luna XVIII* (Thursday, 23 May 205 CE, Apulum, Dacia). *AE* 1941: 77 (= *AE* 1980: 60): *luna XVIII* (Saturday, 20 Nov. 202 CE, Rome). According to Noll (1968), lunar datings were introduced in the 3rd c. under the influence of Oriental religions (and then became predominantly Christian in the 4th c.). However, Noll appears to have overlooked the evidence of lunar datings from as early as 1st-c.-BCE Etruria (see above). It seems that lunar datings represent in fact an ancient Italian tradition: the idiom is also attested in Columella (e.g. 8. 7. 4) and Pliny (e.g. *Natural History* 22. 149), and elliptically in Vergil, *Georgics* 1. 277 (see Servius ad loc.).

[105] For Christian (some only presumed Christian) inscriptions, see index in Diehl (1961) 311. Inscriptions listed by Diehl range from 269 CE (no. 3391, Diehl 1927: 193) to 502 CE (no. 4874, ibid. 413; on which see n. 109 below). Some of Diehl's datings are inferred from fragmentary inscriptions and hence somewhat speculative. Nearly all his inscriptions are thought to come from Rome; no. 4385 may be from Mauretania. For an additional Christian inscription, see *Inscriptiones Christianae Urbis Romae*, NS v, no. 13104; see also ibid., NS vii, no. 17423.

[106] For a good sample, see sources cited by E. Schwartz (1905) 29–104 (chs.2–5). Most common is of course *XIV luna*. The usage of *lunae* (in the genitive), e.g. *XIV lunae*, is also attested but far less commonly.

Christians: detailed dates of death are common in contemporary Christian inscriptions,[107] but rare in Jewish and pagan funerary inscriptions.[108] If, then, Aurelius Samuel was borrowing a Christian funerary formula, the date of *luna octaba* may easily have come together with it; it may thus represent a *Christian* lunar date, rather than one from the Jewish lunar calendar.[109]

Nevertheless, there is a strong case for arguing that this date was taken from a Jewish lunar calendar. First, it does not tally with the lunar dates of most Christian Easter calendars: 20 October would have been the 9th of the lunar month according to the Roman cycle, and the 7th according to the Alexandrian.[110] Secondly, attention must be given to the strikingly Jewish character of this inscription. Jewish features include a line of Hebrew text at the top, *menorot* motifs at the bottom, the dedicator's biblical name (*Samohil* = Samuel), and a reference to 'the law which the Lord gave the Jews' (ll. 11–12). This conspicuous display of Jewishness suggests a strong commitment to Judaism. In spite of the non-Jewish character of the dating, it seems to me unlikely that the lunar date would

---

[107] Shaw (1996) 104–5. Shaw argues that this practice was related to the specifically Christian notion that death was a spiritual new birth, and hence that the time of death was of high significance. On the Roman origin of the mention, in funerary inscriptions, of *age* at the time of death, a practice which was widely adopted by the Jews of Rome, see Rutgers (1995) 101–7.

[108] With the sole exception of funerary inscriptions from Egypt, where date of death is usually given (according to the Egyptian calendar), and from Zoar (dated according to the Jewish Babylonian-type calendar). For Egypt, see Horbury and Noy (1992) 279–81; contrast with Noy (1993–5) i. 332–3 and ii. 540–1. For Zoar, see below section 3.4.2. The Catania Jewish inscription is thus exceptional and unique.

[109] There is certainly no reason to treat a lunar dating (*luna* + *ordinal*) as evidence of Jewish identity. Noy's (1993–5: ii. 331, no. 401) identification of *CIJ* i. no. 81* (= Diehl 1927: 491, no. 4874) as Jewish, solely on the basis of its dating '*luna prim(a)*', must therefore be dismissed. On statistical grounds, this dating would suggest, quite on the contrary, that the inscription is more likely to have been Christian.

[110] According to the *supputatio Romana* (Krusch 1880: 62), 1 Jan. 383 was the 12th of the lunar month; since the lunar months ending in the odd solar months contained 30 days, those ending in the even solar months 29 days, 20 Oct. would have been the 9th. In the authentic Alexandrian calendar as recovered from Ethiopic sources by Neugebauer (1979), as distinct from subsequent Western and Eastern adaptations to the Roman year, the epact of 383/4 (the moon's age on the last day of the preceding year) was 14; since the 30-day lunar months *began* in the odd months of the Alexandrian year, 22 Phaophi (= 20 Oct. in Julian pre-leap year) was the 7th of the lunar month. According to the Easter table of Augustalis (Krusch 1880: 19), in 299, and therefore in 383, 1 January was the 11th of the lunar month, making 20 Oct. the 8th; it is unlikely, however, to have been used in Catania. I am grateful to Leofranc Holford-Strevens for his advice.

have differed from the lunar calendar that must have been reckoned, one assumes, by the Jews in Samuel Aurelius' community.

If the date of *luna octaba* is representative of how the local Jewish calendar would have been reckoned, we may infer that the Jewish calendar of Catania was *not* based on sightings of the new moon. The new moon would have first been visible in Catania on 14 October 383 CE in the evening; in a calendar based on the new moon, 20 October (daylight hours) would have corresponded to the 6th, not to the 8th, of the lunar month.

The conjunction, however, would have occurred on 13 October, in the early hours of the morning. First invisibility of the old moon would have occurred at the same time. In a calendar based on either the conjunction or invisibility of the old moon, 20 October would have corresponded to the 8th day of the lunar month, as in to the inscription.[111]

We may establish, in addition, that the calendar of Catania is likely to have differed from the Palestinian rabbinic calendar of the same period. According to the Palestinian Talmud, indeed, the rule was firmly established that Yom Kippur could never occur on Friday.[112] Yet if 8 Marḥeshwan occurred in Catania on Friday, then Yom Kippur (10 Tishre) would have occurred, four weeks earlier, on the same day of the week.[113]

[111] In support of his translation of the inscription, Libertini mentions that according to the 'Jewish calendar' the 8th of the lunar month would have occurred on 21 Oct. 383 CE (cited by J. B. Frey in *CIJ* i. 467). The 'Jewish calendar' he is assuming is none other but the present-day rabbinic calendar. The use of the present-day rabbinic calendar for ancient Jewish datings is an anachronism which unsuspecting historians, often relying on the tables of Mahler (1916), too frequently commit.

[112] This can be inferred from *Y. Megillah* 1: 2 (70b); see sections 4.2.2 and 4.4.3. The Palestinian Talmud would have been redacted not later than this period: see Sussman (1990) 132–3.

[113] The only way the Catania dating could be accommodated with the contemporary Palestinian rabbinic calendar is by assuming a 29-day month of Tishre, and thus the Day of Atonement occurring one day later, on Saturday. This however is unlikely, because the mean conjunction of Tishre occurred on Wednesday, 13 September. Assuming that Tishre began on that date, the Day of Atonement would have occurred on Friday, and Tishre would have been a 30-day month. On the incompatibility of the Catania inscription and the rabbinic calendar, see Wasserstein (1991/2); his article is marred, however, by an anachronistic assumption that the present-day rabbinic calendar was already in existence.

3.3.3   The *ketubah* of Antinoopolis

We now turn to the marriage contract (*ketubah*) from Antinoopolis, Egypt, dating from 417 CE.[114] Written in Aramaic, it is dated according to consular year, Sabbatical cycle year, perhaps another year count, Jewish month and day, and day of the week. In spite of the fragmentary state of the text, some elements of this date are clearly legible:

1. [הופאטיאס הונוריאו אוגאוסטאוֹ טואֹ] הנדאקאטן
2. [קאי פלאויאו קונס[טאנ]טי[אוֹ קומיטוס טוא]מֹ[גאלוא
3. [פריפסטאטאו קאי] פאטריקיאו בשתה שתיתֹ[יתה] דֹשֹבֹועֹ[ה]
4. [.ה] בירח כסליו בעשרין בה בארֹבֹעה בשֹׁוֹ[בֹתה]

[In the consulate of Honorius Augustus for the] eleventh time
[and   Flavius   Cons]tan[ti]us,   the   most   [magnificent   ($\mu\epsilon\gamma\alpha\lambda o\pi\rho\epsilon\pi\epsilon\sigma\tau\acute{a}$-$\tau o\nu$)] *comes*
[and] *patricius*, in the sixth year of the Sabbatical cycle,
[...] in the month of Kislew, the 20th of it, the 4th day of the week.

We read the 6th year of the Sabbatical cycle, 20 Kislew, and fourth day of the week, i.e. Wednesday (ll. 3–4). The consular year is only fragmentary (ll. 1–3), but comprises the transliterated Greek term *hendekaton* (eleventh), which can only refer to a consul for the eleventh time. This indication, combined with the Sabbatical dating, leads the editors to the only possible year of 417 CE.[115]

Another option considered (but ultimately rejected) by the editors is 425 CE, assuming Wacholder's Sabbatical cycle which runs one year later (see section 2.6.3). But as they show, this year does not suit the other elements extant in the consular dating. The dating of 417 CE must be accepted, therefore, in the absence of any alternative. This document may thus be treated as further evidence in favour of the generally accepted Sabbatical cycle, whereby 417/18 CE would have been the 6th year of this cycle (Sirat *et al.* 1986: 27).

This dating also indicates that the Jews of Antinoopolis kept the same Sabbatical year count as in Palestine (the generally accepted cycle). In this context, the following points should be considered:

(i) Egyptian Jews such as Philo acknowledged that agricultural laws relating to the Sabbatical cycle were restricted entirely to the Land of Israel.[116] Reckoning

---

[114] Sirat *et al.* (1986). The text cited below is from p. 20, ll. 1–4.

[115] Ibid. 25–7; hence the reconstitution of the text, as above. Another year count may be missing, unfortunately, at the beginning of l. 4: see ibid. 29–31.

[116] Philo does not mention this in his account of the Sabbatical year in *Special Laws* 2. 19–21 (86–109), but he does acknowledge it, albeit somewhat elusively, in his account of the Jubilee and of related laws (ibid. 22–4 (110–21)) by referring occasionally to the Land of Israel which he designates simply as 'the land' ($\chi\acute{\omega}\rho a$: ibid. 21 (104), 22 (113), 23 (118–19), and 24 (121)).

of this cycle, therefore, is likely to have been associated, even in Egypt, with Palestinian practice.

(ii) Palestinian influence is evident in the *ketubah*'s language, which is Galilean Aramaic.[117] The very mention in this document of the Sabbatical cycle, a form of dating that is well attested in contemporary Palestine[118] but unparalleled in Egypt until the tenth century,[119] suggests that this dating may have been borrowed directly from Palestinian sources.

Reference to the day of the week enables us to establish how the lunar month would have been reckoned. It could not have been based on sighting of the new moon, which would have been first visible at Antinoopolis on Saturday, 27 October 417 CE, in the evening. Following this, 20 Kislew should have occurred on a Friday.[120]

The mean conjunction, however, occurred on Friday, 26 October, shortly after midday. First invisibility of the old moon, likewise, occurred on that Friday morning. According to this, the 20th of the month would have been on Wednesday, as in the *ketubah*. This suggests that the Jewish calendar of Antinoopolis in the early fifth century was based either on the calculation of the mean conjunction, or on first invisibility of the old moon.

This assumes, of course, that the date in this document is accurate. Sirat and Cauderlier express the view that the day of the month may have been erroneous, as is common in Greek papyri.[121] Their suggestion, however, is only prompted by their determination to reconcile the date of the *ketubah* with the *present-day* rabbinic calendar, according to which 20 Kislew 417 would have been a Friday.[122] This, however, is anachronistic, as the present-day rabbinic calendar was

---

[117] Sirat *et al.* (1986) 9, 12, 31–2. This *may* also indicate rabbinic influence. It must be emphasized, however, that in other respects the *ketubah* displays no evidence of either Palestinian or rabbinic influence. Its text and formula could just as well have been borrowed from Greek Egyptian practices, as frequently pointed out by the editors (ibid. 11–15, 37, etc.).

[118] e.g. in the Zoar inscriptions (see sections 2.6.3 and 3.4.2); also in the mosaic floor of the Horvat Susiya synagogue (together with a dating from the era of creation: Gutman *et al.* 1981: 127).

[119] Sirat *et al.* (1986) 29–30, citing Friedman (1980) i. 102–4.

[120] This is assuming that the day unit began in the evening, and that the *ketubah* document was written in daytime hours (as is indeed most likely). The editors' suggestion that the document was written in the evening after sunset, which would *partially* explain the perceived inconsistency of the *ketubah*'s date with the present-day rabbinic reckoning (Sirat *et al.* 1986: 28), is far-fetched and unconvincing (on writing documents at night, see S. Stern 2000a: 164).

[121] A mistake in the day of the week would have been most improbable for a Jewish scribe: see above section 3.3.2.

[122] Sirat *et al.* (1986) 28, citing again Mahler (1916).

probably not yet in existence;[123] besides, there is no reason to assume that the Jews of Antinoopolis were subservient, in this period, to the rabbinic calendar.

The reliability of the *ketubah*'s dating is defended by Friedman (another of the editors) on the grounds that marriage contracts are generally known, at least in the later period (in Geniza documents), to be accurately dated.[124]

The possibility that the *following* lunar month was reckoned, in Antinoopolis, as Kislew, must also be discarded. First invisibility of the old moon would have occurred on Saturday, 24 November, conjunction on Sunday the 25th in the early morning, and first visibility on the same day in the evening, making the 20th of the lunar month respectively a Thursday, a Friday, or a Saturday. None are compatible with the dating of the *ketubah*.

The significance of this point has been explained above in Ch. 2 (section 2.6.2), but I shall briefly repeat it here. If Kislew began, according to this document, on 26 October 417 CE (and not in the following month), then the previous Nisan (in 417 CE) would have begun on about 4 March (the day on which conjunction occurred, soon after sunrise). This means that Passover, 14 Nisan, would have occurred *c.*17 March, and that the rule of the equinox would have been breached.

3.3.4   Conclusion: the shift to the conjunction

The sources we have examined in this section suggest that in the fourth and fifth centuries major changes had occurred in Jewish calendar reckoning. Whereas in earlier centuries the evidence suggests that the Jewish calendar was based on sightings of the new moon, from the fourth century onwards it had shifted to the calculation of the conjunction. This is evident in the Sardica document, the Catania inscription, and the *ketubah* of Antinoopolis—although in the latter two, invisibility of the old moon cannot be ruled out.

This finding, if correct,[125] is highly significant, because it runs parallel to a similar change that the rabbinic calendar underwent in exactly the

---

[123] As acknowledged by the editors themselves (Sirat *et al.* 1986: 29 n. 22). On the history of the rabbinic calendar, see Ch. 4. The reason why the dates of Kislew in 417 CE, according to the present-day rabbinic calendar, would have occurred two days later than at Antinoopolis—although both calendars are based on the conjunction—is that in the present-day rabbinic calendar, when the conjunction occurs after midday the beginning of the month is usually postponed (the principle of *molad zaqen*). Evidence suggests that in the rabbinic calendar, this principle was not introduced till relatively late (see section 4.4.4). There is no reason to expect it here at Antinoopolis.

[124] Friedman (in Sirat *et al.* 1986: 28–9) suggests that the Jews of Antinoopolis did not follow the present-day rabbinic calendar—which is obviously correct. The editors appear to have remained divided on this matter: see ibid. 7–8.

[125] Caution must be exercised before asserting definitive conclusions. It must be remembered that the sources at our disposal are only sporadic; the *possibility* of calendars based on the conjunction in the earlier period, before the 4th c. CE, cannot be

same period. As early as the fourth century CE, a fixed calendar based
on the conjunction appears to have been adopted in rabbinic circles, as
we shall later see.[126]

Why these changes occurred, and why precisely in this period, are
questions that will be addressed in relation to the rabbinic calendar in
Ch. 5. It is unlikely, as will become evident in that chapter, that the
specific reasons that led the rabbis to the abandonment of the Mishnaic system and the adoption of a fixed calendar would have equally
applied, independently, to the predominantly non-rabbinic communities
that we have surveyed in this chapter (Antioch, Catania, and Antinoopolis). Other explanations must therefore be sought. The first to consider,
however, is whether the calendar of these fourth-century Diaspora communities could have been altered as a result of contemporary rabbinic
influence.

It is widely assumed that Palestinian rabbinic influence began to exert
itself over the Graeco-Roman Diaspora in the course of the third to fifth
centuries, partly as the result of the Patriarch's network of envoys to the
Diaspora communities (Levine 1996: 11, 16, 23–4). The extent of this
influence, however, may have been rather limited (Millar 1992).

The *ketubah* of Antinoopolis is written in Galilean Aramaic and dated,
as in Palestinian sources, according to the Sabbatical cycle, which *may*
suggest a measure of rabbinic influence.[127] But the calendar it assumes
would have been incompatible with the contemporary rabbinic calendar.
Indeed, the rule of the equinox was not observed in 417 CE at Antinoopolis (see section 2.6.2), whereas it had been introduced a century earlier
in the rabbinic calendar (section 4.2.2). In practical terms, this means
that in 417 CE Palestinian and Babylonian rabbis observed Passover one
month later than at Antinoopolis. It seems unlikely, therefore, that use of
the conjunction at Antinoopolis would have been the result of rabbinic
influence.

The same applies to the other sources we have considered. Contacts are known to have existed between Palestinian rabbis and the

ruled out, even if it is not reflected in the evidence. For the persistence of calendars
based on sightings of the new moon in the 4th c. and later, see below section 3.4.

[126] See sections 4.3.1 and 4.4.6. The fixed calendar is already assumed in the
Palestinian Talmud (later 4th c.); but that it was based on the *conjunction* is only
firmly attested in rabbinic sources for the end of the 5th c.

[127] See above, n. 119.

Jews of Antioch;[128] but the Sardica document reveals that the early–mid-fourth-century Jews of Antioch celebrated Passover always in March, in breach of the rule of the equinox. Although their calendar was based on the conjunction and relatively 'fixed', it is unlikely to have been adopted as the result of rabbinic influence.

The Catania inscription does make a reference to the 'patriarchs', perhaps to those of Palestine.[129] But as we have seen, its date implies a Yom Kippur on Friday, which would have been precluded in the rabbinic calendar of the contemporary Palestinian Talmud.

It is important to note that rabbinic influence on Jewish calendar reckoning would have been limited even on Palestinian soil. The Zoar inscriptions, as we have already seen, imply that unlike the rabbis, the Jews of Zoar did not observe the rule of the equinox as late as the fifth century CE. Further differences between the Zoar and the rabbinic calendar will be discussed in the next section. In this context, differences between the rabbinic calendar and the calendar of more distant Diaspora communities come hardly as a surprise.

Since fourth-century Diaspora calendars that are based on the conjunction do not show the mark of rabbinic influence, the possibility of Christian influence should be given serious consideration. For quite some time before this period, the Christians had been using fixed calendar cycles to calculate the date of Easter, which were all based, implicitly, on the mean conjunction. The first of these cycles was designed in the early third century, and began in 222 CE; other cycles were developed in the course of the same century. As we shall see in detail in Ch. 5, the Easter calendar evolved in this way for reasons specific to Christian history, which could not have affected, at least initially, the Jewish calendar. But by the fourth century, once use of these cycles had become well established in Christian communities, the Jewish reckoning of Passover may well have come under their influence.[130]

Christian influence has indeed been noted in the context of the Catania inscription, where the precise date of death, including a lunar dating,

---

[128] See Neaman (1972) 94–7; Wilken (1983) 64–5. *Y. Sanhedrin* 3: 2 (21a), cited by Wilken, is not evidence of a 'rabbinical court' at Antioch, but only that the Jews of Antioch knew of R. Yoḥanan (in Tiberias) and corresponded with his court.

[129] As argued by Noy (1993–5) i. 191. The reference is in l. 10 of the inscription.

[130] See section 5.1.2, where a similar suggestion will be made, albeit more tentatively, with reference to the rabbinic calendar.

is likely to have been borrowed from Christian epigraphic practice. However, the incompatibility of this lunar dating with Christian Easter cycles (see section 3.3.2) suggests that it might have been specifically Jewish.

In view of the early origins of the formula *luna* + ordinal in Italian inscriptions, local *pagan* influence is also a possibility to be considered. The lunar dating in the Pompeii inscription from 60 CE implies a lunar month beginning at the conjunction or at invisibility of the old moon,[131] and so does the Dacia inscription of 205 CE.[132] The same has been inferred as most likely for the inscription of Feretium, Etruria from 67 BCE.[133] These inscriptions precede the advent of Christian Easter cycles. A lunar calendar based on the conjunction or invisibility of the old moon may thus have been borrowed by the Jews of Catania from pagan sources.[134]

Literary sources on an ancient Roman lunar calendar are ambiguous, however, about the beginning of its months. Plutarch claims, not very plausibly, that the Kalends (1st of the month) and Nones (5th or 7th of the month) of the Roman calendar corresponded originally, in the ancient lunar calendar, to the conjunction and the new moon respectively (*Roman Questions* 24 (269B–D)). Elsewhere, however, he implies that the month began one day after the conjunction.[135] Vitruvius writes that the new moon corresponds with the conjunction, but the calendrical significance of this passage is moot.[136] Much later, Macrobius reports that in the early Republican period the new month was declared when the new moon was sighted; the religious ceremony that marked this event is described in detail (*Saturnalia* 1: 15: 9–12).

It must also be noted that the usage of the formula *luna* + ordinal in early Italian inscriptions is not necessarily dependent on the existence of a lunar *calendar*. Particularly significant is the fact that the lunar month itself is never designated

---

[131] *CIL* 4: 4182 (= *AE* 1897: 24): 6 Feb. 60 CE, *luna XVI*. See Deman (1974) 271–3.

[132] *CIL* 3: 1051 (see n. 31): Thursday, 23 May 205 CE, *luna XVIII*. A contemporary inscription from Rome, *AE* 1941: 77 (= *AE* 1980: 60; Saturday, 20 Nov. 202 CE, *luna XVIII*), is more difficult to make out: it implies a month beginning one day after conjunction or invisibility of the old moon, but two to three days before visibility of the new moon.

[133] *CIL* 1(2): 2511 (= *AE* 1922: 91, *AE* 1963: 35, 1983: 394); see Brind'Amour (1983) 51–5.

[134] It must be noted, however, that the lunar dating *luna* + ordinal is not attested, to my knowledge, in Sicilian inscriptions (see Agnello 1953). It is well attested in Italy, particularly in Rome; but this may just be a freak of the evidence.

[135] In *Romulus* 12, he writes that the Roman *noumeniai* (i.e. Kalends) no longer agree with the Greek, but that originally they did; evidence to this is that Romulus founded his city on the last day of a month, which coincided with a conjunction and a solar eclipse. This implies that the Roman *noumenia* originally occurred, as in the early Greek calendar, one day after the conjunction.

[136] Vitruvius, *De Architectura* 9. 2. 3 (Loeb edn. pp. 230–1): 'cum luna est cum sole, nova vocatur'; Pliny, *Natural History* 18. 323. They may be referring to invisibility of the old moon: see Bowen and Goldstein (1994) 707–8 n. 36.

in this formula, either by number or by name. As a form of dating, this formula is clearly insufficient. The absence of any means of distinguishing one lunar month from the next, which one would have expected in a lunar calendar, suggests that a lunar calendar as such did not exist. The formula *luna* + ordinal may just have been, instead, an *astronomical* reference to the moon's monthly cycle.[137]

Christian influence is more likely, however, in the context of the Sardica document. As we have seen, the Jewish calendar in this document was based on the conjunction, and may have been based on a $-11/+19$ scheme. This scheme is characteristic of Christian Easter cycles in the East (Alexandrian and Anatolian).[138]

If the Sardica document reflected the calendar of the Jews of Antioch, we may assume that influence between Christians and Jews would not have been unidirectional. As John Chrysostom's homilies testify, Christians in late-fourth-century Antioch were still prone to observing Easter, as according to the ancient Eastern custom, 'together with the Jews'. Christians at Antioch of either persuasion are likely to have paid close attention to the dates of the Jewish Passover, as the Sardica document itself reveals. In this context, mutual influence between Jews and Christians on calendrical matters is quite likely to have occurred.[139]

Thus to some extent, the emergence in the fourth century of Jewish calendars based on the conjunction may have been the result of Christian calendrical influence. It is only in this period, indeed, that the Christian use of Easter cycles had become firmly ensconced.

3.4 THE LATER PERIOD: THE PERSISTENCE OF DIVERSITY

In spite of the apparent shift of Jewish calendars to calculation of the conjunction, evidence from the fourth century and later suggests that in

---

[137] On the apparent significance of the lunar month to 1st-c.-CE Campanians, see Brind'Amour (1983) 275–83. Astronomical references to the sign of the zodiac are also found in some 4th-c. *luna* inscriptions (Diehl 1927, no. 4377 (= *Inscriptiones Christianae Urbis Romae*, i. 172) and no. 4379); but whether the 'signum' in these inscriptions is one of the zodiac (as Diehl supposes) remains in my view uncertain.

[138] So much so, in fact, that Grumel assumed the Jews to have followed a modified version of the Alexandrian 19-year cycle—a theory which I have rejected above for independent reasons (see section 3.3.1). The $-11/+19$ scheme is also characteristic of western easter cycles.

[139] As also assumed by Grumel (1960), although I cannot accept his own historical account (see discussion in section 2.5.3).

some places, sighting of the new moon continued to form the basis of the Jewish calendar. In this sense, it will be argued, calendrical diversity persisted.

3.4.1 The letter of Ambrose

A brief reference to the Jewish calendar is made in a letter attributed to Ambrose, bishop of Milan, from 387 CE.[140] The context of this letter is itself of interest. In 387 CE, the 14th of the lunar month was considered to occur on Friday, 19 March, according to both the Roman and the Alexandrian Easter cycles.[141] However, the Alexandrian calendar considered that since 19 March was two days before the vernal equinox, Easter had to be postponed to the following month. The 14th of the next lunar month (the 'first month', according to this reckoning) was on 18 April, which happened to be a Sunday. Consequently, Easter had to be celebrated on the following Sunday, 25 April, over a month later than the equinox. This was unacceptably late for Rome, whose own calendar, however, afforded no legitimate date at all.[142]

Because of the exceptional lateness of the Alexandrian Easter, the date of Easter became in that year the object of intense polemical debates.[143] The letter of Ambrose, pro-Alexandrian, was an attack against the Roman Easter calendar.[144]

---

[140] Ambrose, *Epistles*, no. 13 'extra collectionem' in Zelzer (1982), 222–34; no. 23 in *PL* 16; no. 36 in *Fathers of the Church*, vol. 26, trans. M. M. Beyenka, 1954.

[141] See e.g. E. Schwartz (1905) 46.

[142] At Rome, Easter could be celebrated only between 22 March and 21 April, and between the 16th and 22nd of the lunar month; but in 387 the 14th of the next lunar month fell by Roman reckoning on Saturday, 17 April (information courtesy of Leofranc Holford-Strevens).

[143] In the West, it opposed the Alexandrians *versus* the Romans; in the East, it opposed the Alexandrians *versus* the 'Protopaschites' (early Easter observers) who followed the Eastern tradition of observing Easter 'with the Jews'. The latter were the target of John Chrysostom's third homily 'against the Jews', delivered at Antioch early in 387 CE (John Chrysostom, *Adversus Iudaeos*, PG 48: 861–72; see Harkins 1979). The homily implies that the Jews of Antioch, followed by the Protopaschites, were to observe Passover on (or about) 19 Mar.; precise information about the Jewish Passover is not, however, supplied. Another, anonymous homily was written in Asia Minor in the same year with similar objectives (*PG* 59: 747 ff.; Floëri and Nautin 1957, text on pp. 117–25). Both these sources have been referred to above in section 2.5.4.

[144] The letter's adherence to the Alexandrian reckoning is implicit throughout the letter, where the date 18 Apr. for the 14th of the moon, preferred by the Alexandrian cycle, is consistently assumed (Zelzer 1982: 228, 231).

The authenticity of Ambrose's letter has been questioned by a number of scholars. According to E. Schwartz (1905: 54–5) and Frank (1938: 161–2 and n. 96), it is a sixth-century forgery and hence historically 'worthless'. C. W. Jones (1943: 35–6 and n. 3) argues, however, that although the letter contains interpolations (passages from Proterius' letter to Leo, fifth century), still 'much is to be said for its authenticity' (see also Dekkers 1995: 48, no. 160). Strobel (1984: 102–6 and 153) concludes that the attribution to Ambrose may be open to some doubt, but the letter is still securely dated to 387 CE. Finally Zelzer (1978) effectively refutes the objections to the letter's authenticity. These opinions may all be taken into account; they do not significantly affect my conclusions.

The letter refers very briefly to the Jewish Passover as follows:

Denique futurum Iudaei duodecimo, non primo mense celebraturi sunt Pascha, hoc est, decimo tertio Kalendas Aprilis secundum nos . . . (Zelzer 1982: 229).

Finally the Jews are due to celebrate Passover in the twelfth month, not in the first, which is *on XIII Kal. April.* according to us (i.e. according to our Julian calendar) . . .

XIII Kal. April. is 20 March. This date does not agree with any of the Christian cycles, either Alexandrian or Roman. According to these, as stated above, the 14th of the lunar month would have occurred on 19 March. The date in this passage cannot be dismissed as a scribal error. It is corroborated, indeed, by the Egyptian date that the letter (in the same passage) goes on to give as equivalent: 24 Phamenoth, which corresponds precisely to 20 March.

Inasmuch as this date could not have been drawn from any Christian Easter cycle (on the author's assumption that the Jewish cycle was the same), it seems most natural to conclude that it was drawn from an authentic Jewish source. The author must have found out that the Jews in Milan[145] (or possibly elsewhere) were due to celebrate Passover on the 20th of March in that year.

It is unlikely that the author is referring to the *15th* of the lunar month, i.e. the first day of Unleavened Bread, which according to Christian reckoning would have occurred on 20 March. In Christian Paschal literature the Jewish Passover or 'Pascha' always refers to the 14th of the lunar month, when the Passover sacrifice (if applicable) would have been prepared.[146]

This date does not readily agree with calendars based either on the conjunction or on appearance of the new moon. The mean conjunction occurred in 387 CE on 6 March, shortly before noon (local Milan time);

---

[145] For Jews in Milan in Ambrose's period (and later), see Noy (1993–5) i. 1–5.
[146] See above, n. 96.

following this, the 14th of the month should have occurred on the 19th, just as according to Christian reckoning, and one day *earlier* than the Jewish date. The new moon was first visible on 7 March in the evening; following this, the 14th of the month (day time) should have occurred on the 21st, one day *later* than the Jewish date.

A calendar based on the conjunction must therefore be ruled out; sighting of the new moon, however, deserves consideration. Since this letter was written well in advance of Easter, at the beginning of 387 CE, its author could not have known when the new moon, in March, was to be first sighted. He may simply have *assumed*, on the grounds that the Jewish calendar followed appearance of the new moon, that the Jewish Passover would occur one day later than according to Christian reckoning.[147] This would explain why 20 March was entered. If this letter is a sixth-century forgery, the same assumption could have been made, out of ignorance, by someone writing long after the event.

This letter may thus serve as evidence that the calendar of the Jews of Milan, in the later fourth century, was based on sightings of the new moon. This appears to have been, at least, the assumption of the letter's author (whoever he was, and whenever he was writing), and this assumption is presumably significant.

3.4.2 The Zoar inscriptions

A number of inscriptions discovered at Zoar are dated according to day of the month and day of the week. This should enable us to identify when the lunar month, at Zoar, began.[148]

Table 3.3 lists the relevant inscriptions with their dates, in chronological order. Some of the readings are uncertain (as indicated in footnotes below), but this does not affect the overall conclusion. It is evident, indeed, that the beginning of the month at Zoar was completely erratic. In one case, the month begins one day before conjunction (S15);[149] in

---

[147] In actual fact, however, the Christian '14th of the month' and the Jewish Passover would normally have been two days apart, even though the interval between conjunction and first visibility is relatively short at the time of the vernal equinox (see Ajdler 1996: 696–7). For an illustration of the two-day discrepancy between the 14th of the month from conjunction and that from first visibility, see Table 3.1 (in section 3.3.1).

[148] For a general introduction to the Zoar inscriptions, see above, section 2.6.3.

[149] This seems inherently unlikely. S15, however, is problematic in other ways. According to Z88, the previous Tevet (only three months earlier) would have begun on the day after conjunction; it is difficult to understand how a relative difference of 2 days could have built up in such a short interval of time (it would have meant,

Table 3.3. The Zoar inscriptions: beginning of the lunar month.

Inscrip-tion[a]	Year CE[b]	Date on inscription	1st of month[c]	Conjunc-tion[d]	Day of first visibility[e]	Rab-binic calendar[f]
N7	392	Mon. 3 Iyyar	Sat.	Thu. 8/4 22.00	Sun.	Sat.
Z144	429	Fri.[g] 16 Tevet	Thu.	Thu. 12/12 04.00	Sat.	Fri.
N10 = Z315	430[h]	Thu. 17 Elul	Tue.	Tue. 5/8 10.00	Fri.	Wed.
N4	454/5	Fri.[i] 25 Tevet	Tue.	Mon. 6/12 03.00	Tue.	Tue.
S14 = Z177	466[j]	Thu. 20 Elul	Sat.	Thu. 28/7 13.00	Sun.[k]	Fri.[l]
N11	466	Fri. 3 Kislew	Wed.	Tue. 25/10 02.00	Thu./ Fri.[m]	Wed.[n]
Z88	467/8	Tue. 21 Tevet	Wed.	Tue. 12/12 13.00	Fri.	Wed.
S15 = Z308	468[o]	Thu. 6 Nisan[p]	Sat.	Sun. 10/3 03.30	Tue.	Sun.
Z312	471	Thu. 19 Siwan	Sun.	Wed. 5/5 21.00	Sat.	Fri.
S16 = Z306	475	Mon. 10[q] Marḥeshwan.	Sat.	Thu. 16/10 00.30	Sat.	Sat.
N3	503	Tue. 11 Elul	Sat.	Fri. 8/8 13.00	Sun.	Sun.

[a] See Table 2.2 n. *a* (in section 2.6.3).

[b] This year is obtained by adding 68/9 to the year of the era of destruction (the latter amended by one year wherever necessary), according to my conclusions in Ch. 2.

[c] Day of the week when the month would have begun, as inferred from the full date of the inscription (in the preceding column).

[d] Day of the week, Julian date (day/month), and approximate time of mean conjunction (in modern hours, from midnight to midnight).

[e] Day of the week of the first day of a calendar month based on the first visibility of the new moon. This day would have begun on the *previous evening*, when the moon was first visible.

f Day of the week of the first of the month according to the *present-day* rabbinic calendar (merely for reference).

g Perhaps Tuesday (ג instead of ו), which yields Monday for the first day of the month. On calendrical grounds, however, this option is unlikely, as Monday would be two days after visibility of the new moon.

h Year of destruction has been amended in relation to the Sabbatical cycle year (see Table 2.2, in section 2.6.3). In this case, however, it could be the Sabbatical cycle year that is erroneous (i.e. year 4 should be amended to year 5; see my remarks in section 2.6.3). The year would then be 431 CE. See Table 3.4 (below), under the same entry, for the relevant results.

i Naveh (1985 and 1995) reads שובתה, Sabbath, but in a personal communication he advises me that the reading ע]ר[ובתה, Friday (a reading first suggested to me by Shay Walter) is possible and perhaps preferable. This reading is also preferable on calendrical grounds.

j Year of destruction has been amended in relation to the Sabbatical cycle year (see Table 2.2, in section 2.6.3). In this case, however, it could be the Sabbatical cycle year that is erroneous (i.e. year 5 should be amended to year 6). The year would then be 467 CE. See Table 3.4 (below), under the same entry, for the relevant results.

k Saturday is also a faint possibility.

l Month of Av in the present-day rabbinic calendar, because according to the latter the year would have been intercalated. At Zoar, this year would have been common (since the following year, as evident from N11, would have been intercalated: see section 2.6.3).

m Borderline case of first visibility.

n Month of Marḥeshwan in the present-day rabbinic calendar, according to which an intercalation would already have been made (see section 2.6.3).

o Year of destruction has been amended in relation to the Sabbatical cycle year (see Table 2.2, in section 2.6.3).

p The word *Nisan* is fragmentary and hence somewhat conjectural, but no alternative reading is really possible. See S. Stern (1999).

q Perhaps 26 (כו instead of בי): see S. Stern (1999). This yields Thursday for the first day of the month, which corresponds to the day of conjunction.

Note: I have supplied the conjunction and first visibility of the lunar month likeliest to have corresponded to the month of the inscription. This lunar month has been identified on the assumption that the rule of the equinox was not observed and that Passover could occur as early as 17 March (the approximate date inferred from N11), and perhaps even as early as the 15th (see section 2.6.3).

two cases, on the day of conjunction (Z144 and N10[150]); in five cases, between conjunction and day of first visibility (N7, Z177 = S14,[151] N11, Z88, N3); in two cases, on the day of first visibility (N4,[152] S16[153]); and in one case, one day after first visibility (Z312). Even if these results are not entirely secure, the beginning of the month ranges clearly from the day of the conjunction to one day after first visibility, with a majority of cases between conjunction and first visibility.

Table 3.3 is based on my conclusion in Ch. 2, that 68/9 must be added to the year from the destruction in order to convert it into a year CE. This conclusion is based, as explained in Ch. 2, on the generally accepted cycle of Sabbatical years.

According to Wacholder's Sabbatical cycle, 69/70 years must be added to the era of destruction, which leads to totally different results. Although I have shown in Ch. 2 that Wacholder's cycle is unlikely, particularly in the context of the Zoar inscriptions, an attempt has been made in Table 3.4 to consider what his cycle would yield.

This table yields the following distribution, again completely erratic: in one case, between conjunction and first visibility (S15);[154] in one case, on first visibility (N10); in four cases, one day after first visibility (Z144,[155] N11, Z88, N3).

A number of inscriptions, however, yield results that are most unlikely: one day before conjunction (Z312), two days after first visibility (N4,[156] N7), and far worse, three days after first visibility (Z177 = S14, S16).[157]

These unlikely results constitute further grounds for rejecting Wacholder's cycle; I shall not give it, therefore, further consideration.

in practice, three 29 day months in succession, which in a lunar calendar is extremely unusual). The word *Nisan* in S15 is actually fragmentary and hence somewhat conjectural, although no alternative reading is really possible; see S. Stern (1999). If not misread, the date of S15 may simply be erroneous.

[150] If dated 431 CE, between conjunction and first visibility. See Table 3.4 below.

[151] If 467 CE, on or just after first visibility. See Table 3.4 below.

[152] Perhaps one day later: see Table 3.3 n. *i*.

[153] Alternatively, on the day of conjunction: see Table 3.3 n. *q*.

[154] The inconsistency of this inscription with Z88, however, remains (see above, n. 149).

[155] Alternatively, on the conjunction: see Table 3.4 n. *c*.

[156] Perhaps three days after: see Table 3.3 n. *i*. N3 may also be two days after, although visibility of the new moon on Thursday is uncertain.

[157] S16 can be interpreted, alternatively, as two days before conjunction. If the first of the month in S16 is Thursday (Table 3.4 n. *g*), then one day after visibility. If we assume that Passover occurred, according to Wacholder's cycle, in April (as is less likely: see n. *b* to Table 3.4), the results obtained are just as erratic, but comprise a smaller number of problematic cases. Thus in Z312, the 1 Siwan would have occurred either 2 days before conjunction (on Tuesday, 23 May at 17. 30) or 2 days after day of first visibility (Friday, 26 May), both of which are most unlikely.

Table 3.4. The Zoar inscriptions according to Wacholder's Sabbatical cycle.

Inscription	Year CE	Date on Inscription	1st of month[a]	Conjunction[b]	Day of first visibility
N7	393	Mon. 3 Iyyar	Sat.	Tue. 29/3 07.00	Thu.
Z144	430	Fri.[c] 16 Tevet	Thu.	Mon. 1/12 13.00	Wed.
N10 = Z315	431[d]	Thu. 17 Elul	Tue.	Sat. 25/7 19.00	Tue.
N4	455/6	Fri. 25 Tevet	Tue.	Fri. 25/11 12.00	Sun.
S14 = Z177	467[e]	Thu. 20 Elul	Sat.	Tue. 18/7 21.30	Wed.
N11	467	Fri. 3 Kislew	Wed.	Sat. 14/10 12.00	Tue.
Z88	468/9	Tue. 21 Tevet	Wed.	Sat. 30/11 21.30	Tue.
S15 = Z308	469[f]	Thu. 6 Nisan	Sat.	Thu. 27/2 12.00	Sun.
Z312	472	Thu. 19 Siwan	Sun.	Mon. 24/4 05.00	Wed.
S16 = Z306	476	Mon. 10 Marḥeshwan	Sat.[g]	Mon. 4/10 09.00	Wed.
N3	504	Tue. 11 Elul	Sat.	Tue. 27/7 21.00	Thu./ Fri.

[a] As in Table 3.3 above.

[b] As in Table 3.3, but for the following year, i.e. (in all cases) 12 lunar months later. I am assuming that according to Wacholder's cycle, Passover at Zoar could occur between 7 and 30 March (the approximate dates of Passover inferred, according to Wacholder's cycle, from N11 and N12: see section 2.6.3); the relevant lunar month has been selected accordingly. Similarly erratic results are obtained if we assume, as is less likely, that Passover occurred between 5 and 29 April (as *can* be alternatively inferred according to Wacholder's cycle: see section 2.6.3).

[c] Perhaps Tuesday, which yields Monday for the 1st day of the month; see Table 3.3 n. *g*.

[d] Or 432 CE (see Table 3.3 n. *h*), with rather unlikely results: conjunction on Friday 16.30, and first visibility on Sunday (assuming that 431–2 CE must have been intercalated).

[e] Or 468 CE (see Table 3.3 n. *j*), with rather unlikely results: conjunction on Sunday 19.00 and first visibility on Tuesday (assuming that 467/8 CE must have been intercalated).

[f] See Table 3.3 n. *o*.

[g] Or Thursday (see Table 3.3 n. *q*), which on calendrical grounds is preferable.

Thus the beginning of the Zoar month appears to range irregularly from the day of the conjunction to one day after first visibility, with a majority of cases between conjunction and first visibility. This range is problematic and needs to be explained. A high incidence of scribal errors is possible, but perhaps unlikely. Whereas the era from the destruction may have been of limited practical use and hence may have been liable to error, as I have argued elsewhere (S. Stern 1999), the days of the week and the lunar dates are likely to have been well known and accurately inscribed, because of their significance for the observance of the Sabbath and festivals.

Two interpretations can be suggested at present. The first is that the Zoar calendar was based, primarily, on the conjunction. The postponement of the new month by two days (N7, Z177 = S14, S16) or sometimes four days (Z312) would have been due to *extraneous*, i.e. non-lunar reasons, over which it is impossible for us to speculate.[158]

The second is that the Zoar calendar was based on the appearance of the new moon. The high incidence of new months before or after first visibility would have resulted from false or delayed sightings, and perhaps quite often from false *predictions* of when the new moon would first be visible.

It is easy to understand, indeed, why errors of this kind would have been common at Zoar. The site of Zoar, located in the Dead Sea depression at about 300 m below sea level, is particularly unsuitable for sighting the old and the new moons. It is flanked along the east by the Southern Moab mountain range, which rises to heights of over 1000 m above sea level (except for the Zered valley, which rises to over 500 m), and along the west by the Negev hills that rise to over 500 m above sea level. These exceptional elevations cut off the view, at Zoar, of much of the horizon. In order to obtain a reasonable view of the new moon, Zoar inhabitants would have needed to travel some 30 km to the west up mountainous paths; they would have waited for sunset, and then—having sighted the moon—would not have been able to return till the next morning. These difficult conditions might explain why erroneous sightings and predictions would have been so frequent.

However we account for the datings of the inscriptions, the Zoar calendar would have differed substantially from the rabbinic calendar

---

[158] According to this interpretation, the exceptional lateness of Z312 may be dismissed alternatively as a scribal error; whereas the date of S15, one day before the conjunction, may be attributed to an inaccurate calculation of the mean conjunction.

attested in contemporary sources.[159] As we have seen, the Palestinian Talmud precludes the occurrence of Yom Kippur on Friday.[160] Yet N10 (= Z315) is dated Thursday, 17 Elul (430 CE), which means that the following Yom Kippur (10 Tishre) would have been on Friday.[161]

The possibility of scribal error cannot be ruled out. But if this dating is accurate, it would imply that Yom Kippur and the other festivals of Tishre, in 430 CE, would have been celebrated by the Zoar community and the rabbis of Palestine on different dates.

A further incompatibility of this kind was noted regarding N3 as soon as it was first published in 1943. The dating of N3 is Tuesday, 11 Elul (503 CE), which means that the following Rosh ha-Shanah (1 Tishre) would have occurred on Sunday; this is precluded in the present-day rabbinic calendar (Fraenkel 1945). The same applies to the newly discovered Z177 = S14. However, the rule that Rosh ha-Shanah cannot occur on Sunday appears not to have been introduced in the rabbinic calendar till much later, well after the period of these inscriptions (see section 4.4.3). Thus there is no reason to regard these dates as incompatible with the rabbinic calendar of that period.[162]

More generally, the tremendous irregularity of the Zoar dates (with beginning of months ranging from the conjunction to after visibility of the new moon) is unlikely to have conformed to the rabbinic calendar. By the time the Palestinian Talmud was redacted,[163] a fixed calendar based on the regular alternation of 29-day and 30-day months (at least from Adar to Tishre) had been introduced (see sections 4.2.3 and 4.4.2). The Zoar dates show no sign of such regularity; they are likely to have frequently differed, therefore, from the dates of the contemporary rabbinic calendar.

---

[159] It would also have differed from the present-day rabbinic calendar, as evident from the last column of Table 3.3.

[160] See above, n. 112, and below, see sections 4.2.2 and 4.4.3.

[161] This is assuming that Elul was a 29-day month—another rule that had become well established in the rabbinic calendar by this period (see section 4.2.2).

[162] As argued by Akavia (1951/2) 126–8. The reading suggested by Kasher (1949: 176–9) in N3 of תרעסר (i.e. 12 Elul) instead of חדעסר (11th) is paleographically implausible, and has therefore been ignored in the academic literature. Akavia uses N3 as evidence that the postponement of Rosh ha-Shanah from Sunday to Monday must have been introduced in the rabbinic calendar after 503 CE. This is to assume, however, that the Zoar calendar conformed to the rabbinic calendar of this period. Since the newly recently discovered inscriptions reveal that this was not the case (as argued here and in Ch. 2), the Zoar inscriptions cannot inform us about the history of the rabbinic calendar.

[163] The Palestinian Talmud would still have been redacted before the first inscription listed in Table 3.3: see above, n. 112.

This confirms our conclusion in Ch. 2 that the calendar of Zoar differed quite substantially from that of the rabbis in the same period. The historical significance of this finding has already been pointed out. It effectively means that even in fourth- to sixth-century Palestine, the authority of the rabbis did not yet extend to all Jewish communities.

3.4.3 Conclusion

Non-rabbinic evidence pertinent to Jewish calendar reckoning ceases after the sixth century CE. How the Jews, other than the rabbis, reckoned the calendar in this later period remains a matter of conjecture. It is only in the tenth and eleventh centuries that the rabbinic calendar is known to have achieved ascendancy and to have spread to all Jewish communities.

A source occasionally cited as evidence for the seventh century is the Muslim tradition that when Muhammad entered Medina, the Jews were fasting on their Day of Atonement.[164] The date of his entry in Medina is given by early Muslim historians as Monday, 12 Rabiᶜ I.[165]

This date, however, is problematic, as according to the present-day Muslim computation 12 Rabiᶜ I in year 1 (622 CE) would have been a Friday. This large discrepancy cannot be accounted for by assuming that a different lunar calendar was in use.[166]

Moreover, the tradition that this date corresponded to the Jewish Day of Atonement is only recorded in later medieval Muslim sources.[167] It is quite possible that this tradition was construed in this later period on the basis of the *present-day* rabbinic calendar, according to which, indeed, the Day of Atonement would have occurred in 622 CE on a Monday.

Too many uncertainties surround this tradition, therefore, for it to be treated as reliable or authentic.

At the beginning of this chapter, I suggested that calendars based on sightings of the new moon would differ considerably, in their dates, from one community to the next, because of different geographical co-ordinates, variable weather conditions, and variable human observational skills. Calendars based on the conjunction, by contrast, were based on calculations or calendrical schemes that could be shared by disparate

---

[164] Gil (1996) 130–3, with extensive references in n. 21.

[165] Ibn Ishaq, *Sirat Rasul Allah* (Guillaume 1955: 281; ibn Ishaq lived in the early 8th c., but his work was re-edited by ibn Hisham in the early 9th c.); al-Tabari (Watt and McDonald 1988: 162; al-Tabari dates from the late 9th—early 10th cc.).

[166] *Pace* Watt, in Watt and McDonald (1988) p. xlvi.

[167] Ibn Sayyid al-Nas and Ibn Kathir, both from the 14th c.; see references in Gil (1996) 132–3 n. 21.

communities. The latter are more likely, therefore, to have enhanced calendrical uniformity in the Jewish world.

The emergence in the fourth century of Jewish calendars based on
the conjunction, which we have examined in the last section (3.3), may
thus have contributed towards the cohesion of Jewish Diaspora communities in this period. However, we have also seen (in this section, 3.4)
that calendars based on visibility of the new moon appear to have remained in use in the same period, from the fourth century to the sixth,
even in Palestinian communities. Obviously, the sporadic evidence extant precludes any quantification. But if both types of calendars were
used in various communities in the same period, calendrical variety may
have not only persisted in late Antiquity but also *increased*, in comparison with the early period, where only one type of calendar is known to
have existed (section 3.2).

Calendrical uniformity was only achieved in the Jewish world through
the spread and acceptance of the conjunction-based rabbinic calendar, which occurred much later, probably not before the tenth century
CE.[168] Nevertheless, it is possible that the adoption of fixed or conjunction-based calendars in many Diaspora communities of the fourth
century paved the way towards their eventual adoption, much later, of
the present-day rabbinic calendar.

---

[168] According to a Muslim source, calendar dates for a few years in advance were
originally sent out on a regular basis from Baghdad (presumably, from the seat of
the rabbinate) to Spain; then R. Ḥisdai ibn Shaprut introduced in Spain, in the 960s
or 970s, the knowledge of how to reckon the (present-day rabbinic) calendar. The
source is ibn Djoldjol (late 10th cent.) ap. Abu Usaybia in his *History of the Physicians*,
cited in French translation by Munk (1848) 325–6 (hence in English translation in
Munk 1881: 41) and in Hebrew translation by Bornstein (1922*b*) 286–7.

4

The rabbinic calendar:
development and history

The rabbinic calendar is by far the best known of all ancient Jewish calendars. It is described at length in Mishnaic and Talmudic literature, mainly in the tractate *Rosh ha-Shanah*. It is also the main Jewish calendar to have survived till the present day. Yet in spite of this, the origins of the present-day rabbinic calendar are extremely unclear. After more than a century of scholarly research, greatly enhanced by discoveries in the Cairo Geniza, the history of the rabbinic calendar in the first millennium CE, and particularly from the post-Mishnaic to the later Geonic periods, remains shrouded in mystery.

Tradition has it that in 358–9 CE the rabbinic calendar underwent a radical reform. The older calendar, described in the Mishnah and based on empirical sightings of the new moon, was replaced with the fixed, calculated calendar that is in force today. Evidence of such a reform, however, is absent in contemporary sources such as the Palestinian and Babylonian Talmud. It is only first mentioned in late tenth- or early eleventh-century sources, which may cast doubt on the reliability of this tradition.

The present-day rabbinic calendar, likewise, is only fully attested and described in early tenth-century sources, in the polemical correspondence of R. Saadya and Ben Meir. There is thus a gap of about seven centuries between the Mishnah and R. Saadya's period, during which little can be said with certainty about the rabbinic calendar.

The limited evidence that is available has been studied in detail by earlier scholars, although fresh evidence continues occasionally to emerge. Among the earlier scholars, H. Y. Bornstein is worthy of special mention. Of breathtaking scope and proficiency, he published a series of articles in the first decades of the twentieth century, largely based on then recent Geniza discoveries, that had a formative influence on the modern understanding of the rabbinic calendar and its origins. Other scholars to have made significant contributions to this field, in the later nineteenth and earlier twentieth centuries, are H. S. Slonimsky, Z. H. Jaffe, and A. A. Akavia. The work of Bornstein, above all, continues till this day to exercise tremendous authority, in spite of serious attempts in the last two decades to undermine his theories. Although I shall often differ substantially from these early scholars, it is impossible to study the history of the rabbinic calendar without frequently referring to their works.

Earlier scholars have often failed to take account of the considerable diversity that existed between Jewish calendars in late Antiquity. This diversity has been the theme of the last two chapters, and by now should be completely evident. The implicit assumption has often been, instead, that the Jewish calendar was reckoned universally in the same way. As a result, the tombstone inscriptions of Zoar (for instance) have regularly been adduced by calendar historians as evidence for the rabbinic calendar in the early sixth century.[1] Yet there is no evidence that the Zoar community observed the same calendar as the rabbis; as we have seen, recently published material from Zoar indicates in fact the contrary.

For this reason, I have taken care to restrict my study of the rabbinic calendar to purely *rabbinic* sources, from the Mishnaic, Talmudic and Geonic periods. My premiss is that the 'rabbinic calendar' can be treated as a category of its own, within the broader spectrum of early Jewish calendars. Although rabbinic calendar reckoning underwent significant changes in the course of this period, it belonged nevertheless to a cultural movement with relative historical continuity throughout the first millennium CE. Because the extent of rabbinic influence upon the practices of Jewish communities is difficult to assess, it is safer to treat rabbinic evidence as separate and distinct from the sources surveyed in preceding chapters.

Rabbinic sources themselves, however, frequently make the assumption that there is only one Jewish calendar—the calendar of the rabbis—and hence, that festivals must be celebrated everywhere on the same dates. This assumption, I suspect, has adversely affected the perspective of modern historians on the Jewish calendar. It is partly in order to 'restore the balance' that I have delayed discussion of the rabbinic calendar until this chapter. Only after studying the diversity of non-rabbinic Jewish calendars in late Antiquity does one appreciate how peculiar, in this context, the rabbinic concept of calendrical unanimity would have been. This concept, I shall argue in the next chapter, may go some way

[1] See Ch. 3 n. 162.

towards explaining how and why the rabbinic calendar developed in the way it did.

The purpose of this chapter is to establish the *stages* through which the rabbinic calendar evolved, from its Mishnaic origins to the calendar that is in use today. In the next chapter, a historical explanation for this development will be sought.

4.1 THE MISHNAIC CALENDAR

The 'Mishnaic' calendar is represented not only in the Mishnah, but also in other rabbinic sources attributed to the *Tannaim*, i.e. the sages of the first to early third centuries CE. Some of these sources are cited as *baraitot* in the Talmudim; others constitute the bulk of the Tosefta and halakhic Midrashim.[2] For our purposes, it will be sufficient to refer to the Mishnah and Tosefta. Although the Mishnaic calendar belongs undoubtedly to the Tannaitic period, the extent to which it represented actual practice in this period, rather than mere theory, is generally difficult to prove.

4.1.1 The new month

The calendar of the Mishnah is based on the same principles as the Babylonian calendar, as would have been most lunar calendars in the late antique Near East (see Ch. 1). The months are designated, in the Mishnah and other rabbinic sources, by their Babylonian names. They begin, as in the Babylonian calendar, at the first sighting of the new moon. Whoever first sees the new moon must testify before a rabbinic court, which formally declares the beginning of the new month.

The procedure for determination of the new month is described at length in the Mishnah, tractate *Rosh ha-Shanah* (henceforth, *M. RH*).[3] I shall summarize the text (with the omission of some procedural details), rather than cite it verbatim.

Whoever sees the new moon must testify, the next morning, before a rabbinic court consisting of at least three judges.[4] This court was located according to *M. RH* 2: 5 in Jerusalem, but *M. RH* 2: 8–10 suggests

---

[2] See in general Strack and Stemberger (1991).

[3] Some of this description is also found in *T. RH* 1: 14–3: 2 (pp. 210–11).

[4] This detail is not in *M. RH*, but in *M. Sanhedrin* 1: 2.

that by the early second century CE it had been relocated to Yavneh.[5] Witnesses from other cities are also expected to make the journey (*M. RH* 1: 6, 1: 9, 4: 4), perhaps at their own cost; but on their arrival, they are treated to 'large meals' so as to be encouraged, in future, to return (2: 5). Such importance is attached to their testimony, especially regarding the festive months of Nisan and Tishre, that they are allowed to travel from other cities on the Sabbath (1: 4–6 and 1: 9). Originally, anyone's testimony was deemed acceptable (excluding however incompetent witnesses: 1: 7–8); but after that disruptions were caused by 'heretics (*minim*)',[6] only 'known' witnesses were accepted (2: 1). The court interrogate the witnesses to establish whether their testimony is astronomically plausible (2: 6, 2: 8).[7] If it is, the head of the court declares the new month to be 'sanctified' (2: 7): that day is thus *rosh hodesh*, the first day of the month (see 3: 1).

The court's declaration of the new moon was publicized, originally, through a system of beacons which extended from Jerusalem to Syria (2: 4) and to Transjordan.[8] Later, after disruptions had been caused by the Samaritans, calendrical information was transmitted through messengers (1: 3, 2: 2–3).

Although the determination of new months is basically empirical— with the result that Shavuᶜot (Pentecost), the 50th day after Passover, can variously occur on 5, 6, or 7 Siwan[9]—some fixed rules nevertheless exist. The Tosefta stipulates that every month must be 29 or 30 days

---

[5] Usha (in Galilee) is mentioned in *T. RH* 2: 1 (p. 210), for the period following the Bar-Kokhba revolt. For these and subsequent relocations, see Safrai (1965*b*) 27– 38.

[6] According to *T. RH* 1: 15 (p. 210), by the Boethusians. The nature of these disruptions is described in detail in the Tosefta.

[7] Further details are given in *T. RH* 2: 2 (pp. 210–11). On these passages see Wiesenberg (1962); Ajdler (1996) 388–93; Wacholder and Weisberg (1971) 227–42. The latter point out the similarity between Babylonian and rabbinic methods of predicting visibility of new moons, and argue that rabbinic methods were directly borrowed from the Babylonians.

[8] The latter, according to *T. RH* 2: 2 (p. 210). The identity of the hill-tops in *M. RH* and *T. RH* is somewhat obscure; see Rosenthal (1977) 102–4. Syrian hill-tops include the 'Ḥauran'; Transjordanian hill-tops include Gader (Gadara?) and 'Harim' (in Transjordan: see *T. Sheviᶜit* 7: 11, p. 71). Both the Palestinian and Babylonian Talmudim consider the chain of beacons to extend as far as Babylonia (*Y. RH* 2: 2 (58a): the 'palm trees of Babylonia'; *B. RH* 23b: 'Pumbaditha').

[9] *T. ᶜArakhin* 1: 9 (p. 543).

long.[10] In any one year, there cannot be less than 4, or more than 8, full months (of 30 days: *M. ʿArakhin* 2: 2); nor can there be 6 consecutive full months (*T. ʿArakhin* 1: 7, p. 543). These passages imply that in certain cases, the new month would have been declared regardless of when the new moon had been sighted.

Another passage states as follows:

אין עצרת חל אלא ביום הנף.
אין ראש השנה חל להיות אלא ביום הנף וביום עיבורו.
אחרים אומרים: אין בין עצרת לעצרת ואין בין ראש השנה לראש השנה אלא
ארבע ימים בלבד; ואם היתה שנה מעוברת, חמשה.

ʿAtzeret (Shavuʿot) always occurs on the (same) day (of the week as) the day of the waving (of the *ʿomer*, sheaf).

Rosh ha-Shanah always occurs either on the (same) day (of the week as) the day of the waving, or on the following day.[11]

Others say: from one *ʿAtzeret* to the next, and from one Rosh ha-Shanah to the next, there are only four days; and if the year is intercalated, five days (*T. ʿArakhin* 1: 11, pp. 543–4).

The first statement is obvious, as Shavuʿot occurs, by definition, seven weeks after the day of the waving (16 Nisan). The second statement implies, as would be expected of an empirically reckoned calendar, that the dates of Rosh ha-Shanah are flexible: depending on whether there are two or three full months in the six-month period from Nisan to Tishre, Rosh ha-Shanah will occur either on the same day of the week as the *ʿomer* or one day later (respectively). It is unclear, however, why other options are not considered in this passage: for instance, if there are four full months from Nisan to Tishre, Rosh ha-Shanah would occur *two* days after the same day of the week as the *ʿomer*.[12]

More problematic, however, is the third statement (attributed to 'others'), whereby *ʿAtzeret* and Rosh ha-Shanah occur on days of the week that are four days later than in the previous year (or five days later, in an intercalated year).

---

[10] *T. RH* 3: 1–2 (p. 211). For elucidation of this passage see Lieberman (1962) 1037–8. See also *Sifra, ʾEmor* ch. 10: 4; *Y. RH* 3: 1 (58c) and parallels.

[11] For various interpretations of וביום עיבורו, see Bornstein (1908) 92–3. Bornstein favours the view that it means the (notional) 31st day of Nisan, but this is far-fetched on a number of counts. In my translation, I follow the interpretation cited by Bornstein ibid. 93 n. 1.

[12] This possibility is pointed out in *B. ʿArakhin* 9b. The Talmud suggests that the second statement follows the opinion of 'others' (the third statement, see below), whereby the calendar is calculated and consists of a regular alternation of full and defective months. This means that Rosh ha-Shanah normally occurs on the day of the week following that of the *ʿomer*; however, it occurs on the same day as the *ʿomer* in intercalated years, because then—the Talmud suggests—one of the full months in the sequence from Nisan to Tishre is made defective. This interpretation is clearly far-fetched.

This implies that the calendar year is restricted to a *fixed* number of days: 354 days in a plain year, and 383 days in an intercalated year, which amounts to six full and six defective months per annum, with an additional defective month in intercalated years. The statement of 'others' implies, therefore, a calendar that is fixed and calculated in advance, rather than based on empirical sightings of the new moon.[13]

A calculated calendar of this kind, however, would hardly have been functional. Because it assumes an alternation of full and defective months with an additional defective month in intercalated years, its average month length is less than $29\frac{1}{2}$ days. This leads to an annual discrepancy of about half a day from the actual lunar month, which is far worse, for instance, than the lunar calendars of Qumran.[14]

It has been suggested, therefore, that the statement of 'others' refers to a schematic calendar that would only have been used on a *temporary* basis, whenever the decisions of the rabbinic court were not known (Weiss 1995: 188 and n. 14). Provisions of this kind are made, indeed, in another passage of Tosefta that will be studied in detail in the next chapter.[15]

Alternatively, 'others' may simply represent a marginal opinion with which the majority of rabbis disagreed.[16] The marginality of this opinion may be reflected in that it is not cited anywhere in the Palestinian Talmud, nor indeed in any Palestinian source outside the Tosefta.[17]

4.1.2 The intercalation

The procedure of intercalation is described in detail in the Tosefta, tractate *Sanhedrin*. The decision to intercalate is taken by a rabbinic court alone, although *T. Sanhedrin* 5: 2 (p. 423) suggests that witnesses may also be used. The number of judges in this court ranges from three to

---

[13] As inferred in *B. ʿArakhin* 9b. Elsewhere, the Talmud assumes that the calendar of 'others' consists of a fixed and *regular* alternation of full and defective months (except for the extra-sequential defective month in intercalated years: see above, previous n.): *B. RH* 20a, *B. Sukkah* 54b. In *B. RH* 20a, however, the calendar of 'others' is confusingly associated with the empirical calendar: see Weiss (1995) 191–2.

[14] See above, section 1.1.7: in the Qumran 3-year-cycle calendar, intercalated months are full, which partially compensates for this discrepancy. The discrepancy inherent in the calendar of 'others' is noted in *B. ʿArakhin* 9b (Ravina's saying cited below, section 4.4.6). The Talmud suggests that the numbers 'four' and 'five' in the statement of 'others' are not meant to be exclusive, as in some cases, the difference of days from one year to the next would have to be greater. This interpretation ignores, however, the emphatic 'only' (אין אלא בלבד) in the statement of 'others' (see comment of Weiss 1995: 192 n. 30).

[15] *T. ʿArakhin* 1: 8: below, section 5.3.4.

[16] This interpretation is assumed throughout the Babylonian Talmud: see references in n. 13, and also *B. Shabbat* 87b and *B. RH* 6b.

[17] It is frequently cited, however, in the Babylonian Talmud; on the possible implications of this distinction, see section 5.4.2.

seven (*T. Sanh.* 2: 1, p. 416).[18] This court must sit in Judaea rather than in Galilee (2: 13, pp. 417–18).[19]

The additional month that is intercalated is always a second Adar (2: 8 and 2: 11, p. 417).[20] Intercalation can only be made on the basis of two of the following criteria at least (2: 2, p. 416):

(i) *ʾaviv*, the ripeness of the crops, which in the Bible is when Passover must occur,[21] but which is associated here with the offering of the first crop, the *ʿomer* (sheaf), on 16 Nisan.[22]

(ii) the ripeness of the fruits of the tree. The source and definition of this criterion are somewhat unclear.[23]

(iii) the *tequfah*—another biblical term associated with Tabernacles (Exod. 34: 22), and interpreted here as meaning the autumn equinox, or according to one opinion (R. Yose), the vernal equinox.[24]

---

[18] The king and the high priest are excluded from joining it (*T. Sanh.* 2: 15, p. 418).

[19] Zuckermandel's text (following the Erfurt MS) is clearly erroneous: see apparatus (Vienna MS and *editio princeps*). See also *Mekhilta de-R. Yishmael, Bo* 2, end (ed. Horovitz–Rabin, p. 9); *Midrash Tannaim* (ed. Hoffmann, p. 90); and *Targum Onkelos* on Deut. 33: 18, all suggesting a preference for Jerusalem. The Tosefta rules that if the intercalation is made in Galilee, it is still valid; and so does the *baraita* cited in *Y. Sanh.* 1: 2 (18d) (= *Y. Nedarim* 7: 13 (40d)). But according to the *baraita* cited in *B. Sanh.* 11b, Hanania of Ono is of the opinion that intercalation in Galilee is always invalid; and in all manuscript recensions of the *Sheʾiltot de-Rav ʾAhai*, ch. 49 (Mirsky 1964: iii. 80), the opinion of Hanania of ʾOno is presented as normative (likewise at the end of *Midrash Sod ha-ʿIbbur*, Wertheimer and Wertheimer 1953: ii. 44). Mirsky (1964: iii. 80–1 n.) suggests that the tradition whereby intercalation in Galilee is invalid may represent the earlier, original ruling, which would have been abrogated in the late 2nd c. CE when intercalation was forcibly relocated from Judaea to Galilee (according to *Y. Sanh.* 1: 2 (18c); see Safrai 1965b: 31–3). This is quite possible, but it seems to me that the preservation of this 'earlier' tradition in the Babylonian Talmud and the *Sheʾiltot* reflects a specifically Babylonian, anti-Palestinian (or anti-Galilean) polemic, to which we shall return in the next chapter.

[20] As is generally the case in Babylonian-type calendars; the occasional intercalation of Elul, however, does not occur in the rabbinic calendar (see above, section 1.2.2). See also *Mekhilta de-R. Yishmael, Bo* 2 (ed. Horovitz–Rabin, p. 8).

[21] *Ex.* 13: 4, 23: 15, 34: 18; *Deut.* 16: 1.

[22] *T. Sanh.* 2: 2–3, p. 416. This interpretation of *ʾaviv* is possibly based on *Lev.* 2: 14. See R. Hananel on *B. Sanh.* 11b and Rashi ibid. s.v. על האביב.

[23] See Rashi ad *B. Sanh.* 11b, s.v. על פירות האילן, and Maimonides, *Laws of Sanctification of the Moon*, 4: 3.

[24] For various definitions of this criterion, see *T. Sanh.* 2: 7, p. 417. For an expansion of the latter opinion, see *B. Sanh.* 13a–b. On the meaning of the Hebrew term *tequfah*, see section 2.2.2.

According to R. Shimon b. Gamliel, the year can be intercalated on the basis of the *tequfah* alone (2: 2, p. 416), which effectively means the application of some rule of the equinox. His statement, however, is slightly ambiguous and treated as uncertain by the Babylonian Talmud (*B. Sanh.* 11b). The level of ripeness of the crops and of the fruits of the tree is established with reference to at least two of the following three regions: Judaea, Transjordan, and Galilee (2: 3, p. 416).

Additional criteria are also taken into account, but only in a subsidiary manner: the maturity of kids, of lambs, and of birds (2: 4–6, pp. 416–17, presumably because of their demand for Passover sacrifices), the weather, and the progress of pilgrims on their way to Jerusalem (2: 12, p. 417).[25] Some years can never be intercalated: Sabbatical years and first years of the Sabbatical cycle, and for similar reasons, years of famine (2: 9, p. 417).

How the court's decision to intercalate is publicized is not clearly explained. We are told in *T. Sanh.* 2: 6 (pp. 416–17) of a letter dictated by R. Gamliel and the elders to Yoḥanan the scribe on the steps of the Temple Mount, addressed to 'our brothers in exile in Babylonia, in Media, and everywhere else', informing them of the decision to intercalate a 30-day month;[26] but no indication is given as to how regularly letters of this kind were sent.[27]

4.1.3 Theory and reality

As I have argued in Ch. 1, the Jewish calendar of Judaea in the Hasmonaean, Herodian, and early Roman periods is likely to have been similar to that of the Mishnah: a lunar, empirical calendar that had been inherited from the Babylonian calendar of the Persian and Seleucid empires. But whether the procedures described in *M. RH* and in *T. Sanhedrin* were ever fully implemented in all their details remains anyone's guess. It is questionable, for instance, whether the beacon procedure was ever

---

[25] See further *B. Sanh.* 11a, and above, section 2.3.5.

[26] Also in *Y. Sanh.* 1: 2 (18d) and *B. Sanh.* 11b. *Y. Sanh.* adds: 'our brothers in exile in *Yawan*', meaning Greece or perhaps the Greek-speaking east Mediterranean (see also parallel in *Y. Maʿaser Sheni* 5, 56c).

[27] According to the Palestinian Talmud (*Y. Megillah* 1: 4 (71a)), the exilarch Mar ʿUqva (3rd c.) found two letters that had been sent to Babylonia, presumably from the Land of Israel, regarding the intercalation of a second Adar. The fact that he 'found' them suggests perhaps that reception of such letters was actually quite rare.

really carried out, and if so, whether it could have been effective.[28] The effectiveness of the dissemination of rabbinic calendrical decisions in the Diaspora is an important question which we shall return to in the next chapter.

More fundamental, however, is the question of whether the rabbinic court was always in control of the calendar and of calendrical decisions, as assumed throughout *M. RH*. In the Hasmonaean period, calendrical decisions are more likely to have been under the control of the ruling dynasty, as had been the practice in the Persian and Seleucid empires, than under the control of some rabbinic court. Even after the loss of Jewish political autonomy in the Roman period, the high priest is most likely to have been in charge of the calendar, until 70 CE.[29]

After the destruction of the Temple and the end of the high priesthood, it is unclear who in Judaea would have taken charge of the Jewish calendar—which we know continued being reckoned in this period, as evident from the Babatha and Bar-Kokhba documents. The rabbinic court may well have filled the vacuum, but it is questionable whether the rabbis would have commanded sufficient authority in this early period to impose their calendrical decisions upon the entire Jewish community of Judaea and surrounding regions.

By the third century, however, and certainly by the fourth, it is generally believed that the Patriarch's authority in calendrical matters would have considerably increased. Yet even in this period, rabbinic authority did not extend to all parts of Palestine: as late as the sixth century, as we have seen, the Jews of Zoar appear to have reckoned the calendar on their own.

Nevertheless, it is reasonable to assume that an empirical lunar calendar of the kind described in the Mishnah would have been observed by Judaean Jews throughout the Tannaitic period. It is also likely that the

[28] Fire-signals are known to have been used in the biblical period, as attested in *Judges* 20: 38–40 and *Jeremiah* 6: 1. Evidence of a *chain* of beacons, similar to that described in *M. RH*, has been identified in an early-6th-c.-BCE ostrakon from Lakish (Lakish ostrakon no. 4; see Smelik 1991: 125–7, Lemaire 1977: 110–14). According to Ps.-Aristotle, *De Mundo* 398ª31–5 (1st c. BCE–2nd c. CE?), chains of fire-signals were used in the Persian Empire for the communication of urgent messages (see Lewis 1977: 56–7, Graf 1994: 168, Briant 1996: 382–4, 953); this is also suggested in Aeschylus, *Agamemnon* 281–316.

[29] The exclusion of the king and high priest from the calendrical court, according to *T. Sanh.* 2: 15, p. 418 (above, n. 18), may be no more than a rabbinic polemic; this would only confirm the hypothesis that at one time, the high priest was in charge of the calendar.

rabbis determined new moons and intercalations, even if their decisions were not always universally heeded.

The historical reality of an empirical lunar calendar is reflected in a number of additional Mishnaic passages, which take for granted that calendar dates could never be predicted in advance. See *M. Bava Metzi'a* 8: 8, on the uncertain duration of one-year leases (as it cannot be known in advance whether the year will be intercalated);[30] and *M. 'Eruvin* 3: 7–9, on a person's uncertainty as to whether Elul will be full or defective, and hence, when Rosh ha-Shanah (1 Tishre) will occur. According to *M. Megillah* 1: 4, even in the month of Adar it can still be unknown whether the year will be intercalated. Another passage assumes that it takes a few days before the date of the new month is widely known; according to *M. Sanhedrin* 5: 3, witnesses cannot be expected to have known if an incident took place on the 2nd or the 3rd of the month.

4.2 THE TALMUDIC PERIOD

4.2.1 The empirical calendar

The calendar of the Mishnah is discussed and debated in detail in both the Palestinian and the Babylonian Talmudim. This, obviously, is no proof that the Mishnaic calendar continued being reckoned throughout the Talmudic period. The calendar is treated in the Talmudim in the same way as any other portion of the Mishnah, i.e. as a legitimate subject of study regardless of whether it is of current relevance or application.

Nevertheless, the fact that no other calendar system is ever referred to in the Talmudim may be regarded as significant. In the absence of evidence to the contrary, it is reasonable to assume that the Mishnaic system was perpetuated well into the Amoraic period (third to fifth centuries). One passage in the Palestinian Talmud confirms that the calendar was still empirically reckoned in the days of R. Yose:[31] for R. Yose is reputed to have said that he never recited the additional prayer (*musaf*) on the day of *rosh ḥodesh* (new month), because he could never be certain when *rosh ḥodesh* was (*Y. Sanh.* 5: 3, 22d).

---

[30] Also in *T. Bava Metzia'* 8: 31, p. 390.

[31] It is clear from the context of this passage, as well as from the general usage of the Palestinian Talmud, that this R. Yose is the disciple of R. Yoḥanan, from the later 3rd c. For the classification of rabbis into 'generations' and approximate datings, see Strack and Stemberger (1991) 69–110. It should be noted, however, that attributions in rabbinic literature are not necessarily reliable: see *inter alia* my articles, S. Stern (1994*b*, 1995).

It is also assumed in Talmudic sources that calendrical decisions remained under the control of a single rabbinic court. A list of rabbis who composed this calendrical court is given in the Palestinian Talmud, and extends from the first till the penultimate or last generation of Palestinian Amoraim in the mid fourth century.[32] The decisions of this court, presumably based in Tiberias for most or the whole of this period, were widely transmitted to rabbis in other communities: to R. Abbahu in Caesarea,[33] or to R. Naḥman in Babylonia.[34]

4.2.2 Calendrical rules

A distinctive feature of Talmudic sources, however, is a number of additional calendrical rules that were not in the Mishnah or Tosefta, and that are attributed almost entirely to Amoraim. These rules are not necessarily incompatible with the empirical system of the Mishnah—for as we have seen, Tannaitic sources themselves lay down a number of fixed rules. But these additional rules mean that the flexibility of the empirical calendar would have been substantially curtailed.[35]

The Babylonian Talmud frequently cites a saying attributed to Rav (Babylonian Amora, early third century), that since the days of Ezra the month of Elul had never been full (30 days).[36] It does acknowledge that this 'rule' was not always strictly observed,[37] as ʿUlla once explicitly reported.[38] But the reference to Ezra suggests, nevertheless, that this rule existed already in the Mishnaic period, and even long before. This rule

---

[32] R. Ḥaggai, R. Yonah, and R. Yose: *Y. RH* 2: 6 (58b) (see also *Y. Sanh.* 1: 2 (18c)). This R. Yose, among the last generation of Amoraim, is to be distinguished from the earlier R. Yose above mentioned: see Strack and Stemberger (1991) 105. On the composition of the calendrical court, see further Levine (1989) 72–4.

[33] *Y. RH* 3: 1 (58d) (R. Abbahu: late 3rd–early 4th c.).

[34] *B. RH* 21a (R. Naḥman: early 4th c.).

[35] The tension between calendrical empiricism and fixed calendrical rules finds expression in *B. RH* 20a (ll. 1–2: אי אמרת לעולם חסר, אמאי מחללינן? משום דמצוה לקדש על הראייה).

[36] מימות עזרא ואילך, לא מצינו אלול מעובר: *B. RH* 19b and 32a; *B. Betzah* 6a and 22b. For an alternative interpretation, see Wacholder and Weisberg (1971) 238.

[37] *B. RH* 19b ibid. (see *Tosafot*); *B. RH* 21a; *B. Betzah* 22b (MS Munich, see *Diqduqei Sofrim*).

[38] *B. RH* 20a (ʿUlla: Babylonian Amora, early 4th c.). ʿUlla was apparently reporting an actual calendrical decision of the Palestinian court, as he is said to have done on other occasions (*B. RH* 22b).

is also attributed to Rav in the Palestinian Talmud, but without reference to the days of Ezra.[39]

Similar to this is the rule that 'Adar adjacent to Nisan is always defective' (29 days). It is attributed in the same passage of Palestinian Talmud to Rabbi,[40] the redactor of the Mishnah, and elsewhere to R. Yehoshua b. Levi.[41] The attribution to Rabbi suggests that the rule may go back to the Mishnaic period. On this assumption, the Palestinian Talmud interprets two passages from the Mishnah, which imply that either Adar or Elul could be full, as only theoretical.[42] The rule of Adar also appears in the Babylonian Talmud, as a message that was sent (presumably from Palestine) to the exilarch Mar ʿUqva.[43]

Another rule, that appears to have only emerged in the Amoraic period, is that the Day of Atonement cannot occur on a Friday or a Sunday. This rule is mentioned in the Palestinian Talmud[44] as well as in the Babylonian Talmud,[45] although the latter remains uncertain about its extent—for instance, whether it also applies to other festivals. Reasons for this rule are given in the Babylonian Talmud: it was difficult to keep fresh food (ʿUlla's opinion) or an unburied corpse (R. ʾAḥa b. Ḥanina's opinion) over two consecutive days of forbidden work.[46]

This rule is unknown in the Mishnah, where the possibility of the Day of Atonement's occurring after the Sabbath or vice-versa is completely taken for granted.[47] In *Y. ʿAvodah Zarah*, where this rule first appears,

---

[39] *Y. RH* 3: 1 (58c); *Y. Sheviʿit* 10: 2 (39b); *Y. Sanh.* 1: 2 (18d); and in a mutilated version, *Y. Nedarim* 6: 13 (40a). The form and meaning of מימיו, in this passage, is rather unclear. See also *Y. RH* 1 (57b) (= *Y. Ḥala* 1 (57c)).

[40] Ibid.

[41] *Y. Megillah* 1: 7 (71a) (early 3rd-c. Palestinian Amora). R. Yehoshua b. Levi also states that in an intercalated year, Shevat and the first Adar are always full; but if first Adar is made defective, this need not be corrected (ibid.).

[42] References in n. 39. The Mishnaic passages in question are *M. Sheqalim* 4: 5 (Adar) and *M. Sheviʿit* 10: 2 (Elul). The Talmudic interpretation of these passages is not, in itself, implausible.

[43] *B. RH* 19b. The rule of Adar, however, is subject to a Tannaitic dispute in *B. Bekhorot* 58a, and also, implicitly, in *B. RH* 19a. See below, section 5.3.5.

[44] *Y. ʿAvodah Zarah* 1: 1 (39b); *Y. Megillah* 1: 2 (70b).

[45] *B. RH* 20a; *B. Sukkah* 54b. See also R. Ḥananel's inference from *B. Pesahim* 58b that Passover could not occur on Monday (hence the Day of Atonement on Friday), in R. Ḥananel ad loc. (cf Rashi ibid., s.v. בשני בשבת); see, however, Ajdler (1996) 697.

[46] *B. RH* 20a. Both authorities are 3rd generation Amoraim, thus late 3rd–early 4th c.

[47] See *M. Shabbat* 15: 3, *M. Menahot* 11: 7 and 9. Some of these passages may be no more than theoretical (see n. 42 above), but this is unlikely in the case of *M.*

a R. Ḥonia is said to have objected to it and to 'those who remove the Day of Atonement from its right place'. This suggests that the rule may have been, at one time, controversial. R. Ḥonia's opinion is only cited, however, in the context of a date in the book of *Nehemiah*; whether his opinion is deemed to have carried any weight in the Talmudic period is not clarified. The assumption of this passage, however, as well as of another passage in the Palestinian Talmud,[48] is that in the Talmud period the rule of the Day of Atonement was firmly established and normative in the rabbinic calendar.

A similar rule, attested in the Palestinian Talmud, is that neither Rosh ha-Shanah nor the Day of the Willow (21 Tishre) can occur on a Sabbath; in cases of necessity, however, the rule of Rosh ha-Shanah can be waived, but not that of the Day of the Willow.[49] The Babylonian Talmud is aware of the rule of the Willow, but uncertain about its stringency. It cites two conflicting reports, both emanating from Palestine, as to whether this rule was always firmly adhered to (*B. Sukkah* 43b). The possibility of Rosh ha-Shanah occurring on Sunday (hence the Day of the Willow on the Sabbath) is assumed elsewhere in the Babylonian Talmud, although this passage may be no more than theoretical (*B. Niddah* 67b).

A further rule that appears to date from the Amoraic period is that of the equinox. Although the equinox is mentioned already in the Tosefta, it only serves as one of a few criteria involved in the intercalation (see section 4.1.2). The rule that emerges in the Amoraic period is that intercalations can and should be made on the *sole* basis of the equinox.

The rule of the equinox is attested in a single passage of the Babylonian Talmud (*B. RH* 21a), which exists in two different recensions. The first recension, attested in the printed edition of the Talmud, in most manuscript sources, and in a number of medieval secondary sources, implies that 15 Nisan, the first day of Unleavened Bread, cannot occur before the vernal equinox. In this recension, the term *ʾaviv* is treated as synonymous with *tequfah* (equinox):

Menaḥot 11: 7, which appears to refer to actual reality. The Palestinian Talmud makes no relevant comment on *M. Shabbat* 15: 3 (e.g. in *Y. Shabbat* 15 (71d–72a)).

[48] Particularly *Y. Megillah* 1: 2 (70b); this passage will be studied in more detail below.

[49] *Y. Sukkah* 4: 1 (54b), attributed to R. Simon (late 3rd–early 4th c.; see Strack and Stemberger 1991: 99). The statement of *Y. Megillah* 1: 2 (70b) (mentioned above) implicitly contradicts R. Simon's rules, by allowing the occurrence of the Day of Atonement on all but two days (not the same days as R. Simon's). See section 4.4.3.

שלח ליה רב הונא בר אבין לרבא: כד חזית דמשכה תקופת טבת עד שיתסר בניסן,
עברה לההיא שתא ולא תחוש לה, דכתיב: שמור את חדש האביב שמור אביב של
תקופה, שיהא בחדש ניסן.[50]

R. Huna b. Avin sent (the following ruling) to Rava: If you see the winter season prolonging itself till the 16th of Nisan, intercalate that year and do not worry, for it is written:

'Observe the month of *ʾaviv*' (Deut. 16: 1)—observe the *ʾaviv* of *tequfah*, that it occur in (the first half of)[51] the month of Nisan.

The second recension is attested in a few manuscripts and a number of medieval secondary sources (R. Ḥananel and other, mainly Spanish, authors).[52] It implies that the latest possible date for the vernal equinox is 16 Nisan, the day of the waving of the *ʿomer* (sheaf), which is associated elsewhere with the notion of *ʾaviv*:[53]

'שמור את חדש האביב' של אביב, שתהא תקופה נופלת בו.[54]

'Observe the month of *ʾaviv*' (Deut. 16: 1)—of *ʾaviv*, that the *tequfah* occurs on it.[55]

---

[50] Text of Vilna edition.

[51] As interpreted by Rashi, s.v. שמור אביב.

[52] R. Ḥananel (ad *RH* 21a); R. Avraham b. Ḥiyya (*Sefer ha-ʿIbbur* 3: 5); *Yad Ramah* (on *Sanhedrin* 13b).

[53] On *ʾaviv* and the sheaf, see above section 4.1.2. According to Loewinger (1986: 21–2 and *passim*), the precise definition of the rule of the equinox (in this recension) is that the equinox cannot occur more than 16 whole days (24-hour periods) after *molad* Nisan. This definition may be borne out in medieval sources, and thus may represent the view of a number of medieval rabbinic authorities; but it is not the plain meaning of the 'second' recension of *B. RH* 21a, which I have given here in the main text (i.e., that the equinox cannot occur after 16 Nisan). It should be noted, incidentally, that my definition of the rule depends on the *calendar* date of 16 Nisan; a postponement of the beginning of Nisan could thus remove the need to intercalate (for an example, see *B. Sanhedrin* 13b). This would not be possible according to Loewinger's definition.

[54] St Petersburg Geniza fragment, in Katsh (1975) i. 111 (and in facsimile section, p. 112).

[55] In this recension, it is unclear how the notion of *tequfah* is inferred from the verse. For a similar saying in the Palestinian Talmud, attributed to R. Avin, see *Y. Peah* 5: 1 (18d) (= *Y. Sheqalim* 1: 2 (46a)). For a full discussion and assessment of both recensions, see Loewinger (1986) *passim* and especially pp. 84–5 (n. 37) and p. 113 (n. 71). Loewinger argues that the original version would have been that of 16 Nisan, but this remains largely speculative.

Whatever the recension, the exact definition of the rule of the equinox,[56] and the exegetical inference, it is clear that the concepts of *aviv* and of *tequfah*, clearly distinguished in the Tosefta, have been conflated here into a single rule.[57] This rule entails that the year be intercalated on the sole criterion of the vernal equinox.

The emergence of the rule of the equinox in this particular period—if the attribution to R. Huna b. Avin and Rava is reliable—is of the highest historical significance. Rava belongs to the early or mid fourth century, at a time when the rule of the equinox was being propagated among the Christian Churches of the Near East (see sections 2.5.1 and 2.5.4). It is also in this period that according to later rabbinic traditions, the fixed rabbinic calendar was instituted.[58]

The implications of this passage will be considered in detail in the next chapter. At present it is important to stress, however, that this passage does *not* imply that a fixed calendar had yet been instituted. On the contrary, the formulation of R. Huna b. Avin suggests that the decision whether or not to intercalate depended entirely on an annual calculation of the equinox. Had a fixed cycle (e.g. of 19 years) been instituted, it would have been far simpler, and far more reliable, for Rava to have been given it.[59]

Moreover, this passage does not necessarily indicate how the *Palestinian* rabbinic court would have made intercalations. Even if this rule was sent to Rava from Palestine,[60] it may have been no more than a *guideline* for Rava to rely on whenever the calendrical decisions of the Palestinian court had not been received. This may be implicit, indeed, in the phrase 'intercalate that year and do not worry'. This phrase suggests that there *could* have been something to worry about, because in some cases, the rule of the equinox might not have been observed by the

---

[56] A further question that is not clarified in this source is how the equinox itself is to be defined: is it the astronomical true equinox, the mean equinox, or is it notional and based on some simplified calculation? See my remarks at end of section 4.4.5.

[57] See parallel *baraita* in *B. Sanh.* 13b, *Targum Ps.-Jonathan* on Deut. 16: 1, and contrast with *Sifre Deut.* 127 (ed. Finkelstein, p. 185), *Midrash Tannaim* (ed. Hoffmann, p. 89), and *Y. Peah* 5: 1 (18d) (= *Y. Sheqalim* 1: 2 (46a)), where the same verse is similarly interpreted but without reference to the *tequfah*.

[58] See e.g. Maimonides, *Laws of the Sanctification of the Moon*, 5: 3, where Rava is mentioned as being at the end of the period of the empirical Mishnaic calendar. For full discussion see below.

[59] See Karelitz (1973) section 130: 1.

[60] As the phrase שלחו ליה usually means—even though R. Huna b. Avin did spend some time of his life in Babylonia (Strack and Stemberger 1991: 103).

Palestinian court—but that Rava did not need to concern himself about this unusual contingency. The phrase 'do not worry' may thus imply that the equinox was not yet established as a fixed rule.[61]

Nevertheless, I would argue that the emergence of calendrical rules in the Amoraic period represented the embryonic beginnings of a fixed rabbinic calendar.

4.2.3　The fixed calendar

By the later Amoraic period, a fixed calendar was introduced. Evidence of this radical change is surprisingly sporadic. But a clear sense that something had changed in calendar reckoning is conveyed, to begin with, in the Babylonian Talmud.

A statement is made in the Babylonian Talmud that 'now, we know the fixing of the (new) moon'.[62] This meant that it was now possible, even in Babylonia, to be *certain* about the dates of new moons that had been set by the Palestinian court. On the strength of this statement, indeed, the Talmud goes on to question the necessity of two festival days. Now that the dates of festivals were no longer doubtful, there was no reason for Diaspora communities to observe a second festival day:

והשתא[דידעינן בקביעא דירחא], מאי טעמא עבדינן תרי יומי? משום דשלחו מתם:
הזהרו במנהג אבותיכם בידיכם, זמנין דגזרו שמדא ואתי לאקלקולי.

But now [that we know the fixing of the (new) moon],[63] for what reason do we (in the Diaspora) observe two (festival) days?

Because they sent (a message) from there (from the Land of Israel): 'Give heed to the customs of your fathers which you are keeping, lest a persecution be decreed,[64] which would lead to disruption (of the calendar)'.

Thus the observance of a second festival day was still justified because calendrical disruption remained a possibility. How a 'persecution' could have disrupted the calendar will be discussed in the next chapter (section 5.1.1). But it is clear that in the Talmud's mind, only a catastrophic

---

[61] A different interpretation is suggested by Loewinger (1986) 85–6 (n. 38): 'do not worry' about the Tannaitic opinions (listed in *B. Sanh.* 13a-b) that define the criterion of the equinox in a different manner.

[62] דהאידנא ידעינן בקביעא דירחא: *B. Betzah* 4b, a statement attributed to R. Zeira.

[63] The text in square brackets is only attested in the printed editions (starting from the Soncino edition, which I have quoted in my citation); it is absent in all the manuscripts, except as a marginal note in Oxford, Bodleian Library, MS Opp. Add. fol. 23 (Neubauer 366). But although of doubtful authenticity, this clause can be justified by the wider context of this passage.

[64] Later editions read: זמנין דגזרו המלכות גזרה, but this is a censorial substitution.

event such as a persecution could have led to calendrical disruption; the possibility of mere *error* is not even considered.

This Talmudic assumption only makes sense in the context of a fixed calendar. So long as the Mishnaic system was in place, there was no way of predicting, without the risk of error, the empirical calendrical decisions of the Palestinian rabbinic court.[65] But as the Talmud emphasizes, the situation had *'now'* changed. The removal of any risk of error could only have been the result of a fixed calendar,[66] or at least, of a calendar that was substantially more predictable than in the Mishnaic system.

The existence of a fixed calendar in the late Amoraic period is confirmed beyond doubt in a passage of the Palestinian Talmud. The context is a *mishnah* (*M. Megillah* 1: 2) which assumes that Purim (14 Adar) can occur on every day of the week. The Talmud comments as follows:

אמר רבי יוסה: לית כאן 'חל להיות בשני' ולית כאן 'חל להיות בשבת'. חל להיות בשני, צומא רבא בחד בשובא; חל להיות בשבת, צומא רבא בערובתא.

R. Yose said: 'if (Purim) occurs on Monday' (in the *Mishnah*) does not apply; and 'if (Purim) occurs on the Sabbath' (in the *mishnah*) (also) does not apply. (For) if it occurs on Monday, the great fast will be on Sunday; and if it occurs on the Sabbath, the great fast will be on Friday.[67]

This passage assumes that the 'great fast', i.e. the Day of Atonement, cannot occur on Sunday or on Friday—a rule which has been discussed above. This passage also assumes, however, that there are a fixed number of days between Purim (14 Adar) and the Day of Atonement (10 Tishre), so that if Purim occurs on Monday, the Day of Atonement will necessarily occur on Sunday. This is only possible if defective and full

---

[65] *Pace* Rashi, who appears to have understood that the Babylonians were able to predict when the new moon, in Palestine, would have been visible (Rashi ad *B. Betzah* 4b s.v. קים לן בקביעא; see *Ḥiddushei Ḥatam Sofer* ad loc.). This is not in itself implausible, but knowledge of the new moon's astronomical visibility would not necessarily have informed them when it was actually sighted (see section 3.1.7). The possibility of error, therefore, must have remained. Rashi's interpretation, moreover, does not account for the sense of historical *change* that is implicit in the term 'now' (והשתא).

[66] This is the interpretation of most medieval commentators, who assume however that the fixed rabbinic calendar instituted then was the same as it is today: see Ritva on this passage in his *Novellae* ad *B. Sukkah* 43a. For a modified account, see Bornstein (1920) 250–1 and below, section 5.1.1.

[67] *Y. Megillah* 1: 2 (70b). R. Yose's view that the occurrence of 14 Adar on the Sabbath is 'impossible' is reiterated in *Y. Megillah* 1: 4 (70b).

months, from Adar to Tishre, are regularly alternated. This passage implies, therefore, that the sequence of new months from Adar to Tishre was permanently fixed.

The emergence of a fixed rabbinic calendar, or at least of a *partially* fixed calendar, can thus be dated to no later than the fourth century, when the Palestinian Talmud is most likely to have been redacted.[68] The attribution to R. Yose may also be taken into account: 'R. Yose' generally refers to a later third-century Amora.[69] However, this attribution is problematic, as the same R. Yose is attributed elsewhere a saying implying that the calendar was still, in his period, entirely empirical and unpredictable (see section 4.2.1). It is possible that 'R. Yose' in the *Y. Megillah* passage refers in fact to another Amora from the mid fourth century,[70] but this is obviously speculative.

Evidence of the new calendar can also be found in another passage, where R. Simon is said to have instructed 'those who made calculations' (אילין דמחשבין) not to set Rosh ha-Shanah or the Day of the Willow on a Sabbath.[71] This phrase suggests that the calendar was no longer dependent on an empirical procedure, but rather on calculations;[72] and that the calendar was no longer set by a rabbinic *court*, but rather by 'those who made calculations', i.e. *experts* in calendrical calculation.

Inasmuch as the wording of this passage is not attributed directly to R. Simon, but is rather the redactor's, it is safest to date this passage to when the Palestinian Talmud was redacted, not later than the fourth century.[73]

Further Palestinian sources have been adduced as evidence of a fixed, calculated calendar, but they are inconclusive. One recension of *Lamentations Rabba* states, rather enigmatically, that 'the eve of the first day of *Pesaḥ* [i.e. of 15

---

[68] Sussman (1990) 132–3; cf Strack and Stemberger (1991) 188–9. It is important to stress that at this stage, the calendar may only have been *partially* fixed. Evidence of some outstanding flexibility will be considered in the next section, on the Geonic period.

[69] See above, n. 31.

[70] See above, n. 32.

[71] *Y. Sukkah* 4: 1 (54b), see above section 4.2.2. For textual variants, see secondary sources such as *Tosafot* ad *B. Sukkah* 43b, s.v. לא, and D. Metzger (1994) 86 (see n. 30).

[72] See, however, Ran (R. Nissim) ad Rif, *Sukkah* 21b–22a.

[73] See n. 68.

Nisan] is the eve of 9 Av'.[74] This has been interpreted as meaning that they always occur on the same day of the week, which would imply a fixed number of days between Nisan and Av, with the regular alternation of full and defective months throughout this period (Kasher 1949: 175). However, this interpretation is doubtful because in other recensions, the comparison between *Pesaḥ* and 9 Av is explicitly and only related to the eating of bitter herbs.[75]

The following passage deserves more detailed investigation:

רבי אבהו אזל לאלכסנדריאה, ואטעינון לולבין בשובתא. שמע רבי מי, מר: מן מייבול להון[76] רבי אבהו בכל שתא? רבי יוסי מישלח כתיב להון: אף על פי שכתבנו לכם סדרי מועדות, אל תשנו מנהג אבותיכם נוחי נפש.

R. Abbahu went to Alexandria, and they took the palms (*lulavin*) on the Sabbath.
R. (A)mi heard, and said: who will bring them R. Abbahu every year?
R. Yose sent them a letter: although they have written to you the order of festivals, do not change the custom of your fathers, whose souls are at rest (*Y. ʿEruvin* 3: 9, 21c).

This passage, and especially R. Ami's statement, implies that the taking of palms on the Sabbath at Alexandria was the direct result of R. Abbahu's visit, and would be contingent, in future years, on further visits of this kind.

This only makes sense in relation to a halakhic ruling of the Babylonian Talmud (*B. Sukkah* 43a). According to *M. Sukkah* 4: 2, the *lulav* may only be taken on the Sabbath if it coincides with the first day of Tabernacles. According to the Babylonian Talmud, however, in the Diaspora the *lulav* may not be taken on the Sabbath even on the first day of the festival, because in the Diaspora the dates of festivals are treated as uncertain (with the observance, for instance, of two festival days). Although this ruling is not mentioned in the Palestinian Talmud,[77] it may have been known to Palestinian Amoraim. This must be assumed, at least, if we are to make sense of the passage above. R. Ami assumed that the Jews of Alexandria had taken the *lulav* on the Sabbath on the first day of the festival on the strength of R. Abbahu's visit, who would have told them

---

[74] *Lamentations Rabbah*, *petiḥta* 18 and 3: 5 (printed edition). This Midrash is assumed to have been redacted in the 5th c.: see Strack and Stemberger (1991) 309–11.

[75] Buber (1899), p. 64b, but cf ibid. p. 8a; T.–S. C1.58, col. 3, l. 3, published by Rabinovitz (1976) 122 (cited by Weiss 1995: 188 n. 14).

[76] Following the recension of a Geniza fragment, in *Seridei Yerushalmi* and Lieberman (1929) 8.

[77] See Lieberman (1934a) 277–8. That Palestinian Jews took the *lulav* on the Sabbath on the first day of Tabernacles—a practice going back to *M. Sukkah* 3: 13–14, 4: 2, and 4: 4—whereas Babylonian Jews did not, is well attested in Geonic and later sources: see Lewin (1942) 104–5; Aptowitzer (1964/5) ii. 221 (and on the passage in *B. Sukkah* 43a, ibid. iii. 732–4); also Elkin (1996/7).

the exact dates of the festival, as had been set by the rabbinic court in Palestine. R. Ami remarked that they could not rely on such visits every year.[78]

The statement of R. Yose has been interpreted in a similar vein. According to R. Yose, the Alexandrians had been sent a written list of the exact dates of the festivals, thus removing any area of uncertainty; R. Yose instructed them, however, to keep their ancestral custom of not taking the *lulav* on the Sabbath on the first day. The availability of a written list of the dates of festivals suggests that in R. Yose's period, the calendar was fixed and disseminated well in advance— thus corroborating the statement attributed to (perhaps) the same R. Yose in *Y. Megillah* (see above).[79]

However, it is unlikely that in the period of R. Abbahu (late third–early fourth century), the community of Alexandria observed the Babylonian rabbinic prohibition of taking the *lulav* on the Sabbath, even on the first day of the festival. As explained above, the rationale behind this custom was the same as for the observance of two festival days: uncertainty as to when exactly the new month had been set in Palestine by the rabbinic court. In previous chapters I have shown, however, that this uncertainty would not have existed in non-rabbinic communities, where the calendar was reckoned and set independently of the Palestinian rabbinic court (see in particular section 3.2.1). In the case of Alexandria, calendrical independence is attested by the letter of Peter of Alexandria—R. Abbahu's contemporary (see section 2.5.3). These communities had no reason to observe two festival days, which explains why this custom is unattested outside rabbinic sources; consequently the Jews of Alexandria would not have had the Babylonian rabbinic reason to prohibit the taking of the *lulav* on a Sabbath.

---

[78] Traditional and modern commentators are unanimous in this interpretation. See *Penei Moshe* and *Korban ha-ʿEdah* ad loc.; Lieberman, Lewin, and Aptowitzer ibid.

[79] See Bornstein (1920) 250–1. Traditional commentators (*Penei Moshe* and *Korban ha-ʿEdah* ad loc., also implicitly Lieberman 1934a: 277–8, and myself in S. Stern 1994a: 51) go further and suggest, by association with *B. Betzah* 4b, that R. Yose's injunction concerned the Diaspora observance of a second festival day, that was to be maintained even after the institution and dissemination of the fixed calendar. This interpretation, however, is out of context and unwarranted. There is no indication that the story of R. Abbahu in Alexandria had anything to do with the second festival day. Earlier in the text (*Y. ʿEruvin*, loc. cit.) there is a reference to the second festival day of Rosh ha-Shanah, but it is unlikely to be relevant to R. Yose's statement. The identification of R. Yose's statement in *Y. ʿEruvin* with the citation in *B. Betzah* is also unconvincing, as the phrase אל תשנו מנהג אבותיכם נוחי נפש (do not change the custom of your fathers, whose souls are at rest) is not unique to this passage but also found, in a totally different context, in *Y. Pesaḥim* 4: 1 (30d) (= *Song Rabbah* 1: 12, see Rabinovitz 1976: 98). It is interesting to note, however, that this traditional interpretation of *Y. ʿEruvin* may go back to R. Hai Gaon (early 11th c.), who uses the phrase, ולא ישנו ממנהג אבותיהם נוחי נפש ('they should not change the custom of their fathers, whose souls are at rest'), at the end of his responsum on the two festival days—this citation, however, referring specifically to the observance of two days of Rosh ha-Shanah in Palestine (*Teshuvot Geonim* (Lyck) 1; Lewin 1931: 9).

Y. ʿEruvin should thus be interpreted in a completely different manner. The Alexandrians had not taken the *lulav* on the Sabbath on the strength of R. Abbahu's report, as R. Ami *erroneously* understood, but simply because this was their ancestral custom. R. Yose correctly understood this. In his subsequent letter to the Alexandrians, he wrote that although Palestinian rabbis had sent them the 'order of festivals'—which does not mean the *dates* of the festivals, but rather a compendium of the *laws* relating to festivals, including perhaps the rabbinic ruling not to take the *lulav* on the Sabbath in the Diaspora—they should nevertheless observe their ancestral custom, and thus take the *lulav* even on the Sabbath.

According to this interpretation, which in my view is more simple and far more plausible, this passage of *Y. ʿEruvin* would have no bearing on the institution of a fixed calendar.

Other Talmudic passages are similarly inconclusive. In *Y. ʿAvodah Zarah* 1: 1 (39b–c), R. Yoḥanan b. Madaya claims to have worked out that the 24th of the seventh month in *Nehemiah* 9: 1 would not have been on the day after the Sabbath (Sunday). How he worked this out is unclear, particularly as no year is given in *Nehemiah* for this event. But in any case, R. Yoḥanan b. Madaya's ability to work out a date so far back in time does not necessarily imply that a fixed calendar was in existence in his period. His calculation may have been based on a *theoretical* schematic calendar, or on some mean length of the month and/or of the year.[80]

4.2.4   The Hillel tradition

It is widely accepted that the fixed rabbinic calendar was instituted by Hillel the Patriarch in 358/9 CE.[81] This institution, however, is not mentioned or recorded in any of the contemporary rabbinic sources, such as the Palestinian or Babylonian Talmud. The earliest reference to it appears in a responsum of R. Hai Gaon (early eleventh century) cited by R. Avraham b. Ḥiyya:[82]

עד ימי הלל בר׳ יהודא בשנת תר״ע לשטרות, שמאותה שנה לא הקדימו ולא אחרו,
אלא אחזו הסדר הזה אשר היה בידם

---

[80] *Pace* Lieberman (1934*b*). See on this passage Weiss (1995) 186. Other passages cited in Lieberman's article (1934*b*) are even less conclusive, and do not require further discussion.

[81] This tradition is frequently cited even in academic works, for instance Strack and Stemberger (1991) 104; Schürer (1973–87) i. 594.

[82] In his *Sefer ha-ʿIbbur* 3: 7 (Filipowski 1851: 97), written in 1123 CE; cited in Lewin (1932/3) 17. R. Avraham b. Ḥiyya is sometimes referred to by his titles, either 'ha-Nasi' or 'Savasorda'. Mann (1925) has argued, though not quite convincingly, that this section of R. Hai's responsum is actually an interpolation by R. Avraham b. Ḥiyya himself, and hence, that the tradition regarding Hillel should be attributed to the latter (see on this Kasher 1949: 24).

... until the days of Hillel b. R. Yehuda in the year 670 of the Seleucid era (358/9 CE), from when they did not bring forth or postpone, but kept to this cycle which was at hand ...

The topic of R. Hai's responsum is the 19-year cycle of intercalations, and this is clearly what this passage refers to. Thus it cannot be inferred from this passage that the fixed calendar *in its entirety* was instituted by Hillel. Even after the adoption of the 19-year cycle, new months could still have been set on a purely empirical basis, following the procedure of the Mishnah.

Later medieval authors, however, understood this tradition to mean that the entire fixed calendar, in its present-day form, was instituted by Hillel in 358/9 CE. This interpretation is first found in R. Zeraḥiah ha-Levi's *Ha-Ma'or ha-Qatan* (mid twelfth century), with explicit reference to the institution of the calculation of new months.[83] Later still, in the mid thirteenth century, Nahmanides went as far as suggesting that Hillel sanctified in advance all the new months to occur between his time and the end of history.[84]

Yet it is important to realize that the Hillel tradition was not universally known or endorsed by medieval rabbinic authorities. Maimonides (writing *c*.1178 CE) ignores it altogether, although he does write that the Mishnaic calendar remained in practice 'until the days of Abaye and Rava',[85] which is chronologically compatible with the dating of 358/9 CE.

R. Isaac Israeli (early fourteenth century), however, gives in one place a *later* dating for the institution of the fixed calendar: 'near the end of the period of the sages of the Talmud ... approximately 4260 years according to the era of Creation', i.e. 499/500 CE.[86] The basis of this dating is clear: according to the epistle of R. Sherira Gaon, 499/500 CE corresponds

---

[83] R. Zeraḥiah ha-Levi, *Ha-Ma'or ha-Qatan* ad *RH* ch. 1 (5b at the top, in the Vilna pagination of the *Rif*).

[84] Nahmanides, השגות לספר המצוות להרמב׳ם, positive mitzvah no. 153; id., ספר הזכות, on *B. Gittin* 36a. This view was reiterated by his disciple R. Yom Tov Ishbili (Ritva), in his *Novellae* on *B. Sukkah* 43a, and has become the dominant view in rabbinic literature ever since. See also Rashba (another disciple of Nahmanides), *Responsa* 4: 254, who states, however, that he does not know the origin of the Hillel tradition.

[85] Maimonides, *Laws of Sanctification of the New Month*, 5: 3.

[86] R. Isaac Israeli, *Yesod 'Olam* 4: 5 (Goldberg 1848: ii. 7b). However in 4: 9 (ibid. 16b), he writes: 'about 300 years after the destruction' (i.e. of 70 CE), and goes on to cite the Hillel tradition which he attributes to 'our rabbis' (רז׳ל). The Hillel tradition is also assumed by Israeli in ibid. 4: 14 (29b) and 4: 18 (35b–36a).

to the end of the Amoraic period (i.e. in Israeli's terms, 'the end of the period of the sages of the Talmud').[87] Israeli may have exploited a contradiction in the passage of Maimonides above mentioned, which states that the calculated calendar was instituted 'from the end of the sages of the Talmud'—thus considerably later than the days of Abaye and Rava.

Other traditions ascribe the institution of the fixed calendar to a variety of periods and ancient authorities. R. Hai 'the head of the yeshiva (*metiva*)' is cited by a number of Karaite writers as ascribing the institution of the fixed calendar to R. Yitzḥaq Napḥa (late third-century Palestinian Amora).[88] The identity of this Rabbanite 'head of the yeshiva' is uncertain, but it can only be either R. Hai b. David, gaon of Pumbadita in 890–7, or R. Hai b. Naḥshon, gaon of Sura in 889–96.[89]

Another tradition appears in a *baraita* that is cited only by Karaites, but ostensibly a genuine, albeit late, rabbinic work. This *baraita* is a sequel to *M. RH* 2: 8–9, and describes how the dispute between R. Gamliel of Yavneh (early second century) and his opponents regarding the date of the Day of Atonement led to the institution, by R. Gamliel himself, of the fixed rabbinic calendar.[90]

---

[87] *Iggeret R. Sherira Gaon*, in Lewin (1920) 95, the year of the death of Ravina (on this date in the *Iggeret*, see further below). But R. Isaac Israeli himself gives the slightly different date of 504/5 CE as the end of the Talmudic period (ibid. 4: 18, p. 34a).

[88] This passage from R. Hai's work is cited *inter alia* by the later 10th-c. Karaite Yefet b. Ali. For this and other sources, see Pinsker (1860) ii. 148–51; also Bornstein (1904) 144 and 159–60, (1922a) 361–2; Lieberman (1992) 18–19; Ankori (1959) 350–1 n. 138. R. Hai 'the head of the yeshiva' is also mentioned by al-Qirqisani (*c*.930 CE) in *The Book of Lights and Watch-Towers*, 1. 3. 27 (Nemoy 1930: 342; Chiesa and Lockwood 1984: 114), but only as ascribing to R. Yitzḥaq Napḥa the institution of the rule that Passover cannot occur on Monday, Wednesday, and Friday. Ankori (ibid.) raises the possibility that this R. Yitzḥaq Napḥa may be a later Babylonian figure, distinct from the Amora of the 3rd c.; but his evidence should be treated with caution. Even more conjectural is Bornstein's (1922a: 362 n. 1) emendation to 'R. Yoḥanan Napḥa'.

[89] Nemoy (1930) 328 n. 37, and 397 on n. 37. Nemoy appears to favour R. Hai b. David; Bornstein (1904: 158 n. 1, 1922a: 361 n. 4) favours R. Hai b. Naḥshon because his father, R. Naḥshon Gaon, is associated in later medieval sources with a calendrical cycle (the עיגול דרב נחשון, on which see Bornstein 1922a: 354–8 and below, section 4.4.1).

[90] The *baraita* is cited by the Karaite Sahal b. Matzliaḥ (later 10th c.) in his תוכחת מגולה, published by Pinsker (1860) ii. 25–43, on pp. 41–2; see Bornstein (1922a) 358–61; Lieberman (1992) 19–20. As Lieberman points out, the rule that Rosh ha-Shanah cannot occur on Sunday, Wednesday, or Friday is attributed to R. Gamliel by Ben Meir (early 920s CE: see Friedlander 1893: 197, Bornstein 1904: 65 and 165 n. 1), as

Yet another tradition ascribes the institution of the fixed calendar to R. Yehudah ha-Nasi, the redactor of the Mishnah (late second–early third centuries): it is found in the epistle of the late eleventh-century Palestinian Gaon Aviatar.[91]

Al-Biruni (*c*.1000 CE) writes that some Rabbanites date the institution of the fixed calendar to approximately 200 years after Alexander the Great; whereas according to other Rabbanites, it was instituted after the destruction of the Second Temple by one Eliezer b. Paruaḥ.[92] This name is unknown in rabbinic literature, but there are some grounds for accepting it as a genuine Rabbanite tradition. Indeed, the name b. Paruaḥ is found in 1 Kgs. 4: 17 as Solomon's governor (נציב) of the region of Issachar; the tribe of Issachar is associated, in rabbinic literature, with calendar reckoning,[93] and the term נציב, according to the Babylonian Talmud (*B. Sanhedrin* 12a), was used by the calendrical court as a code word for 'month'. In a rabbinic context, therefore, the name b. Paruaḥ has clear calendrical connotations. As to the name Eliezer, Lieberman suggests that it may be connected to yet another rabbinic tradition which ascribes to R. Eliezer (early second century) the rule that Rosh ha-Shanah cannot occur on Sunday, Wednesday, or Friday.[94]

Some medieval rabbinic authorities, finally, imply uncertainty about the origins of the fixed calendar. Maimonides' vagueness and inconsistency, in the passage above mentioned, may conceal an element of such uncertainty. But uncertainty is more evident in a responsum of his father's teacher, R. Yosef ibn Migash, in which both the questioner and the responder have no clear idea as to why and when the fixed calendar was instituted (*Teshuvot Ri Migash*, no.146). Rashi's disciple R. Yaʿaqov

well as by the Jewish apostate Petrus Alfonsi (late 11th c.) in his *Dialogi* (*PL* 157, p. 655).

[91] *Megillat Aviatar*, p. 9, ll. 6–11 (Schechter 1902: 472); cited by Bornstein (1904) 163–5; Lieberman (1992) 21. R. Yehudah ha-Nasi is also mentioned by Ben Meir (see references in previous n.), but together with R. Gamliel.

[92] Al-Biruni (1879) 67–8. Although a Muslim writer, al-Biruni is generally considered to have gathered his information from reliable sources.

[93] e.g. *Targum Onkelos* ad *Deut*. 33: 18. The basis of this tradition is *1 Chron*. 12: 33; see *Targum* ad loc., and *Pesiqta de-Rav Kahana* 1 (= *Esther Rabbah* 4: 1, *Song Rabbah* 6: 4).

[94] Lieberman (1992) 21. The R. Eliezer tradition is found in a liturgical poem by Binyamin b. Shemuel, רשות לשבת הגדול, in *Maḥzor Romi* (cited by Bornstein 1904: 164 n. 2).

b. Shimshon (writing in 1123/4) ascribes the institution of the fixed calendar to the rather nebulous 'sons of Issachar',[95] and so does R. Mosheh ha-Darshan (early eleventh century), implying that the 'sons of Issachar' were active after the Tannaitic period.[96] This notion of 'sons of Issachar' is also, perhaps, a euphemism for ignorance.

A further tradition has been adduced from Maoza b. Shelomoh al-Ladani's monograph on the calendar (fourteenth century, Yemenite), according to which it was the Geonim who calculated and instituted the fixed calendar.[97] This, however, is a misinterpretation of the passage. All Maoza says is that the calendar tables and algorithms that were in use in the later Middle Ages were formulated by the Geonim, but not that the basic principles of the fixed calendar were instituted by them.[98]

Late medieval rabbinic traditions about the foundation of the fixed calendar are thus so numerous and diverse that one wonders whether the Hillel tradition deserves the privileged status which, in the course of time, it eventually achieved. It is worth noting, besides, that apart from R. Hai's responsum[99] the figure of Hillel b. R. Yehuda or Hillel the Patriarch is unknown in early rabbinic sources. 'Hillel' is occasionally found in early rabbinic sources as the name of a late Palestinian Amora, but without any indication that he was a *nasi* or patriarch (Hyman 1964: i. 373–5). The identification of 'Iulus (Ἴουλος) the Patriarch', mentioned by the emperor Julian in an edict of 363 CE, with 'Hillel' is insufficiently substantiated.[100] The very existence of a 'Hillel the Patriarch' in the mid fourth century may thus be treated as uncertain.

[95] *Sefer ha-ʿIbbur*, a part of *Sefer ha-ʾAlqushi*, Oxford, Bodleian Library, MS Opp. 317 (Neubauer 692), fos. 88a–99b (unpublished), in chs. 31, 32, and 37. See citations in Bornstein (1922*a*) 328 n. 1 and ibid. 363; Kasher (1949) 111. The phrase 'sons of Issachar' is taken from *1 Chron.* 12: 33 (see n. 93). On R. Yaʿaqov b. Shimshon's *Sefer ha-ʾAlqushi*, see Grossman (1995) 418–23.

[96] In a text attributed to him by the author of an early 14th-c. MS, itself copied and published by Luzzatto (1854) 37 (cited in Bornstein 1922*a*: 328, but with an incorrect reference). The authenticity of this text is obviously questionable.

[97] Sar-Shalom (1988) 27–8, citing from Maʿoza b. Shlomo al-Ladani's עיבור השנים published by Tobi (1981) 210 and 216.

[98] Algorithm: a set of steps designed to achieve a complex mathematical operation (*New Encyclopaedia Britannica, Micropaedia* i. 239). All the Geonim would have instituted were *methods* for performing the calculation of the fixed calendar.

[99] And then later sources, e.g. *Maḥzor Vitry* (early 12th c.: Hurwitz 1923: 478 and 482 *bis*).

[100] Cited in M. Stern (1974–84) ii. 559–68, no. 486a (see discussion pp. 562–3, 508–10), from Wright (1949–59) iii. 176–81, no. 51. See however Epiphanius, *Panarion* 30: 4 ('Ellel').

4.2.5   The 'institution' of the fixed calendar

The absence of any information in rabbinic sources from before the tenth or the eleventh centuries regarding the institution of the fixed calendar casts considerable doubt on the historical reliability of the Hillel and other traditions. Not only is it uncertain who instituted the calendar, but also, I would suggest, whether such an institution was ever made at all. Although the Talmudic evidence we have surveyed above (in particular, the passage from *Y. Megillah*) indicates that elements of a fixed calendar had been adopted by the mid or later fourth century, this was not necessarily the result of a formal 'institution' or decree.

Indeed, the transition from the empirical Mishnaic calendar to the fixed, calculated calendar was not necessarily as radical as is commonly assumed. On the one hand, the Mishnah suggests that calculations were already made as part of the Mishnaic calendrical procedure: visibility of the new moon must have been calculated and predicted in order to verify the testimony of witnesses.[101] A fixed calendar of full and defective months in alternation was also used in this period, according to the Tosefta, whenever the new moon had not been sighted.[102]

On the other hand, lunar observations were still being made long after the 'institution' of the fixed calendar, in order to verify its accuracy. *Baraita de-Shemuel* ch. 5 indicates that solar and lunar observations were carried out for this purpose in Tishre of 776 CE,[103] even though it is unlikely that the calendar designed in this *Baraita* on the basis of these observations was ever intended to be applied in practice (S. Stern 1996).

Another indicator of the importance of moon sighting as late as the ninth century can be found in the letter of the exilarch of 835/6 CE—an important document from the Cairo Geniza, to which we shall often return in this and the next chapter.[104] The exilarch's letter must be treated as significant, even if it was written by a person who, of his own admission, was not involved in calendrical decisions, and hence whose views did not necessarily represent those of the calendrical court. Out

---

[101] As explicit in *M. RH* 2: 6 and 2: 8; *B. RH* 20b, 25a; *Y. RH* 2: 6–8 (58a–b) (on which see Weiss 1995: 193–8). It is possible that for the purpose of intercalation, calculation of the equinox would also have been regularly carried out.

[102] *T. ʿArakhin* 1: 8 (p. 543); see Bornstein (1908) 83.

[103] See Akavia (1955) 129–30.

[104] TS 8 G7¹ (not J7¹, as erroneously in Mann and hence in subsequent publications), first published by Mann (1920–2) ii. 41–2 (for discussion, see ibid. i. 52–3), then in Bornstein (1922a) 346–8 and Lewin (1932/3) 35–6. A new transcription of the text is presented below in the appendix.

of the three possibilities that are considered in this letter for the date of Passover (15 Nisan) in 836 CE—Tuesday, Wednesday, or Thursday—Tuesday is preferred not because it is the day of the conjunction,[105] as would be expected in the context of a calculated calendar, but only by elimination of the other two. Wednesday is eliminated because of the rule of *lo BaDU*,[106] and Thursday—most significantly for us—because in the West (Palestine), the new moon of Nisan 836 CE would have been visible before Thursday; if Passover, by now 15 Nisan, and hence 1 Nisan, was set on Thursday, the new moon might have been sighted beforehand, which would have invalidated the calendar.[107] This demonstrates a persisting concern, in this period, for the calculated calendar to agree, to some extent at least, with empirical observation—in a way that was no longer to apply in the present-day rabbinic calendar.[108]

It is conceivable, therefore, that the transition from an empirical to a fixed calendar was only gradual and progressive. The introduction of calendrical rules in the Amoraic period, such as the rules of Tishre, Adar, the Day of Atonement, and the equinox (see above), may have been critical to this transitional process. For as we have seen, these rules would have had the effect of restricting the flexibility of the Mishnaic empirical calendar. By reducing the options available to the calendrical court, these rules would have contributed to the formation of an increasingly rigid and 'fixed' calendar, which would have begun to take shape, eventually, by the fourth century CE.[109]

The *gradual* nature of such a process would thus explain why the 'institution' of a fixed calendar is not mentioned at all in early rabbinic literature.

---

[105] Even though the letter refers *en passant* to this conjunction, recto, ll. 9–10.

[106] i.e. that Passover cannot occur on Monday, Wednesday, or Friday: recto, l. 13 to verso, l. 7. On this rule, see below section, 4.4.1.

[107] Recto, ll. 11–13; verso, ll. 7–9. In actual fact, the new moon of Nisan 836 CE would not have been visible before Wednesday night (i.e. Thursday); but with limited scientific knowledge, such a prediction (on the part of the exilarch or of the Palestinian authorities) would not have been unreasonable.

[108] In the present-day rabbinic calendar, early visibility of the new moon is no longer a concern: see Ajdler (1996) 221–2. Still in 922 CE, Ben Meir appears to have used the argument of early visibility of the new moon to support his earlier date of Rosh ha-Shanah (see section 5.4.4): Bornstein (1922*b*) 244-7, Jaffe (1931) 196-8 (I am grateful to Yaaqov Loewinger for drawing my attention to this).

[109] This suggestion will be explored in further detail in section 5.3.5.

4.3 THE GEONIC PERIOD

4.3.1 Evidence of divergences from the present-day rabbinic calendar

Although a fixed calendar had begun to take shape by the fourth century CE, it was not identical with the Jewish rabbinic calendar of today. A number of documents and texts from the Geonic period reveal that the rabbinic calendar was reckoned differently till as late as the ninth century. It is only in the tenth century, in R. Saadya Gaon's extensive correspondence with Ben Meir, that we find evidence of the rabbinic calendar in its full present-day form.

The passage from *Y. Megillah* that indicates, as we have seen, that a fixed calendar was in place in the fourth century, implies in itself a different calendar from that which is observed today. By stating that Purim could not occur on either Monday or the Sabbath, R. Yose was implying that all other days of the week were possible.[110] According to the present-day rabbinic calendar, however, Wednesday should also have been excluded.[111]

Later evidence suggests that in the early sixth century, it was still possible for Purim to occur on Wednesday. This can be inferred from the epistle of R. Sherira Gaon, in which the date of death of R. ʾAḥai b. R. Huna is recorded as Sunday, 4 Adar 817 (of the Seleucid era, i.e. 505/6 CE).[112] This implies that 14 Adar, Purim, would have been on Wednesday. Provided R. Sherira's records are correct, this date would suggest that the calendar reckoned in Babylonian rabbinic circles in 506 CE was not the same as it is today.[113]

Various attempts have been made to explain away the dating of 'Sunday, 4 Adar', but none are particularly convincing. Some have suggested that ובחד בשבא (Sunday) be emended to ובתרי בשבא (Monday), which would reconcile the date

---

[110] R. Yose implicitly ignores R. Simon's rule in *Y. Sukkah* 4: 1 (54b) (see above, section 4.2.2). R. Simon's rule appears not to have been formally incorporated into the calendar until much later, with the rule of *lo ADU Rosh* (see below, section 4.4.3).

[111] If Purim occurs on Wednesday, the subsequent Rosh ha-Shanah will occur on Sunday, which is proscribed in the present-day calendar under the rule of *lo ADU Rosh* (see below section 4.4.1).

[112] *Iggeret R. Sherira Gaon*, in Lewin (1920) 98.

[113] R. Sherira Gaon's epistle was written in 987 CE. On the reliability of his chronology, see Gafni (1987). The date of R. ʾAḥai b. R. Huna's death implies, furthermore, that the rule of *molad zaqen* was not observed: see argument below, section 4.4.4.

with the present–day calendar.[114] This emendation is possible, but arguably unwarranted.

Lewin (1920: 98 n. 3) suggests that in this period, the days of the month were counted from the first day of *Rosh Ḥodesh*, i.e. from the 30th of the previous month—in other words, that what was really 3 Shevat would have been called '1 Adar', what was really 1 Adar would have been called '2nd', etc., so that '4 Adar' really meant the 3rd. This rather confusing method of dating is attested in halakhic sources, but only from twelfth–century Ashkenaz (Germany);[115] it appears to have been generally rejected.[116] It would be extremely far-fetched to apply this method of dating to early sixth–century Babylonia, for the sole purpose of reconciling R. Sherira's date with the present-day rabbinic calendar.[117]

Bornstein (1922*a*: 370–1) suggests that 505/6 CE could have been intercalated, and hence that R. 'Aḥai's death could have been in the *first* month of Adar. Indeed, 4 Adar I can occur on Sunday without breaching any rule of the present–day rabbinic calendar (such as the rule of the Day of the Willow). However, this solution remains incompatible with the present-day rabbinic calendar, according to which the year 505/6 CE would *not* have been intercalated.[118]

According to some recensions of the 'French' version of R. Sherira's epistle, the year of R. 'Aḥai's death reads 816 (i.e. 504/5 CE). This reading, however, must be rejected on calendrical grounds.[119] In 505 CE, the conjunction of Adar occurred on a Saturday in the afternoon. This is incompatible with the 1st of the month occurring on a Thursday, whether it is based on conjunction or on visibility of the new moon.

The date of R. 'Aḥai b. R. Huna's demise does confirm, however, that in the early sixth century the rabbinic calendar was based on the conjunction. If 4 Adar 506 CE occurred, as stated, on Sunday, the 1st of

---

[114] Rapaport (1914) 166–7, s.v. *Alexander Moqdon*, section 19.

[115] The earliest reference I have found to this method of dating is in *Sefer Ra-'avya* (Aptowitzer 1964–5: iv. 275–7, ch. 919). By contrast, this method appears to be unknown in the (perhaps) contemporary *Tosafot Yeshanim* ad RH 19b, s.v. מימות (Hirschler 1984: 25), *Sefer Ra'avan*, responsum 48: 6 (Albeck 1904: 39–40), and *Midrash Sekhel Tov* (Buber 1901: ii. 87). For 14th-c. sources, see responsa of R. Shlomo b. Aderet (*Teshuvot ha-Rashba*) 6: 151; R. Nissim, ad *B. Nedarim* 50b (incorrectly referenced in Lewin 1920: 98 n. 3).

[116] See Aptowitzer (1964–5) iv. 275–7, and later works cited there in editors' nn.; for a 14th/15th-c. source, see responsa of R. Shimon b. Tzemaḥ Duran (*Tashbetz*), 1: 153.

[117] Bornstein's (1922*b*: 281–4) attempt to infer a similar method of dating (i.e. starting from the first day of *Rosh Ḥodesh*) from tractate *Sofrim* (end of ch. 20) is totally unconvincing.

[118] Bornstein explains, furthermore, that intercalation would have been based in this period on *tequfat Shemuel*. That 505/6 CE was intercalated remains possible regardless of whether Bornstein's explanation is accepted.

[119] *Pace* Lewin (1920: 98 n. 4), who endorses it as the correct reading.

the month would have been on Thursday; this is the day of the week when the conjunction occurred.[120]

That the calendar was based on the conjunction is corroborated by another date in R. Sherira's epistle, that of the death of Ravina. Ravina died on Wednesday, 13 Kislew 811 (i.e. 499/500 CE), which implies the 1st of the month on Friday; this, again, is the day of the week when the conjunction occurred.[121] The fact that this date is compatible with the present-day rabbinic calendar is insignificant, as coincidences between various lunar calendars are always bound to occur quite frequently.[122]

The divergence of the early Geonic from the present-day rabbinic calendar is possibly confirmed later on in the Palestinian *Sefer ha-MaᶜᵃƂ asim*. The date of this work is somewhat uncertain, but the mid seventh century is likely (Strack and Stemberger 1991: 205). Reference is made in this work to Rosh ha-Shanah occurring on Saturday night/Sunday, ostensibly as a practical possibility. This is proscribed, however, in the present-day rabbinic calendar.[123]

Of far greater importance, however, is a much later document from the Cairo Geniza: a letter of a Babylonian exilarch—one of the main leaders of the Rabbanite community—with detailed calendrical instructions for the year 835/6 CE.[124] This letter reveals that Passover (15 Nisan) in that year was due to occur on a Tuesday; whilst according to the present-day rabbinic calendar, it should have occurred on Thursday. According to the exilarch, the setting of Passover on Tuesday was dictated by a concern to avoid visibility of the new moon before the first day

[120] The mean conjunction occurred more precisely on Wednesday night, just before midnight.

[121] Lewin (1920) 95. The mean conjunction occurred on Friday, in the early hours of the morning.

[122] As argued by Bornstein (1922*a*) 370; *pace* Kasher (1949) 166–7 and Gil (1996) 130–3, who argue on the basis of this dating that the present-day rabbinic calendar was already in existence.

[123] For the same reason that Purim cannot occur on Wednesday; see below section 4.4.1 (the rule of לא אד״ו ראש). See Herr (1979/80), whose argument depends on the assumption (pp. 76–8) that the passage of *Sefer ha-Maᶜasim* (cited at p. 63 from Rabinovitz 1972: 287–8, Margaliot 1974: 45; see also Yudlov and Havlin 1992: iii) cannot be referring to the second day of Rosh ha-Shanah, as the custom in Palestine, throughout the first millennium CE, was to observe only one day of this festival. This assumption, however, is questionable and possibly unfounded, since some Palestinian evidence from the 7th and 8th cc. suggests the observance of two days: see Fleischer (1983) 249–53 and (1984*c*); Herr (1984).

[124] See appendix. The year 835/6 is given in the document according to both the Seleucid era and the era of creation, which excludes the possibility of any mistake.

of the month. This concern does not exist in the present-day rabbinic calendar.[125]

Once discovered and published in 1922, the exilarch's letter proved beyond doubt that almost five hundred years after R. Yose and 'Hillel the Patriarch', the fixed calendar in its present-day form had still not been instituted.

Scholars arguing for the early origins of the present-day rabbinic calendar have found this difficult to refute. Kasher (1949), in his monograph on the calendar, simply ignores this aspect of the exilarch's letter. Langermann (1987: 161–2) calls for a 're-examination' of the manuscript in Cambridge. The manuscript, however, is clearly legible and in good condition; it is hard to believe that re-examination would alter significantly our accepted reading.[126]

Langermann's argument rests on a work by the Muslim astronomer al-Khwarizmi, dating from 823/4 CE, in which the present-day rabbinic calendar is almost fully described.[127] This important text indicates, as Langermann argues, that the present-day rabbinic calendar existed before the date of the exilarch's letter. The existence of this calendar, however, does not prove that it was observed *in practice*; the exilarch's letter of 835/6 CE is certainly evidence to the contrary. All al-Khwarizmi proves is that the present-day rabbinic calendar has already been conceived of *in theory*.

It is also questionable whether the section in al-Khwarizmi's work that describes, in algorithmic form, the present-day rabbinic calendar (Langermann 1987: 164–5), is authentic and not a later interpolation (as argued by Sar-Shalom 1988: 42–7). This section of the work, indeed, is completely out of place: it comes in the middle of an account of the mean lengths of the lunar and solar years. Moreover, al-Khwarizmi's algorithm is useless as it stands, because the epochs of the 19-year cycle and of the *molad* (mean conjunction) are not supplied. The absence of these epochs in al-Khwarizmi's text suggests either that something is missing from the text, or that the algorithm—without which the text would become completely coherent and intelligible—is excessive and a late interpolation.

Further sources have been adduced to prove that the rabbinic calendar in the early and mid Geonic period differed from today's, but these are considerably less conclusive. The *Baraita de-Shemuel* (beginning of ch. 5), written in the late eighth century, presents a fixed calendrical calculation that is based on a year

---

[125] See above, section 4.2.5 and n. 108. The date of Passover 836 CE implies, furthermore, that the rule of *molad zaqen* was not observed: see argument below, section 4.4.4.

[126] Mann's (1920–2: ii. 41–2) transcription was actually full of minor errors, but they did not affect the general meaning of the text. For a more accurate transcription, with photographs of the manuscript, see appendix below.

[127] The text is published in Hebrew translation by Langermann himself (1987). Langermann's precise dating of this work to 823/4 CE (ibid. 160, read '4584') is based on a reference to that year in the text (ibid.165), which is presumably more than just a *terminus post quem*.

length of 365¼ days and a lunation of 29½ days and two-thirds of an hour. These values differ considerably from those of the present-day rabbinic calendar, where the lunation is taken as 29½ days and 793/1080 of an hour (see below, section 4.4.1). However, I have shown elsewhere that the *Baraita de-Shemuel* itself would not have believed its values to be functional or accurate, nor would it have been the intention to apply this calendar in practice; the calendar of the *Baraita de-Shemuel* was only theoretical and, in some respects, fictitious (S. Stern 1996).

The same argument is likely to apply to the *Pirqei de-R. Eliezer*, which belongs to the same period[128] and which assumes, in chs.6–7, the same simplified values for the year and the lunation as in the *Baraita de-Shemuel*.

4.3.2   The Geonic calendar(s)

Except that it was different from today's, little is known about the rabbinic calendar of the early and mid Geonic periods. Some of its most fundamental features remain totally unknown: for instance, what cycle of intercalations was used, or what conjunction was it based on.

The nature of the rabbinic calendar in this period has been, among earlier scholars, a matter of intense controversy. Bornstein saw the calculation of the calendar as going through a rigid succession of changes, from the second to the ninth centuries, each change bringing about a further improvement in its astronomical and mathematical accuracy. The calculation of the lunation and of equinoxes, in particular, were gradually refined until the values of the present-day calendar were reached. This model was given its most extreme formulation by Jaffe, a colleague of Bornstein, in his posthumously published history of the Jewish calendar.[129]

Akavia rejected this model, largely because it was excessively speculative. In his view, the calendar calculation in the early Geonic period was basically *undefined*. For a long time, lunations and equinoxes were calculated on the basis of only approximate values, such as are found in the *Baraita de-Shemuel* (see above, section 4.2.5); from time to time, calendar dates were adjusted with the help of astronomical observations.[130]

---

[128] 8th or 9th c.: Strack and Stemberger (1991) 356.

[129] Jaffe (1931). The critical remarks of Akavia in his foreword to this work are worthy of note (pp. 11–16). Jaffe—a mathematician rather than a historian—devised a brilliant reconstruction of the 'stages' in the evolution of the calendrical calculation, but his approach was excessively speculative (and often reliant on spurious evidence) to command scholarly credibility. For a convenient epitome of the Bornstein–Jaffe theory, see Sar-Shalom (1984) 17–30.

[130] Such as the observation carried out in Tishre 776 CE, which is recorded in *Baraita de-Shemuel*, ch. 5: see Akavia (1955) and S. Stern (1996).

Thus the calendar may have been based, in larger part, on calculation, but this calculation was far from standard or 'fixed'. It was only in the mid or later ninth century that a standard calculation, based on accurate values—i.e. the present-day rabbinic calendar—was instituted. This theory is attractive, but actually no less hypothetical than that of Akavia's predecessors.[131]

As we shall see, some elements of the rabbinic calendar lend themselves better to the 'evolutionary' model of Bornstein/Jaffe, while others are more suited to the 'fluid' model of Akavia.

A passage from the *She'iltot* of R. 'Aḥai (mid eighth century) has often been cited to illustrate the fluid or transitional character of this period:

אבל היום שאין חכמים בקיאין בחשבון תולדות לבנה ובדיקדוקי סוד העיבור

But today the Sages (i.e. rabbis) are not expert in the calculation of the lunar conjunction and in the minutiae of the calendrical court . . .[132]

The passage from which this is cited is obscure on a number of counts.[133] At first sight, the purpose of this passage is to explain why Purim no longer occurred in this period on the Sabbath, whereas in the Mishnaic period it did. The meaning of the citation above would thus be that since the calendar was no longer based on accurate predictions and sightings of the new moon, there was no harm in postponing the beginning of the month so as to prevent Purim occurring on the Sabbath.

However, the wording of the citation above suggests a different interpretation. It appears to be a paraphrase of the Talmudic argument that because 'we (i.e. in Babylonia) are not expert in the determination of the new moon' (אנן לא ידעינן בקיבועא דירחא), and hence our calendar dates are uncertain, the *lulav* should not be taken on the Sabbath.[134] Following the same logic, R. 'Aḥai would be arguing in this passage that the scroll of *Esther* should not be read on the Sabbath, in case the 'real' date of Purim is on some other day. If this second interpretation is correct, it would imply that R. 'Aḥai considered that in his own day ('today'), calendar dates were still to be treated as uncertain.

Bornstein (1904: 154–5, 1922*a*: 351) considers R. 'Aḥai's attitude to reflect the fact that the calculated calendar was not yet finalized or fixed. Against this, it

[131] The evidence from *Baraita de-Shemuel*, ch. 5 is not entirely convincing. Although the results of the observation of 776 CE were clearly used for the purposes of calendrical calculation, I have argued that the calendar constructed in *Baraita de-Shemuel* was only theoretical and not intended to be applied in practice (S. Stern 1996).

[132] *She'iltot de-Rav 'Aḥai*, ch. 79 (Mirsky 1964: 224). On my translation, see below section 4.3.3. On the *She'iltot* in general, see Brody (1997) 202–15.

[133] As noted by rabbinic commentators: see for instance Berlin (1955) i. 439–43; Kasher (1949) 156–65.

[134] *B. Sukkah* 43a; see above, section 4.2.3.

has been argued that a perception of uncertainty does not necessarily contradict the existence of a fully developed calculated calendar.[135]

Evidence of the flexibility of the calendar calculation in the early-mid Geonic period can be found, however, in the exilarch's letter of 835/6, in which he states:

ולא[מי]בעיא בהכי הדין מעשה דלא איפשר לשוויינון לא כסדרן ולא שלמין; אלא אפילו זמנין דאי עבדינן כסדרן ושל[מין] או חסרין, דאמי להדדי, ולעולם עליהון סמכינן.

This applies not only in this present case ... where it is impossible to make them (the months of 835/6 CE) regular or full, but even when it makes no difference whether (the months) are made regular, full, or defective, we always rely on them (the Palestinian authorities) ...[136]

This implies that in some years, the calendar could have been set in more than one way (with the year being either regular, full, or defective), and that an arbitrary decision had to be taken by the Palestinian authorities. In the present-day rabbinic calendar, by contrast, this multiplicity of options is totally precluded (Bornstein 1922a: 347).

4.3.3 The calendrical court

An assumption over which there appears to be widespread agreement is that until the ninth century, the Palestinian rabbinic court retained an exclusive monopoly over all calendrical decisions, just as in the earlier, 'Mishnaic' period. The continuity of the Palestinian calendrical court well after the 'Mishnaic' period appears to be borne out by all the sources. Already in the Palestinian Talmud the list of rabbis composing the calendrical court extends till the penultimate or last generation of Palestinian Amoraim, including R. Yose, who elsewhere assumes the existence of a fixed calendar. This passage suggests that the calendrical court continued functioning, with all its ceremonial, after the Mishnaic system had been abandoned.[137]

Much later, in the early tenth century, Ben Meir reports that every year, at the end of the feast of Tabernacles, the head of the Palestinian academy would ascend the Mount of Olives and announce the calendar dates that had been calculated for the forthcoming year. These dates

[135] Kasher (1949) 161–5. Less convincing is Kasher's argument that the term 'today' (היום) in this citation is merely the rewording of a similar term in *B. Sukkah* 43a (האידנא), and hence that the citation is not meant to refer to R. ʾAḥai's own period, but rather to that of the Talmud.

[136] Exilarch's letter (see appendix), verso, ll. 9–14. A 'regular' year is when full and defective months are regularly alternated; a 'full' year is when the months of Marḥeshwan and Kislew are both full; a 'defective' year is when both are defective.

[137] *Y. RH* 2: 6 (58b). R. Yose: *Y. Megillah* 1: 2 (70b) (see above).

would then have been disseminated across the Diaspora, in good time before the next Passover. This old tradition demonstrated, in Ben Meir's view, that the Palestinian court had always retained supreme authority over calendrical decisions.[138]

Further sources confirm that the authority of the Palestinian court in calendrical matters was recognized by rabbinic Jews, in Babylonia and *a fortiori* in Palestine, at least as late as the ninth century. This was, indeed, the main argument put forward by the (Babylonian) exilarch in his letter of 835/6 CE: that for the sake of calendrical unanimity, the decisions of the Palestinian court should always be obeyed.[139] Conversely, Pirqoi b. Baboi (writing in the late eighth or early ninth century) makes no apparent reference to the calendar, in spite of his vehement opposition, in other areas of halakha, to Palestinian rabbinic authority—which suggests, *e silentio*, that on this matter he concurred.[140]

The survival of this Palestinian rabbinic monopoly, from the Mishnaic and early Amoraic periods until at least the ninth century, was not a mere archaism but an inherent necessity. Because the calendar calculation was not yet fully standardized or fixed, the responsibility for calculating calendar dates had to be restricted to a single authoritative body, so as to safeguard the rabbinic principle of calendrical unanimity.[141] This authoritative body not only calculated and announced the dates of the calendar, but also decided, at its discretion, *how* the calendar calculation was to be carried out.

To a large extent, the account I have outlined must be considered correct. However, we shall see in the next chapter that the relationship between the Babylonian rabbinic community and the Palestinian court was actually far more complex; the possibility of other rabbinic courts engaging, officially or unofficially, in calendar calculation is not to be entirely excluded.

It is also widely assumed that in this period, the Palestinian court kept its calculation of the calendar as a well-guarded secret.[142] This is

---

[138] Guillaume (1914–15) 553, ll. 12–15. See also Bornstein (1904) 105–6, (1922*b*) 238 n. 2; Gil (1992) 562–3.

[139] Verso, ll. 9–17 (see appendix).

[140] The fragments of Pirqoi's work have been published sporadically. For a bibliography see *Encyclopedia Judaica*, xiii. 560–1, s.v. Pirqoi ben Baboi (Brody 1997: 113 n. 45). Most sources are now available in Yudlov and Havlin (1992) vii. 687–782.

[141] On this principle of unanimity, see section 5.3.1.

[142] Bornstein (1922*b*) 286; Jaffe (1931) 55–6. According to Bornstein, the calendar calculation may have remained secret till as late as the mid 10th c., even after the R. Saadya–Ben Meir controversy.

not impossible, but the evidence is meagre. All it consists of is a single expression in rabbinic sources, סוד העיבור, which is commonly translated as 'the secret of intercalation'.

This, however, was not the original meaning of this expression. In the Babylonian Talmud, where the expression is first found, סוד העיבור has the very specific sense of '*council* of intercalation', i.e. the rabbinic panel or court in charge of setting the calendar.[143] In the passage quoted above from the *She'iltot* of R. 'Aḥai (mid eighth century) it is also to be understood in the sense of 'council'.[144]

Only in *Pirqei de-R. Eliezer* (ch. 8, *passim*), a source from around the eighth or ninth century (Strack and Stemberger 1991: 356), the phrase takes on, perhaps for the first time, a connotation of secrecy (the translation 'council of intercalation' is just about possible, but less likely); and in the perhaps contemporary *Kiddush Yeraḥim* of R. Pinḥas, the meaning of 'secret of intercalation' becomes unambiguous.[145] In a later source, a responsum of R. Hai Gaon (early eleventh century), סוד העיבור in the

---

[143] סוד, a biblical Hebrew term, translates as 'secret' but also as 'assembly' or 'council'. The expression סוד העיבור appears to have been originally coined in *B. Ketubot* 112a (*bis*), on the basis of an interpretation of *Ezekiel* 13: 9 (see parallel in *Y. RH* 2: 5 (58b), but without the expression סוד העיבור); its meaning there is clearly 'council of intercalation'. The expression is then found in *B. RH* 20b, but there its meaning is more ambiguous: דתניא בסוד העיבור could mean 'it has been taught at the council of intercalation', but equally 'it has been taught (as part of) the secret of intercalation'. However, the fact that this teaching could be cited in *B. RH* by a Babylonian Amora, R. Simlai's father, suggests that it would not have been particularly secret (even if Shemuel happened not to have known it: see ibid.). In *B. Ketubot* 111a (Vilna edn., l. 13), many recensions read סוד העיבור rather than הסוד *tout court* (the latter in the printed edition, and as Rashi's text evidently read: see Hirshler 1977: 538–9 and n. 20); in this context, the meaning of סוד העיבור would have to be 'secret of intercalation'. However, the reading סוד העיבור in this passage is more likely to be a later interpolation (the reading סוד, which implies an unspecified secret, is paralleled in *Song Rabbah* 2: 7; see also the En Gedi inscription in Levine 1981: 140–5).

[144] See above, section 4.3.2. What R. 'Aḥai means is that 'today' the rabbis do not know the minutiae that used to be involved in the decision-making process of the calendrical court (דיקדוקי סוד העיבור). The same sense *may* also be meant in a Babylonian letter of the early 920s, thus translating: 'many years ago, sages from Babylonia went up to the land of Israel, and investigated (דקדקו) with the sages of the land of Israel at the "court of intercalation" . . .' (Bornstein 1904: 88–9, Guillaume 1914–15: 546–7; see full citation in section 5.4.4).

[145] Marmorstein (1921) 254 (אדר שני, fo. 8b, l. 4). For the date of this work, see below, n. 164. The term סוד is also used in this sense in one of Ben Meir's letters (Friedlander 1893: 197, Bornstein 1904: 65).

sense of 'secret of intercalation' comes to refer to the calendar calculation itself;[146] and this usage becomes even more explicit in R. Ḥananel's
Talmudic commentary (mid eleventh century).[147]

The notion of calendrical secrecy, romantic as it is, should thus be
treated with a measure of circumspection. Even if a policy of secrecy
existed in the Geonic period—perhaps as a ploy to protect the Palestinian court's monopoly—the exilarch's letter of 835/6 CE suggests that
it could not have been particularly effective. Although the exilarch was
not a member of the calendrical court, and was happy instead to sub-
mit to the Palestinian authorities, he shows himself in this letter to have
been well versed in the calendrical calculation (including, for instance,
the calculation of the mean conjunction).

4.4 THE EMERGENCE OF THE PRESENT-DAY RABBINIC CALENDAR

By the early 920s, at the time of the R. Saadya–Ben Meir controversy,
the present-day rabbinic calendar had been in existence for some time.
Some elements of this calendar went back to the Talmudic period, but
others were not instituted before the mid or later ninth century. As we
have seen, although the calendar implicit in the exilarch's letter of 835/6
CE was in some ways remarkably similar to the present-day rabbinic calendar, the dates that were set for that year would have been at variance
with the present-day rabbinic computation.

In the last section of this chapter I propose to establish, wherever possible, in which period the various elements of the present-day rabbinic
calendar would have been instituted. For the sake of clarity, I shall first
provide a concise outline of the present-day calendrical computation.

4.4.1 The present-day rabbinic calendar: an outline

(i) The conjunction (*molad*) is calculated on the basis of two values:

---

[146] In *Teshuvot Geonim* (Lyck) 1; Lewin (1931) 5. The same usage is implicit in
Midrashic works that can be assumed to be contemporary with, or later than, R. Hai:
Midrash Tehilim (ed. Buber) 19: 10, p. 84b (for the date of this work see Strack and
Stemberger 1991: 350–1); *Exodus Rabbah* 15: 27 (for the date, see ibid. 335–7).

[147] R. Ḥananel ad *RH* 20a: 'why was it called סוד העיבור? Because the court
only revealed it [i.e. the '*secret* of intercalation'] to its appointed members'. See also
R. Ḥananel ad *Sukkah* 54b.

(*a*) the mean lunation (duration of the lunar month) of 29 days, 12 hours, and 793 parts (there are 1080 parts to an hour).

(*b*) *molad* of Tishre year 1 (of the era of creation, i.e. the first Tishre in 'history'), which is given as 2nd day (Monday), 5 hours (of the 24-hour period beginning in the evening), 204 parts, or in its Hebrew acronym: בהר״ד (*BaHaRaD*). This corresponds to Sunday, 6 October 3761 BCE at 23 hours, 11 minutes, and 20 seconds (assuming the day begins at 18 hours).

The *molad* of Tishre year 1 functions as an epoch (reference point). Any subsequent *molad* can be worked out by adding the right number of lunations to this epoch. As an alternative to *BaHaRaD*, the *molad* of the following Tishre (year 2) can also be used. This molad is 6th day (Friday), 14 hours, no parts (acronym: ו״ד, *WeYaD*).[148] The fact that this epoch is a round figure (with no parts of the hour) suggests that this was the original epoch to have been in use (see further below, sections 4.4.7 and 5.4.6).

　　(ii) The month begins, *a priori*, on the day of the *molad*. Sometimes it is postponed by one or more days, because of the rules that follow (3–4, which are hence known as 'postponement' rules, דחיות).

　　(iii) Rosh ha-Shanah, 1 Tishre, cannot occur on Sunday, Wednesday, or Friday. This rule is known by its Hebrew mnemonic: לא אד״ו ראש (*lo ADU Rosh*).[149] If the *molad* of Tishre occurs on any of these days, the 1st of the month must be postponed.

　　(iv) If the *molad* of Tishre occurs on or after the 18th hour (i.e. midday), the 1st of the month must be postponed.[150] This is known as *molad zaqen* ('late conjunction').

　　(v) The calendar consists of a fixed alternation of 29- and 30-day months: there are always 30 days in Nisan, 29 days in Iyyar, etc. Only the months of Marḥeshwan and Kislew are subject to variation: they can be 'regular' (i.e. 29–30), 'full' (i.e. 30–30), or 'defective' (i.e. 29–29) (כסדרם, שלמים, חסרים). This variation makes it possible for rules (iii)

---

[148] On the vocalization of *WeYaD*, see Ibn Ezra (1874) p. 3b, suggesting a derivation from Deut. 23: 13 (Loewinger 1986: 70).

[149] Ibn Ezra (1874: p. 2a) suggests that the correct vocalization should be *lo IDO Rosh*, derived from Ezra 8: 17. I shall use, however, the common vocalization. The rule that Pesaḥ cannot occur on Monday, Wednesday, and Friday (לא בד״ו פסח) is derived from לא אד״ו ראש, and basically another formulation of the same rule. For the rationale of this rule, see above, section 4.2.2, and below, section 4.4.3.

[150] If the following day is either Sunday, Wednesday, or Friday, Rosh ha-Shanah must be postponed till the day after, hence a postponement of two days.

and (iv) to be observed, i.e. for the subsequent Rosh ha-Shanah(s) (sometimes more than one year ahead) not to occur on the wrong days. This variation also makes it possible to compensate for the discrepancy between the mean lunation under rule (i)(*a*) and the average month length of 29½ days resulting from a pure alternation of 29- and 30-day months.

(vi) The intercalation is based on a fixed 19-year cycle, which starts at year 1 (from the creation) and within which the following seven years are intercalated: 3, 6, 8, 11, 14, 17, 19. Intercalation consists of an additional 30-day month, which is inserted before Adar and called 'first Adar'.

From the late Geonic period until the present day, a number of tables and algorithms have been designed and formulated on the basis of these fundamental principles, so as to facilitate the calendar calculation and remove unnecessary complications. Among the earliest of these algorithms were the cycle attributed to R. Naḥshon (gaon of Sura, 871–9), עיגול דרב נחשון,[151] and the table known as לוח ארבעה שערים ('four gates' or 'four parts' table) which was already in existence and apparently widespread in R. Saadya's time. The 'four parts table' represents the earliest formulation of the normative rabbinic calendar, with which it corresponds down to the finest detail. All it requires is knowledge of the *molad* and of the cycle of intercalations; on this basis, calendar dates can be worked out with the greatest of ease.[152] But the history of these

---

[151] R. Naḥshon's 247-year cycle (of 13 × 19 year cycles) does not quite conform, however, to the present-day rabbinic calendar which by definition is not cyclical (see Sar-Shalom 1984: 51–2). The authenticity of its attribution to R. Naḥshon is doubtful, because it is not mentioned in any Geonic source; its earliest mention is by Abraham ibn Ezra (early 12th c.; see reference in Bornstein 1922*a*: 354–8, especially p. 355 n. 1). R. Naḥshon's cycle is not known ever to have been used, except in Yemen between the 12th and early 14th cc. (Tobi 1981; reference courtesy of Tzvi Langermann). It was also erroneously printed in some editions of R. Yaʿaqov b. Asher's *Arbaʿah Turim*, *ʾOrah Ḥayim* 428, thus leading on occasion to some calendrical confusion (Kasher 1949: 39, Silber 1993: 200–1).

[152] See Bornstein (1904) 37–40, with references on p. 37 n. 1; Bornstein (1922*b*) 231–6, with references on p. 232 n. 1; Sar-Shalom (1984) 46. This table is firmly attested in the R. Saadya—Ben Meir correspondence of the 920s CE: see Friedlander (1893) 198–9 (= Bornstein 1904: 66–70), Schechter (1902) 498–500 (= Adler 1914: 45–9; Bornstein 1904: 113–16), Levi, Adler and Broyde (1900) 225–7 (= Bornstein 1904: 75–8). It is also attested as a work in verse by Yose al-Naharwani, perhaps to be identified with Nissi al-Naharwani, R. Saadya's contemporary in Babylonia (Epstein 1901: 204–10; I am grateful to Jean Ajdler for pointing out this source to me). My preferred translation of ארבעה שערים is 'four parts' (as in the equivalent usage of the Aramaic term בבא); others prefer the more literal rendering of 'four gates', i.e. the four days of the week when the year can begin (all days other than אד"ו—item 3 above) and hence that serve as 'gateways' to the year (Epstein 1901: 204;

tables and algorithms belongs largely to a later period (from the tenth century onwards), and hence lies outside the scope of this present study.

Because different elements of the present-day rabbinic calendar were instituted at various times and various stages, it is necessary to address each of these elements separately. For my own convenience, I shall refer to them below in a different order.

4.4.2   The sequence of months

The regular alternation of full and defective months (above, section 4.4.1, rule (v)), at least between Adar and Tishre, was already in place by the late Amoraic period, as evident from the Palestinian Talmud (*Y. Megillah* 1: 2 (70b), see above). It is *possible* that the 'variable' months in this period were already Marḥeshwan and Kislew, as they were later to be in R. Saadya's and the present-day rabbinic calendar.[153]

The rationale for treating the months of Marḥeshwan and Kislew as variable is that they are far away in time from the major biblical festivals (the next one being Passover), which provides plenty of opportunity for errors to be rectified. It is not impossible, however, that other winter months were also variable before R. Saadya's period.

4.4.3   The rule of *lo ADU*

The same passage from the Palestinian Talmud (*Y. Megillah*) informs us that already in the later Amoraic period, Rosh ha-Shanah could not occur on Wednesday or on Friday. But this implies that Rosh ha-Shanah *could* occur on any other day of the week, including Sunday (as noted above, section 4.3.1). In the present-day rabbinic calendar, however, Sunday is proscribed under the rule of *lo ADU* (above, section 4.4.1, rule (iii)).

The present-day prohibition of Rosh ha-Shanah on Sunday draws its origin from another passage of the Palestinian Talmud (*Y. Sukkah* 4: 1 (54b)), where R. Simon prohibited the Day of the Willow (21 Tishre) from being set on the Sabbath (hence, Rosh ha-Shanah on Sunday). But evidence from the Palestinian and Babylonian Talmudim (not least, the

see also R. Avraham b. Ḥiyya, *Sefer ha-ʿIbbur* 2: 9, Filipowski 1851: 63—courtesy of Jean Ajdler). The usage of the term לוח (lit. 'table') in the sense of 'calendar' may have originated from here. Further reference will be made to the 'four parts table' in the context of the R. Saadya–Ben Meir controversy (section 5.4.5).

[153] Evidence for R. Saadya is in his fragmentary monograph on the calendar, in Schechter (1902) 48 (= Bornstein 1904: 73).

passage from *Y. Megillah* itself) suggests that in the Talmudic period, this rule was not consistently obeyed.[154]

Later evidence confirms that the occurrence of the Day of the Willow on the Sabbath was still possible as late as the sixth century. As we have seen, the date of death of R. ʾAḥai b. R. Huna is recorded in the epistle of R. Sherira Gaon as Sunday, 4 Adar 506 CE, which implies that the subsequent Rosh ha-Shanah occurred on Sunday (see section 4.3.1). Furthermore, the Palestinian *Sefer ha-Maʿasim* possibly implies that as late as the seventh century, when this work is thought to have been written, the occurrence of Rosh ha-Shanah on Sunday remained a practical possibility (see ibid.).

The rule of *lo ADU Rosh*, which excludes Rosh ha-Shanah on Wednesday and Friday, as well as Sunday, is first recorded—in the form of this mnemonic—in the mid-eighth-century *Halakhot Pesuqot* of R. Yehudai Gaon.[155] That this passage is a later interpolation cannot be entirely ruled out.[156] But the rule of *lo ADU* is undoubtedly attested in the exilarch's letter of 835/6 CE, where it is stated and explained in considerable detail.[157]

4.4.4 The rule of *molad zaqen*

The origins of the rule of *molad zaqen* (above, section 4.4.1, rule (iv)) are as obscure as is its rationale. However, we know that its introduction into the rabbinic calendar was relatively late.

The date of R. ʾAḥai's death in 506 CE, as given in R. Sherira's epistle, entails not only that Rosh ha-Shanah occurred on Sunday (see above), but also that the rule of *molad zaqen* would have been breached. If 4 Adar 506 CE was a Sunday, the subsequent 1 Tishre (also a Sunday) would have coincided with the day of conjunction; conjunction, however, would have occurred at least four hours after midday.[158] Unless the calculation of the conjunction was grossly inaccurate in this period, and the conjunction was believed to occur on Sunday, 1 Tishre *before*

---

[154] See above, section 4.2.2. R. Simon's additional rule, prohibiting Rosh ha-Shanah on a *Sabbath*, appears never to have been accepted.

[155] Sassoon (1950) 187; Abramson (1971) 290. Also in Schlossberg (1886) 135. On the *Halakhot Pesuqot* in general, see Brody (1997) 207–33.

[156] The equivalent rule of *lo BaDU Pesaḥ* is also mentioned in one recension of the liturgical poem of R. Pinḥas, from the same period or slightly later (Marmorstein 1921: 254), but this is likely to be an interpolation.

[157] Exilarch's letter (see appendix), recto, l. 13 to verso, l. 7.

[158] As noted by Bornstein (1904) 32.

midday, we may conclude that the rule of *molad zaqen* was not yet in observance.

That *molad zaqen* was not observed is confirmed beyond doubt in the exilarch's letter of 835/6 CE, in which the time of *molad* Nisan (836 CE) is explicitly given as Tuesday 'in the daytime . . . at four hours', i.e. approximately 10 a.m.[159] This *molad* is sufficiently accurate[160] to warrant the assumption that the lunation in use in this period was also reasonably correct. This means, therefore, that the subsequent *molad* of Tishre, according to the exilarch's reckoning, would have been on a Thursday at least 4 hours later, thus well into the afternoon. But since Passover of 836 CE was to occur on a Tuesday (according to this same letter), the subsequent Rosh ha-Shanah would have been on Thursday—on the day of the conjunction, when this conjunction occurred in the afternoon. This demonstrates that as late as 835/6 CE, the rule of *molad zaqen* was not yet observed.[161]

Molad zaqen was well established, however, by the time of the R. Saadya–Ben Meir controversy in the 920s CE. In fact, their argument hinged entirely on the definition of this rule: Ben Meir was of the view that *molad zaqen* did not apply from noon, but only from 642 parts thereafter.[162]

4.4.5 The 19-year cycle

Evidence of a 19-year cycle of intercalations (above, section 4.4.1, rule (vi)) is totally absent in early rabbinic sources. As we have seen, the saying of R. Huna b. Avin in *B. RH* 21a would imply, if the attribution is reliable, that no cycle of intercalations was yet instituted in the early fourth century (see section 4.2.2).

---

[159] Recto, ll. 9–10 (cited below, section 4.4.6), as correctly interpreted by Mann (1931–5) i. 52 (although in other respects, Mann largely misunderstood the calendrical elements of this letter). Bornstein (1922a: 347–9) interpreted this phrase as meaning the 4th hour of the 24-hour period, i.e. Monday night at approximately 10 p.m. On this basis, Bornstein inferred that whilst *molad zaqen* might well have been observed, the calculation of the *molad* in this period would have been completely different. This interpretation is highly unlikely, however, for reasons which will be explained below (section 4.4.6).

[160] See section 4.4.6.

[161] It is precisely for this reason that according to the present-day rabbinic calendar, Passover of 836 CE would have been postponed till Thursday (Wednesday being excluded because of *lo ADU Rosh*, hence *lo BaDU Pesah*).

[162] This led to a dispute between R. Saadya and Ben Meir regarding the dates of Passover of 922–4 CE (see further in the next chapter, section 5.4.4).

The earliest mention of the 19-year cycle is in *Pirqei de-R. Eliezer* (end of ch. 8),[163] a work which is generally dated to the eighth or ninth century (Strack and Stemberger 1991: 356). It is also mentioned in the *Kiddush Yeraḥim* of R. Pinḥas, which was written not earlier than the mid eighth century.[164] It is then found in later sources, such as al-Khwarizmi's monograph on the Jewish calendar, dating from 823/4 CE.[165]

The 19-year cycle may be already implicit in the liturgical works of R. Eleazar ha-Qallir (seventh century). The evidence, however, is very tenuous. The *piyyut* רבות עשית, in the קרובות לפרשת החודש, states that in 2448 years (i.e. from the creation to the Exodus) there had been 900 intercalations. This round figure fits best the 19-year cycle, according to which there would have been, more precisely, 901 or 902 intercalations; whereas other cycles (8-year, 25-year, 30-year cycles) yield results that are far more discrepant (respectively 918, 881, 897 intercalations).

In the סילוק לפרשת שקלים (אז ראית), R. Eleazar ha-Qallir *possibly* refers, implicitly, to twice the great cycle of 532 years, which represents the 19-year cycle of intercalations multiplied by the 28-year cycle of equinoxes or *tequfot*.[166]

It has been argued on purely *astronomical* grounds that the 19-year cycle currently in use must have been instituted in the course of the fourth century,

---

[163] As well as in parallel recensions, which are cited in the later medieval monographs on the calendar: see Bornstein (1922*a*) 337–8. The printed version of *Pirqei de-R. Eliezer* is itself corrupt; see manuscript and other recensions of this passage in Horovitz (1972) 40–1.

[164] See Marmorstein (1921) 254, אדר שני, fo. 8b, ll. 1–3. The *terminus post quem* of R. Pinḥas is based on his reference, in the same text, to the fast commemorating the earthquake of January/Shevat 748 CE (ibid. p. 251, fo. 14a, ll. 11–12; see Gil 1992: 89–90, Elizur 1999: 324–7). How much later than 748 CE R. Pinḥas was writing is impossible to know, but it was certainly well before R. Saadya's period (early 10th c.). Indeed, in his work *Ha'Egron* (fo. 3b, ll. 68–72) R. Saadya mentions Pinḥas as an 'early' poet, distinct from the poets 'close to us (in time)': Allony (1969) 154–5, and with English translation, Davidson (1919) xliii–xlvi; cf Gil (1992) 179 n. 53.

[165] Langermann (1987) 164. For the dating, see above, n. 127. This is not part of the section that may have been later interpolated (see above, section 4.3.1).

[166] For an explanation of this 28-year cycle, see for instance S. Stern (1996) 105 and below, section 5.4.2. The great cycle of 532 years is attested in Slavonic *Enoch* (see section 1.1.4), and was used from the 5th c. CE in Eastern and Western Christian Paschal calendars (Grumel 1958: 127 and 137). It must be emphasized that the figure 532 is not at all explicit in R. Eleazar ha-Qallir's text: all that is stated is that the 'cycle' (מחזור) corresponds (perhaps, approximately) to 22 jubilees (perhaps of 49 years each, yielding 1078 years), or to 6 millennia divided by $5^2/_3$ (which makes 1059 years). A double cycle of 532 years, i.e. 1064 years, is possibly what the passage means.

because only in this period the cycle would have conformed to the true vernal equinox.[167] Indeed, the 19-year cycle assumes an average year length that is slightly longer than the tropical solar year; as a result, it accumulates a discrepancy of approximately one day in 216 years. Nowadays, the discrepancy appears to have reached about 7 days. This suggests that the cycle was instituted in the fourth century, when the discrepancy would have been nil.

This argument—which I shall refer to as the 'astronomical argument'—depends, however, on precisely which rule of the equinox the 19-year cycle would have been based. It is reasonable to assume, indeed, that the 19-year cycle was initially set in such a way as to conform with the rule of the equinox, which was one of the earlier principles of intercalation.[168] Early rabbinic sources are divided, however, as to the exact definition of this rule.[169] Even if we take the ruling of R. Huna b. Avin as definitive for the Babylonian Talmud,[170] the Palestinian rabbinic court, which presumably instituted the 19-year cycle now in use, may have ruled in favour of some other opinion.[171]

Furthermore, as we have seen, the rule of R. Huna b. Avin exists in two very different recensions in our sources, and hence is itself uncertain. If R. Huna b. Avin's rule was that the equinox could not occur after 16 Nisan, the Day of the Sheaf,[172] then in the fourth century, the 19-year cycle would have conformed to the rule of the equinox.[173] But if it was that the equinox could not occur

[167] Wiesenberg (1961) 593–4 and in *Encyclopedia Judaica* v. 48, s.v. Calendar; Loewinger (1998).

[168] Particularly from the 4th c. CE: see above, section 4.2.2.

[169] It is subject to an extensive Tannaitic dispute in *B. Sanhedrin* 12b–13b.

[170] *B. RH* 21a, cited above, section 4.2.2. R. Huna b. Avin's saying may be interpreted as a halakhic decision regarding the Tannaitic dispute: Loewinger (1986) 21, 85–6 (n. 38).

[171] Parallel passages in the Palestinian Talmud are of uncertain interpretation: see *Y. Peah* 5: 1 (18d), *Y. Sheqalim* 1: 2 (46a), *Y. Sanhedrin* 1: 2 (18d). Loewinger (1986: 113–16 nn. 71–2) considers these passages to agree with R. Huna b. Avin's saying in *B. RH* 21a, but this remains debatable. We can safely assume, however, that the 19-year cycle was not based on the Tannaitic opinion that the rule of the equinox depended on the *autumn* equinox (namely that the autumn equinox should not occur after the last day of Tabernacles, 21 Tishre—see above, section 4.1.2). Indeed, the present-day 19-year cycle would have been in violation of the rule of autumn equinox until as late as the early 15th c. (assuming that this rule was based on the astronomical true autumn equinox): Loewinger (1986) 172–4 (n. 131).

[172] As according to the 'second' recension of R. Huna b. Avin's saying, and as I have interpreted it above (section 4.2.2).

[173] Within the 19-year cycle, the 16th year is when Passover occurs the earliest (in relation to the solar year); this year alone is sufficient to establish whether the rule of the equinox is observed. In 378/9 CE (the 16th year of a 19-year cycle, as reckoned in the present-day rabbinic calendar), the vernal equinox (20 March) would have coincided with 16 Nisan, in conformity to the 'second' recension of R. Huna b. Avin's saying. Nowadays, by comparison, in 1993/4 (16th year of the cycle) 16 Nisan was on 28 March, whilst the vernal equinox was on the 20th (at 22: 25), thus a discrepancy of about 8 days. I am assuming that in the 4th c. the month of Nisan

after 14 Nisan, the day of the Passover sacrifice,[174] then the 19-year cycle would not have conformed to the rule of the equinox till the eighth century.[175]

The 'astronomical argument' also depends on the assumption that the 19-year cycle was based on the *astronomical true* equinox. It may have been based, however, on a mean equinox,[176] or even on a simplified schematic calculation. The schematic calculation of the equinox that is found in the Babylonian Talmud[177] is unlikely to have been used as the basis of the present-day 19-year cycle, because then the rule of the equinox would have been regularly breached.[178] But it is not impossible that some other scheme was used.[179] The assumption that the 19-year cycle was based on the astronomical equinox remains therefore to be confirmed.

The 'astronomical argument' depends furthermore on the assumption that the institutors of the 19-year cycle knew exactly when the astronomical true

would have begun on the day of the conjunction; but this was not necessarily the case. If the month began at the sighting of the new moon, the 19-year cycle would have conformed to the rule of the equinox even earlier than in the 4th c. According to Loewinger's definition of the 'second' recension (see section 4.2.2), which is not contingent on the beginning of the calendar month, the 19-year cycle would have conformed to rule of the equinox in the middle of the 4th c. exactly (Loewinger 1998).

[174] As according to the first recension, which is interpreted by medieval commentators as meaning that either 14 or 15 Nisan is the limit of the equinox: see Rashi and *Tosafot* ad *RH* 21a, and with further references, Loewinger (1986) 23–4, 81 nn. 29–30, 86–97 nn. 39–55, 93–4 nn. 52–3. On Maimonides' opinion (*Laws of Sanctification of the New Moon*, 4: 2), see Loewinger (1986) 25–6, 98–111 nn. 58–69, 175–6 nn. 136–7.

[175] In 758/9 CE (the 16th year of a 19-year cycle), the vernal equinox (17 March) would have coincided with 14 Nisan. Loewinger (1986) argues that the 'second' recension (i.e. the rule of 16 days or of 16 Nisan) is more authentic, but this remains largely speculative. See section 4.2.2.

[176] A mean equinox is determined in such a way that the time interval between spring equinox and autumn equinox is the same as between autumn equinox and spring equinox (note that Meeus 1991: 137, 378 uses the term 'mean equinox' in an astronomical, and totally different, sense). In reality, the interval between *true* spring equinox and *true* autumn equinox (the 'summer') is longer than between the *true* autumn equinox and *true* spring equinox (the 'winter'). Consequently, the *mean* spring equinox occurs almost two days after the *true* spring equinox (see Maimonides, *Sanctification of the Moon*, 10: 7).

[177] B. *ʿEruvin* 56a and B. *Berakhot* 59b, later known as *tequfat shemuel*. See section 5.4.2.

[178] According to the calculation of *tequfat shemuel*, the vernal equinox always occurs on 25 or 26 March (of the Julian calendar: see section 2.6.3). But 15 Nisan in the 16th year of the cycle would have occurred, in the 4th c., on 18 or 19 March (e.g. in 341, 360, 379 CE), and in later centuries even earlier in March.

[179] For instance, the fixed dates of 21 or 22 March, assumed in the 4th-c. Alexandrian and Syrian Easter computations (respectively) for the vernal equinox (see section 2.6.3). One of these may conceivably have been borrowed by the rabbinic institutors of the 19-year cycle.

equinox occurred. This could have been roughly determined, with a margin of error of about one day, by observing the azimuths of sunrise and sunset, which are in a straight line with the observer on the day of the equinox.[180] Better results might have been achieved with the help of instruments. A sundial or a gnomon[181] should have made it possible to determine the exact Eastern and Western points on the horizon, where the sun rises and sets on the day of the equinox. However, the gnomon is an instrument that is prone to many imprecisions, as noted by ancient astronomers themselves.[182] Another instrument used by astronomers like Ptolemy for the determination of equinoxes consisted of a ring bronze placed in the plane of the equator (Pedersen 1974: 131 n. 7). However, even an astronomer of Ptolemy's eminence was unable, with these methods, to obtain accurate measurements of the equinox: his results frequently erred by as much as $1\frac{1}{2}$ days.[183] It is thus rather improbable that the rabbinic institutors of the 19-year cycle were able to measure the equinox with sufficient precision.

It should be remembered that a margin of error of one day, in the calculation of the equinox, is sufficient to alter the putative date of the 19-year cycle by as much as two centuries (according to the 'astronomical argument').[184] Thus on a number of accounts, the 'astronomical argument' is far less 'factual' and reliable than at first appearance. Because of the uncertainties that surround this argument, any date between the fourth and eighth centuries could equally be considered.

4.4.6   The calculation of the *molad*: the evidence

The calculated calendar that was adopted by the fourth century (see evidence in section 4.2.3) would probably have been based on the conjunction.[185] This is confirmed, at least, by the epistle of R. Sherira Gaon for the years 499/500 and 505/6 CE (section 4.3.1).

We do not know, however, how exactly the conjunction was calculated by the calendrical court in this period. In the absence of evidence, modern scholars have preferred to ask instead whether, or how early, the present-day *molad* calculation (item 1 in section 4.4.1 above) could have been *known* in rabbinic circles. This question is worthy of attention, even if it does not necessarily indicate when this calculation would have been

---

[180] A method suggested to me by Bernard Yallop.

[181] On this simple astronomical instrument and on its applications, see Ptolemy, *Almagest* 3: 1 (Toomer 1984: 132–4) and 5: 14 (ibid. 252); Pedersen (1974) 105–6; and generally, Evans (1999).

[182] Ptolemy, *Tetrabiblos* 3: 2 (Robbins 1940: 228–31). I am grateful to Uwe Glessmer for the reference.

[183] Petersen and Schmidt (1968) 83–91; Pedersen (1974) 128–32, 148–9. I am grateful to Yaaqov Loewinger for the references.

[184] Since, as noted above, the discrepancy of the 19-year cycle is of approximately one day in 216 years.

[185] As is likely of any calculated lunar calendar: see explanation in section 3.1.2.

used for calendrical purposes *in practice*. In this context, two elements
of the *molad* calculation must be considered: the mean lunation of 29
days, 12 hours, and 793 parts, and the epoch of Monday, 5 hours, 204
parts (*BaHaRaD*) for the molad of Tishre in year 1 (or its equivalent in
the next year: *WeYaD*).

Both these elements, lunation and epoch, are absent in early rabbinic
sources. Although the lunation is mentioned in *B. RH* 25a, this is almost
certainly a later interpolation. The text as we have it reads as follows:

תנו רבנן: פעם אחת נתקשרו שמים בעבים, ונראית דמות לבנה בעשרים ותשעה
לחדש. כסבורים העם לומר ראש חדש, ובקשו בית דין לקדשו. אמר להם רבן
גמליאל: כך מקובלני מבית אבי אבא, אין חדושה של לבנה פחותה מעשרים ותשעה
יום ומחצה ושני שלישי שעה וע״ג חלקים.

Our rabbis taught: once the sky was covered with clouds, and the likeness of the
moon was seen on the 29th of the month. The people were minded to declare
(this day) a new moon, and the court wanted to sanctify it, but R. Gamliel said
to them: 'I have received as a tradition from my father's house, that the renewal
of the moon does not occur after less than 29 days and a half, two-thirds of an
hour, and 73 parts'.

Assuming that the '73 parts' refer to the 1080 parts of the hour, this
lunation is the exactly same as in the present-day rabbinic calendar.[186]
However, the phrase אין חדושה של לבנה פחותה ('not ... less than'),
which implies a *minimal* value, is inappropriate for what should represent
a *fixed* value.

Moreover, the mean lunation is totally out of context in this passage.
The context of this passage is the Mishnaic, empirical calendar, which
is based on the appearance of the new moon; calculation of the *molad*
is therefore irrelevant. R. Gamliel was only establishing that the moon
could not have been sighted on the 29th day of the previous month. All
he could have stated, therefore, was the *minimal number of days* in an
empirical lunar month.

The text before us is likely, therefore, to have been interpolated. This
has been recognized by both ancient and modern scholars.[187] Originally
the text would have read: אין חדושה של לבנה פחותה מעשרים ותשעה יום

---

[186] 793 parts = $2/3$ hour + 73 parts.

[187] R. David Gans (1743) 213 (late 16th c.); Slonimsky (1852) 32 n.; Bornstein
(1904) 129; Jaffe (1931) 40–1. Gans argued slightly differently, that R. Gamliel would
have been referring to the minimal true lunation (i.e. the shortest possible period of
time from one *true* conjunction to the next), which is no less than (approximately) 29
days (more precisely, 29 days and $6\frac{1}{2}$ hours: Meeus 1991: 324; Ajdler 1996: 701).
This suggestion is less likely, because the minimal true lunation is not *entirely* relevant

('not after less than 29 days')—and no more. The interpolation of ומחצה
ושני שלישי שעה וע'ג חלקים ('and a half, two-thirds of an hour, and 73
parts') would have been made by an editor who thought that the mean
lunation—not the minimal number of days in the month—was meant in
this passage. The absence of manuscript evidence does not undermine
this argument; it only suggests that the interpolation must have been
made relatively early, perhaps in the late Geonic period.[188]

Another passage in the Babylonian Talmud implies a lunation that is
very close to that of the present-day. In *B. ʿArakhin* 9b, Ravina suggests
that the regular alternation of 29-day and 30-day months leads to an
error of one day every 3 years, and an additional day every 30 years:

מתקיף לה רבינא: והאיכא יומא דשעי, ויומא דתלתין שני!

Ravina objected: but there is one day (made up) of hours, and one day (in) thirty
years!

Even if Ravina's statement was only based on calendrical experience,
it may have been possible to infer from it the mean lunation of 29½ days,
two-thirds of an hour, and one-fifteenth of an hour. Indeed, the monthly
accumulation of two-thirds of an hour leads to one day every 3 years
(more precisely, every 36 months); whilst the monthly accumulation of
one-fifteenth of an hour leads to one day every 30 years (more precisely,
every 360 months).

The phrase 'one day made up of hours'—rather than 'one day in three
years'—suggests perhaps a calculation based on the monthly addition of
two-thirds of an hour. This would suggest that Ravina's statement was
not merely based on calendrical experience, but also on a calculation,
which may have assumed the mean lunation of 29½ days, two-thirds of
an hour, and one-fifteenth of an hour.

This lunation of 29½ days, two-thirds of an hour, and one-fifteenth of
an hour, which we may convert into 29 days, 12 hours, and 792 parts, and
which could well have been known to Ravina or the Talmudic redactor,
differs from the lunation of the present-day calendar by only one part.

to the length of a month based on sightings of the new moon. Either way, however,
the original text would have read: '29 days' (see below).

[188] The text as we now have it was already cited *c*.1122/3 CE by R. Avraham b.
Ḥiyya, *Sefer haʿIbbur* 2: 2 (Filipowski 1851: 37–8). The inappropriate interpolation of
this mean lunation (or of values derived therefrom) is common in sources of this kind.
It is likely to have occurred in manuscripts of *Pirqei de-R. Eliezer*, ch. 7 (see below),
and definitely occurred, more recently, in Lipkin's edition of *Baraita de-Shemuel ha-
Qatan* (Lipkin 1902: 19a).

This does not prove, however, that the present-day lunation was not known. For this passage is not giving the length of the mean lunation: it is only explaining why a calendar consisting of a regular alternation of 29- and 30-day months is inadequate. The evidence of this passage, therefore, remains somewhat inconclusive.

Also worth noting is Slonimsky's suggestion (1852: 32 n.) that the second half of Ravina's statement ('one day (in) thirty years'), which is inconsistent in wording with the first ('one day made up of hours'), might have been a later interpolation. Bornstein (1904: 130) endorses this view, and argues that the interpolation would have been made in the Arab period, under the influence of the Muslim calendar which intercalates 11 days in 30 lunar years (360 months) of alternate 29- and 30-day months.[189]

As late as the eighth century, there is still no clear evidence of the present-day *molad* calculation. The *Baraita de-Shemuel*, ch. 5, an astronomical work from the later eighth century, appears to have no knowledge of it. Although the *molad* it supplies for Tishre 776 CE, i.e. the beginning of the 4th day of the week, is quite close to that of the present-day rabbinic calendar,[190] the *molad* calculation it is based on in the *Baraita* is substantially different. The epoch of this calculation is Tishre of year 1, beginning of the 4th day (as opposed to *BaHaRaD* in the present-day calculation); the lunation is $29\frac{1}{2}$ days and two-thirds of an hour (i.e. 73 parts short).[191]

The same lunation is implicit in the astronomical sections of the *Pirqei de-R. Eliezer* (chs. 6–8), which dates from around the same period.[192] A large part of ch. 7 presents a 21-year lunar cycle at the end of which the *molad* recurs at the same time and on the same day of the week. This

---

[189] Cf Jaffe (1931) 41–2. The division of the hour into 15 parts (called *ḥil*) is attested in the undatable *Baraita de-Sod ha-ʿIbbur* (Wertheimer and Wertheimer 1953: ii. 39–40), and in an equivalent astronomical sense in *B.Berakhot* 32b (the sphere is divided into 12 signs of the zodiac, each of which is subdivided into 30 *ḥil*).

[190] The *molad* of Tishre 776 CE as reckoned today would have been 4th day, 3 hours, 363 parts: see S. Stern (1996) 120–2.

[191] In the light of the Talmudic passage we have examined above (Ravina's statement), which assumes a considerably more accurate lunation, it is unlikely that the late 8th-c. authors of the *Baraita* believed their own lunation to be accurate. As I have argued elsewhere, the *molad* calculation of the *Baraita* was probably not intended to be used, for practical calendrical purposes, for more than one or two decades (S. Stern 1996: 126–8). Although the *molad* of Tishre 776 CE was clearly calculated on the basis of this inaccurate lunation (ibid. 121–2), this does not mean that the authors of the *Baraita* could not have also corroborated it through more accurate means.

[192] See above, n. 128.

cycle necessarily implies a lunation of 29½ days and two-thirds of an hour, just as in the *Baraita de-Shemuel.*

In the same chapter of *Pirqei de-R. Eliezer*, references are made to the present-day lunation of 29½ days, two-thirds of an hour, and 73 parts, as well as to other values derived from it. This lunation is inconsistent with the 21-year cycle that dominates this chapter. It is likely, therefore, that all the references to 'parts' (e.g. 73 parts) are later interpolations.[193] The references to 'parts' are omitted, indeed, in a number of manuscript recensions,[194] and appear to have been absent in the text of R. Avraham b. Ḥiyya.[195] The original text would thus have read: '29 days, 12 hours, and two-thirds of an hour'.

One element of the present-day *molad* calculation is attested beyond doubt, however, in a liturgical poem of R. Pinḥas, which refers to the division of the hour into 1080 parts.[196] This division of the hour was specifically designated for the lunation of 29 days, 12 hours, and 793 parts; it is not known to have been used in any other context.[197] R. Pinḥas's reference to this division of the hour implies, therefore, knowledge of the present-day lunation. The most likely date for R. Pinḥas is the late eighth or early ninth century, although this remains somewhat conjectural.[198]

An element of the present-day *molad* calculation is also found in *Targum Ps.-Jonathan* ad *Genesis* 1: 16:

ועבד ה׳ ית תרין נהוריא רברביא, והוון שוין באיקרהון, עשרין וחד שעין בציר
מנהון שית מאה ותרין שובעין חולקי שעתא.

And the Lord created the two great luminaries, and they were of equal glory, twenty-one hours less 672 parts of the hour.

---

[193] As argued by Luria (1852), ch. 7 n. 12 (pp. 15b–16a).

[194] In MS Parma 563/41 (Askhenazi script, 13th–14th cc., cited in Horovitz 1972: 40–1), and in MS London, British Library, Or. 11120/1 (Institute of Microfilmed Hebrew Manuscripts, no. 6076; Yemenite, later 17th c.).

[195] *Sefer ha-ʿIbbur* 2: 2 (p. 36) and 2: 4 (p. 40) (cited as the '*baraita* attributed to R. Eliezer').

[196] Fleischer (1984a) 129 (reference courtesy of Shulamit Elizur).

[197] Elsewhere in rabbinic sources, the hour is divided into fractions and sub-fractions of 24, as follows: 1 hour = 24 עונה = 24^2 עת = 24^3 רגע (*T. Berakhot* 1: 3, p. 1, *Y. Berakhot* 1: 1 (2d), *Lamentations Rabbah* 2: 19). The same division, but expressed differently, is mentioned by R. Eleazar ha-Qallir in the סילוק לפרשת שקלים (אז ראית); he mentions there that some subdivide the hour even further. For an apparently different division of the hour, see *B. Berakhot* 7a (see Lieberman 1956: 2).

[198] For the dating of R. Pinḥas, see above, n. 164.

There can be no doubt that this is a cryptic reference to a *molad* of (4th day), 20 hours, 408 parts (since 1080 − 672 = 408), which corresponds exactly to the *molad* of the 12th month before *BaHaRaD*. Ps.-Jonathan appears to have agreed that the *molad* of what is generally termed 'year 1' was *BaHaRaD*; however, he assumed that the world was created 12 months earlier, in such a way that the first *molad* would have coincided with a Wednesday (4th day), the day of the week when the luminaries were created. Ps.-Jonathan appears to ignore the fact that according to the present-day 19-year cycle, the year before *BaHaRaD* would have been intercalated, so that the Tishre before *BaHaRaD* should actually have occurred *13* months earlier. Nevertheless, it is clear that Ps.-Jonathan assumed the same lunation and the same conjunctions (e.g. *BaHaRaD*) as in the present-day *molad* calculation; he only differed as to when the luminaries were created.

The value of this source depends again on our ability to date it. The *Targum Ps.-Jonathan* is generally ascribed to the seventh or eighth century,[199] but in this kind of text, later interpolations are never to be excluded. There are good reasons, indeed, to believe that this passage is an interpolation. The negative wording of this passage ('21 hours less 672 parts'), when the Targum could more easily have said '20 hours and 408 parts', suggests perhaps that the reference to parts is a later addition, whereas the original text would simply have read: '21 hours'. The origin and meaning of these 21 hours would remain, however, unclear.

The earliest *datable* reference to the present-day *molad* calculation is in the work of the Muslim astronomer al-Khwarizmi on the Jewish calendar, dating from 823/4 CE, where the lunation of 29 days, 12 hours, and 793 parts, is explicitly given.[200] As stated above, all this indicates is that the present-day lunation would have been *known*, if al-Khwarizmi is to be believed, by the Jews in his period; but it does not necessarily prove that it was used for calendrical purposes *in practice*.[201] The *theoretical* nature of al-Khwarizmi's work may be confirmed by the fact that the epoch of *BaHaRaD* (or some equivalent), just as the epoch of

---

[199] Shinan (1985) 87. See, however, Hayward (1991).

[200] Langermann (1987) 164. For the dating, see above, n. 127. Al-Khwarizmi's reference to the lunation is *not* part of the section that may have been later interpolated (see above, section 4.3.1).

[201] See above, section 4.3.1, and my general remarks at the beginning of this section (4.4.6).

the 19-year cycle, is omitted entirely in this work—which effectively renders the calculation of the *molad* impossible.[202]

Nevertheless, the exilarch's letter of 835/6 CE suggests that already in this period, the rabbinic calendar may have been based on the same *molad* calculation as today. For the exilarch gives the *molad* of Nisan 836 CE as follows:

משום סיהרא דניסן דקא מיתליד ביממא דתלתה בש[ב]ה בארבע [ש]עות[203]

... because the moon of Nisan is to be born[204] on the day of the 3rd of the week (Tuesday) at 4 hours ...

According to the present-day calculation, the *molad* of Nisan 836 CE would have occurred on Tuesday, 15th hour, and 861 parts. On this basis, Bornstein (1922*a*: 347–9) simply inferred that the exilarch's *molad* was discrepant from ours (in the present-day rabbinic calendar) by 11 or 12 hours. An error of 12 hours, however, is most unlikely to have been made by someone who had an interest, even if moderate, in the cycle of the moon. The correct interpretation, which most scholars have endorsed,[205] is that the '4 hours' in this letter relate to the 12-hour period of *daytime*, and not to the 24-hour night-and-day period.[206] Accordingly, the exilarch's *molad* would be very close to ours—ours occurring at the 3rd hour of day time and 861 parts, thus only 1080 − 861 = 219 parts before the exilarch's 4 hours.

It is possible, therefore, that the present-day calculation of the *molad* was already in use in the exilarch's period: for the exilarch's 'four hours' may simply be a round expression of the *molad* as calculated today.

---

[202] See Sar-Shalom (1988) 41–7. In datable sources, the epoch of the *molad* is only expressed for the first time in the 10th c. It is implicit throughout the correspondence of R. Saadya and Ben Meir, whose *moladot* were identical with those of the present-day rabbinic calendar (see section 5.4.6). The epoch of *WeYaD* is explicitly given in the monograph on the intercalation by Yehoshua b. ʿAllan, an apparent contemporary of R. Saadya, ed. A. Harkavy, *Ha-Goren* 4 (1903), pp. 75–80, see pp. 75–6.

[203] Recto, ll. 9–10, in my reading (see appendix).

[204] This expression, just like the substantive *molad* (lit. 'birth'), refers to the conjunction (see *B. RH* 20b).

[205] First proposed by Mann (1920–2) i. 52.

[206] The word ביממא ('on the day of') would thus be a specific reference to *daytime*. This interpretation does not contradict the exilarch's prediction (recto, ll. 11–13; verso, ll. 7–9) that the new moon would be visible on the following evening (i.e. Tuesday evening)—*pace* Akavia (1951/2) 124; see my remarks above, n. 107.

4.4.7 The origins of the present-day rabbinic *molad*

Already in the early twelfth century, R. Avraham b. Ḥiyya acknowledged that the rabbinic mean lunation of 29 days, 12 hours, and 793 parts, was identical with Ptolemy's in his second-century-CE classic work of astronomy, the *Almagest*.[207] The coincidence was too remarkable to be fortuitous. R. Avraham b. Ḥiyya explained it away, rather apologetically, by claiming that Hipparchos (second century BCE, Ptolemy's source) had taken this lunation from the early Jewish sages—the ancestors of R. Gamliel referred to in *B. RH* 25a.[208]

In modern historical terms, it seems far more plausible to assume, on the contrary, that it was the rabbis who borrowed their lunation from Ptolemy. It also appears, indeed, that the epoch assumed in the rabbinic calculation of the *molad* (*BaHaRaD* or *WeYaD*) was based on that of Ptolemy.

The epoch assumed by Ptolemy for the mean conjunction is $0^d\ 44^i\ 17^{ii}$ after noon on 24 Thoth in year 1 of Nabonassar, which is equivalent to 22 March 747 BCE at 5.42 a.m.[209] The *molad*, according to the rabbinic computation, would have occurred on the same day and almost at the same time: 6.30 a.m. Consequently, all the *moladot* in the rabbinic calendar occur only about 50 minutes later than Ptolemy's mean conjunctions.

This discrepancy of about 50 minutes can be partly explained by the fact that Ptolemy's figures were based on the longitude of Alexandria, whereas the rabbinic *molad* would have been based on a longitude further east, perhaps that of Jerusalem. This would reduce the discrepancy by over 20 minutes.[210]

In addition, Loewinger has correctly pointed out that account must be taken of the equation of time (in modern terms: the difference between true and mean time), which Ptolemy himself was aware of and tabulated in his works (Pedersen 1974: 154–8). Ptolemy's equation of time would have necessitated an

---

[207] R. Avraham b. Ḥiyya, *Sefer ha-ʿIbbur* 2: 2 (Filipowski 1851: 37), referring to Ptolemy's *Almagest* 4: 2 (Toomer 1984: 176). Ptolemy expresses his lunation in the Babylonian sexagesimal system, as $29^d\ 31^i\ 50^{ii}\ 8^{ii}, 20^{iv}$—where 1^i represents $1/60$ of the day, 1^{ii} represents $1/60$ of 1^i, etc. (see Pedersen 1974: 50–2). It amounts to exactly the same as the rabbinic lunation. The figures supplied by R. Avraham b. Ḥiyya for Ptolemy's lunation are actually different: see on this the pertinent remarks of Bornstein (1927) 18–19 n. 3, and Wiesenberg (1961) 568–9.

[208] R. Avraham b. Ḥiyya, *Sefer ha-ʿIbbur* 2: 2 (Filipowski 1851: 37–8). On *B. RH* 25a, see above section 4.4.6. Isaac Israeli argued that Ptolemy obtained his lunation independently from the rabbis, on the grounds that Ptolemy's lunation was actually slightly shorter (see Wiesenberg 1961: 568–9; Isaac Israeli, *Yesod ʿOlam*, 3: 12 (Goldberg 1848: i. 49a–50a), also 4: 7 (ibid. ii. 12a)).

[209] *Almagest* 6: 2 (Toomer 1984: 275). For an explanation of this epoch, see also Toomer (1984) 9; Pedersen (1974) 125–7.

[210] Bornstein (1904) 34–5, (1922a) 353; Jaffe (1931) 106–9; Sar-Shalom (1984) 29.

adjustment of the time of *molad* Tishre (the rabbinic epoch). Assuming that this adjustment was made, the discrepancy between the rabbinic epoch of *BaHaRaD* or *WeYaD* and Ptolemy's would be reduced to only a few minutes.[211]

It may also be presumed, finally, that the epoch of *WeYaD*, being a round figure (i.e. days and hours, but no parts), was deliberately rounded off.[212] This would account for any minor discrepancy between Ptolemy's mean conjunction and the rabbinic *molad*.

There are strong grounds, therefore, to conclude that the rabbinic epoch is in substance identical to Ptolemy's, and thus that it was directly derived from the latter.

The assumption that the *molad* calculation of the present-day rabbinic calendar was taken from Ptolemy led Bornstein, Jaffe, and others to conclude that it could not have been instituted before the ninth century. This is because Ptolemy's *Almagest* was not known to astronomers in the Near East before its translation into Arabic in the early ninth century, under the initiative of the Abbasid Caliphs.[213] It is likely that knowledge of Ptolemy's calculation of the conjunction was only then transmitted to the Jews, who soon incorporated it into the fixed rabbinic calendar.[214] Although somewhat conjectural, this theory remains completely plausible, particularly as evidence of the present-day *molad* calculation only begins to emerge in the early ninth century.

Other options, however, must also be considered. More recent scholars have drawn attention to the fact—largely unnoticed by Bornstein and Jaffe—that the Babylonian astronomers employed exactly the same mean lunation as Ptolemy, centuries before Ptolemy composed his work.[215] It is most likely, indeed, that Ptolemy's lunation was borrowed from Babylonian astronomy.[216] This raises the possibility that the rabbinic calendar-makers may have taken their lunation directly from the Babylonians, without resorting to Ptolemy's *Almagest*. If so, the rabbinic lunation could have been adopted long before the early ninth century.[217]

This theory—equally conjectural—depends on the extent to which Babylonian astronomy would have survived after the first century CE,

---

[211] Y. Loewinger, unpublished paper.

[212] Artificially rounded figures were also assumed in the rabbinic calendar for the epoch of the *tequfot* (equinoxes and solstices), according to both the schemes of Shemuel and of R. ʾAda. See S. Stern (1996) 104–11.

[213] On which see Pedersen (1974) 14–15.

[214] Bornstein (1904) 33, (1922*a*) 344–6, 349–53; Jaffe (1931) 102–8 (chs. 16–17).

[215] i.e. $29^d\ 31^i\ 50^{ii}\ 8^{iii}\ 20^{iv}$: Neugebauer (1955) i. 70, 78.

[216] Pedersen (1974) 162–3; Toomer (1988).

[217] Neugebauer (1949) 323–4; Langermann (1987) 159–60.

when cuneiform writing, including Babylonian astronomical records, appear to have completely ceased. Contacts between rabbis and Babylonian astronomers are unlikely to have developed before the Amoraic period. Shemuel, a first-generation Babylonian Amora (early third century) is known in the Talmud for his astronomical interests, and may have conversed with (pagan) Babylonians about these matters (see below, section 5.4.2). However, there is no evidence that classical Babylonian astronomy was still practised or known in this later period.[218]

On purely astronomical grounds, Loewinger has argued that the *molad* of the present-day rabbinic calendar must have been instituted in the fourth century, when it would have coincided with an astronomically accurate mean conjunction (nowadays, they are about two hours apart).[219]

This 'astronomical argument' assumes, however, that fourth-century rabbis were able to carry out their own astronomical observations, and to calculate on this basis an astronomically accurate mean conjunction. In my view, this assumption is unwarranted (cf above, section 4.4.5).[220]

This theory, moreover, only accounts for the *epoch* of the rabbinic *molad*. That the lunation of 29 days, 12 hours, and 793 parts was borrowed from either Ptolemy or the Babylonian astronomers remains, however, almost irrefutable.

Whether the *molad* calculation was borrowed from Babylonian astronomers, or from an Arabic translation of Ptolemy's *Almagest* that would have been made at the ninth-century Abbasid capital of Baghdad, in the heartland of Babylonia, the *geographical* origins of this *molad*

---

[218] See Neugebauer (1949) 323. Geller (1997) argues for the survival of Babylonian cuneiform knowledge until the beginning of Sasanian rule in the 3rd c.; he also contends (1997: 56–8) that Shemuel would have learnt astronomy from Babylonian scholars. On both points, however, his argument is entirely conjectural and lacks concrete substantiation. For a more cautious assessment, see Millar (1993) 489–523. The rabbinic division of the day into fractions and subfractions of 24, which is attested in a number of Palestinian sources (see above, n. 197) and which differs from the Babylonian sexagesimal system of fractions and subfractions of 60 (see above, n. 207), indicates at least that the influence of Babylonian time-reckoning over *Palestinian* rabbis would have been limited.

[219] This present-day two-hour discrepancy between the *molad* and the accurate mean conjunction is the cumulative result of a slight inaccuracy in the rabbinic (i.e. Ptolemy's) mean lunation. See Loewinger (1998).

[220] Moreover, Loewinger's argument depends entirely on the reliability of his Δt (see Ch. 3 n. 33): in this context, indeed, an error of minutes could severely undermine his theory. The speculative nature of Δt casts further doubt on Loewinger's theory. According to Bernard Yallop, however, the correction for Δt is unlikely to change much in the future (pers. comm.).

would have been the same. It was in Babylonia, indeed, that this *molad* would have become known to the Jews and incorporated into the present-day rabbinic calendar.

This comes rather as a surprise. For it was the *Palestinian* rabbinic court, as we have seen, that set and controlled the calendar until as late as the ninth century—as explicitly indicated in the exilarch's letter of 835/6 CE. It is paradoxical, therefore, that the *molad*, one of the most fundamental principles of the present-day rabbinic calendar, should have drawn its roots from Babylonia, the seat of Palestine's rival rabbinic schools.

To understand this paradox, we must evaluate the history of the rabbinic calendar in its wider social context. As we shall see in the next chapter, the calendar came to epitomize the complex relations between the Palestinian and Babylonian centres of the Amoraic and Geonic periods.

5

Calendar and community: the emergence of the normative Jewish calendar

The most significant development in the rabbinic calendar of the first millennium CE was its transition from an empirical system to a fixed, calculated scheme. This change has been described in some detail in the previous chapter; but why it occurred remains entirely to be explained.

The traditional explanation is that the fixed calendar was instituted because of persecutions and unfavourable political conditions. This theory, together with others, will be assessed in detail in this chapter. It will become clear that the change that occurred to the rabbinic calendar was less the result of external pressures than of internal historical processes. As I shall argue, the emergence of the fixed rabbinic calendar went hand in hand with the development of the rabbinic community of the late Roman period.

One of the distinctive characteristics of the rabbinic community in late Antiquity and the early Middle Ages was its gradual geographic expansion. From being mostly confined to Judaea until the early second century CE, the rabbinic community had spread to Galilee by the middle of this century, after the Bar-Kokhba revolt of 132–5 CE; it then spread to Babylonia in the early third century, with the first generation of Amoraim. In the course of the Geonic period, rabbinic Judaism was to expand further afield to Egypt, North Africa, and southern and western Europe, and eventually to dominate the whole of world Jewry. Throughout this period of expansion, the question of solidarity, cohesion, and *communitas* between the various rabbinic communities became increasingly pressing. In this context, I shall argue, the calendar came to play a decisive role. The institution of a standard, fixed calendar was a significant contributor to the unity of the rabbinic community or—as the rabbis saw it—of the Jewish people.

Central to this process, throughout this period, was the Babylonian rabbinic community. Its complex relationship with the Palestinian community, which remained nominally in charge of the calendar until the end of the Geonic period, will prove critical to our understanding of the evolution of the rabbinic calendar in this period, and of the dominance which it eventually achieved in the later medieval and the modern period.

5.1 WHY THE RABBINIC CALENDAR CHANGED: SOME THEORIES

A variety of theories have been suggested, since the higher medieval period, as to why the Mishnaic system was abandoned in favour of a calculated calendar. These theories, which will be examined in the first part of this chapter, are not mutually exclusive; indeed, each may contain an element of truth. On further examination, however, these theories often turn out to be either implausible or inadequate.

5.1.1 The persecution theory

The traditional and generally accepted theory accounting for the institution of the fixed calendar is what I shall call the 'persecution theory'. This theory does not have a single formulation, but its numerous variants all share the following notions in common:

(i) The change from an empirical to a fixed calendar was the result of a situation of *crisis*, which was precipitated by social and/or political conditions in Palestine of the fourth century.[1] This crisis consisted, according to most accounts, of persecution at the hands of the Romans or Christians. However, not all accounts imply an actual *persecution*. In this respect, the name I have given this theory—purely for convenience—can sometimes be misleading.

(ii) The upshot of this crisis was that the empirical calendar system became unmanageable and impossible to maintain. This may have been due to the demise of the rabbinic, calendrical court, upon which the empirical calendar had hitherto depended; to Roman disruption of the rabbinic calendrical procedure; to poor communications, making it difficult for witnesses to travel to the court and for messengers to travel to

---

[1] For the date of the change to a fixed calendar, see above, section 4.2.3.

Diaspora communities; or to any other factor which may have hindered the proper functioning of the empirical calendar.

(iii) In these circumstances, the rabbinic court decided to do away with empirical procedures, and to institute instead a fixed calendar calculation.

The first proponents of this theory go back to the twelfth century. Maimonides gives it a terse but clear formulation. In his view, the fixed calendar was instituted because of the destruction of the land (i.e. of the Jewish community in Palestine) and the complete cessation of the rabbinic court:

בעת שחרבה ארץ ישראל ולא נשאר שם בית דין קבוע

(Calculation was instituted) . . . at the time when the Land of Israel was destroyed and no permanent court was left.[2]

According to R. Tuviah b. Eliezer, writing earlier in the twelfth century, the cessation of the rabbinic court was not the result of destruction, but rather of exile abroad:

ובזמן שהיו ישראל שרוין על אדמתם, היו מקדשין את החדש על פי ראיית העדים; וכשגלו, אין בית דין קבוע לחקור ולדרוש עמדו ישראל על תקנות סוד העיבור שהיו מחשבין מאדם

When Israel were settled in their land, they used to sanctify the month on the basis of observation by witnesses; but when they went into exile, there was no permanent court to investigate and examine (the matter) . . . they followed the rules of the secret of intercalation which had been calculated since the day of Adam . . .[3]

---

[2] Maimonides, *Laws of Sanctification of the New Month*, 5: 3. Cf Maimonides' *Book of Commandments*, positive commandment 153: 'observation (of the new moon) is no longer in practice nowadays, because of the absence of a High Court'. Maimonides' view is accepted by Nahmanides (13th c.), who only differs in that it was rabbinic ordination, rather than the rabbinic high court, which (in his opinion) ceased: see Nahmanides' comments on Maimonides' *Book of Commandments*, ibid.; Nahmanides, *Sefer ha-Zekhut*, on *B. Gittin* 36a; also the *Novellae* of his disciple, R. Yom Tov Ishbili (Ritva), on *B. Sukkah* 43a. Maimonides' view is also accepted by Meiri, *Beit ha-Behirah* on *B. Sanhedrin* 13a (A. Sofer ed. 40), who emphasizes the impossibility of observing the Mishnaic calendar after the cessation of the rabbinic courts.

[3] R. Tuviah b. Eliezer, *Midrash Leqah Tov*, on Exod. 12: 2 (Buber 1884: ii. 27b); cited in full with translation by Ankori (1959) 270 and n. 53. In this context, 'secret of intercalation' clearly means the fixed rabbinic calendar, which the author believes was known, at least as a theoretical calendar, since the beginning of history (see Ankori ibid.; on the phrase 'secret of intercalation', see above, section 4.3.3).

Decline of the rabbinic court is also assumed, in the same period, by R. Yaʿaqov b. Shimshon (writing in 1123/4), although he does not specify whether this was due to destruction of the land or exile. Referring to the 'sons of Issachar', by which he designates the institutors of the fixed calendar,[4] he states:

כי ראו סנהדרין בטלה והולכת, וחקרו בסוד העיבור לדעת מה יעשה ישראל, וציינו להם שערים לתכונת המועדים וראשי השערים (צ'ל: השנים?).

For they saw that the Sanhedrin was declining, so they studied the 'secret of intercalation' to know what Israel should do, and designed tables for the calculation of festivals and new (?) years.[5]

A different approach is taken by R. Zeraḥiah ha-Levi in his *Sefer ha-Maʾor*. According to him, it was not cessation of the court, but rather poor communications in fourth-century Palestine that led the empirical procedure to be discontinued:

מימי הלל בן יהודה בן רבינו הקדוש, שהנהיג לקדש על פי החשבון ו<לא> על פי הראייה, מדוחק הגלות, שלא היו העדים מצויין ללכת להעיד לפני בית דין, ולא השלוחים לכל המקומות יכולין לצאת להודיע קידוש בית דין, משום שבוש דרכים.

... in the days of Hillel b. Yehudah son of our holy Rabbi,[6] who instituted a calendar based on calculation and not on observation, because of the pressure of exile, (i.e.) that there were no witnesses to go and testify before the court, and court envoys were not able to go to all places and announce the court's decisions, because of the disruption of the roads.[7]

A further, earlier version of the 'persecution theory' is cited by al-Biruni (1879: 67, written c.1000 CE) as one of the Rabbanite views: namely that the fixed calendar was instituted because the Samaritans had disrupted the beacons system (through which calendrical decisions were disseminated, according to *M. RH* 2: 2–4). This, however, is clearly a misinterpretation of *M. RH* 2: 2, which states that disruption of the beacons system at the hands of the Samaritans led only to its replacement with the sending of messengers.[8]

---

[4] See above, section 4.2.4.

[5] *Sefer ha-ʿIbbur* (see Ch. 4 n. 95), ch. 32 (fo. 94a–b), cited in Bornstein (1922a) 328 n. 1 and 363; see also ch. 37 (fos. 98a–99a), cited in Bornstein ibid. 328. On R. Yaʿaqov b. Shimshon's *Sefer ha-ʾAlqushi*, see Grossman (1995) 418–23.

[6] For a critical assessment of this tradition, see section 4.2.4. When and by whom the new calendar was instituted does not concern us here; all I wish to address is *why* it was instituted.

[7] *Ha-Maʾor ha-Qatan* on *RH*, ch. 1 (5b at the top, in the Vilna edition of the *Rif*).

[8] As pointed out by Akavia (1950) 339–40.

This theory has been repeated in later rabbinic monographs on the calendar until the modern period.[9] Most modern scholars have also endorsed this theory (e.g. Baron 1952: ii. 209), though not without modifications. Indeed, some medieval assumptions about fourth-century Palestine have had to be discarded in the light of modern scholarship. The notion of *decline or death* of the Palestinian rabbinic court in the fourth century, a centrepiece of Maimonides' argument, has been proved wrong by sources from the Geonic period, many of which have come to light in the Cairo Geniza, that reveal continuous rabbinic activity in Palestine throughout the first millennium CE.[10]

Likewise, the notion that *exile* precipitated the institution of a fixed calendar has been ignored in modern scholarship, because of the absence of evidence of Jewish emigration from Palestine in the fourth century, when the fixed calendar was introduced.[11] Quite on the contrary, archaeological evidence suggests the persistence of populous Jewish communities in Palestine in the fourth and fifth centuries.[12]

Furthermore, as Lieberman (1946) has demonstrated, there is little or no evidence of Roman *persecution* in third- and fourth-century Palestine. Contemporary Palestinian rabbinic sources make no references to such persecutions.[13] The large number of monumental Palestinian synagogues dating from the fourth to the sixth centuries suggests a prosperous Jewish community that was far from contemplating destruction.[14] Its economic success must have depended on safe communications and reasonable standards of political security. This casts considerable doubt

---

[9] For the later medieval period, see e.g. Nahmanides, ibid. (above, n. 2); Isaac Israeli, *Yesod 'Olam*, 4: 6 (Goldberg 1848: ii. 10b), 4: 9 (ibid. 16b), 4: 14 (29b), 4: 18 (35b–36a).

[10] Because of the importance of this question for the history of the rabbinic calendar, H. Y. Bornstein devoted an entire article to it (Bornstein 1919). It is true that for an unknown reason the Patriarchate came to an end in 429 CE, but this has little bearing on the continuity of the rabbinic calendrical court, which is still documented, for instance, in the exilarch's letter of 835/6 CE (see below, appendix). See in general Gil (1992).

[11] Exile *may* have been forced upon Jews of Palestine in the 1st and 2nd cc., in the aftermath of the great Jewish revolts against Rome; but there is no evidence of substantial emigration in later centuries.

[12] See for instance the evidence in Levine (1981), E. Stern *et al.* (1993).

[13] Only later rabbinic sources refer to large-scale persecutions in 4th-c. Palestine: *Iggeret R. Sherira Gaon* (written in 987 CE), in Lewin (1920) 61 (cited by Ajdler 1996: 695).

[14] See above, n. 12.

on R. Zeraḥiah ha-Levi's notion of 'disruption of the roads', as well as on Maimonides' notion of 'destruction' of the Palestinian settlement.

Nevertheless, one incident of persecution and destruction is known to have occurred on a fairly large scale in the early 350s, in retaliation for the Jewish insurrection under Constantius and Gallus. The coincidence of this date with that of Hillel's institution (359 CE) provided reasonable grounds for Graetz to hypothesize that these events were linked. To cite:

The deplorable condition of Judaea led the then patriarch Hillel II to perform a deed of great self-denial. The method hitherto in vogue (i.e. the empirical calendar) . . . had become impracticable and often impossible on account of Constantius' persecutions. . . . As a consequence, the days on which the most important festivals were to fall remained in doubt. To put an end to all the difficulties and uncertainties, Hillel II introduced a fixed calendar for all time . . . (Graetz 1919: ii. 410–11).

The 'persecution' theory was thus reinstated in a modern, revised form. Among other scholars who since reiterated this theory is Jaffe, who argues that the foundations of the fixed calendar were already laid down by R. Akiva, under the pressure of Roman persecutions during and after the Bar-Kokhba revolt of 132–5 CE, but that it was similar persecutions in the mid fourth century that led Hillel to institute a permanent fixed calendar.[15]

But even if the Hillel tradition is considered reliable—which, as I have argued in the previous chapter, is by no means certain—it is difficult to accept that the short-lived crisis of the Gallus revolt, which appears to have been exceptional, and from which the Jewish community appears to have recovered soon after, would have led Hillel to institute a *permanent* change in the Jewish calendar. For this reason, Lieberman (1946: 330–4, 1974: 113–17) rejects Graetz's explanation and suggests instead that the persecutions which led to Hillel's institution consisted of *specific* decrees by the Christian Imperial authorities against the Jewish *calendar*. Lieberman argues that in order to prevent the dissident churches of the East, after the council of Nicaea, from observing Easter at the same time as the Jews,[16] the Christian Roman emperors prohibited

the Patriarch to compute and proclaim in advance the date of Passover; and especially to dispatch messengers, who had to take roads to the Jewish diaspora in the East, which ran through Syria and Mesopotamia. The sectarian churches of these

---

[15] Jaffe (1931) ch. 4. See also Sar-Shalom (1984) 25, for an endorsement of his views.

[16] See on this above, sections 2.5.1 and 2.5.4.

countries would thus be deprived of information about the date of Passover...
the Patriarch concluded that the measure was not a temporary one and consequently created a permanent calendar.[17]

Lieberman's theory, however, is completely unsubstantiated. The absence of any external evidence, in either Christian or Roman legal
sources, of any imperial prohibition against Patriarchal calendar reckoning, casts considerable doubt on its historical validity.[18]

Internal evidence from contemporary rabbinic sources is also, at best,
sporadic, although it deserves more detailed examination. Lieberman's
main source—also adduced by other modern scholars in support of the
'persecution theory'—is a cryptic message, cited in the Babylonian Talmud, that was sent from Palestine to Rava—significantly, perhaps, as he
lived at the same time or not long before Hillel. This message appears
to have conveyed, in riddles, that envoys of the rabbinic court had been
intercepted by the Roman authorities:

שלחו ליה לרבא: זוג בא מרקת, ותפשו נשר, ובידו[19] דברים הנעשים[20] בלוז - ומאי
ניהו? תכלת. בזכות הרחמן[21] ובזכותם יצאו בשלום. ועמוסי יריכי נחשון בקשו
לקבוע נציב אחד, ולא הניחן אדומי הלז. אבל בעלי אסופות נאספו, וקבעו לו
נציב אחד בירח שמת בו אהרן הכהן.

They sent (this message) to Rava:

A couple was coming from Raqat, but an eagle captured it. In its hands were
things made in Luz—and what are these? purple.[22] Through the merit of the
Merciful and through their own merit, they got out safely.

And the offspring of Naḥshon's loins wished to establish a *netziv*, but that
Edomite did not allow them. However, the members of assemblies assembled
and established one *netziv* in the month in which Aaron the Priest died (*B.
Sanhedrin* 12a).

---

[17] Lieberman (1946) 334 (1974: 117). This theory is endorsed by Schäfer
(1995) 179.

[18] The prohibition, under Justinian, on Jews' celebrating Passover too early was
issued two centuries after the institution of a fixed calendar, and is anyway unlikely,
for reasons explained above, to have had the rabbinic calendar as its principal target:
see above, section 2.6.1.

[19] So in the Soncino edition (1495) and most manuscripts. Venice and other editions read: ובידם, i.e. in their (the couple's) hand.

[20] So in all manuscripts. Printed editions read, ungrammatically: הנעשה.

[21] So in all manuscripts and Soncino edition. Venice and other editions: הרחמים.

[22] This is a Talmudic gloss.

Some elements of this message can be decoded, although the general meaning remains somewhat unclear. Raqat is presumably Tiberias,[23] the seat of the Jewish Patriarchate in Palestine. The eagle represents the Roman authorities—owing perhaps to its effigy on Roman army standards—as does the 'Edomite' further below. The couple in question, presumably two men, were captured by the Romans for a reason that is not made explicit; perhaps, for attempting to smuggle 'things made in Luz', i.e., according to the Talmudic gloss, the special purple required for the manufacture of *tzitzit*.[24] Why Rava needed to be told of their capture and eventual release is not explained.

The message goes on to report what is perhaps, or perhaps not, a separate incident, involving the attempt to establish a *netziv*. This term generally means 'officer'; but 'officer' does not fit the verb 'establish', לקבוע ('appoint' would have been more suitable). The Talmud (further on) interprets the term *netziv* as 'month', on the basis of 1 Kgs. 4: 7–19. Accordingly, the descendants of Nahshon—i.e. the Patriarchate[25]—would have been prevented by the Romans from establishing a thirteenth month,[26] i.e. from intercalating the year; but the 'members of assemblies'—perhaps the same as the 'offspring of Nahshon'— successfully intercalated the year, during the month of Av.[27]

Why the Romans objected to this intercalation is not explained. The Talmud's interpretation of this message appears rather implausible, because intercalation is unlikely to have been, to the Romans, a matter of concern.[28] The original meaning of this cryptic message may actually have been different. It is perhaps more likely, in historical terms, that the message originally referred to the appointment of an officer (*netziv*) by the patriarch, to which the Romans may have objected for whatever

[23] So in R. Hananel and Rashi's commentaries, on the basis on *B. Megillah* 6a; also in the Talmudic commentary attributed to R. Nahshon (later 9th c.), in Assaf (1942) 154.

[24] See Rashi, citing *B. Sotah* 46b. *Tzitzit* are the fringes referred to in Num. 15: 37–41.

[25] So R. Hananel and Rashi. The patriarchs traced themselves to the house of David: see *B. Sanhedrin* 5a; *Genesis Rabbah* 98: 8.

[26] The phrase נציב אחד ('one *netziv*') might be a direct citation from 1 Kgs. 4: 19, where it corresponds to the thirteenth.

[27] Aaron died on the first day of the 5th month: Num. 33: 38. See Wacholder and Weisberg (1971) 237. The commentary attributed to R. Nahshon (later 9th c.) reports that until his day, intercalations were made in the month of Av (Assaf 1942: 154, see comments on p. 147).

[28] Justinian's decree (in the 6th c.) suggests, if anything, that the Christian authorities would have preferred the Jews to intercalate the year: see section 2.6.1.

political reasons. On balance, the obscurity of this passage prevents us from reaching any firm conclusions.

More conclusive perhaps is another passage cited by Lieberman and others,[29] in *B. Hullin* 101b, where the Talmud attempts to explain a ruling that was sent (presumably, from Palestine) by R. Yitzhaq b. Yaʿaqov b. Giyore in the name of R. Yohanan. This ruling suggests, surprisingly, that when the day of Atonement occurs on the Sabbath, a person who transgresses by working would not be liable on account of the day of Atonement, but only on account of the Sabbath.[30] After rejecting Abaye's explanation, Rava suggests that this ruling was referring to exceptional circumstances:

אמר רבא: שמדא הוה, ושלחו מתם דיומא דכפורי דהא שתא שבתא הוא. וכן כי אתא רבין וכל נחותי, אמרוה כרבא.

Rava said: there was a persecution, and they sent (a message) from there (from Palestine) that the day of Atonement, that year, was on the Sabbath.

And so, when Ravin and all the immigrants came (to Babylonia from Palestine), they explained (this ruling) like Rava.

In the context of this passage, Rava appears to mean that because of a 'persecution', the *wrong* message was sent from Palestine to Babylonia: in truth, the day of Atonement was not meant to occur, in that year, on a Sabbath. Because the day of Atonement did not *really* occur on that Sabbath, one would not have been liable, on that day, for transgressing the day of Atonement.

Rava's account, however, is difficult to comprehend. Medieval commentators are at pains to explain why persecution should have caused the wrong message to be sent. It must be noted, moreover, that Rava's saying is not a statement of historical fact, but only a *hypothesis* for resolving the Talmudic problem (i.e. the meaning of R. Yitzhaq b. Yaʿaqov b. Giyore's ruling).

Medieval commentators have explained the *B. Hullin* passage, and in particular the precise nature of the 'persecution', in a variety of ways. According to Rashi and Ps.-R. Gershom (ad loc.), the Romans had prohibited the observance of the day of Atonement; in order not to forget it entirely, the rabbis decided to observe it on another day, on a Sabbath, when its observance would be less conspicuous. Because the day of Atonement did not *really* occur on that Sabbath, one would not have been liable, on that day, for transgressing the day of Atonement.

---

[29] e.g. Graetz (1919) ii. 407–8.

[30] The halakhic argument is actually more complex, but this simplified rendition is sufficient for our purposes.

According to this interpretation, Rava would be implying that a false message had been *deliberately* sent from Palestine about the date of the day of Atonement (see also *Arukh*, s.v. *shemad*). Other commentators suggest, along similar lines, that the Romans prohibited calendar reckoning entirely.[31]

Others understand this passage completely differently: Rava only meant that the envoys of the calendrical court were *delayed* because of a persecution, as in the passage in *B. Sanh.* 12a, so that the news that the day of Atonement coincided with the Sabbath only arrived in Babylonia after the day was over.[32] In such a case, liability for transgressing the day of Atonement would not have applied.[33]

Even if the passages from *B. Sanhedrin* and *B. Ḥullin* suggest that persecution could occasionally disrupt the calendar, there is no indication whatsoever that this would have led to the institution of a fixed calendar. Disruptions of this kind could have occurred in any period, and were not restricted specifically to the fourth century. There is no indication in this passage that persecution occurred with sufficient frequency, at any given time, to justify a change in the way the calendar was reckoned.

The notion that persecution (שמדא) could occasionally disrupt the calendar occurs again in another passage, in *B. Betzah* 4b. There it is stated that the reason for observing the two festival days in the Diaspora is 'lest a persecution be decreed, which would lead to disruption (of the calendar)' (זמנין דגזרו שמדא ואתי לאקלקולי). The context of this passage, however, is quite different, as it refers to the period when the dates of the new moons were known in the Diaspora (והשתא דידעינן בקביעא דירחא), which probably means, after a fixed calendar had already been instituted.[34]

That disruptions could still occur in this period can be accounted for in a number of ways. R. Hai Gaon suggests that even after the institution of the fixed calendar, false calendrical information could still be sent occasionally to the Diaspora in order to avert, somehow or other, a 'persecution'.[35] Bornstein (1920: 250–1) points out that long after the institution of a fixed (or partially fixed) calendar, calendrical decisions

[31] Ritva ad loc.; see also Halevy (1901) 313–16.

[32] *Arukh* s.v. שמד, Ritva citing *Tosafot*, and Meiri ad loc. For a related but different interpretation—and considerably more far-fetched—see Nahmanides ad loc.

[33] This, again, is a simplification of the halakhic argument.

[34] See discussion above, in section 4.2.3.

[35] Responsum of R. Hai Gaon in *Teshuvot Geonim* (Lyck) 1, Lewin (1931) 8. Cf. another responsum of his in Lewin (1932/3) 40, but perhaps in a different sense, as this apparently refers to the period of the empirical calendar.

remained in the hands of the Palestinian rabbinic court; the Diaspora depended on receiving the news of their calendrical decisions (as evident, for instance, from the exilarch's letter of 835/6 CE).[36] At times of persecution, therefore, transmission of these decisions and hence festival observance in the Diaspora could still have been disrupted.[37]

The passage in *B. Betzah* 4b alerts us, however, to a further weakness in the 'persecution theory'. The main point of this theory, indeed, is that the institution of a fixed calendar was designed to remove the risk of calendrical disruption. But if disruption to the calendar was still possible after the institution of the fixed calendar, it is difficult to understand how this institution could have been justified. It is true that under the new system, the court would no longer have depended on the testimony of witnesses; moreover, envoys to the Diaspora would not have needed to be sent so frequently.[38] However, the persistence of a risk of disruption means that this institution would only have been a half-measure.

The 'persecution theory' fails to convince, therefore, for three different reasons: (i) the notion of fourth-century insecurity and/or persecution is unsubstantiated by, and indeed contradictory to, external historical evidence; (ii) internal evidence from the Babylonian Talmud

[36] According to 10th-c. sources, these calendrical decisions were disseminated to the Diaspora on an annual basis: see section 4.3.3. The passage in *B. Hullin* 101b (above quoted) may also imply an *annual* announcement, when it states: 'the day of Atonement, *this year*, is on the Sabbath'.

[37] Bornstein's interpretation appears to have been anticipated, however, by R. Shlomo b. Shabtai 'Anav (13th c.) in his commentary on the *She'iltot* (in Mirsky 1964: iii. 81), as well as by a scribal gloss in MS Vatican Ebr. 109 (on *B. Betzah* 4b), apparently inserted in the wrong place in the text, but referring unmistakably to a 'cancellation of envoys' as a result of persecution. By R. Hai's period (early 11th c.), the Diaspora was no longer dependent on the Palestinian court, as the calendar calculation had been completely standardized for more than one century. In his period, the danger of disruption would thus have been almost completely eliminated. R. Hai's interpretation of this passage appears to relate to the earlier period, and may have been received by him through tradition; it is questionable to what extent he himself, living in a later period, would have fully understood it (these remarks also apply to R. Shlomo b. Shabtai 'Anav and to the scribal gloss in the Vatican MS). R. Ḥananel (ad loc.) writes that a persecution could have caused the calendar calculation to be forgotten, but this is perhaps far-fetched (Rashi offers a similar interpretation, but he appears to be referring to the period of the empirical calendar: see Ch. 4 n. 65). See further section 4.2.3, and S. Stern (1994*a*).

[38] Only once a year (see above, n. 36), as opposed to six times a year in the Mishnaic system (*M. RH* 1: 3).

is only sporadic, and does not suggest that 'persecution' led to the institution of a fixed calendar; (iii) the institution of a fixed calendar would not have been justified as a fully appropriate solution.

5.1.2   The Christian influence theory

This theory, by contrast, has found almost no adherents, although it deserves in my view as much attention as the theory discussed above. It is based on the fact that a change from empirical to fixed calendars also occurred among the Christians, in their reckoning of the date of Easter, but already one century earlier. This raises the possibility that the rabbinic adoption of a fixed calendar in the fourth century was the direct result of Christian influence.

A survey of the historical development of the date of Easter is most instructive in this respect. Little is known about the date of Easter in the first two centuries of the Christian era, but it is generally assumed to have coincided, in this period, with the Jewish Passover. Indeed, Easter was no more, at first, than a Christian reinterpretation of the latter (Simon 1986: 310–22).

Evidence to this effect can only be found for the later second century, when the first Paschal controversy is known to have erupted. This controversy involved the 'Quartodecimans' in Asia Minor, so called because they observed Easter on the 14th of the lunar month; the churches of Rome and elsewhere observed Easter on the subsequent Sunday (Eusebius, *Ecclesiastical History* 5:23:1). The issue, it seems, was only the *day of the week* when Easter should be observed; but the definition of the 14th of the lunar month was taken for granted by both parties.

The 14th of the lunar month was defined by Polycrates, bishop of Ephesus and leader of the Quartodecimans in the 190s CE, as 'the day when the people (i.e. the Jews) dispose of the leaven'.[39] This statement suggests first-hand experience of the Jewish Passover, rather than a merely theoretical notion of it. To outside observers like Polycrates, disposal of the leaven would have been the most public and most visible

---

[39] Ap. Eusebius, ibid. 5: 24: 6, following Rufinus' Latin translation: 'quo fermentum Iudaeorum populus aufert'; the Armenian version renders, similarly, 'swept out the leaven'. Eusebius' original in Greek reads: ὅταν ὁ λαὸς ἤρνυε(ν) τὴν ζύμην or in other recensions ὅταν ὁ λαὸς ἤρτυε(ν) τὴν ζύμην (Schwartz and Mommsen 1908: i. 492–3), neither of which are comprehensible. Schwartz suggests instead ἦρεν (was destroying); Mohrmann (1962: 170 n. 53) suggests ἦρε (destroyed).

action carried out by the Jews of Ephesus on that day;[40] whereas other rituals, carried out in the privacy of the home, would have been less visible. Polycrates' reference to a real-life event, disposal of the leaven, suggests that he and the Christians obtained the date of the 14th of the month by *actually* observing on which day the Jews around them prepared for the celebration of their festival.

The Quartodecimans were not necessarily the only Christians to rely on the Jews, in this manner, for the date of Easter. Evidence from Ps.-Cyprian, which we will presently consider, suggests that in this early period, the Christians elsewhere would also 'follow the Jews' for determining the date of Easter[41]—except that Easter was observed by them on the following Sunday. In this sense, the date of Easter would have been determined by all Christians, in this period, on the *empirical* basis of the Jewish calendar.

This changed, however, in the early third century, when calculated cycles for the date of Easter first begin to appear. The earliest of these is the 112-year cycle of Hippolytus, formulated in Rome in 222 CE;[42] this cycle was slightly modified in Ps.-Cyprian's *De Pascha Computus*, a treatise on the calculation of the date of Easter written in North Africa in 243 CE.[43] The purpose of the Easter cycle is explicitly stated, in the latter, as follows:

volumus ... ostendere nunquam posse Christianos a via veritatis errare et tanquam ignorantes quae sit dies Paschae, post Iudaeos caecos et hebetes ambulare (Ps.-Cyprian, *De Pascha Computus*, PL 4. 1025B).

We wish ... to show that it is possible for Christians never to stray from the way of truth and trail after the blind and stupid Jews, as if not knowing on which day Easter should occur.

---

[40] For evidence of Jews in Ephesus in the 2nd c. CE, see Schürer (1973–87) iii. 22–3.

[41] The practice of 'following the Jews' is also well attested in Syria from the early 3rd c., but there it lasted for many centuries, long after the introduction elsewhere of calculated Easter cycles: see above, section 2.5.1.

[42] The Easter tables of Hippolytus (c.170–236 CE) were discovered on a chair, now supporting a statue; 222 CE is actually the first year of his cycle, hence presumably the approximate year when it was formulated. See E. Schwartz (1905) 29–36. Possibly earlier paschal computations are attributed in 10th-c. sources to Demetrius of Alexandria (c.188–230 CE): see Richard (1974) 308.

[43] See E. Schwartz (1905) 36–40. For a German translation of this work, see Strobel (1984) ch. 2. The original text can be found in *PL* 4. 1023ff.

This passage does not necessarily mean that the Jews observe Passover on the wrong date,[44] or, as it has often been interpreted (Simon 1986: 315–16), that Easter should always occur on a different date from the Jewish Passover. Ps.-Cyprian's point is rather that Christians should no longer *depend* on the Jews for their dates of Easter; his cycle will enable the dates of Easter to be determined without reference to when the Jewish Passover is observed.[45] Ps.-Cyprian's purpose in developing a fixed cycle is thus for the Christians to part ways and become free from dependence on Jewish practice.[46]

Cycles for the date of Easter were also developed in this period in the East. Eastern computations of the date of Easter were based on the rule of the equinox, first attributed to Dionysius of Alexandria in the mid third century with an 8-year cycle,[47] and then reiterated in *c.*277 CE by Anatolius, also from Alexandria but residing in Laodicea (Syria), with a more accurate 19-year cycle.[48] The purpose of the rule of the equinox may have been, again, to part ways with the Jews (Grumel 1960: 172–3), many of whom in this period observed Passover before the equinox (see above, section 2.5.1). However, it is equally possible that the rule was adopted by Alexandrian Christians because of their native interest in astronomy;[49] or because of a genuine belief that this was the correct method of determining the date of the biblical Passover; or finally, because the equinox was perceived as a universal, objective criterion that was most suited for a standard calendrical calculation.

[44] However, this may be implicit further on in the *De Pascha Computus*, where a contrast is drawn between the Jews of today and the Hebrews of the biblical period who benefited from divine inspiration.

[45] The same intention appears to characterize the decisions taken at the Council of Nicaea, in 325 CE: the point was not to celebrate Easter on different dates, but rather, to reckon the date of Easter independently from the Jews (see Constantine's letters, cited above in sections 2.5.1 and 2.5.4).

[46] See Richard (1974) 309. Al-Biruni (1879: 302) writes (c.1000 CE) that the Christians devised their own Easter cycles because the Jews used to lie to them about the date of Passover. It is also possible that the system of 'following the Jews' was becoming impractical in Christian communities where there were no Jews (suggestion of Martin Goodman).

[47] Eusebius, *Eccl. Hist.* 7: 20; his cycle was of 8 years.

[48] Eusebius, ibid. 7: 32. On the rule of the equinox, see Ch. 2. In the 3rd–4th cc. this rule was not endorsed by the Western churches (it is ignored, for instance, by Ps.-Cyprian), although in the 4th c. it was observed *de facto*: see Duchesne (1880) 18–21, 42; Richard (1974) 310.

[49] Anatolius' interest in astronomy is evident from the rest of his work, which partially cited by Eusebius (ibid.).

We do not know how early the Easter cycles were used in practice by Christian communities, but by the early fourth century, and certainly by the Council of Nicaea (325 CE), the Roman cycle of 8 or 84 years had become standard in the West (Richard 1974: 316–19, E. Schwartz 1905: 40–71), and so the Alexandrian cycle of 19 years[50] in the East.[51]

Against this background, it is intriguing to note that the rabbinic calendar underwent a similar development in the same period, or more precisely, in the immediately *following* period. For as we have seen in Ch. 4 (sections 4.2.2–3), it is in the course of the fourth century that a fixed (or partially fixed) calendar was adopted in rabbinic circles, together with the rule of the equinox. This raises the possibility that the rabbis were influenced by the recent changes in the Christian Easter computation.

Easter cycles would not have been used in parts of northern Syria where the Christians perpetuated the custom of 'following the Jews' well after the Council of Nicaea. In Palestine, however, there is no evidence to suggest that the Christians did not follow the normative Easter cycles (either Alexandrian or Anatolian), in conformity to the Council of Nicaea.[52] It is quite possible, therefore, that the rabbis of Palestine would have been aware of the existence of these cycles.

The extent to which the rabbis would have been generally exposed to Christian influence is difficult, admittedly, to measure. Evidence of Christian influence is hard to find in rabbinic sources, and the rabbis of late Antiquity are known, in general, for their cultural insularity.[53] But although explicit references to Christianity are rare in rabbinic sources,

[50] An adaptation of Anatolius' cycle, probably dating from the beginning of the 4th c.: Grumel (1958) 36, Richard (1974) 315, E. Schwartz (1905) 3–29.

[51] With some notable exceptions, e.g. the Syrian Christian communities that continued observing Easter 'with the Jews' (i.e. in the month when the Jews observed Passover): see above, section 2.5.1. Quartodecimans also reappear, it seems, in Western Asia Minor in the later 4th and 5th cc.: see Socrates, *Hist. Eccl.* 6. 11, 7. 29 (*PG* 67. 697 c, 805 a), and perhaps implicitly 5. 22 end (*PG* 67. 645 a; on which see Daunoy 1925: 428); Sozomen, *Hist. Eccl.* 7. 18 (*PG* 67. 1472 b); but see, with considerable reservations, Floëri and Nautin (1957) 38–9, 117. Even if Quartodecimans did exist in this period, they may well have relied on the Easter cycles (rather than on the Jews) for determining the dates of the 14th of the moon. Alternative Easter cycles were developed in the course of the 4th–6th cc. (e.g. at the council of Sardica: see section 2.5.3), but this is beyond our scope.

[52] See above section 2.5.1, and with some reservations, Ch. 2 n. 144.

[53] See in particular Lieberman (1963) 123–41, S. Stern (1994*c*) 139–98.

Palestinian rabbis were undoubtedly aware of this new religion, particularly in the fourth century, after Constantine's conversion and the expansion of Christianity in the Holy Land.[54] It would be wrong to assume that the rabbis were completely immune to their influence.[55]

Obviously, the parallelism between Christian and rabbinic calendars does not necessarily prove that the former influenced the latter, even if the Christians preceded the rabbis by about one century. Similar traits can often develop at the same time but independently in different cultures, as the result of commonly shared historical conditions.

In this case, however, the change from empirical to fixed calendars was clearly not due to commonly shared historical conditions. The reason that led Christians to alter their reckoning of the date of Easter was specific to early Christianity; it responded to a need to dissociate Christianity from its Jewish origins and from Jewish practice—this, at least, is the explanation that Ps.-Cyprian explicitly gives. The change of the rabbinic calendar could not have been motivated, independently, by any similar concern: the adoption of a fixed calendar would have been completely irrelevant to parting ways from the Christians.[56]

Thus it is quite conceivable that whilst the Christians were attempting, through their calendar, to part ways with the Jews, the rabbis in turn were influenced by the Christian Easter cycles of the Christians. The weakness of this theory is not intrinsic implausibility, but only that it is based on inference and lacks positive substantiation. It is also unclear why the rabbis should have succumbed to the influence of this particular Christian practice.

[54] See for instance Simon (1986) 179–201, Levine (1975) 70–85.

[55] The possibility of Christian influence over the Jewish calendar has been raised above in the context of non-rabbinic calendars (section 3.3.4). We may assume, however, that the Jews of non-rabbinic communities, e.g. in Antioch, were less culturally insular than the rabbis of Palestine. See Meeks and Wilken (1978), Wilken (1983).

[56] If anything, the rabbis' imitation of the Christian calendar would have frustrated the Christians attempt to part ways—but only in a limited measure: for the rabbinic fixed calendar was bound to differ from Christian Easter cycles, so that reliance of Christians on Jews (or vice versa) for the date of the festival would have been permanently precluded.

5.1.3　The scientific progress theory

This theory proposes that the change from the 'primitive', empirical calendar of the Mishnah to a more 'scientific', calculated calendar was the outcome of general scientific progress in late Antique society.[57]

This theory rests on the assumption that the Mishnaic, empirical calendar would have been thought more 'primitive'. Since it was based on sightings of the new moon (for the month) and seasonal observations (for the intercalation), this calendar was irregular (because new moons are not visible at regular intervals), unreliable (because of its dependence on weather conditions, trustworthy witnesses, and other uncontrollable factors), and hence completely unpredictable from one month to the next, and all the more so over longer periods. This calendar was also dependent on a specific *social* context: the existence of a rabbinic court that could exercise sufficient authority, and that could effectively communicate its decisions to all the Jewish communities.

The calculated calendar, by contrast, would have been far more 'advanced'. It was regular (consisting of the regular alternation of 29- and 30-day months; alternatively, being based on the mean conjunction which occurs at regular intervals), reliable (because unaffected by any extraneous factors), and completely predictable over long periods of time, even *ad infinitum*). As it was based on a purely mathematical calculation, it was free from any social constraint; it did not depend, in principle, on anyone's authority. Even if in practice, the Palestinian court retained control of this calculated calendar in the first few centuries, this calendar was eventually to become 'democratic' and accessible to all.

Thus the functional advantages of the calculated calendar, as well as its greater accuracy, would explain why the Jews eventually adopted it, along with many other ancient societies. The switch to calendar calculation would only have become possible, in late Antiquity, once the required knowledge in astronomy and mathematics had been attained.

This theory is problematic, however, on a number of counts. Firstly, scientific progress in astronomy and mathematics had reached an adequate level long before the fourth century CE. The 19-year cycle was known in the Near East as early as the fifth century BCE. The mean conjunction was also calculated by Babylonian and Greek astronomers from

---

[57] For earlier proponents of this theory, see Schürer (1973–87) i. 594 (from Schürer 1898–1902: i. 753–4), Bornstein (1922*a*) 361. I think it is unlikely, however, that Bornstein regarded this as the main explanation for the switch to a calculated calendar. For a more recent proponent, see H. Ben-Sasson ap. Sar-Shalom (1984) 25.

this early period (see above, section 4.4.7). It is difficult to understand why it would have taken so long for Palestinian rabbis to find out about these values.

Secondly, the 'scientific progress theory' does not take sufficient account of the *halakhic* nature of the Mishnaic calendar. In rabbinic sources such as the Mishnah and the Talmudim, the Mishnaic calendar was treated as part of the halakha (law). Any change of calendar would have been contradictory, therefore, to the conservatism inherent in rabbinic law. 'Scientific progress' is unlikely to have justified, on its own, a radical halakhic change of this nature.[58]

Thirdly, the notion that the Mishnaic calendar was 'primitive' and therefore *destined* to be superseded by a more 'advanced', superior system, is based on an outdated, nineteenth-century concept of cultural evolutionism that is no longer acceptable. It is questionable, indeed, to what extent fourth-century rabbis would have regarded the Mishnaic calendar as 'primitive'.

They could not have denied that the Mishnaic calendar was functionally inconvenient. Because the intercalation was largely unpredictable, Tannaitic sources consider the possibility of a house being let for 'one year' without anyone knowing whether that year would last for 12 or 13 months.[59] The observance of festivals, likewise, would occasionally have been disrupted. We are told that if the scroll of *Esther* was read on 14 Adar (the festival of Purim), but then the year turned out to be intercalated, *Esther* would have to be read again on the 14th of the second Adar.[60]

This unpredictability was compounded by the rabbinic court's tendency to wait until Adar before deciding whether or not to intercalate,[61] because many of the empirical criteria that determined this decision could only be known and

---

[58] Some proponents of the 'scientific progress theory' acknowledge that for many centuries 'stubborn' religious conservatism prevented the Jews (as well as others, such as the Babylonians) from abandoning their old method and adopting a more advanced, calculated scheme: Schürer (1973–87) i. 594. They fail to explain, however, why the old method should eventually have given way.

[59] *M. Bava Metzia*ᶜ 8: 8; *T. Bava Metzia*ᶜ 8: 31 (p. 390).

[60] *M. Megillah* 1: 4; *T. Megillah* 1: 6 (p. 222); *Y. Megillah* 1: 7 (70d); *B. Megillah* 6b.

[61] Although the decision to intercalate the year could be taken by the court as early as Rosh ha-Shanah (i.e. six months before the intercalation, though not beforehand: *B. Sanhedrin* 12a), it could also be taken *in extremis*, at the very end of the month of (first) Adar (*M. ᶜEduyot* 7: 7; *T. Sanhedrin* 2: 13 (p. 418); *Y. Megillah* 1: 7 (71a); *B. RH* 7a; *B. Sanhedrin* 87a).

ascertained in the spring.[62] These empirical criteria include, as we have seen (section 4.1.2), ripeness of the crops and fruits,[63] size of the lambs, kids, and birds,[64] weather conditions (cold, rain, snow), state of the roads, bridges, and (earthenware) ovens, and last but not least, whether pilgrims who had left for Jerusalem would make it on time for the Passover celebration.[65] R. Gamliel's letter informing of his decision to intercalate, in which many of these criteria are mentioned, would have been written in the spring, not long before the intercalation was to be made.[66]

The uncertain length of months in the Mishnaic system would also have been disruptive. Because it took a few days for people to find out whether the previous month had been of 29 or 30 days, witnesses could not be expected to know if the date of an incident was the 2nd or the 3rd of the month (*M. Sanhedrin* 5:3). Although the Mishnah does not explicitly mention it, we may assume that a house could also be let for a specific month, without anyone knowing how long this month would last. Indeed, the Palestinian Talmud reports that R. Hoshaya used to warn the witnesses at Ein Tav (where the calendrical court was at one time located) as follows: 'be aware of the weight of your testimony—how house rents will be affected by it'.[67]

In this respect, the calculated calendar would have been much preferable. Regularity, predictability, and 'democratic' access (as opposed to dependence on the decisions of an exclusive court) would have represented, at least in functional terms, considerable progress over the earlier system.

Yet in other ways, the Mishnaic system would have been regarded as preferable to a calculated calendar. The rabbis may have felt that the empirical calendar was *astronomically* more accurate, as it was based on regular observations of the moon and hence did not suffer, in the long term, from the slight or greater discrepancies from astronomical reality which calculated calendars always, unavoidably, entail.[68]

---

[62] As correctly assumed by Thornton (1989*a*) 403 n. 6.

[63] *T. Sanhedrin* 2: 2 (p. 416); *Y. Sanhedrin* 1: 2 (18d); *B. Sanhedrin* 11b.

[64] *T. Sanhedrin* 2: 4–6 (pp. 416–17); *Y. Sanhedrin* 1: 2 (18d); *B. Sanhedrin* 11a.

[65] *T. Sanhedrin* 2: 12 (p. 417); *Y. Sanhedrin* 1: 2 (18d); *B. Sanhedrin* 11a.

[66] *T. Sanhedrin* 2: 6 (pp. 416–17) and parallels; see section 4.1.2. Although his letter was sent as far out as Babylonia and Media, it is unlikely to have reached the more distant Jewish Diaspora communities in time for the intercalation (Thornton 1989*a*: 403 n. 5).

[67] *Y. Sanhedrin* 1: 2 (19a); *Y. Nedarim* 6: 13 (40a). On Ein Tav, see Safrai (1965*b*).

[68] See my general remarks in section 2.1.1. On the discrepancies of the present-day rabbinic calendar from astronomical reality, see sections 4.4.5 and 4.4.7.

More importantly, the empirical calendar system was an effective way of imposing and maintaining rabbinic authority upon the Jewish community. In this respect, it would have been *politically* expedient for the rabbinic class to maintain the *status quo*, and to resist any change in the way the calendar was reckoned.

The Mishnaic system had also intrinsic *ideological* value. By controlling the dates of the calendar from month to month, the rabbis perceived themselves as exerting control over the entire cosmos, and even over the Divine order. Thus we are told in a number of sources that God and his angelic court would not sit in judgement at the New Year (1 Tishre) until the rabbinic court had sanctified it and declared it the first day of the month.[69] To cite a longer version of this tradition, which exemplifies the cosmic power which the calendrical court was perceived to have exerted:

'This month will be unto you' (Exod. 12: 2)—that is, the reckoning of time will be turned over to you. Consider, said R. Yehoshua b. Levi, the analogy of a king who had a timepiece and turned the timepiece over to his son when his son grew up . . .

R. Hoshaya taught: When a court on earth decrees and says, 'New Year's Day is today', the Holy One tells the ministering angels: 'Raise up the dais. Summon the advocates. Summon the clerks. For the court on earth has decreed and said: New Year's day is today.'

But if the witnesses are delayed in coming, or if, for any reason, the court decides to put off the beginning of the year by one day, the Holy One tells the ministering angels: 'Remove the dais, dismiss the advocates, dismiss the clerks, since the court on earth has decreed that the New Year will not begin till tomorrow'.

And the proof from Scripture? 'When it is a decree of Israel it is an ordinance for the God of Jacob' (Ps. 81: 5: therefore what is not a decree of Israel is not—as it were—an ordinance for the God of Jacob.

R. Pinḥas and R. Ḥilkiya taught in the name of R. Shimon: When all the ministering angels gather before the Holy One and ask Him, 'Master of the universes, when does the New Year begin?' He replies: 'Are you asking Me? Let us, you and me, ask the court on earth.' . . .[70]

---

[69] *T. RH* 1: 12 (p. 209); *B. RH* 8b. The Tosefta adds that during the 40 years in the wilderness, the court's decisions regarding the dates of festivals would have determined when the Manna would have fallen (just as the Manna did not fall on the Sabbath (*Exodus* 16: 21–30), it is assumed in this passage that it did not fall on festivals).

[70] *Pesiqta de-Rav Kahana* 5: 13 (Buber 1868: 54a; Mandelbaum 1987: 102–3); cited from translation of Braude and Kapstein (1975) 114–15 (with modifications). Parallel source in *Y. RH* 1: 3 (57b).

Similarly remarkable may be another passage in the Palestinian Talmud, although its interpretation remains somewhat uncertain. Rabbinic legal sources consider a girl's loss of hymen to be irreversible from the age of three, but reversible in her first three years. The passage in question contends that this three-year period can be extended *in extremis*, if the court decides to prolong the third year with an intercalatory month.[71]

According to the commentary *Penei Moshe* (ad loc.), this means that if a girl became three in the month of Adar, and then lost her virginity—irreversibly—in the same month, but then subsequently the court decided to intercalate, her birthday would be postponed to the next month and hence, her virginity would be miraculously restored. This would suggest that the rabbinic court is capable, through its calendrical decisions, of altering the very course of nature.[72]

According to Meiri, however, all the passage means is that for purely legal purposes, loss of virginity would be *treated* as reversible in a situation where the year was intercalated—without any reference to actual, physiological reality.[73]

The ability of the rabbinic court to interfere with time, the cosmos, and the Divine explains perhaps why the determination of new months is referred to in the Mishnah (*M. RH* 2:7, 3:1, etc.) as an act of 'sanctification'. The sanctification of the new month appears, indeed, to have been treated as a religious ceremony of some significance.[74]

In this light, the Mishnaic, empirical calendar is unlikely to have been treated by the rabbis as 'primitive' or as deficient. In spite of its functional disadvantages, this calendar was the basis of an entire ideology and world-view. On the one hand, it meant that man—or more specifically, Israel, and more specifically still, the rabbinic court—was empowered over time and the cosmic order. On the other hand, it implied a concept of time that was flexible, man-made, and in a sense, *sacred*. This ideology was not merely theoretical: it would have affected, in practice, the daily experience of time and of its flow.

After the institution of a calculated calendar, this experience of time would have been radically redefined. Because the calendar was now governed by fixed, mathematical rules, time was eventually to be experienced as rigid, objective, and 'desacralized'.

---

[71] *Y. Ketubot* 1: 2 (25b); *Y. Nedarim* 6: 13 (40a); *Y. Sanhedrin* 1: 2 (19a).

[72] In support of this interpretation, which is otherwise less plausible than that of Meiri (below), is the citation of Ps. 57: 3 as proof-text in our passage. This verse is cited in an entirely different context, but with an ascription of meaning that is analogous to our passage as interpreted by *Penei Moshe*, in *Y. Sanhedrin* 6: 9 (23d) (*Y. Kiddushin* 4: 1 (65c)).

[73] Menaḥem ha-Meiri (1947) 53 on *Ketubot* (11b).

[74] The liturgy (blessings) to be recited, apparently, at this ceremony, is given at some length in minor tractate *Soferim* 19: 7; see Fleischer (1973).

From a modern perspective, this new concept of time may seem more 'advanced'. But there is no reason to treat the earlier world-view as deficient, less legitimate, or 'primitive'. World-views are not easily discarded. Why the rabbinic calendar was so radically altered remains, therefore, to be explained.

5.2 THE 'ONE CALENDAR' THEORY

5.2.1 The theory in Geonic and later medieval sources

The 'one calendar' theory, to put it briefly, is that the fixed rabbinic calendar was instituted in order to enable the observance of a single, identical calendar in all the Palestinian and Diaspora communities.

Under the empirical system, indeed, calendrical unity would have been virtually impossible. Different communities would have sighted the new moon at different times, resulting in festivals being observed on different days. As we have seen in Ch. 3, this situation was prevalent in the ancient Jewish world. Some communities, mainly in Palestine and in Babylonia, may have chosen to follow the decisions of the Palestinian calendrical court; but knowledge of these decisions was not always easy to obtain. The Mishnaic system of beacons or messengers would have been, at best, of limited effectiveness, especially as it could not reach the more distant Babylonian communities.[75] By necessity, distant or outlying communities would have been forced to make their own calendrical arrangements, with the result that festivals would have been observed on different days.

The institution of a fixed calendar would have made it possible for all Jewish communities to observe the festivals on exactly the same days. Indeed, the same calendrical calculation could be carried out by any Jewish community, anywhere in the world. Even if the calendar calculation was not initially fully fixed (as we have seen in Ch. 4), the existence of some fixed rules would have enabled distant communities to make fairly reliable predictions.[76] A calendar based on the conjunction, in particular, was far easier to predict than one based on sightings of the new moon. Later, when the calendar calculation became fully fixed and was widely

---

[75] The limited effectiveness of the messenger system is confirmed with internal evidence from rabbinic sources: see below, section 5.3.2.

[76] This will be explained in detail below.

disseminated—as it has been, nowadays, for more than a millennium—festivals could be celebrated universally, without error, on exactly the same dates.

The theory that the fixed calendar was instituted by the rabbis precisely for this purpose, i.e. to enable the same calendar to be observed universally by all Jewish communities, is not entirely new. It finds expression as early as in the Geonic period, in a work attributed to R. Hai 'the head of the yeshiva', identified either as R. Hai b. David or as R. Hai b. Naḥshon, both Geonim from the end of the ninth century.[77] This passage is cited verbatim by the Karaite Yefet b. Ali, as follows:

> The festivals used to be a matter of division and dispute, because in the days of the early sages they used to (make) sightings of the (new) moon, and those who lived in cities on mountain tops would sight it on its day (on the 30th day of the last month), and declare (the date of) the (subsequent) festival (accordingly), whereas those who lived in cities in the plain would sight it (the new moon) on the next day, and declare (the date of) the festival one day later, (in accordance with) when they had sighted (the new moon). And the people of Israel (עדת ישראל) were very distressed at this, because the festivals were distorted, some (observing them) on one day and others on the next.
>
> When R. Yitzḥaq Napha saw this, he decided in his wisdom to institute a system whereby all the people of Israel would observe the same day. And he justified this on the basis of Scriptures ... from Hezekiah ... proving that it was desirable to Him (God) that the festival be (celebrated) by the assembly of the congregation, by one assembly (אסיפה) and one band (אגודה), without division, for division is a sin ...
>
> When R. Yitzḥaq Napha saw that some would observe the festival on one day and others on the next, he was very distressed and so were the whole of Israel, until the Holy One gave him the wisdom to institute this system. He made this institution for the sake of Heaven, and because of this all Israel accepted it and obeyed it. Thus the whole of Israel, from one end of the world to the other, and until the days of the Messiah, conduct themselves accordingly.[78]

---

[77] See Ch. 4 n. 89.

[78] My translation, based on the text published by Pinsker (1860) ii. 149–50 (appendix 11). The text is in some places incomprehensible or corrupt, but this does not affect its general meaning. Pinsker's text is cited with some conjectural emendations by Bornstein (1904) 144, 159–60, (1922a) 361–2; Ankori (1959) 350 n. 138. The words in brackets are mine, to facilitate comprehension of the passage. On the attribution of the fixed calendar to R. Yitzḥaq Napha, see above, section 4.2.4. This citation of R. Hai 'the head of the yeshiva' is quoted by other Karaite authors, in paraphrase or in abbreviated form: for references see Pinsker, ibid. and Ankori, ibid.

A similar theory is reported by al-Biruni (1879: 68) as one of the Rabbanite opinions.[79] According to this, calendrical diversity was caused by the dispersion of the Jews after the destruction of the Temple in 70 CE, when the Jews settled in different countries where the new moon would be visible on different days. The calendar based on sightings of the new moon was abolished in this period, so as to avoid the danger of schisms.

In historical terms, the notion that Jewish dispersion was caused by the destruction of the Temple is obviously an over-simplification; but this point is not essential to al-Biruni's theory. His main point is that exile entailed calendrical diversity, so long as the empirical system was in place; and thus that the fixed calendar was instituted, just as according to R. Hai, for the sake of Jewish unity.[80]

The same idea is also implicit in the otherwise very different works of R. Yaʿaqov b. Shimshon and of R. Tuviah b. Eliezer (both early twelfth century). Both consider the empirical system to have been abandoned because the Jews went into exile and the calendrical court was consequently discontinued—a theory which I have rejected above (section 5.1.1), under the heading of 'persecution theory', as historically implausible. However, these authors also argue that exile and dispersion would have led the Jews to observe the festivals on different dates, and that the fixed calculation was instituted so as to ensure the observance of a single calendar. Thus their argument is not only that exile rendered the Mishnaic system unmanageable—as according to the 'persecution theory'—but also that it would have led to calendrical disunity. To cite from R. Tuviah b. Eliezer:

וכדי שלא יהו ישראל עושין ב' ימים טובים בשינוי זה מזה, האב היום והבן מחר
ואחיו למחרת, עמדו ישראל על תקנות סוד העיבור ולכן ראוי לסמוך על סוד
העיבור ולא לעשות ישראל אגודות אגודות להיות זה מחלל שמירת יום קודש של
זה וכבר ישראל נפוצים בארצות שאין הלבנה נראית כדרך שהיתה נראית בארץ
ישראל

And in order that Israel should not observe (the same festival) on two different days, the father today, the son tomorrow, and the brother the day after, Israel instituted the secret of intercalation . . . therefore it is right to rely on the secret of intercalation, and not to split Israel into factions (*agudot agudot*), whereby one would desecrate the holy day of the other . . . For Israel are now dispersed in

---

[79] For the other opinion, more akin to the 'persecution theory', see above, section 5.1.1.

[80] The institutor of the calendar, according to this tradition, was Eliezer b. Paruaḥ: see above, section 4.2.4.

lands where the (new) moon is not visible in the same way as it is in the land of Israel ...[81]

The thesis put forward by R. Hai 'the head of the yeshiva', and later, by R. Tuviah b. Eliezer, was largely intended as an anti-Karaite polemic. The Karaites, indeed, rejected the Rabbanite fixed calendar; they observed instead a calendar that was based on sightings of the new moon and on annual inspections of *ʾaviv*, the ripeness of the crops, as the sole legitimate criterion for intercalation.[82] Because of the empirical nature of their calendar, different Karaite communities would often observe the festivals at different times from one another[83]—a situation which the Rabbanites exploited to their own, polemical advantage. It is in this context that R. Hai and R. Tuviah b. Eliezer both argued that unity was preferable to schism, and that only a fixed calendar could guarantee that festivals would be observed by everyone on the same day. In a certain sense, indeed, their argument was that the Rabbanite fixed calendar had been designed to do away with calendrical sectarianism.[84]

[81] R. Tuviah b. Eliezer, *Midrash Leqaḥ Tov*, on Exod. 12: 2 (Buber 1884: ii. 27b–28a), partially cited above, section 5.1.1, and cited in full with translation by Ankori (1959) 270 and n. 53. See also *Midrash Leqaḥ Tov*, on Gen. 17: 13 (Buber 1884: i. 39b), on Deut. 14: 1 (ibid. iv. 22a), and on Deut. 33: 4 (iv. 63a). The passage from R. Yaʿaqov b. Shimshon, *Sefer ha-ʿIbbur*, ch. 32 (see references above, n. 5), is cited by Bornstein (1922a) 363. Similar intimations can be found in Isaac Israeli, *Yesod ʿOlam*, 4: 9 (Goldberg 1848: ii. 16b). The phrase אגדות אגודות (which comes from *B. Yevamot* 13b–14a) is also used by R. Yaʿaqov b. Shimshon (ibid.), as well as in the exilarch's letter of 835/6 CE (verso, l. 15), albeit in a slightly different context.

[82] As explained in the preface to this work, the Karaite calendar will not be systematically discussed. For a general introduction, see Gil (1992) 795–9, Olszowy-Schlanger (1998) 248–50. For primary sources, see e.g. al-Qirqisani, *The Book of Lights and Watch-Towers*, 1. 13. 2, 1. 14 (Nemoy 1930: 384, 387; Chiesa and Lockwood 1984: 146, 148).

[83] See for instance Olszowy-Schlanger (1998) 300–2 (text no. 7 = T.–S. J3.47ᵛ), a Karaite betrothal document from 1033 CE dated to 'the month of Av, or Ellul according to other Karaites'. For evidence of Karaite calendrical diversity from the 15th c., see Bartenura (1922) 26 (in translation, Adler 1930: 226). Differences among the Karaites were not only due to empirical factors, but could also be the result of disagreement as to how the calendar should be reckoned: see al-Qirqisani, *The Book of Lights and Watch-Towers* 1. 19 (Nemoy 1930: 392–4; Chiesa and Lockwood 1984: 153–4); Gil (1992) 798. The Karaites of Babylonia, for instance, did not intercalate according to the criterion of *ʾaviv*, but simply relied on the fixed 19-year cycle of the Rabbanites (see sources cited by Ankori 1959: 311–12, Gil 1992: 796 and n. 12).

[84] See on this Bornstein (1922a) 362 n. 1 (with reference to R. Hai); Ankori 1959: 269–75 and 348–53 (with particular reference to R. Tuviah b. Eliezer). Evidence of this anti-Karaite polemic is also implicit in al-Qirqisani, *The Book of*

Yet in spite of its polemical character, the 'one-calendar theory' of R. Hai and his successors has much to be commended. There can be no doubt that under the empirical system, various Jewish Diaspora communities would have celebrated the festivals on different dates. The evidence we have studied above, in Chs. 2–3, confirms the existence of such calendrical diversity. What remains to be established, however, is whether this diversity would have justified, on its own, the rabbinic institution of a fixed calendar, and if so, why in the fourth century more than in any other period.

5.2.2 'One calendar': the Christian parallel

In answer to this last question, it may be relevant to note that in the fourth century the ideal of 'one calendar' is known to have been decisive to the formation of the Christian Easter calendar. As I have already pointed out (section 2.5.4), one of the main purposes of Constantine's Council of Nicaea (in 325 CE) was to unify the Churches in their observance of Easter. Although the Council refrained from a clear formulation of how the date of Easter was to be reckoned,[85] the existence of Easter cycles, as from the early third century, undoubtedly facilitated the implementation of the Council's policy. Because the same Easter cycles could be shared by a large number of Christian constituencies (for instance, the Alexandrian cycle in the Eastern Mediterranean region), it became possible for the date of Easter to be substantially standardized and unified in the course of the fourth century.

We may be entitled to wonder, again, whether these developments did not exert some influence on rabbinic Jewry. Palestinian rabbinic leadership of the fourth century, and in particular, the Patriarch, may have drawn some inspiration from Constantine's unification policy. To counter Constantine's accusation that the Jews observed Passover 'twice in the year', which probably meant, as I have argued (section 2.5.4), that the Jews were divided over the dates of the festival, the Patriarch may have sought to emulate the Christian example and unify Jewish observance through the institution of a fixed calendar.

Lights and Watch-Towers, end of 1: 19 (Nemoy 1930: 396; Chiesa and Lockwood 156); for al-Qirqisani's response, see ibid. and 1. 3. 26–36 (Nemoy 1930: 342–4; Chiesa and Lockwood 1984: 114–17). See also Sahal b. Matzliaḥ (later 10th-c. Karaite) in his תוכחת מגולה (published by Pinsker 1860: ii. 25–43), apparently responding to this polemic by recalling the Rabbanite calendrical schism that broke out in the early 920s between R. Saadya and Ben Meir (ibid. 36).

[85] For reasons which have been discussed above, section 2.5.1.

5.2.3 Unification as a rabbinic policy

To verify the 'one-calendar theory', we must consider whether policies of this kind are likely to have been adopted by the Patriarch or the rabbis of the fourth century.

Much has been written in recent years on the political function of the Jewish Patriarch in the third and fourth centuries. Besides exercising authority over many aspects of social and religious life in Jewish Palestine, the Patriarch appears to have extended his influence abroad by regularly sending envoys to Diaspora communities.[86] Whether he had aspirations of 'converting' Diaspora communities to rabbinic Judaism is impossible, however, to prove.[87] But there is evidence in rabbinic sources that with regard to the calendar, attempts were made to bring Diaspora communities in line with Palestinian rabbinic practice.

This is implicit, first and foremost, in the beacon system, later superseded by the sending of envoys, that are both described in detail in the Mishnah. The purpose of these was to disseminate as far as possible the calendrical decisions of the Palestinian rabbinic court. Whether these procedures were ever fully implemented, and whether indeed they were effective, are questions which I have raised but which do not concern us here.[88] What is important to us at present is the *expectation*, implicit in the Mishnah, that Diaspora communities should follow the Palestinian rabbinic calendar, and that the rabbinic court should provide Diaspora communities with the means to do so.

Another tradition confirms the rabbis' concern to communicate calendrical decisions to distant Diaspora communities. R. Gamliel is described as sending letters from Jerusalem proclaiming his decision to intercalate the year; these letters were addressed to his 'brethren' in Galilee, the 'South' (Judaea), Babylonia, Media, and the 'whole Diaspora', including according to one version *Yawan*, meaning Greece or perhaps the

---

[86] See in particular Levine (1996), who refers on pp. 11, 16, and 23–4 to rabbinic, epigraphic and patristic sources on the Patriarch's envoys.

[87] A passage in Jerome's commentary on Gal. 1: 1 (*PL* 26. 335) suggests that the Patriarch's envoys would encourage Diaspora Jews to observe the law. It is difficult to tell, however, whether this is an accurate reflection of reality, or simply a Christian-biased assumption of what the mission of the Patriarch's envoys (or *apostoli*) should be. Epiphanius suggests that *apostoli* could dismiss unworthy synagogue officials in Diaspora communities (*Panarion* 30. 11, *PG* 41. 424), but the implications of this are not entirely clear. Internal rabbinic evidence is also insufficiently informative.

[88] Section 4.1.3, and below, section 5.3.2.

Greek-speaking East.[89] Again, the authenticity of this tradition does not really matter. What is important is the notion, in the sources where the story is cited, that R. Gamliel considered himself responsible for ensuring that his decisions be followed by all Diaspora communities.

One story suggests, furthermore, that Palestinian rabbis prevented Diaspora communities from reckoning their own, independent calendars. When Ḥananiah nephew of R. Yehoshua, a mid-second-century sage of Palestinian origin, began setting his own calendar in Babylonia, two sages from Palestine were dispatched by 'Rabbi', i.e. the Patriarch, with instructions to put an end to his activities. Their vigorous intervention forced Ḥananiah to cancel his calendrical decisions.[90]

Finally, the story is told, in a number of rabbinic sources, of various second- and third-century Palestinian rabbis travelling abroad for the stated purpose of 'intercalating the year' (לעבר את השנה): R. Akiva to Nehardea (Babylonia),[91] R. Meir to 'Asia',[92] and R. Ḥiyya b. Zarnuqi with R. Shimon b. Yehotzadaq, again to 'Asia'.[93] The purpose of these journeys is somewhat unclear, as it would have been perfectly possible and normal to intercalate the year in Palestine.

These journeys would in fact have contravened the Tannaitic rule that intercalation could only be made in Judaea, or failing this, in Galilee.[94] In these stories,

---

[89] *T. Sanhedrin* 2: 6 (pp. 416–17); *Y. Sanh.* 18d (with reference to *Yawan*); *B. Sanh.* 11b. The identity of this R. Gamliel is somewhat unclear, but it is probably R. Gamliel (I) the Elder.

[90] *Y. Sanhedrin* 1: 2 (19a) (*Y. Nedarim* 7: 13 (40a)); *B. Berakhot* 63a–b; for translation and discussion of these passages, see Neusner (1965–70) i. 122–30, Gafni (1997) 107–11. The Patriarch (on whom see Gafni ibid. 108; Oppenheimer 1995: 127 n. 52) is only mentioned in the Palestinian Talmud version. The precise activities of Ḥananiah, and the basis of the Palestinians' objection to him, will be considered in further detail below.

[91] *M. Yevamot* 16: 7.

[92] *T. Megillah* 2: 5; *B. Megillah* 18b; for parallels with no reference to the intercalation, see *Y. Megillah* 4: 1 (74d) and *Genesis Rabbah* 36: 8 (ed. Theodor–Albeck 343).

[93] *B. Sanhedrin* 26a. This story belongs to the 3rd c., as it involves the figures of R. Yoḥanan and Resh Lakish.

[94] *T. Sanhedrin* 2: 13 (pp. 417–18), and further sources cited in section 4.1.2. See further below, section 5.3.1.

the procedure of intercalation seems to have been carried out entirely in Nehardea or Asia.[95] For some reason, the Tannaitic rule was waived.[96]

As to the purpose of these journeys, the traditional view is that R. Akiva
and the others were forced to flee from Palestine and declare the intercalation
abroad because of political persecutions.[97] This theory, as the other 'persecution
theories' discussed above, is unsubstantiated and historically unlikely.

Others have suggested that the purpose of these journeys was 'to investigate
the need for an intercalated year, i.e. in order to see how the seasonal conditions
in Babylonia should be considered in the Palestinian debates regarding intercalation' (Herr (1976) 857; cf Alon (1980) i. 245–6). This theory is unconvincing,
because it contradicts the Tannaitic rule that intercalation could only be based
on the seasonal conditions of Judaea, Galilee, and the Transjordanian region.[98]

The purpose of intercalating the year abroad would probably have
been to inform the communities in Nehardea or Asia that the year was
due to be intercalated,[99] or alternatively, to make sure that this intercalation was duly observed. For as we have seen in Ch. 2, the practice
of intercalation varied considerably from one Jewish community to the
next. Many communities, not least in 'Asia' (i.e. Asia Minor—see below),
observed Passover quite early, often before the vernal equinox (see section 2.5.1). In such cases, Palestinian rabbis might well have advocated
an intercalation, and hence the observance of Passover one month later
than in these communities.[100] These stories thus suggest that Palestinian
rabbis would travel abroad to *convince* the communities of Asia and elsewhere to intercalate the year and observe Passover at the same time as
them.

---

[95] This is almost explicit in the case of R. Ḥiyya b. Zarnuqi and R. Shimon
b. Yehotzadaq in *B. Sanhedrin* 26a, as pointed out by Alon (1980) i. 243–4 (despite
Tosafot on *B. Sanh.* 26a, s.v. לעבר). This is also how the Babylonian Talmud understood the story of R. Akiva, since according to *B. Berakhot* 63a this story was cited
as a precedent in support of Ḥananiah nephew of Yehoshua's activities.

[96] For a justification of R. Akiva's action, see *B. Berakhot* 63a. See also Alon
(1980) i. 247. Gafni (1997: 105–6) suggests that the prohibition on intercalating outside the land of Israel was not explicitly formulated in R. Akiva's period.

[97] *Tosafot* on *B. Yevamot* 115a, s.v. אמר, a theory developed in detail by Burstein
(1955/6).

[98] *T. Sanhedrin* 2: 3 (p. 416); *Y. Sanh.* 1: 2 (18d); *B. Sanh.* 11b.

[99] See the remarks of Graetz (1890–1909) iv. 442–3.

[100] This is possible regardless of whether the rabbis observed the rule of the
equinox. Note that the rule of the equinox was only introduced in the rabbinic calendar in the 4th c. (see section 4.2.2), whereas these stories are set in the 2nd and 3rd
cc.; inasmuch as these stories are found in the Mishnah and Tosefta, they would not
have been redacted much later than the 3rd c.

This interpretation, if correct, might explain why—according to the same sources—R. Meir remained in Asia until the festival of Purim, whereupon he was unable to find a scroll of Esther written in Hebrew (*T. Megillah* 2:5, *B. Megillah* 18b). He may have wanted to ensure that the 14th of that month would be celebrated in these communities *as Purim*, and not as Passover, which following the intercalation would only be celebrated one month later.

The identification of 'Asia' with Asia Minor is plausible, and certainly preferable to Alon's assumption (1957: i. 320–7, and briefly 1980: i. 231, 243) that the term refers in *all* rabbinic sources to the locality of Aila or Aqaba on the Red Sea. Although it is quite possible that the calendar observed by the Jews of Aila did not conform to rabbinic norms—as was the case, indeed, in contemporary Zoar (see sections 2.6.3 and 3.4.2), not far to the north of Aila—it is unlikely that these eminent rabbis would have singled out the tiny community of Aila for their mission. Asia Minor is also more likely to be the place where R. Meir could not find a scroll of Esther written in Hebrew.[101]

My interpretation is not incompatible with the suggestion of a number of scholars that intercalation was carried out by R. Akiva and the others, in either Nehardea or in Asia, in *co-operation* with the local communal authorities so as to secure their loyalty to the Palestinian rabbinic calendar.[102] This suggestion, however, is not substantiated by the sources and perhaps unnecessary.

In spite of all these sources, it remains uncertain whether there ever was a *systematic* attempt by Palestinian rabbinic authorities to bring Diaspora communities in line with their own calendrical practices. The 'one-calendar theory' we have outlined above, according to which the fixed calendar was instituted for the sake of calendrical unity, assumes a 'grand strategy' which is not necessarily warranted by the evidence we have considered, and may be out of character with what is otherwise known about the rabbis and rabbinic Judaism in this period.

The 'one-calendar theory' remains in my view most plausible, but in the light of these remarks, its medieval formulation (e.g. of R. Hai 'the head of the yeshiva') must be radically revised. Attention must also be given to the fact that the medieval 'one-calendar theory' assumes that the fixed calendar was formally 'instituted' by the rabbinic court, at a given moment of rabbinic history;[103] whereas in Ch. 4, section 4.2.5, I have suggested that the transition from empirical to fixed calendar may have been slow and gradual.

---

[101] See at length Bar-Kokhba (1997), especially pp. 55–69. In *B. Sanhedrin* 26a, the reference to the Sabbatical year does not necessarily mean that the *destination* of R. Ḥiyya b. Zarnuqi and R. Shimon b. Yehotzadaq ('Asia') was in the land of Israel.

[102] Alon (1980) i. 245–8, Gafni (1997) 106, Oppenheimer (1995) 122–3. The notion of local cooperation is suggested already by R. Meir Abulafia, *Yad Ramah* on *B. Sanhedrin* 26a.

[103] This assumption is also implicit in all the 'persecution theories'.

In the rest of this chapter, therefore, I shall accept the theory that the fixed calendar was adopted for the sake of unifying the Jewish community. However, I shall argue that this policy did not originate from above, as a 'grand strategy' of the Patriarch and the rabbinic calendrical court, but rather from below. It was, I shall argue, a slow and gradual process, that resulted from the complex relations between Palestine and the Diaspora, and more specifically, between the Palestinian and the Babylonian rabbinic communities.

5.3   PALESTINE AND BABYLONIA: THE SINGLE RABBINIC COMMUNITY

5.3.1   The ideal of calendrical unanimity

The 'one-calendar theory' discussed above assumes a notion that was perhaps unique, in Antiquity, to rabbinic Judaism: that all Jews were meant to follow the same calendar and observe the festivals on the same dates. The notion of calendrical unanimity is easy for us to take for granted. Nowadays, we are used to the fact that there is only one Jewish calendar all over world; in the secular domain, likewise, the Gregorian calendar has become *lingua franca* across the globe.

In the ancient world, by contrast, calendrical diversity—Jewish and non-Jewish—was completely the norm.[104] Since new months and intercalations were reckoned independently by various Jewish communities, festivals could often be observed on totally different dates. This situation would not have been perceived as divisive or schismatic. There is no suggestion, in any of the Jewish non-rabbinic sources we have examined in Chs. 2–3, that calendrical diversity was regarded by the Jews as 'problematic'. Everyone was aware that a calendar based on empirical data, such as sightings of the new moon, was bound to differ from one locality to the next. If one community observed Passover one month later than the others, this was not necessarily perceived as an expression of sectarianism, disagreement, or rift.[105]

---

[104] On the diversity of non-Jewish calendars, see above, especially section 1.2.4.

[105] The same attitude prevailed in the 15th c. among the Karaites, according to R. Ovadia Bartenura, who writes that the Karaites of Egypt, Jerusalem, and Constantinople see nothing wrong in celebrating the festivals at different times from one another (see reference above, n. 83).

Not so, however, in rabbinic Judaism, where the assumption was that new moons and festivals should be observed by everyone on the same dates. This assumption is not explicit in rabbinic sources, nor is it clearly substantiated or justified. But it is implicit in the rules that intercalations can only be made in Judaea or in Galilee,[106] only by a single, appointed rabbinic court,[107] and only with the approval of the Patriarch.[108] The setting of the new months, likewise, is assumed to be the prerogative of a single rabbinic court.[109] This implies that the same calendar must be followed by all Jews. This assumption also lies behind the story of Ḥana-niah nephew of R. Yehoshua, who was prevented from setting his own calendar in Babylonia;[110] and the famous story of R. Yehoshua's dispute with R. Gamliel over one new moon, where R. Yehoshua was coerced into obeying R. Gamliel's decision and desecrating the day which, in his view, should have been that of the Day of Atonement (*M. RH* 2: 8–9).

The ideal of calendrical unanimity, which may have been peculiar to rabbinic Judaism, gave rise to unique calendrical practices that were un-heard of in other Jewish circles. One of these was the dissemination of the court's calendrical decisions, according to the Mishnah, through a system of beacons or envoys—an almost incredible scenario which finds no parallel in any other, non-rabbinic source. Rabbinic sources suggest that calendrical decisions were disseminated in practice to communities

---

[106] *T. Sanhedrin* 2: 13 (pp. 417–18), and parallel sources cited and discussed in section 4.1.2. Scriptural support is given to this rule in *B. Sanhedrin* 11b, from Deut. 12: 5. See also *Y. RH* 2: 6 (58b), citing Ezek. 13: 9 (cf *Y. Sanhedrin* 1: 2 (18c); *B. Ketubot* 112a). According to *Midrash Tannaim* (ed. Hoffmann, p. 90), citing *Deut.* 16: 1 in support, intercalations can only be made in the Temple. According to the Palestinian Talmud, intercalation may be carried out outside the land of Israel if no one inside the land can do it; this explains how Jeremiah, Ezekiel, and Barukh could intercalate while they were in exile (*Y. Sanhedrin* 1: 2 (19a); *Y. Nedarim* 7: 13 (40a). This exception also applied to R. Akiva, but not to Ḥananiah nephew of R. Yehoshua (*B. Berakhot* 63a; cf *Y. Sanhedrin* and *Y. Nedarim* ibid.). For a lengthy homily on this whole theme, see *Pirqei de-R. Eliezer* 8; see also *Midrash ha-Gadol* on Exod. 13: 10 (Margaliot 1956: ii. 234–5).

[107] *B. Sanhedrin* 10b–11a. It is identified with the 'great court in Jerusalem' in *Mekhilta de-R. Yishmael, Bo* 2, end (ed. Horovitz–Rabin 9), with scriptural support from Exod. 12: 2.

[108] According to one *baraita* in *B. Sanhedrin* 11a.

[109] See *Y. Sanhedrin* 1: 2 (18c); *Y. RH* 2: 6 (58b). According to the Targum to S. of S. 7: 5, intercalations, new moons, and new years are set 'at the gate of the great Sanhedrin' (see Marx 1910–11: 65–6). *Targum Onkelos* to Deut. 33: 18 implies that calendar decisions are taken only in Jerusalem.

[110] See above, section 5.2.3. Note, in the version of *B. Berakhot* 63b, the citation of scriptural support from Isa. 2: 3.

in Palestine—e.g. to Caesarea, where R. Abbahu resided[111]—as well as in the Diaspora, as we shall see below.

Another practice unique to rabbinic Judaism was the Diaspora observance of two festival days, to prevent the inadvertent desecration of the date observed in Palestine. This practice, to repeat, was totally unheard of in non-rabbinic sources.[112]

The concept of two festival days was, in itself, a paradox. For it meant that the Diaspora would observe a *different* calendar—with two-day rather than one-day festivals—in order to observe the *same* calendar, i.e. celebrate the festivals on the same day. This paradox was perhaps the clearest expression of the impossibility, at least in the context of the ancient world, of implementing world-wide calendrical unity with an empirical calendar. Calendrical unanimity was bound to remain, in this sense, an unfulfilled ideal.

The earliest reference to the two festival days of the Diaspora is in one brief passage of the Tosefta;[113] it appears more frequently in the Talmudim, with a full treatment in *B. Betzah* 4b.[114]

Related to the notion of calendrical unanimity is also the observance of two days of Rosh ha-Shanah. This custom also applied to the Jews of Palestine, because the date of this festival, which coincides with the new month (1 Tishre), could not have been transmitted in time to other Palestinian communities outside the rabbinic court. This may explain why the two days of Rosh ha-Shanah, unlike the two festival days of the Diaspora, receive extensive treatment already in the Mishnah. One passage in the Mishnah suggests that the two days of Rosh ha-Shanah were only observed when there was reason to be doubtful about its date.[115] Other passages appear to assume that the two days were regularly observed.[116]

By the Geonic period, however, it is possible that only one day of Rosh ha-Shanah was observed in Palestine, this custom remaining unchallenged until

---

[111] *Y. RH* 3: 1 (58d). R. Berakhya is also mentioned in this passage, but his place of residence, presumably in Palestine, is unknown. The location of the calendrical court, in R. Abbahu's period (late 3rd–early 4th cc.), is likely to have been Tiberias, where the Patriarch resided: see Safrai (1965*b*).

[112] The second festival day was unknown to non-rabbinic writers such as Josephus: see section 3.2.1. See also section 4.2.3, on the taking of the *lulav* on the first day of Tabernacles that occurs on the Sabbath.

[113] *T. 'Eruvin* 5: 3 (p. 144); parallel in *B. 'Eruvin* 39b.

[114] See further S. Stern (1994*a*).

[115] *M. 'Eruvin* 3: 7.

[116] *M. Shabbat* 19: 5; *M. 'Eruvin* 3: 9; also ibid. 3: 8, unless it is read as a continuation of ibid. 3: 7 (cited in previous n.); *M. Menaḥot* 11: 9; *M. 'Arakhin* 2: 5 (and implicitly, 2: 2); *T. 'Eruvin* 5: 3 (p. 144). See Gandz (1949–50) 256–67.

the eleventh century.[117] The standard observance of only one day may have developed as a result of the introduction of a fixed calendar in the fourth century, but this is only speculation.

5.3.2 Calendrical unanimity and the Babylonian community

Calendrical unanimity was not a mere *desideratum* of the Palestinian calendrical authorities. It was shared and accepted by all rabbinic communities, not least the rabbinic community of Babylonia. This community, unlike all other Diaspora communities, had enough in common with the Palestinian rabbis to accept, for the sake of unity, Palestinian authority over calendrical decisions.

The uniqueness of the Babylonian community was sensed and appreciated by the Palestinian authorities. It is no wonder that most of their efforts to disseminate calendrical decisions were directed specifically at the Babylonian community. The beacon-chain described in the Mishnah faced only the north-eastern direction, towards Syria; both the Palestinian and the Babylonian Talmudim consider it to have extended to Babylonia.[118] Likewise, the calendar envoys that succeeded this system were largely sent, according to our sources, in the direction of Syria and Babylonia.[119] Some excursions were made, as we have seen, to 'Asia' (Asia Minor). But no envoys are known to have been sent to Egypt, even though it was closer to Palestine than Babylonia and Asia, and comprised among the largest Jewish communities in this period.

A number of rabbinic sources confirm that calendrical information was never sent to Egypt, in spite of its considerable Jewish population;[120] this point is also noted by Maimonides (*Sanctification of the New Month*, 5:10). Most revealing is *Y. 'Eruvin* 3:9 (21c), which has already been cited and discussed in section 4.2.3 When R. Abbahu visited Alexandria during the festival of Tabernacles, he apparently informed the Alexandrians of the 'correct' date of the festival. R. Ami

---

[117] See Herr (1979/80) 76–8. The earliest evidence of this custom is found in early Geonic sources, cited by Lewin (1942) 81–2. See also Ajdler (1996) 670, who suggests that this can also be inferred by comparing *B. Niddah* 67b with *Y. Megillah* 4: 1 (75a). Against this, see Fleischer (1983) 249–53 and (1984c).

[118] *Y. RH* 2: 2 (58a) (the 'palm trees of Babylonia'); *B. RH* 23b ('Pumbaditha').

[119] As implicit in *T. Peah* 4: 6 (p. 23) and parallels: *T. Ketubot* 3: 1 (ibid. 263), *Y. Ketubot* 2: 7 (26d), and *B. Ketubot* 25a. Similarly, *T. Sanh.* 2: 6 (pp. 416–17) and *B. Sanh.* 11b (R. Gamliel's letter regarding the intercalation: see above, section 5.2.3). It may be relevant to note, however, that a similar assumption—but in this case, historically false—is made in *M. Sheqalim* 3: 4 and *T. Sheqalim* 2: 3-4 (p. 175) regarding the half-shekel contributions from the Diaspora, which are assumed in these sources to have come only from Syria, Babylonia, and Media.

[120] See sources cited in previous n.

heard about this and exclaimed: 'who will bring them R. Abbahu every year?', which clearly implies that calendrical information was not normally sent to the Jews of Egypt.[121]

The extent to which the Mishnaic beacons or the sending of envoys were ever implemented in practice, and if so, whether these systems could ever have been effective, are questions which have already been raised (section 4.1.3) and which cannot really be answered. A number of passages in the Babylonian Talmud suggest that calendrical information from Palestine was, at least occasionally, received. The date of the new moon was once transmitted to Babylonia by the sage ʿUlla.[122] A false message[123] and a cryptic message[124] are also said, on other occasions, to have been received.

But this does not prove that the transmission of calendrical information to Babylonia was either regular or reliable. We are told in the Palestinian Talmud that the exilarch Mar ʿUqva found two letters that had been sent to Babylonia, presumably from the Land of Israel, regarding the intercalation.[125] The fact that he only 'found' these letters, which may have even dated from before his period, suggests that reception of such letters was actually quite rare. According to the Babylonian Talmud, Levi once happened to be in Babylonia and saw the Jews observing the Day of Atonement one day too early; he refused to correct them, however, because he had not heard the announcement of the new moon directly from the rabbinic court (*B. RH* 21a). This story, together with other similar accounts,[126] conveys the impression not only that mistakes could occur, but also that the transmission of calendrical information

---

[121] On the meaning of R. Yose's letter to the Alexandrians (in the same passage) which stated: 'they have written to you the order of festivals', see discussion in section 4.2.3. Egypt's failure to conform to the Palestinian rabbinic calendar in the Talmudic period is evident in the letter of Peter of Alexandria (early 4th c.: see section 2.5.3) as well as in the *ketubah* of Antinoopolis (early 5th c.: see section 2.6.2), which both indicate that the rule of the equinox would not have been observed.

[122] *B. RH* 22b; perhaps also, on another occasion, ibid. 20a.

[123] *B. Hullin* 101b; see above, section 5.1.1.

[124] *B. Sanhedrin* 12a; see above, section 5.1.1.

[125] *Y. Megillah* 1: 7 (71a). Mar ʿUqva was exilarch of Babylonia in the 3rd c., and hence most likely to be in possession of such letters.

[126] Other, similar stories are cited in *B. RH* 21a, but note that the text of the Vilna edition is incomplete. See *Diqduqei Sofrim* ad loc., MS JTS cited by Kasher (1949) 127, and secondary sources including the *Sheʾiltot de-Rav ʾAḥai* (Mirsky 1964: 82–3), a Geonic responsum (Marmorstein 1928: 31–2, Lewin 1932/3: 38), the commentaries of R. Ḥananel and Ps.-Maimonides ad loc., and Isaac Israeli, *Yesod ʿOlam* 4: 5 (Goldberg 1848: ii. 9a).

from the Palestinian rabbinic court to the Babylonian Diaspora was haphazard and, at best, sporadic.[127]

The same stories, however, illustrate the degree to which Babylonian Jews were willing to accept, in spite of these difficulties, the authority of Palestinian calendrical decisions.[128] Calendrical information from Palestine was not only accepted, but also actively sought out. In the Levi episode just mentioned, the Babylonians begged him to testify as to the 'correct' date of the Day of Atonement—i.e. when it was observed in the Land of Israel—so that they might amend their calendar accordingly (in this occurrence, unfortunately, he refused).[129]

The most visible expression of Babylonia's unique dependence on Palestinian authority was the precautionary observance of the second festival day, in areas of the Diaspora which the calendar envoys would not have had time to reach.[130] Its desecration was apparently treated with severity (*B. Pesaḥim* 52a). Actual observance in Babylonia of this second festival day is attested throughout the Babylonian Talmud.[131] The trouble which Babylonian Jews took to observe it was a clear indication of their commitment to the Palestinian calendar.[132] Some Amoraim went as

---

[127] Note also that ʿUlla appears to have reported the new moon in Babylonia without acting as regular or official envoy: *B. RH* 22b.

[128] ʿUlla's report on the new moon was accepted in Babylonia not merely because he was an important person, but rather, as R. Kahana explains, because calendrical information from the Land of Israel could always be treated as reliable and authoritative (ibid.).

[129] *Theoretical* knowledge about the calendar is also often said, in the Babylonian Talmud, to have emanated from Palestine: see in particular *B. RH* 20b (R. Zeira), *B. Sukkah* 43b (Bar Hadya, Ravin and 'all those who came down' from Palestine; cf *B. RH* 20a, ʿUlla), and the calendrical rules that were sent to Babylonia from Palestine (see references below, section 5.4.1). However, this may be insignificant, because in general rabbinic teachings were far more frequently transferred from Palestine to Babylonia than in the opposite direction: see Dor (1971).

[130] In areas within reach of the envoys, one day only would have been observed: see *B. RH* 21a.

[131] See *B. ʿEruvin* 39b; ibid. 40a; *B. Pesaḥim* 51b–52a; *B. RH* 20b–21a; *B. Sanhedrin* 26b; and at length, *B. Betzah* 4b. The liturgy and biblical readings for the second festival days are discussed in detail in *B. Taʿanit* 4b–5a (cf *Y. Taʿanit* 1: 1 (63d)); *B. Taʿanit* 28b (= *B. ʿArakhin* 10a; contrast *T. Sukkah* 3: 2 (p. 195), *Y. Sukkah* 4: 5 (54c)); *B. Megillah* 31a. The Diaspora observance of the two festival days has survived all vicissitudes until the present day: see S. Stern (1994*a*).

[132] The onerous nature of the second festival day may find expression in *Y. ʿEruvin* 3: 9 (21c), according to which it was inflicted on Diaspora Jewry as a punishment for having transgressed the festival whilst still in the Land of Israel. This passage, however, is obviously polemical.

far as fasting two days for the Day of Atonement; the Palestinian Talmud criticizes this practice as dangerous and unnecessary, and recalls that it once cost the life of the father of a Babylonian Amora;[133] but the Babylonian Talmud reports that Rava, who used to fast two days, was rewarded one year for his caution, as his second fast day proved to be correct.[134]

It is only in the Tannaitic and early Amoraic periods, when its function was to prevent the inadvertent desecration of the date observed in Palestine, that the observance of the second festival day would have signified Babylonia's loyalty to the Palestinian calendar. From the fourth century onwards, when a fixed calendar was instituted and hence the dates set by the Palestinian court were largely known in the Diaspora, the second festival day was only retained as a custom.[135] From this point onwards, the Babylonian observance of the second day would only have become, if anything, an expression of *difference* from the Palestinian community.

Babylonian loyalty to the Palestinian calendar persisted well into the Geonic period. As late as 835/6 CE, the Babylonian exilarch confirmed the authority of the Palestinian court in all calendrical decisions; this, he explicitly wrote, was essential for calendrical unanimity (see above, section 4.3.3). It is only in the late ninth or early tenth centuries that Babylonian loyalty to Palestine began to crumble, for reasons which will be examined further below.

5.3.3 Calendrical dissidence in Babylonia

This is not to say that before the ninth century calendrical dissidence had never existed in Babylonia. Mention has already been made of the story of Ḥananiah nephew of R. Yehoshua (above, section 5.2.3). As evident in the Palestinian version of this story, Ḥananiah's calendar was not merely independent from that of Palestine, but also substantially different; for when it was rescinded, the more distant communities that could not be informed in time observed a festival, following Ḥananiah's calendar, on the 'wrong' date.[136]

The precise activities of Ḥananiah nephew of R. Yehoshua are worthy of further attention. According to the Palestinian version, all Ḥananiah appears to

---

[133] *Y. RH* 1: 4 (57b) (= *Y. Ḥallah* 1 (57c)).

[134] *B. RH* 21a. See also *B. Pesaḥim* 54b and *Tosafot* ibid. s.v. לקביעא.

[135] So according to *B. Betzah* 4b: see above sections 4.2.3 and 5.1.1, and S. Stern (1994*a*).

[136] All the text actually refers to is a 'disruption', but this can only mean that a festival was celebrated on the 'wrong' date.

have done was *intercalation*, i.e. the occasional proclamation of a second month of Adar.[137] This would only have involved a *calculation* of when intercalation was due, as is implicit at the end of the story: R. Yehudah b. Betyra persuaded Hananiah that the Palestinians' ability to *calculate* was not inferior to his.[138]

According to the Babylonian version, however, Hananiah was both 'intercalating years' and 'setting months';[139] thus he had taken charge of the whole calendar. Even so, 'setting months' (קובע חדשים) implies something different from the Mishnaic procedure of 'sanctifying months' (מקדש חדשים). However Hananiah set his new months—perhaps, again, purely through calculation—the Babylonian Talmud may be suggesting that he refrained from the Mishnaic procedure because it was restricted to the land of Israel.[140]

Yet although the accounts of the Palestinian and Babylonian Talmudim differ in significant ways,[141] the Babylonian Talmud essentially agrees that Hananiah was wrong to have violated the prerogative of the Palestinian court.

The observance of Hananiah's 'erroneous' dates in some of the more distant communities is indicative, perhaps, of the geographical scope of his authority. But Diaspora rabbinic leaders did not all approve of his activities. According to the Palestinian version, it was R. Yehudah b. Betyra in Nisibis who persuaded Hananiah to give in to Palestinian authority.[142]

The story of Hananiah—whether 'historical' or not—alerts us at least to the *possibility* of calendrical dissidence among the rabbis of Babylonia. Intimations of dissidence can also be found in connection with the early Amora Shemuel. Shemuel is said to have boasted that he could set the calendar for the entire Diaspora (*B. RH* 20b); and as proof of his knowledge, he once sent to R. Yohanan, his leading Palestinian contemporary,

---

[137] חנניה בן אחי רבי יהושע עיבר בחוצה לארץ: *Y. Sanhedrin* 1: 2 (19a) (= *Y. Nedarim* 7: 13 (40a)). In the context of this passage, עיבר refers specifically—as is indeed the more general usage—to intercalation of the *year* (and not to intercalation of the month, i.e. the addition of a 30th day).

[138] Compare the texts of *Y. Sanhedrin* 1: 2 (19a) and *Y. Nedarim* 7: 13 (40a). This section of the story is not included in Gafni's translation (1997: 108).

[139] היה מעבר שנים וקובע חדשים: *B. Berakhot* 63a.

[140] The same phrase, קובע חדשים, is used in a similar context in *B. Megillah* 12b, with reference to the rabbis in Susa (in the story of Esther).

[141] See further Gafni (1997) 107–11, who points out that the Palestinian version assumes the primacy of Palestinian calendrical authority to be permanent and intrinsic to the land of Israel, whereas according to the Babylonian version, it is contingent on the greater erudition of the Palestinian sages.

[142] On the location of this 'Nisibis', as well as on Hananiah's own location in Babylonia, see Oppenheimer (1995) especially pp. 127–8.

a list of intercalations for a sixty-year period.[143] Unlike Hananiah, Shemuel is not known to have put his knowledge into practice. But this did
not prevent the Palestinian Talmud from suspecting him of calendrical
dissidence, as it implies, in a rather enigmatic passage, that he was guilty
of the same sin as Hananiah who intercalated the year outside the land
of Israel.[144]

Calendar dissidence, however, is extremely rare in Talmudic literature. The case of Hananiah would have been considered exceptional; in
the Talmud, it functions purely as a cautionary tale. Hananiah, moreover, was a Tanna from the mid second century CE; he belonged to a
period when rabbinic activity in Babylonia had not yet begun to flour-
ish. The Babylonian Talmud certainly does not sympathize with him.
The impression conveyed is that by the Amoraic period, and certainly
after the generation of Shemuel (early third century), calendrical loyalty
to Palestine had become the norm in rabbinic Babylonia. There is no
reason to doubt the historical truth of this impression. Calendrical dissidence is no longer heard of until the very end of our period, with the
R. Saadya–Ben Meir controversy of the 920s. Why calendar dissidence
did not arise until this later period will be explained below.

5.3.4   Calendar prediction in Babylonia

The tradent of the Hananiah story in the Babylonian Talmud, R. Safra,
may have had a special interest in calendar reckoning outside the land
of Israel, for in *B. Pesahim* 51b–52a he is reported as claiming to have
known the 'fixing of the new moon'. As the context of this passage makes
clear, R. Safra meant that although he lived in Babylonia, in a place
beyond reach of the calendar envoys, he was able to know, or rather
to *predict*, when the new moon had been declared in Palestine.[145] On

---

[143] *B. Hullin* 95b. According to Bornstein (1887: 303, 1924: 319–20), this constituted a 60-year cycle of intercalations, equivalent perhaps to double the 30-year
cycle of the Sardica document (on which see section 2.5.3). The *cyclical* nature of
Shemuel's intercalations is not explicit, however, in the text. Moreover, the number
'60' may simply be used in this passage in an approximate or hyperbolical sense, to
indicate an indeterminate large number of years (for similar usages of '60' in the
Talmud, see Chajes 1952: 226–7, ch. 30).

[144] *Y. Ketubot* 2: 6 (26c), as correctly interpreted by Gafni (1997) 111 and Ajdler
(1996) 692.

[145] This is the plain meaning of the passage, as interpreted by Rashi (ap. *Tosafot*
on *B. Sukkah* 43a, s.v. ולא ידעינן) and R. Isaiah of Terrani the Elder (13th c.) in *Pisqei
ha-Rid* on *B. Pesahim* 51b–52a (Isaiah of Terrani 1966: 270). The interpretation of
Rabbenu Tam (in *Tosafot*, loc. cit.) is exceedingly far-fetched.

this basis, he sought to be exempted from the observance of a second festival day. Unlike Ḥananiah, R. Safra had no intention of publicizing his knowledge to the local community. His question was only whether *in private* (or 'in the desert') he could be exempted from the observance of a second festival day, since to him the date of the festival was certain.

The Talmud does not clarify on what basis R. Safra was able to predict the dates of the new moon.[146] What is important about this passage, however, is that although R. Safra recognized the Palestinian prerogative over the calendar, and thus refrained from any public act of calendrical dissidence, he still attempted to reckon the calendar without resort to the envoys of the Palestinian court.

R. Safra's interest in predicting the new moons declared in Palestine was not merely academic. To some extent, predictions of this kind would have been necessary for rabbinic Diaspora communities, for the simple reason that calendrical information from Palestine could not always be relied upon to reach them. If the date of the Day of Atonement, in particular, could not reach them on time, a prediction of it would have been needed, because the custom was generally not to fast, in doubt, over two days.[147] The ability of R. Safra, and possibly of other experts such as Shemuel, to calculate and predict the Palestinian 'fixing of the new moon' would thus have been essential.

For similar reasons, people at sea needed ways of predicting the dates of the festivals. Calendar envoys could obviously not reach them; but they had the advantage, at sea, of clear horizons to the west as well as to the east. R. Naḥman is said to have advised them as follows, with reference to Passover: 'When you observe that the moon sets as the day rises, destroy your leaven'. The Talmud continues: 'When does it set (as the day rises)? On the fifteenth (of the lunar

---

[146] If, as one would assume from the context of this passage, the Palestinian calendar still followed the empirical Mishnaic system, it is unclear how R. Safra could have had the confidence never to commit an error in his predictions. Calendrical rules, which may have been introduced in the Amoraic period, would have assisted him in his predictions; see further below. According to R. Isaiah of Terrani (1966: 270), the fixed calendar was already instituted in R. Safra's period, but not yet widely known; this also is possible, even if R. Safra belongs to the beginning of the 4th c. However, although of similar expression, this Talmudic passage must be distinguished from *B. Betzah* 4b, where the Talmud suggests that since the 'fixing of the moon' is known, the second festival day should be *completely* abolished. There the Talmud is ostensibly referring to a later period when the fixed calendar had been instituted and was already widely known (see above, section 4.2.3).

[147] In some cases, indeed, mistakes could still be made, as in the story of Levi: see above, section 5.3.2. People who fasted over two days were rare: see ibid.

month)! And yet we destroy (our leaven) on the fourteenth! From their perspective, as the world is revealed to them (they have a clear horizon), it sets (as the day rises) already on the fourteenth.'[148]

Although it would be quite easy for people at sea to make their own sightings of the *new* moon, and thus to set their own independent calendar, R. Naḥman refrains from giving them such advice. All they are required is to *predict* the date of Passover, on the basis of the coincidence of moonset and sunrise in the *middle* of the lunar month.

A passage from the Tosefta explains, indeed, how Diaspora communities should reckon the calendar when calendrical information from the Palestinian court has failed to reach them.[149] Full and defective months, it rules, should be reckoned in alternation. The Tosefta adds that if Siwan has been reckoned in the Diaspora as defective (29 days) and Tammuz as full (30 days), but then it emerges that Tammuz was actually made defective (by the Palestinian court), the error need not be corrected.[150]

The reason for this perhaps surprising ruling is presumably that there are no major festivals in Av, and thus that no harm will arise if the Diaspora is one day behind the land of Israel; this is preferable to a correction of the calendar, which may cause unnecessary confusion. The assumption appears to be that eventually, by the month of Tishre, the discrepancy with the land of Israel will be naturally rectified.

This passage constitutes an explicit recognition, on the part of a Palestinian source, of a calendar system that can be reckoned independently by Diaspora Jews, and can occasionally deviate from the official calendar of the Land of Israel. Nevertheless, it is evident from this passage that this calendar system should not be treated as a substitute for Palestinian calendrical decisions: it is only to be used on a temporary basis, whenever the latter have not been received. Its purpose is only for the Diaspora to keep up, if only approximately, with the calendar of the Land of Israel.

Calendar reckoning in Babylonia is bound to have been a historical reality. For it would have been almost inconceivable, in practical terms, for

---

[148] *B. RH* 21a.

[149] *T. ʿArakhin* 1: 8 (p. 543): במקום שאין מכירין זמנו של חדש, נוהגין אחד מעובר ואחד שאינו מעובר. וכן בגליות, נוהגין אחד מעובר ואחד שאינו מעובר. היו נוהגין תמוז בזמנו והאב מעובר, ואחר כך נודע להן שאב בזמנו, מניחין אותו, ומונין מכאן ואילך אחד מעובר ואחד שאינו מעובר.

[150] As correctly interpreted by Bornstein (1908) 88–93; see also Weiss (1995) 187 n. 7. 'The error need not be corrected' is the only possible translation of מניחין אותו, as rightly interpreted by Pardo (1994: vii. 495) and Abramsky (1965: 42a). See also Weiss (1995) 187 n. 8. The interpretation of Herr (1976: 852) is incorrect.

Babylonian or other communities to depend entirely on the Palestinian calendar without ever making their own calendrical decisions. These decisions would not have contradicted the ideal of calendrical unanimity and the authority of the Palestinian court, so long as it was clear that their purpose was only to *predict* the Palestinian decisions (as in the case of R. Safra), or at least to *keep up* with the Palestinian rabbinic calendar (as in the Tosefta passage). In this way, Babylonian communities could have run their own calendar without betraying their loyalty to the Palestinian rabbinic community.

The assumption that Babylonian communities must have reckoned their own calendar in the Amoraic period is also found in a Geonic source. Referring to the story of Levi, in which a Babylonian community had observed the Day of Atonement on the wrong date but Levi was unable to correct them,[151] the Geonic responsum explains:

ולא היה בזאת כלום על הבבליים, כי אחזו את דרכם שהיא ירושתם, או שהראשים
שבהן כך קבעו וכך עליהם לעשות.[152]

But the Babylonians were not at all wrong in this matter, because they were following the way (i.e. calendar) they had inherited, or because their leaders had decided on these (dates) and so they were to conduct themselves.

This responsum, however, may be less a reflection of Levi's period than of late Geonic Babylonia, in which it was presumably written. The growing calendrical independence of Babylonia in the later Geonic period will be discussed in sections 5.4.3 and following.

Isaac Israeli goes much further than this Geonic responsum. He suggests that the Jews of Babylonia observed a calculated calendar that was based on the conjunction; their calendar differed by one day from the Palestinian calendar, as the latter was based on sightings of the new moon. This explains why Levi and others (in the same passage of *B. RH* 21a) had found the Jews of Babylonia observing the Day of Atonement one day too early (*Yesod 'Olam* 4:5; Goldberg 1848: ii. 8b–9a). This theory is most ingenious, but fails to explain why the Babylonians accepted, whenever available, the Palestinian dates (as evident in the Levi story, and as acknowledged by Israeli himself); these dates would have been incompatible with their own calendar. Israeli's theory is perhaps excessively radical; in the context of the Levi story, it is more likely that Babylonian Jews carried out their own sightings of the new moon, or calculated the likelihood of its visibility in the Land of Israel.[153]

---

[151] See above, section 5.3.2.

[152] Marmorstein (1928) 32; Lewin (1932/3) 38.

[153] See also Rashba, *Responsa* 4: 254.

5.3.5 From calendrical rules to the fixed calendar

It is for the sake of Diaspora Jewry, I shall now argue, that calendrical rules were formulated around the beginning of the Amoraic period, well before the fixed calendar was instituted.[154] These rules did not abolish the Mishnaic system; but they reduced the range of dates when new moons and festivals were able to occur. Knowledge of these rules would have enabled the Babylonians, therefore, to *predict* with much greater ease the Palestinian calendrical decisions. Thus the importance of these rules to the rabbinic Babylonian community would have been considerable.

The rules that the months of Elul and Adar (adjacent to Nisan) are always defective (of 29 days) are likely to have been formulated, indeed, for no other purpose but this.[155] Since Elul and Adar preceded the main festival months (Tishre and Nisan, respectively), knowledge that they could only be defective would have enabled Diaspora Jews to *predict*, to a high degree of accuracy, when the festivals were due to be observed.[156] Although the Talmud acknowledges that the rule of Elul was not always strictly observed (see section 4.2.2), this rule could have been used as a *guideline* for predicting the dates of Tishre with reasonable certainty.

The connection between these rules and calendar reckoning in the Diaspora is explicit, perhaps not surprisingly, in the Babylonian Talmud. In this passage, the rule of Adar is subject to a dispute:[157]

דרש רב נחמן בר חסדא: העיד רבי סימאי משום חגי, זכריה ומלאכי על שני אדרים,
שאם רצו לעשותן שניהן מלאין, עושין, שניהן חסרין, עושין, אחד מלא ואחד חסר,
עושין; וכך היו נוהגין בגולה. ומשום רבינו אמרו: לעולם אחד מלא ואחד חסר, עד
שיוודע לך שהוקבע ראש חודש בזמנו. שלחו ליה למר עוקבא: אדר הסמוך לניסן
לעולם חסר.

R. Naḥman b. Ḥisda made the following discourse:

R. Simai testified in the name of Haggai, Zechariah, and Malachi concerning the two Adars (in an intercalated year), that if they (the court) desired they could make both of them full, and if they desired they could make both of them defective, and if they desired they could make one full and the other defective; *and this was the custom in the Diaspora.*

---

[154] See detailed discussion in section 4.2.2.

[155] The origin of these rules may be much earlier than the Amoraic period: see ibid.

[156] Cf Beckwith (1996) 288–9. In Palestine itself, the rule of Elul would have helped to justify the observance of a single day of Rosh ha-Shanah. See above, section 5.3.1.

[157] Another Tannaitic dispute on the rule of Adar is recorded in *B. Bekhorot* 58a.

And in the name of our teacher, they said: one is always full and the other always defective, *until you are informed that the new month was on time* (i.e. both defective).[158]

They sent to Mar ʿUqva (a message): Adar adjacent to Nisan is always defective (*B. RH* 19b).

The statement that 'this was the custom in the Diaspora' (which I have emphasized) presumably refers to making the first Adar full and the second defective.[159] The statement cited 'in the name of our teacher' appears to mean, therefore, much the same thing: that the sequence full–defective should 'always' be followed until information to the contrary is received; we may assume that this statement is also addressed, primarily, to the Diaspora. It implies that although the sequence full–defective was not always observed by the Palestinian court, it could be used in the Diaspora as a *guideline* for predicting when the new month of Nisan, and hence the date of Passover, would have been fixed.

The rule of the equinox, apparently sent to Babylonia in the early to mid fourth century, would have fulfilled a similar function with regard to intercalation. As an astronomical phenomenon, the equinox could be determined anywhere in the world and did not depend on agricultural or other criteria (e.g. ripeness of the crops) that would have been specifically tied to the land of Israel. The rule of the equinox thus made it possible for Diaspora Jews, wherever they were, to predict with virtual certainty whether or not the year had been intercalated by the Palestinian court. That this was the purpose of the rule may be implicit, indeed, in the Talmudic passage where it is cited: this passage implies, as I have argued in Ch. 4 (section 4.2.2), that the rule was only meant as a *guideline* for Babylonians to rely on in the absence of firm information from the Palestinian court.

Additional rules, such as the prohibition of the Day of Atonement's occurring on a Friday or a Sunday, would have been instituted in the

---

[158] The term בזמנו ('on time') is technical and refers to the new moon occurring on the 30th day of the previous month. The possibility that both months may have been full is not raised. However, the second festival day, observed in the Diaspora, would have covered for such an eventuality, so that no immediate correction of the calendar would have been needed. It is also possible that 'our teacher' (*rabbenu*) is of the view that 'the Adar adjacent to Nisan is always defective', so that it can never happen that both months are full (note that this view is attributed to 'Rabbi', presumably R. Yehudah ha-Nasi, in *Y. RH* 3: 1 (58c) and parallels; in our passage, however, *rabbenu* is identified by Rashi as Rav).

[159] As per Bornstein (1908) 91 n. 2.

Amoraic period for primarily different reasons (see section 4.2.2). Nevertheless, all these rules would have had the effect of reducing the range of dates when the Day of Atonement could occur, which would have helped Babylonian Jews to predict the dates of that and the other festivals in Tishre.

It is important to note that the origin of these rules was not Babylonia but Palestine. According to the Babylonian Talmud, many of these rules were purposely sent from Palestine to the leaders of the Babylonian community. Thus we are told that the rule of Adar—which is also attested in the Palestinian Talmud[160]—was 'sent' to the exilarch Mar ʿUqva, i.e. from Palestine.[161] The rule of the equinox was sent to Rava by R. Huna b. Avin, who did spend part of his life in Babylonia, but who would have sent this teaching from the land of Israel.[162] These passages confirm Babylonia's continuous dependence, in calendrical matters, on the authority of Palestine. However, the Palestinian origin of these rules comes hardly as a surprise, if we consider that throughout this period, the rabbinic calendar remained under the firm control of the Palestinian court. What is important about these passages is that the Palestinian authorities appear to have been willing to *alter* their calendar, with the introduction and propagation of such rules, for the sake of assisting Babylonians in their calendrical predictions.

As I have already suggested (sections 4.2.2, 4.2.5), calendrical rules were the first step towards the eventual formation of the fixed calendar. We know from the Palestinian Talmud that a (partially) fixed calendar, with a regular alternation of full and defective months from at least Adar to Tishre, was already in place by the end of the fourth century (section 4.2.3). The effects of this new calendar were soon to be realized in Babylonia. Now that the calendar was 'known' in the Diaspora—in the sense that the dates of the festivals had become almost completely predictable, or that they could be calculated and disseminated by the Palestinian court well in advance[163]—the Babylonian Talmud was able to question whether the observance of a second festival day was still

---

[160] As well as the rule of Elul: see section 4.2.2.

[161] As the phrase שלחו ליה (they sent to him) is usually taken to mean (cf passage from *B. Sanhedrin* 12a, cited in section 5.1.1): *B. RH* 19b, cited above in this section.

[162] See section 4.2.2. On R. Huna b. Avin, see Strack and Stemberger (1991) 103.

[163] See section 5.1.1, on *B. Betzah* 4b. On the annual dispatch of calendar dates by the Palestinian court, attested in late Geonic sources, see section 4.3.3.

necessary.[164] For its ability to follow the Palestinian calendar was now virtually guaranteed.

It is arguably for this very purpose that the fixed calendar had been introduced. The shift to a fixed calendar was more radical than any other change, such as the institution of fixed rules, that had preceded. But it did not represent a fundamental change of direction or policy. As I have argued in Ch. 4, the transition from empirical calendar to calculated system may have been quite gradual. Ever-multiplying calendrical rules, including eventually the alternation of full and defective months from Adar to Tishre, may have simply overrun the old Mishnaic system. This would have brought the empirical observation of the moon to an effective end, and ushered in a fixed calendar that was eventually to be based entirely on the calculation of the mean conjunction. The fixed calendar was thus the culmination of a process, in which the Mishnaic calendar was gradually adapted to enable Diaspora communities to predict and follow the same calendar as in the Land of Israel.

The evidence we have considered suggests that this process began in the third century, when the rule of Adar was first sent to the exilarch Mar ʿUqva, and culminated with the fixed calendar some time in the fourth century. Why these developments took place in this period is easy to understand. As soon as the rabbinic community of Babylonia began to grow and expand, at the beginning of the Amoraic period, the problem of rabbinic solidarity and, more precisely, of Babylonian rabbinic loyalty to its Palestinian motherland, needed urgently to be addressed. The earlier episode of Ḥananiah nephew of R. Yehoshua—if indeed historical—could not be allowed to be repeated. What was at stake, besides political considerations, was the very cohesion of rabbinic Judaism; and this, it was felt, depended largely on homogeneity of calendrical observance.

So long as the Mishnaic system remained in place, calendrical homogeneity would have been impossible. The rabbinic calendar was gradually adapted in the early Amoraic period, so as to ensure that Babylonian rabbis were able to observe the same calendar as in the Land of Israel. The end result of this process was the fixed, rabbinic calendar, eventually to develop into its present, normative form.

---

[164] *B. Betzah* 4b; that this passage refers to the fixed calendar is likely, even if not absolutely certain. See discussion above, section 4.2.3, and my remarks at the end of section 5.3.2.

5.4 THE BABYLONIAN ORIGINS OF THE NORMATIVE JEWISH CALENDAR

Traditional proponents of the 'one-calendar theory', starting with R. Hai 'the head of the yeshiva', assumed that the fixed calendar was instituted by the Palestinian court for the sake of calendrical unity. In previous section, I have argued that the shift from empirical to fixed calendar was not the result of a single 'institution', but rather a gradual process. The purpose of this process, nevertheless, was to enable Palestinian and Babylonian rabbinic communities to observe the festivals on the same dates.

In this section, I shall question the assumption that the Palestinian court alone would have been responsible for this process. I shall argue that the Babylonian community played a critical role in the formation of the normative rabbinic calendar.

5.4.1 Calendrical rules in Babylonia

As we have seen, the concept of calendrical unanimity was not a Palestinian imposition upon a reluctant Babylonian community. The Babylonians were fully committed to this ideal; their subservience to the Palestinian calendrical court persisted in Babylonia, at least in principle, until as late as the exilarch's letter of 835/6 CE. Thus it was in the interest of the Babylonians, as much perhaps as of the Palestinians, to find ways of keeping up with the Palestinian calendar whilst in the Babylonian Diaspora.

The development of calendrical rules, we have also seen, was designed to facilitate this purpose. Calendrical rules were of much greater importance to Babylonians than to Palestinians, because it was the Babylonians who needed to predict the calendar of the Palestinian court. It is to be expected, therefore, that fixed rules were adopted and used in Babylonia *before* they become standard in the Palestinian calendar.

Evidence to this effect is scant, but we may point to a passage in the Babylonian Talmud that has been quoted above (*B. RH* 19b, in section 5.3.5). This passage states that although, in the Mishnaic system, the two months of Adar (in an intercalated year) could be either full–full, defective–defective, or full–defective, the custom in the Diaspora was always to reckon them as full–defective. The observance of this rule in the Diaspora (or rather, perhaps, in Babylonia) must have put pressure, eventually, on the Palestinian calendrical court to accept it as a standard rule—otherwise calendrical schism would have become in some years inevitable. Although we have no evidence of when and how it became a standard rule in Palestine, it has certainly become one in the normative rabbinic calendar.[165]

If this example is representative of a more general trend, the Babylonians may well have been the prime movers in the development and use of fixed calendrical rules. In this respect, they would have launched the process that eventually led to the adoption of a fixed calendar.

According to the Babylonian Talmud, as we have seen, a number of calendrical rules (e.g. the rule of the equinox) were 'sent' from Palestine to Babylonian leaders (see above, section 5.3.5); this is what would have given these rules their necessary legitimacy. There is no reason, *a priori*, to doubt the Palestinian origin of these rules. However, when sent from Palestine, these rules were often no more than *guidelines* which were not strictly followed by the Palestinian court itself (see section 4.2.2). My point, therefore, is that the Babylonians were the first to rely on these rules and use them *in practice*. This is what would have later led the Palestinians, in turn, to adopt these rules as *standard* in their calendar.

5.4.2   Calendar calculation in Babylonia

This may go some way towards explaining the particular interest of Babylonian sources in calendar calculations. This interest, unique to Babylonia, is evident in the case of a few individual Amoraim, but also in Babylonian rabbinic literature as a whole.

To begin with individual Amoraim, the figure of Shemuel (early–mid third century) is worthy of special mention. As we have seen (section 5.3.3), Shemuel boasted that he could set the calendar for the entire Diaspora, and sent to R. Yoḥanan a list of intercalations for sixty years. He is also attributed a cycle for calculating equinoxes and solstices (*tequfot*),[166] and elsewhere, the notion that the length of the lunar calendar year (not intercalated) is not less than 352 and not more than 356 days (*B. ʿArakhin* 9b). Evidently, his calendar expertise was related to his knowledge of astronomy, as he is said to have exclaimed: 'the paths of heaven are as clear to me as the streets of Nehardea, except for comets— I do not know what they are'.[167] Knowledge of astronomy, or ability to

---

[165] See for instance Maimonides, *Laws of Sanctification*, 8: 5.

[166] *B. ʿEruvin* 56a. This cycle may have been instrumental in setting his 60-year schedule of intercalations.

[167] *B. Berakhot* 58b; cf *Y. Berakhot* 9: 3 (13c). Nehardea was his home town in Babylonia.

calculate the lunar calendar, may have earned him elsewhere the name שמואל ירחינאה, 'Shemuel of the moon' (*B. Bava Metzia*ᶜ 85b).

Knowledge of the calendar, however, is not restricted in the Babylonian Talmud to him. R. Naḥman, a leading late-third-century Babylonian figure, is attributed an intriguing formula regarding the visibility of the new moon in Babylonian and in Palestine,[168] and Ravina, a much later figure, is attributed elsewhere the notion that the regular alternation of full and defective months leads to a discrepancy of one day in three years and an additional day in thirty years.[169]

The Babylonian Talmud as a whole, moreover, has an interest in calendrical calculation that is not paralleled in Palestinian sources. A lengthy passage in *B. ᶜArakhin* (8b–10a) is devoted entirely to this topic, but without any parallel in the Palestinian Talmud. Shemuel's cycle of *tequfot* is mentioned twice in the Babylonian Talmud (*B. Berakhot* 59b and *B. ᶜEruvin* 56a), but nowhere in the Palestinian.[170] A passage in the Babylonian Talmud extolling those who calculate *tequfot* and *mazalot* (the rise of constellations?) is completely unparalleled in Palestinian sources.[171]

Most distinctive is the Babylonian Talmud's obsession with a schematic calendar that is attributed in a Tannaitic source to 'others', and that has been analysed in detail in Ch. 4 (section 4.1.1). This source assumes that 'from one *ᶜAtzeret* to the next, and from one Rosh ha-Shanah to the next, there are only four days, and if the year is intercalated, five days', which implies a fixed calendar based on a rudimentary alternation of full and defective months.[172] Although it represents a marginal opinion which would not have been heeded in the Tannaitic period by the rabbinic court, as argued in Ch. 4, the saying of 'others' is frequently cited and discussed in the Babylonian Talmud, often as a hermeneutic device for explaining away difficult passages.[173] In the Palestinian Talmud,

---

[168] *B. RH* 20b, but see manuscript variations in *Diqduqei Sofrim*.

[169] *B. ᶜArakhin* 9b, cited above in section 4.4.6.

[170] It does appear in later Palestinian sources: see S. Stern (1996) 105–7. The mean length of tropical seasons is supplied, however, by R. Eleazar ha-Qallir in his סילוק לפרשת שקלים (אז ראית), a Palestinian work which is perhaps contemporary with the Babylonian Talmud (7th c.).

[171] *B. Shabbat* 75a. Most of the sayings in this passage are attributed, however, to chains of Palestinian sages. Contrast with *Avot*, end of ch. 3, a Palestinian source where *tequfot* are described as a mere 'side-dish' to wisdom.

[172] *T. ᶜArakhin* 1: 11 (pp. 543–4).

[173] Mainly in *B. ᶜArakhin* 9b; also in *B. Shabbat* 87b, *B. RH* 6b and 20a, *B. Sukkah* 54b.

by contrast, the opinion of 'others' is not mentioned once; the Tosefta is the only Palestinian source where it is mentioned. It is possible that the calendar of 'others' was designed specifically for Diaspora Jews, as a scheme to be followed whenever Palestinian calendrical decisions were not known.[174] In any case, the frequent mention of the calendar of 'others' in the Babylonian Talmud reflects the special interest Babylonians would have had in calculated calendrical schemes.

Babylonian interest in calendar calculation finds further expression in its interpretation of the blessing on the sun, which according to the Babylonian Talmud (*B. Berakhot* 59b) is to be recited at the beginning of the 28-year cycle of *tequfot* (attributed elsewhere to Shemuel). According to the Palestinian Talmud, by contrast, this blessing is not contingent on any calendrical cycle: it is recited whenever the sun re-appears after having been hidden by clouds for three continuous days (*Y. Berakhot* 9:3 (13d)).

In a similar vein, the Babylonian custom was to start praying for rain on the 60th day after the autumn equinox; the Palestinian custom, by contrast, was to start this prayer on the calendar date of 7 Marḥeshwan. The 60th day after the autumn equinox was not contingent on the empirical lunar calendar of Palestine; it represents, perhaps, the only element of the liturgical calendar that could have been reckoned in Babylonia independently of Palestinian calendrical decisions. No wonder, this Babylonian custom is attributed in both Talmudim to Ḥananiah nephew of R. Yehoshua, famous for his calendar dissidence. It is also endorsed, not surprisingly, by Shemuel.[175] Preference for a date based on the equinox reflects an interest in calendar calculation that was unique to the Babylonian rabbinic community.

---

[174] Weiss (1995) 188 and n. 14, suggesting that this passage of *T. ʿArakhin* is similar in purpose to *T. ʿArakhin* 1: 8 (see above section 5.3.4, and n. 149) which just precedes it; see section 4.1.1.

[175] *Y. Taʿanit* 1: 1 (63d); *B. Taʿanit* 10a. Shemuel's cycle of equinoxes may have been formulated for the very purpose of determining the starting date of the prayer for rain (Loewinger 1986: 75). All other dates in tractate *Taʿanit*, which relate to the rainfall season and the order of fasts in periods of drought, are given according to the lunar calendar; these fasts, however, would not have been observed in Babylonia (according to *B. Taʿanit* 11b). This is not to say that Palestinian sources do not take any account, in this context, of the discrepancy between the lunar calendar and tropical seasons: see *T. Taʿanit* 1: 2 (p. 214); *Y. Taʿanit* 1: 3 (64b) and 1: 9 (64d). See also *Y. Bikkurim* 2: 5 (65a–b); and see discussion between Palestinian sages in *B. RH* 15a.

It has been argued that Babylonian rabbis such as Shemuel developed their interest in astronomy and calendrical schemes because of the influence of Babylonian culture. This suggestion is not implausible, even if the extent to which rabbis exposed themselves to non-Jewish influence, and the extent to which the Babylonian tradition of astronomy survived into the late Antique period, remain somewhat unclear.[176] A distinction, however, must be drawn between astronomy and calendars. Interest in astronomy can also be found in rabbinic sources from Palestine, far away from Babylonian influence. Besides citing Shemuel's sayings about comets,[177] the Palestinian Talmud has a description of the courses of the sun and the moon that is not paralleled in the Babylonian Talmud.[178] It also has an unparalleled discussion on the relationship between the cardinal points on the horizon and the azimuths of sunrise and sunset at the equinoxes and solstices.[179] What is distinctive, therefore, of the Babylonian Talmud is not its interest in astronomy, but rather its interest in *calendrical calculation*: for instance, as I have shown above, the cycle of *tequfot* and the schematic calendar of 'others', neither of which are mentioned in the Palestinian Talmud.

This *specific* interest in calendar schemes cannot be simply attributed, therefore, to non-Jewish Babylonian influence. It was probably motivated by the Babylonian Amoraic need to predict the dates of the Palestinian calendar, or in the absence of information from Palestine, to rely on standard calendrical schemes. In this respect, the Babylonian rabbinic community may again be seen as the prime movers in the conception and development of fixed, calculated calendars.

The attributions of many of these sources to Shemuel—if it is reliable—suggests that Babylonian interest in calendar calculations went back to the beginning of the Amoraic period. Thus the difference between the Palestinian and Babylonian Talmudim which I have outlined cannot be put down to the fact that the Babylonian Talmud was redacted *later*, in a period when the fixed calendar had become more prominent.

Even after a fixed calendar was adopted by the Palestinian calendrical court, Palestinian interest in calculated schemes appears to have remained minimal. R.

[176] See above, section 4.4.7 and n. 218.

[177] *Y. Berakhot* 9: 3 (13c), which parallels *B. Berakhot* 58b–59a.

[178] *Y. RH* 2: 4 (58a), see S. Stern (1996). In this article I refer to this passage as a 'calendar', but only in a loose sense of the term (see ibid. 112 n. 16). Inasmuch as the passage is concerned with the courses of the sun and the moon, it is far more astronomical in character than calendrical.

[179] *Y. ʿEruvin* 5: 1 (22c), cited with textual variations by R. Ḥananel on *B. ʿEruvin* 56a.

Eleazar ha-Qallir (seventh century?), in his קרובות לפרשת החודש, deals almost exclusively with the empirical procedure of the Mishnah; the only intimation of a calendrical calculation comes in his statement that from the Creation to the Exodus, there were 900 intercalated years (see section 4.4.5).

By the end of the eighth century, however, we find a calculated calendar in the *Baraita de-Shemuel* (ch. 5), a work of presumably Palestinian origin which is otherwise entirely devoted to astronomical themes; the same applies to the probably contemporary *Pirqei de-R. Eliezer*, in chs. 6–8.[180]

Yet even if the Babylonians were the prime movers in the adoption of calendrical rules and then of a fixed calendar, as I have argued above, they are unlikely to have contributed *directly* to the fixed calendar that the Palestinian authorities chose, in the fourth century, to adopt. Early Babylonian Amoraim could hardly have participated in a decision-making process that was restricted exclusively to the Palestinian rabbinic court.

The case of Shemuel confirms this point. His astronomical statements are cited in the Palestinian Talmud (*Y. Berakhot* 9:3 (13c)), but not his statements relating to the calendar. When he sent his sixty-year schedule of intercalations to R. Yoḥanan, the leading authority in Palestine, the latter retorted that this was 'mere calculation' (*B. Ḥullin* 95b). And when he boasted that he could set the calendar for the entire Diaspora, Abba the father of R. Simlai—a local sage from Nehardea—was quick to show him that his calendrical knowledge was actually incomplete (*B. RH* 20b). Even Babylonian sages were anxious to protect, in the third century, the Palestinian monopoly over calendrical decisions.

The 28-year cycle of *tequfot*, attributed in the Babylonian Talmud to Shemuel, became a dominant part of the rabbinic calendar, and is found in Palestinian sources from the Geonic period.[181] However, Shemuel would not necessarily have been its only inventor. This cycle derives in large measure from the Julian calendar, with which it shares, on the whole, the same dates for solstices and equinoxes.[182] It could have been formulated in rabbinic Palestine independently from Shemuel; its appearance in Palestinian Geonic sources, where it is not attributed to Shemuel, is thus no evidence that Shemuel contributed this cycle to the Palestinian calendrical authorities.

---

[180] See S. Stern (1996) on the fictitious nature of these calendars.

[181] e.g. *Baraita de-Shemuel*, ch. 5 (late 8th c.). For Babylonian sources, see e.g. R. Hai's responsum ap. R. Avraham b. Ḥiyya, *Sefer ha-ʿIbbur* 3: 7 (Filipowski 1851: 97–8); cited in Lewin (1932/3) 16–18. In later medieval sources, this cycle is often referred to as *tequfat Shemuel*, to distinguish it from *tequfat R. ʾAda*, a calculation of *tequfot* attributed in some sources to R. ʾAda that by the 12 c. had largely superseded it (see for instance R. Avraham b. Ḥiyya, ibid. 3: 3–5). See S. Stern (1996) 105–110.

[182] See S. Stern (1996) 105–6, and above, section 2.6.3.

The treatment which Shemuel appears to have received at the hand of Palestinian leaders as well as of his own colleagues suggests that there was little chance, in the Amoraic period, for Babylonians to contribute directly to the making of the fixed rabbinic calendar. By the ninth century, however, things had dramatically changed. This was the result of a gradual erosion of Palestinian calendrical authority, which I shall now explain.

5.4.3   The erosion of Palestinian authority

The purpose of adopting a fixed calendar in the fourth century was, as I have suggested, to secure Babylonian loyalty by enabling Babylonians, or anyone elsewhere, to observe the same calendar as in Palestine. But this policy turned out to be a double-edged sword. For the fixed calendar had the inevitable effect, at the same time, of increasing Babylonia's autonomy, and hence, of diminishing its dependence on the Palestinian court.

Palestine's loss of authority over Babylonia would not have been immediate. It is possible that in the early stages, the calendar calculation was kept secret by the Palestinian court;[183] it may also have been undefined, and subject to unpredictable adjustments and changes by that court.[184] Thus Diaspora Jews would not have known how to reckon it. The dates of forthcoming festivals would still have been sent to Babylonia, though now on an annual basis, thus ensuring at once calendrical unanimity and Babylonian dependence on Palestinian authority.[185]

In the course of time, however, and certainly by the ninth century, the Palestinian calendrical calculation came to be known in Babylonia. This was either the result of direct disclosure, or of a careful analysis of the calendar dates that had been sent, over the years, from Palestine. Babylonian sages may have relied, for this purpose, on the help of non-Jewish astronomers. The study of astronomy received a considerable boost in Baghdad at the turn of the ninth century, under the patronage of the Abbasid Caliphs.[186] This may have assisted Babylonian rabbis to further their traditional knowledge of calendar schemes, and to infer the calendar system in use by the Palestinian court. It is perhaps no coincidence

---

[183]   See discussion above, in section 4.3.3.

[184]   See discussion above, in section 4.3.2.

[185]   See section 4.3.3.

[186]   Pedersen (1974) 14–15; Bornstein (1904) 33 n. 4, (1922*a*) 324–7 and 344–5. See also Abraham Ibn Ezra's account in Goldstein (1967) 147–9.

that we find a detailed account of the normative Jewish calendar in the work of the Muslim astronomer al-Khwarizmi (himself a product of the Abbasid period, writing in 823/4 CE),[187] which *may* have been based entirely on inference.[188]

The exilarch's letter of 835/6 CE indicates quite clearly that by this period, Babylonian leaders were well versed in the Palestinian calendar calculation.[189] At this stage, they could have declared complete independence from Palestine and reckoned the calendar completely on their own. For political reasons, perhaps, the exilarch chose otherwise. But the polemical tone of his letter is indicative that calendar dissidence was on the rise in Babylonia, presumably even in rabbinic (or 'Rabbanite') circles. Clearly, Palestinian calendrical authority had become considerably eroded. This erosion of Palestinian calendrical authority was symptomatic, no doubt, of Babylonia's general ascendancy over the Palestinian rabbinic community in this period. But it was also the natural result of the adoption and use of a fixed calendar.

Calendar dissidence finally erupted in the early 920s, when R. Saadya and the Babylonian leadership rejected the calendrical decisions of Ben Meir in Palestine, and claimed supreme authority in the fixation of the calendar. Dissidence, however, was not the sole consequence of calendrical independence from Palestine in the ninth century and beyond. Evidence from the R. Saadya–Ben Meir correspondence suggests, as we shall now see, that in the course of this period the Babylonians became actively involved in the formulation of the fixed rabbinic calendar—in a way which would have been impossible in Shemuel's period. Indeed, their contribution to the present-day rabbinic calendar may have been decisive.

5.4.4 The R. Saadya–Ben Meir controversy

It seems appropriate to conclude our study with the event that marks the end of our period. This event was hardly known to historians until the discovery of documentary evidence from the Cairo Geniza, first

---

[187] See Ch. 4, section 4.3.1 and n. 127.

[188] As suggested by Sar–Shalom (1988) 44. Note however that a substantial part of al-Khwarizmi's work may be a later interpolation, as argued by Sar–Shalom (1988) (see section 4.3.1). It is also in this cultural context that R. Nahshon's cycle, if authentically attributed, may have been composed: see above, section 4.4.1.

[189] See my remarks at the end of section 4.3.3, and appendix.

published in full by Bornstein in his seminal work of 1904.[190] The authorship of the documents, their chronological order, as well as a number of broader historical questions have since been subject to arguments that lie beyond our scope. For our purposes, a general outline will suffice.[191]

In the summer of 921 CE, the Palestinian Gaon, or his son Ben Meir, made known the calendar dates for the next three years; the next Passover, in 922 CE, was to occur on a Sunday. The Babylonian leaders, however, had worked out that the next Passover was to occur on Tuesday.[192] A lengthy, polemical correspondence was subsequently exchanged between both camps, in which R. Saadya, newly arrived in Babylonia, played an active role. Some communities followed Ben Meir, and others, perhaps the majority, the Babylonian leadership.[193] As a result, Passover in 922 CE was observed in each camp on different dates. The schism may have prolonged itself to Rosh ha-Shanah of the same year (922 CE). After that, the Babylonian calendar of R. Saadya appears somehow to have prevailed.[194]

The calendrical dispute arose from the definition of *molad zaqen*. In the present-day rabbinic calendar, the same as upheld by R. Saadya, *molad zaqen* is a *molad* of Tishre that occurs on or after the 18th hour of the 24 hour period (i.e. noon), in which case the beginning of the month must be postponed (see section 4.4.1, item 4). The anticipated occurrence of such a *molad* in 924 CE should have dictated, already in 922 CE, the postponement of Passover to Tuesday. Ben Meir, however, defined the *molad zaqen* as occurring only on or after 18 hours and 642 parts. The difference between his calendar and R. Saadya's was thus only slight, but in this case, significant, for in 924 CE, the *molad* of Tishre was to occur on a Saturday at 18 hours 237 parts. Since Ben Meir considered this not

---

[190] Bornstein (1904). Sources were also sporadically published by Friedlander (1893), Levi (1900), Levi, Adler, and Broyde (1900) (with French translation), Schechter (1902), Hirschfeld (1903–4) (with English, but inadequate, translation), Adler (1914) (with French translation), Guillaume (1914–15) (including more complete editions of the texts cited by Bornstein 1904, which were later cited in full by Bornstein (1922*b*), and Fleischer (1984*b*: 375–85).

[191] For more detailed accounts, see Bornstein (1904) 21–8, (1922*b*) 238–41; Malter (1942) 69–88; Gil (1992) 562–9; Brody (1997) 118–19.

[192] According to Ben Meir, the year 921–2 CE was to be defective, whereas the Babylonians argued is was to be full (on 'defective' and 'full', see section 4.4.1, item 5).

[193] The schism did not follow consistent geographical boundaries: some communities in Babylonia, for instance, were loyal to the Palestinian calendar.

[194] See Malter (1942) 85–6. In the wake of this controversy R. Saadya composed a monograph on the calendar, most of which is now lost, which was widely cited or referred to in later medieval works: see references in Bornstein (1922*b*) 253 n. 1.

to be a *molad zaqen*, he ruled that the calendar dates from 922 CE to 924 CE should *not* be postponed; Passover of 922 CE was hence to occur on time, on Sunday.

Not unexpectedly, the argument between Ben Meir and the Babylonians shifted to questions of authority. Ben Meir asserted the ancient Palestinian monopoly over calendrical decisions, and cited, in support, the Talmudic prohibition against intercalating outside the Land of Israel.[195] He reminded the Babylonians that they and their ancestors had always accepted the Palestinian calendrical decisions that were announced every year on the Mount of Olives (Guillaume 1914–15: 553).

R. Saadya and his colleagues defended their position by claiming the authority of the 'four parts table', an algorithm which they had relied on for their calculation (see above, section 4.4.1). This table, they claimed, was an 'ancient' tradition inherited from their fathers, and which was followed, according to R. Saadya, by 'all Jews in the east, west, north, and the islands'.[196] Moreover, the *molad zaqen* of 18 hours, implicit in the algorithm, could find support in the Talmud,[197] whereas Ben Meir's addition of 642 parts was, in R. Saadya's view, absurd and purely fabricated.[198]

As to the question of Palestinian authority, R. Saadya or one of his colleagues replied in a letter as follows:

ובודאי שרבותינו שבבבל בדורות הראשנים היו שולחין ודורשין מרבותינו שלארץ
ישר׳ קביעת חדשי שנה בשנה, לפי שלא היו בקיאין בסדר העיבור כמותן, לפיכך
היו כותבין אליהם. אבל מן שנים רבות, כבר עלו כמה חכמים מבבל אל ארץ ישר׳,
ודקדקו עם חכמי ארץ ישר׳ בסוד העיבור, ופשפשו וחיפשו בזו עד שנתבוננו בו ויפה
יפה. וכבר הם קובעים חדשים בבבל זה שנים רבות לבדם, וגם חכמי ארץ ישראל
מחשבים וקובעים חדשים לבדם. וכבר בכל השנים האלה עלה חשבונם אחד; לא
נמצא ביניהם חילוף, אלא החשבון על מכונו ועל תיקונו, והמועדים מתקדשים
חוקה אחת ותורה אחת, מפני שהחשבונות כולם כאחד ניתנו מרועה אחד. ולא
ראינו קילקול כזה ולא פירצה כזאת הנה נא יש בישיבות זקנים שהגיעו לגבורות

---

[195] See Ben Meir's letters in Schechter (1902) 42 (= Bornstein 1904: 61–2; Adler 1914: 50–2); Levi (1900) 262–3 (= Bornstein 1904: 64–5).

[196] Levi, Adler, and Broyde (1900) 225–6 (= Bornstein 1904: 75–7).

[197] *B. RH* 20b (the inference, however, is by no means certain): Schechter (1902) 500 (= Bornstein 1904: 116; Adler 1914: 47 and 49).

[198] Schechter (1902) 62 (= Bornstein 1904: 94–5); Hirschfeld (1903–4) 292 and 296 (= Bornstein 1922*b*: 247–8); Guillaume (1914–15) 547–9 (= Bornstein 1904: 90–1); ibid. 550–1 (= Bornstein 1904: 93–4). To this Ben Meir retorted that *his* rule of 642 parts was the ancient tradition: Friedlander (1893) 197 (= Bornstein 1904: 65); Guillaume (1914–15) 555. The argument could have gone on endlessly.

וגם הזקינו מאד, וכולם אין אחד מהם זוכר שהוצרכו אנשי בבל לשאול עיבור שנים
וקביעת חדשים מארץ ישר', אלא אתם מעברים כמנהגכם, וגם אנחנו מנהג אבותינו
בידינו, ואנחנו מעברים כדרכינו, וחשבון אחד הוא. [199]

To be sure, in earlier generations the rabbis of Babylonia would send and ask
for the Palestinian rabbis' yearly decisions regarding the months of the year,
because they (the Babylonians) were not expert in the order of intercalation [200]
in the same way as (the Palestinians). Therefore, they used to write to them.

But already many years ago, sages from Babylonia went up to the land of
Israel, and investigated with the sages of the land of Israel in the 'court [201] of
intercalation', and searched and inquired into this matter, until they understood
it very well. And now, for many years already, they set the months on their own
in Babylonia, and the sages of the land of Israel also calculate and set the months
on their own. And in all these years, their calculation has been the same and there
has been no difference between them; [202] for the calculation is well established,
the festivals are sanctified according to the same rule and the same principle, and
the calculations were all given by the same shepherd. We have never seen such a
disruption or breach ... Behold, there are elders in the yeshivot (of Babylonia)
who have advanced in years and who are very old, and none of them remembers
that Babylonians ever needed to ask the Palestinians for the intercalation of years
and the setting of months. Rather, you set the calendar according to your custom,
and we also follow the custom of our fathers and we set the calendar in our own
way, but the calendar is one and the same.

The argument was, in other words, that a meeting had been held some
time in the past between Palestinian and Babylonian sages, at which the
Babylonians had studied the calendar in detail and had been given the
right to reckon the calendar autonomously. Autonomy, however, would
not mean divergence: as the letter emphasizes at length, both communities were to reckon exactly the same calendar, based on a completely
standard calculation. It was the existence of this standard calendar, indeed, that made Babylonia's autonomy possible. Calendrical unanimity
was, as ever, paramount; dependence on Palestine, however, had become
irrelevant.

[199] Guillaume (1914–15) 546–7 (= Bornstein 1904: 88–9, in more fragmentary
form); Mann (1920–2) i. 51 n. 2.

[200] 'Intercalation' is used here in a broad sense, and refers specifically to the setting
of months.

[201] Or 'committee', or again: 'investigated ... the secret of intercalation'. See
above, section 4.3.3.

[202] This point is also made in the letter published in Schechter (1902) 62 (= Bornstein 1904: 96–7), in which the writer refers to evidence available to him from earlier
dated documents.

Calendar historians have commonly accepted the story of a Palestinian–Babylonian meeting at face value. This meeting would have happened a long time before the 920s, since according to the letter, contemporary Babylonian elders had no first-hand memory of it. But it could not have happened more than a few generations earlier,[203] certainly not before 835/6 CE, when according to the exilarch's letter, Babylonia was still dependent on Palestine. On this basis, Bornstein and others opted for a date in the middle of the ninth century. It is at this meeting that the standard calendar would have been released, thus marking the final stage in the institution of the present-day rabbinic calendar.[204]

However, the polemical character of this letter should not be overlooked. Although a meeting between Palestinians and Babylonians is not historically impossible, this story—for which we have no other record—could equally have been a piece of fictitious Babylonian self-legitimization.[205] We do not know Ben Meir's response to this letter, but he is likely to have vehemently rejected its claims. It would be wrong, therefore, to believe the Babylonian story at face value without taking account of Ben Meir's position.

5.4.5 The 'four parts table'

Central to the Babylonians' contention was that the 'four parts table', on which they relied, was an ancient and legitimate tradition. At the end of the letter just quoted, however, the Babylonians appear to have acknowledged that this tradition was specifically Babylonian, and that a different algorithm was used in Palestine. To cite again: 'rather, you set the calendar according to your custom, and we also follow the custom of our fathers and we set the calendar in our own way, but the calendar is one and the same'. Thus although the calendar was essentially the same, Babylonians and Palestinians employed different algorithms for its calculation.

---

[203] As correctly inferred by Bornstein (1904) 43–4, (1922a) 349–50, from the wording of the letter.

[204] Bornstein, ibid.; cf Mann (1920–2) i. 51–4, Sar-Shalom (1988) 37–8. Bornstein saw this meeting as a 'working party' to which the Palestinians contributed their ancient, rabbinic calendrical traditions, and the Babylonians their astronomical expertise acquired in Baghdad under the Abbasids (see also Jaffe 1931: 103).

[205] Katz (1979) 45; also Langermann (1987) 159.

This finds confirmation from Ben Meir's response. Ben Meir did not use the 'four parts table' of his Babylonian opponents,[206] but another algorithm instead.[207] He despised the 'four parts table', with the claim that as an algorithm it was incomplete.[208] Indeed, he even went as far as ruling that any calendar based on the calculation of the conjunction and on the 'four parts table', without deference to the Palestinian calendrical court, was intrinsically invalid.[209] At one point, Ben Meir did present a revised version of the 'four parts table', which he had adapted by adding 642 parts to it;[210] but this, clearly, was only for the polemical purpose of responding to the Babylonians in their own terms.[211]

The evidence suggests, therefore, that the 'four parts table' of the Babylonians was not Palestinian in origin, and had not yet gained Palestinian acceptance in the early tenth century.[212] This algorithm was probably formulated in Babylonia, perhaps some time in the ninth century. It may have been the outcome of a Palestinian–Babylonian meeting,

[206] As he is said himself to have stated in Guillaume (1914–15) 548 (= Bornstein 1904: 90).

[207] Ben Meir's algorithm was based on the formula שו'ח כה'ז חד'ז, mentioned in his letter in Friedlander (1893) 198–9 (= Bornstein 1904: 67–9). See explanatory tables in Bornstein (1904) 71, Sar-Shalom (1984) 45 and (1988) 39. For a discussion, see Bornstein (1922*b*) 253–7. The algorithm is not found elsewhere, except in *Midrash Tehilim* 20: 5 (Buber 1889: 175–6), a contemporary Midrash of presumed Palestinian origin (see Strack and Stemberger 1991: 350–2). Another formula used by Ben Meir, and also unparalleled elsewhere, was totally unknown to his Babylonian opponents: see the Babylonians' letter in Schechter (1902) 62–3 (= Bornstein 1904: 98), and discussion in Bornstein (1922*b*) 254.

[208] Guillaume (1914–15) 550 (= Bornstein 1922*b*: 259–60). This claim was actually unfounded.

[209] Schechter (1902) 249 (= Bornstein 1904: 108–9). The text, however, is somewhat fragmentary.

[210] Friedlander (1893) 198–9 (= Bornstein 1904: 65–70); see also Adler (1914) 51. For a tabulation of Ben Meir's amended 'four parts table', see Bornstein (1922*b*) 235. Ben Meir's account of his amended table is actually more complex, as it also integrates his own algorithm of שו'ח כה'ז חד'ז: see Bornstein (1922*b*) 247–8, 258–9, 269, and 279.

[211] The Babylonians had no trouble recognizing that Ben Meir had artificially superimposed his 642 parts on their traditional 'four parts table': see Levi, Adler, and Broyde (1900) 227 (= Bornstein 1904: 78); Hirschfeld (1903–4) 296 (fo. 2ᵛ) (= Bornstein 1922*b*: 247–8); Schechter (1902) 498–500 (= Bornstein 1904: 113–16; Adler 1914: 45–9). Ben Meir himself appears not to have denied the charge.

[212] The 'four parts table' in verse by Yose al-Naharwani, perhaps R. Saadya's contemporary in Babylonia (Epstein 1901: 204–10, see above Ch. 4 n. 152), was certainly composed in Babylonia: it uses the Babylonian era of *WeYaD* (on which see section 5.4.6 below).

but there is no necessity to make such an assumption. By the ninth century, Babylonians leaders were quite capable of assuming calendrical autonomy and designing their own calendrical algorithm without seeking permission from Palestine. It is conceivable that the algorithm was not formulated till after 835/6 CE, as in that year the Babylonian exilarch was still dependent on Palestinian authority. But it may have existed already beforehand. The exilarch may indeed have been polemicizing against its use.[213]

If R. Saadya is to be believed, the 'four parts table' was in widespread use across the Diaspora ('all Jews in the east, west, north, and the islands') already in his period.[214] It certainly became so later. Whereas Ben Meir's algorithm fell into oblivion, the 'four parts table' eventually became standard in the normative rabbinic calendar, even in Palestine itself.[215] In this respect, the Babylonians made a lasting contribution to the present-day rabbinic calendar.

5.4.6   The calculation of the *molad*

By the time of the R. Saadya–Ben Meir controversy, the *molad* calculation of the present-day rabbinic calendar was already firmly in place. Both parties assumed the same *moladot* for the years 922–4 CE, and these corresponded exactly to the present-day computation. The nature of their controversy, however, informs us that the present-day *molad* computation was originally instituted by the Babylonian rabbinic community.

The strangest feature of the R. Saadya–Ben Meir controversy was Ben Meir's addition of 642 parts to *molad zaqen* (see above). Ben Meir himself was apparently unable to explain it: all he could say was that it was the tradition he had received. There is no reason to doubt, on this point, Ben Meir's sincerity. Had he known the reason for these 642 parts, it would surely have been in his interest to reveal it; this would

[213] If true, this would provide a historical context to Al-Khwarizmi's description of the Jewish calendrical algorithm. It is also possible that the exilarch's claim of dependence on Palestinian calendrical authorities, in his letter of 835/6 CE, was only an excuse to fend off the new Babylonian algorithm, which he may have perceived as a threat to his own authority. Obviously, all this is only speculative.

[214] Levi, Adler and Broyde (1900) 225–6 (= Bornstein 1904: 75–7); mentioned above, section 5.4.4.

[215] So in the late-11th-c. Palestinian *Megillat Aviatar*, p. 9, l. 8 (Schechter 1902: 472). The 'four parts table' is then cited in various forms by later authorities such as R. Avraham b. Ḥiyya, *Sefer ha-ʿIbbur* 2: 9; R. Isaac Israeli, *Yesod ʿOlam*, 4: 10 (Goldberg 1848: ii. 19a–23a); and R. Yaʿaqov b. Asher, *Arbaʿah Turim*, *ʾOraḥ Ḥayim* 428. Ben Meir's algorithm is not found in any of these sources (see above, n. 207).

have added much weight to his otherwise implausible argument. It may be assumed, therefore, that the rule of 642 parts was formulated some time before Ben Meir, for reasons that he no longer knew.[216]

The rationale behind Ben Meir's tradition can be conjectured, however, with a fair degree of certainty. The number 642 is familiar in the present-day rabbinic calendar—already reckoned in the period of R. Saadya and Ben Meir—as part of the *molad* of Nisan year 1 (six months before *molad WeYaD*), which is 4th day (Wednesday), 9 hours, 642 parts. This correlation is too obvious to be ignored.

To understand Ben Meir's addition of 642 parts to *molad zaqen*, it is important to realize that this addition did not merely affect *molad zaqen*, but rather the calendar calculation as a whole. It effectively meant that any *molad* could occur up to 642 parts later, without causing a postponement of the new month. This is why Ben Meir had to add 642 parts to almost every value of his (adapted) 'four parts table'. In this respect, Ben Meir could have expressed his disagreement with the Babylonians in terms of the *molad* itself: he could have retained the *molad zaqen* on the 18th hour (as according to the Babylonians), but assumed that the *molad* itself, according to his reckoning, really occurred 642 parts *earlier*.

This, it seems, was the *original* formulation of Ben Meir's (or rather, his predecessors') position. The epoch they chose for the *molad* calculation was 642 parts earlier than in the normative rabbinic calendar, and corresponded exactly to the *molad* of Nisan, year 1, at 4th day, 9 hours. This round figure (with whole hours and no parts) would have been chosen for reasons of convenience—just as in the case of the *molad* epoch of the normative rabbinic calendar, i.e. *molad* of Tishre year 2, at 6th day, 14 hours exactly (*WeYaD*). Both these epochs, indeed, must have been artificially rounded off (as argued above, section 4.4.7). The result of choosing *different* epochs, however, was that the epoch of Ben Meir's predecessors occurred 642 parts earlier. Although hypothetical, this theory is the most plausible explanation of Ben Meir's 642 parts rule.[217]

---

[216] See references above. The Babylonian accusation that Ben Meir had arbitrarily invented the rule of 642 is somewhat unreasonable. See Bornstein (1922*b*) 255–6.

[217] See Jaffe (1931) 109–10 (ch. 18; see also pp. 182–98); Bornstein (1922*b*) 252; Loewinger (1986) 72–3 (n. 21a); Sar-Shalom (1992/3); and for a similar argument, Cassuto (1943). Lasker and Lasker (1990/1: 126) argue that the number of 642 parts was chosen because of its intrinsic calendrical importance, due to its (allegedly) common occurrence in the 'four parts table'. In actual fact, it is only common in a 'four parts table' based on Nisan (attested only in later sources: see below, n. 219), for the simple arithmetical reason that any *molad Nisan* preceding a *molad Tishre* at 18 hours

Why Ben Meir's predecessors preferred the epoch of Nisan year 1, and hence a *molad* 642 parts earlier, is a matter of pure speculation. Various theories have been suggested, and I shall briefly review them below. Most of these theories assume, as indeed is likely, that the epoch of the present-day calendar (*We YaD*) was Babylonian, whereas the epoch of Ben Meir's predecessors represented a specifically Palestinian tradition.

According to one theory, an epoch in Nisan year 1 was preferred by Ben Meir's predecessors for the simple reason that the epoch of Nisan, rather than of Tishre, was traditionally preferred in Palestinian calendars (Bornstein 1904: 126–9; Cassuto 1943). Evidence to this effect is limited, but perhaps sufficient. The calendrical algorithms of Ben Meir and of *Midrash Tehilim* (of putative Palestinian origin) use the *molad* of Nisan as epoch.[218] By contrast the 'four parts table', of Babylonian origin (see above), was based on the *molad* of Tishre. There is also evidence of a different 'four parts table' based on the *molad* of Nisan, which *may* have been Palestinian in origin.[219]

This theory is slightly problematic, however, because the Palestinians are known to have used Tishre as epoch for chronological eras. Until the end of the Geonic period, the era 'from the Creation' was taken in Babylonia to begin at the *molad* of Tishre *We YaD* (i.e. the beginning of what we should nowadays call 'year 2');[220] in Palestine, the custom was also to begin the era in Tishre, but one year earlier (as is normative today).[221] This one-year discrepancy, recorded in medieval monographs as a division between 'East' (Babylonia) and 'West'

(the 'limit' of *molad zaqen*) occurs at 13 hours 642 parts. Lasker and Lasker's argument is somewhat self-defeating, because Ben Meir himself did not accept a *molad zaqen* at 18 hours, and hence in his calendar the number 642 parts would not have had the same significance: in Ben Meir's amended 'four parts table' (see above), 642 parts do not appear at all (see table in Bornstein 1922*b*: 235)! See also Sar-Shalom's refutation (1992/3: 122–3) of Lasker and Lasker's argument.

[218] Ben Meir's relevant algorithm is cited by his opponents in Guillaume (1914–15) 548 (= Bornstein 1904: 90), and again in Schechter (1902) 62 (= Bornstein 1904: 95). See Bornstein (1922*b*) 256–7. The passage from *Midrash Tehilim* (above, n. 207) states explicitly: 'from Passover to Passover'.

[219] This table was apparently unknown to both R. Saadya and Ben Meir, and may well have been a later composition. It is first found in a number of early-12th-c. works from Northern France and Italy: *Sefer ha-ʿIbbur* of R. Yaʿaqov b. Shimshon (ch. 36), *Mahzor Vitry* (Hurwitz 1923, supplement pp. 10–12), and *Midrash Sekhel Tov* (Buber 1901: ii. 90–2; Bornstein 1904: 117–21 (appendix 10)). On the latter, see Strack and Stemberger (1991) 390. The *Midrash Sekhel Tov* also provides 'four-column tables' based on *molad Tishre* (Buber 1901: ii. 92–3). See Bornstein (1922*b*) 233–6 and 273–9; Loewinger (1986) 51–2 (n. 17). The Palestinian origin of this Nisan-based table remains, however, speculative.

[220] This reckoning appears to be used in *B. ʿAvodah Zarah* 9b. It is then found in the exilarch's letter of 835/6 CE (see Bornstein 1922*a*: 348 n. 1).

[221] This reckoning is first found in the *Baraita de-Shemuel*, ch. 5, of putative Palestinian origin. See Akavia (1955) 123–5.

(Palestine),[222] led also to different ways of expressing the 19-year cycle of inter-calations.[223] It has been argued that the *original* Palestinian custom was to reckon the era of Creation from the *Nisan* preceding *WeYaD*, i.e. (in Palestinian terms) from *molad* Nisan 4th day, 9 hours; later, this epoch shifted to the preceding Tishre. This, however, is completely conjectural.[224]

The question of whether to use Nisan or Tishre as calendrical epochs may go back to the famous Tannaitic dispute between R. Eliezer and R. Yehoshua, on whether the world was created in Tishre or in Nisan (respectively).[225] It may also have depended on various Tannaitic traditions regarding the beginning of the calendar year.[226]

Another theory proposes that the *molad* of Ben Meir's predecessors, 642 parts earlier, was designed to make up, at least approximately, for the time difference between the longitude of Babylonia, on which the (now normative) *molad* would have been based, and the longitude of Palestine.[227] In actual fact, this correction would not have been necessary. Not only is it highly unlikely that any *molad* calculation would have been based on the longitude of Babylonia,[228] but it has

---

[222] R. Avraham b. Ḥiyya, *Sefer ha-ʿIbbur* 3: 7 (Filipowski 1851: 96–7), citing R. Saadya Gaon (also in Lewin 1932/3: 14–15); Isaac Israeli, *Yesod ʿOlam*, 4: 14 (Goldberg 1848: ii. 26b–27a). See Bornstein (1921*b*) 223–4.

[223] Yehoshua b. ʿAllan (early 10th c.?), in his monograph on the intercalation published by Harkavy (1903) 79 (which I should not interpret like Jaffe 1931: 88–90); R. Hai Gaon, responsum cited in R. Avraham b. Ḥiyya, *Sefer ha-ʿIbbur* 3: 7 (Filipowski 1851: 97); al-Biruni (1879) 165; Isaac Israeli, *Yesod ʿOlam*, 4: 14 (Goldberg 1848: ii. 26); anonymous commentary on Maimonides' *Laws of Sanctification of the New Moon*, 6: 8. Note the 19-year cycle from *WeYaD* in one of the Babylonian letters to Ben Meir (Guillaume 1914–15: 546). According to Bornstein (1922*a*: 337–42), this also accounts for the different cycles in *Pirqei de-R. Eliezer*, ch. 8 end (Horovitz 1972: 40–1) and in the *baraita* cited by Isaac Israeli, *Yesod ʿOlam*, 4: 2 (Goldberg 1848: ii. 3); but Jaffe (1931: 84) sees these passages as evidence of some earlier, fundamental disagreement about the nature of the 19-year cycle.

[224] It is worth noting, incidentally, that eventually the Palestinian era from the Creation became normative in Babylonia, at least by R. Hai Gaon's period (early 11th c.). As a result, the epoch of *molad Tishre WeYaD* was superseded in the normative calendar by the epoch of *molad Tishre BaHaRaD* (i.e. one year earlier than *WeYaD*; this did not affect the times of the *molad*, but only the method used to calculate it). See various Geonic responsa in Lewin (1932/3) 15–22; then all medieval calendar monographs, e.g. R. Avraham b. Ḥiyya, *Sefer ha-ʿIbbur* 2: 6. This suggests that in some areas of calendar reckoning, Palestine may still have exerted some influence over Babylonia, till at least the end of the Geonic period.

[225] *B. RH* 10b–12a (and parallels); *Y. RH* 1: 1 (56b); *Y. ʿAvodah Zarah* 1: 2 (39c). See Jaffe (1931) 109.

[226] *M. RH* 1: 1, and Palestinian and Babylonian Talmudim ad loc. See at length Bornstein (1904) 135–42; this topic, however, requires further study.

[227] Bornstein (1904) 28–9, 34–5, (1922*a*) 353–4; and for a recent reinstatement, but with some refinements on the longitude difference, Lasker and Lasker (1990/1). On Bornstein's position, see Sar-Shalom (1992/3) 119–20.

[228] Sar-Shalom (1992/3) 114–15; see also Malter (1942) 79 (citing Epstein).

also been shown that if the (now normative) *molad* calculation was derived from Ptolemy, as appears quite likely, it would have conformed almost exactly to the longitude of Jerusalem.[229] Nevertheless, Ben Meir's predecessors may have *believed*—albeit erroneously—that the *molad* calculation of the Babylonians was illegitimately based on the longitude of Babylonia; if so, from their perspective, a correction would have been justified, and the round figure of *molad Nisan* 4th day, 9 hours would have been preferred.

This theory assumes again that the *molad* calculation that is now normative was *Babylonian* in origin. This explains why the *molad* would have been *perceived* by Ben Meir's predecessors to be based on the longitude of Babylon. By adjusting it to that of Jerusalem, the Palestinians would have been reasserting their calendrical authority; they would have been appropriating the *molad* calculation of the Babylonians and giving it a 'Palestinian' identity. To some extent, the correction of the *molad* to the Jerusalem longitude would thus have been *polemical*.

Yet another theory has been recently proposed by Loewinger: that the *molad* epoch of Ben Meir conformed almost exactly to a mean conjunction inferred from the work of the Arab astronomer al-Battani, and may have been regarded as more accurate than Ptolemy's conjunction, upon which the normative *molad* was based.[230] However, the correspondence between Ben Meir's *molad* and al-Battani's astronomical data remains debatable. Al-Battani, moreover, is unlikely to have published his works before the beginning of the tenth century; whereas Ben Meir's tradition of 642 parts must have been sufficiently ancient for its original rationale to have been forgotten.[231]

The Babylonian origins of the present-day *molad* calculation (642 parts later than Ben Meir's), already suggested above in Ch. 4,[232] are thus confirmed by the R. Saadya–Ben Meir controversy. This controversy also suggests that in this area of calendar calculation, the Babylonians had taken the lead in the ninth century, some time before the period of Ben Meir. Indeed, although the disagreement between Babylonians and Palestinians was, originally, about the epoch of the *molad*, the Palestinians chose early on to accept the Babylonian *molad* calculation, and to limit their disagreement to the definition of *molad zaqen*, by redefining it as 18 hours 642 parts.

[229] As recently argued by Loewinger (see above, section 4.4.7).

[230] Unpublished paper (see section 4.4.7). Jaffe (1931: 181) may have allusively anticipated this theory.

[231] See above in this section. It is possible, though in my view unlikely, that Ben Meir followed al-Battani but deliberately concealed this.

[232] In section 4.4.7, I have argued that whether the *molad* calculation was derived from Ptolemy or from Babylonian astronomy, it is most likely to have been formulated in Babylonia.

The reason why Ben Meir's predecessors chose to reformulate their position in terms of *molad zaqen* was perhaps to give the *appearance* of reducing the extent of their disagreement with the Babylonian calendar. To maintain a different epoch (at Nisan year 1, 4th day, 9 hours) would have meant that the *molad* calculation, each month, would have been different from the Babylonian. By contrast, the addition of 642 parts to *molad zaqen* would only have been noticed in years when *molad Tishre* occurred between 18 hours and 18 hours 642 parts. Thus the formulation of *molad zaqen* gave the *impression* of reducing their disagreement to only rare occurrences. For the sake of calendrical unanimity (or near unanimity), it was preferable to keep the same *molad* calculation and to disagree with the normative calendar only in these rare occurrences.

The fact that *they* (the Palestinians) submitted to the Babylonian *molad*, rather than the Babylonians submitting to theirs,[233] must be regarded as significant. Although R. Saadya's Babylonian calendar was eventually to prevail in the 920s, in the ninth century the battle had already been half won.

Inasmuch as the present-day *molad* calculation and the 'four parts table' were both Babylonian in origin, the contribution of the Babylonian rabbinic community to the normative Jewish calendar would thus have been considerable: for the *molad* calculation and the 'four parts table' constitute the foundation of the present-day rabbinic calendar. There is thus a case to argue that the calendar in use nowadays—R. Saadya's—is essentially a Babylonian calendar.

[233] The Babylonians could equally have submitted to the Palestinian *molad*, by redefining *molad zaqen* as 18 hours *minus* 642 parts.

Appendix

The exilarch's letter of 835/6 CE, from the Cairo Geniza (TS 8 G7[1]), was first published by Mann in 1922.[1] All subsequent studies relied entirely on Mann's edition.[2] Because of its importance for the history of the rabbinic calendar, I offer below a new transcription of the document, with, for the first time, an English translation. Mann's transcription was unfortunately marred by errors, which have been corrected here (as indicated in the footnotes). Most of Mann's conjectural reconstructions, however, have been retained (in square brackets). I include photographs of the document which, to my knowledge, have been published only once before.[3]

Recto

1   דלי הוי⁴ כולן וכל יש׳ אגודה [אחת בח⁵]דשים

וכל מועדים כבהדין מנהגא ק[א מ]דבריןֿ⁶ א׳ ⁷

אבהתן ומתיבאתא עד הינא והי[נא] שתה דהוה

שנת אלפא ומאה וארבעין ושבע שנין לש׳⁸

5   לשטרות⁹ והיא שנת ארבעת אלפים וחמש

מאות ותשעים וחמש שנים לבראשית

אף על גב¹⁰ דילעינין מרחשון וכסליו

וטבת מתאחר סהרא דילהון אפילו הכין

---

[1] Mann (1920–2) ii. 41–2 (document 13), erroneously identified as TS 8 J7[1]—an error that has been carried over in most subsequent publications.

[2] Albeit with some conjectural emendations: Bornstein (1922*a*) 346–8; Lewin (1932/3) 35–6; Sar-Shalom (1984) 27.

[3] S. Stern (1997) 4.

[4] i.e. דליהוי (Mann).

[5] So Mann. An alternative might be [אחת בכל ח]דשים. The left vertical stroke of [ח is visible in the manuscript (although unclear in the photograph). The lower horizontal stroke apparent in the same area in the photograph is only a crack in the vellum, which does not appear to be the result of ink penetration.

[6] Mann: מ]דברי.

[7] First letter of next line, to fill up space (Mann).

[8] Mann: ושבע שתיןֿ (without לש׳). The letter שׁ (at the end of the line) is incomplete. לש׳ are again the first letters of the next line (see previous n.), a scribal convention (perhaps, but not necessarily, to fill up space).

[9] The letter ט is completely disjointed (by contrast with the same letter in l. 8).

[10] Mann: עלגב (probably just a printing error).

The exilarch's letter of 835/6 CE (TS 8 G7[1]): recto (courtesy of Cambridge University Library)

The exilarch's letter of 835/6 CE (TS 8 G7[1]): verso (courtesy of Cambridge University Library)

משום סיהרא דניסן דקא מיתליד[11]

ביממא דתלתה בש[נ]ב]ה בארבע [ש]עות[12]   10

אי מעברינן שלימ]ני]ן האוי קבעיה דניסן

בחמשה ומתחזי מן קמי קבעיה במערב

ומיקלקל מידי ושוינין[13] כסדרן לא איפשר

דמיתרמי פסח בארבעה בשבה ולא בדו

פסח ולמה לא ב[דו] פסח וא[14] ולא גהז עצרת   15

משום לא אדו ראש השנה ואי עבדינן

פסח בתרין בתר]ין[15] ב]שבה מתרמיא ראש

שתא בארבעה ו]יום כ]פור[16] במעלי

Verso

ולית איפ]שר משו]ם[17] שכבה וא]נ]י ע]בדינן פסח   1

בארבעה [אתיא] ראש שתא בארבעה[18] [ב]מעלין] ו]י]ום

כפור בחד ב]ש]בה[19] ולית איפשר משום שכבה

למיבת תרי יומי דשבת שבתון ואי עבדינן פסח

במעלי אתיא ראש שתא בחד בשבה ולית איפש]ר]ן[20]   5

משום יום טוב גדול של ערבה דלא ליתרמי[21]

ערבא[22] בשבתא ולא סגיא דלא לשוינון[23]

לירחי חסירין משום ניסן דלא ליקלקל

סיהרא ולא [מי]בעיא בהכי הדין[24] מעשה

---

[11] Mann: מיתלי (i.e. 'is hung', which makes little sense); but the letter ד is clear and as legible as the rest. מיתליד appears to be a misspelling of מיתיליד; alternatively, the second י of מיתיליד may be omitted because it is a weak letter, as in the form איתמר for איתאמר (suggestion of Emmanuel Silver).

[12] Mann: שע]ות], but this is over-cautious: the letter ע is clearly legible, and part of the ש is also visible. Jaffe's alternative conjectures of יד]ות] or שת]ות] (Jaffe 1931, ch. 15) are therefore unjustified.

[13] Mann: דשוינון.

[14] Omitted by Mann; the letter א has a stroke on top, indicating that it is a scribal error.

[15] Unnecessary repetition (Mann).

[16] Mann: ו]יום כ]פורים. The letter כ is visible but unclear. As the lacuna is actually much longer, an alternative might be ו]יומא דכ]פור (E. Silver).

[17] Mann: משום].

[18] This word has faint dots on top, indicating that it should be deleted (Mann). The scribal error is clear.

[19] Mann: בש]בה].

[20] Mann: אי]פשר].

[21] Mann: לית]ר]מי.

[22] Mann: ערבה.

[23] Mann: לשוינין.

[24] Mann: בהכדין.

דכ[ו]דין[²⁵] עבדו.²⁶ לקמי ראש החבורה   10
ובנ[ין] החבורה חסירין דנ[ס]מכינן²⁷ עליהון דלא
דלא²⁸ איפשר לשוויונון לא כסדרן ולא שלמין
אלא אפילו זמנין דאי עבדינן כסדרן ושלנ[מין]
או חסירין דאמי להדדי ולעולם עליהון סמכינן
דלא ליהוי ישראל אגודות אגודות ואנא וראשי   15
מתיבאתא²⁹ ורבנין וכל יש׳ אממכנן³⁰ על עיבורא
דאישתדר לקמי חנ[ב]רין. לבר.³¹ היכין
דאמרו קמי אית. קא דחלין³² מן שמיא

Recto

1   . . .that we and all Israel be [one] band [in all] months
and all festivals. This custom has been followed
by our fathers and by the *yeshivot* until now, which is the year
1147
5   of the Seleucid era, and the year
4595 from the Creation.³³
Although as regards Marḥeshwan, Kislew
and Tevet, their moon (will be) delayed,³⁴ nevertheless—
since the moon of Nisan is to be born³⁵

²⁵ The letters ד and ן are fairly legible.

²⁶ Mann reads [ושדרנ[ו, but there is no evidence of a ש, and the rest of the word is equally unclear. Mann's reading is based on l. 17.

²⁷ Mann: [דס]מכינן, but this is overcautious. Even the letter ס is slightly legible.

²⁸ Unnecessary repetition (Mann).

²⁹ Mann: מתיבאתה.

³⁰ Text and meaning unclear. Mann reads אסמכינן, but this is clearly not in the manuscript.

³¹ A number of additional letters are visible at this point, but illegible; it is difficult to make sense of these last two lines.

³² Mann: קה דהלין (probably just a printing error).

³³ i.e. 835/6 CE, according to the Babylonian era of Creation, which begins from *molad WeYaD* (see sections 4.4.1 and 5.4.6).

³⁴ i.e. although later on, in the winter months of 836/7 CE, the new moon (or the conjunction) will be delayed in relation to the first day of the month, if the previous year (835/6 CE) will have been defective.

³⁵ i.e. the conjunction (cf *B.ʿEruvin* 56a, *B. RH* 20b). The purpose of this parenthetical clause ('since . . . four hours', in ll. 9–10), somewhat out of place, is apparently to explain why the new moon of Nisan 836 CE will be visible in the West before Thursday (l. 12), i.e. already on Tuesday evening after sunset: the conjunction, indeed, will occur some 8 hours beforehand. In actual fact, however, the mean conjunction is only marginally relevant to the first visibility of the new moon (see above, sections 3.1.1 and 3.1.7). Indeed, the exilarch's prediction that the new moon of Nisan 836 CE would already be visible on Tuesday evening was wrong: see Ch. 4 n. 107.

10   in the daytime of the third (day) of the week (Tuesday) at four hours—
      if the (months of 835/6 CE) were intercalated and made full, then the be-
         ginning of Nisan would be set
      on the fifth (Thursday), whereas (the new moon) would be visible in the
         West[36] before the beginning of the month,
      and (hence) this matter (the calendar) would be disrupted. And it is im-
         possible to make (the months of 835/6 CE) regular,
      for then Pesaḥ would occur on the fourth of the week (Wednesday), and
         (this would contravene) *lo BaDU*

15   *Pesaḥ.*[37] And why *lo BaDU Pesaḥ* and *lo GaHaZ ʿAtzeret?*[38]
      Because *lo ADU Rosh ha-Shanah.* For if we make
      Pesaḥ on the second of the week, the new year
      occurs on the fourth, and the Day of Atonement on Friday,

Verso

1   and this is impossible because of the dead.[39] And if we make Pesaḥ
      on the fourth, the new year occurs on Friday, and the Day of Atonement
      on the first of the week, and this is impossible because of having to leave
      the dead unburied for two days of sabbath rest.[40] And if we make Pesaḥ

5   on Friday, the new year occurs on the first of the week, and this is impossible
      because of the great festival of the Willow—the Willow should not
      occur on the Sabbath.[41] Thus we can only make
      the months (of 835/6 CE) defective, so that in Nisan, the new moon be not
         disrupted. And this applies not only in this present case,

10   where they have so decided and ... before[42] the head of the *ḥavurah*
      and its members[43] (that the months shall be) defective—for (in this case)
         we rely on them (the assembly) because it is

[36] i.e. Palestine, as frequent in the Babylonian Talmud and later Babylonian sources.

[37] i.e. the rule that Pesaḥ (Passover, 15 Nisan) cannot occur on Monday, Wednesday, or Friday.

[38] i.e. the rule that *ʿAtzeret* (Shavuʿot, Pentecost) cannot occur on Tuesday, Thursday, or the Sabbath. Both rules amount to the same as *lo ADU Rosh.* See sections 4.4.1 and 4.4.3.

[39] If the Day of Atonement and the Sabbath were contiguous, a person who died on the first of these days could not be buried till the third day, which is not acceptable (see ll. 3–4).

[40] A citation from Lev. 23: 32.

[41] See sections 4.2.2 and 4.4.3.

[42] According to Mann's reconstruction (see n. 26), the text would read: 'sent before', or rather perhaps, 'sent from before', as in l. 17: see below, n. 46.

[43] The *ḥavurah* ('assembly'), distinct in ll. 15–17 from the author of the letter (the exilarch) and the heads of the (Babylonian) *yeshivot*, refers in all likelihood to the Palestinian academy or *yeshivah* (Mann 1920–2: i. 54 n. 2; Gil 1992: 492 n. 6, 567).

impossible to make them (the months of 835/6 CE) regular or full,
but even when it makes no difference whether (the months) are made
regular, full, or defective, we always rely on them (the *havurah*),
15   lest Israel be split into factions. I, the heads
of the *yeshivot*, the rabbis, and all Israel,[44] rely (?) on the calendar[45]
that was sent from before the *haverin*[46]. . . as
they said before . . . they fear heaven

[44] That the author of this letter is the exilarch can be inferred with reasonable
certainty from this self-referential sentence.

[45] Literally, the intercalation. This usage of עיבור was to become very common
in the later medieval period.

[46] Members of the *havurah* (above, ll. 10–11), or 'our colleagues', i.e. the
Palestinian rabbinic authorities. The text literally means 'sent *before* the *haverin*', suggesting that they were the calendar's *recipients*. This, however, is unlikely, since the
Palestinian academy is presented in l. 11 as the calendrical authority upon whom everyone relies. It is possible, therefore, that the term לקמי is used in a looser sense,
as suggested in my translation.

References

ABRAMSKY, Y. (1965). חזון יחזקאל, תוספתא בכורות-ערכין. Jerusalem.

ABRAMSON, S. (1971). *Sefer Halachot Pesuqot (Facsimile Edition of Codex Sassoon 263)*. Jerusalem.

ADLER, E. N. (1914). 'Nouveaux documents sur la dispute entre Ben Méir et Saadia'. *REJ* 67: 44–52.

—— (1930). *Jewish Travellers*. London.

AGNELLO, S. L. (1953). *Silloge di iscrizioni paleocristiani della Sicilia*. Rome.

AJDLER, J. J. (1996). הלכות קידוש החודש על-פי הרמב׳ם. 4th edn. Jerusalem.

AKAVIA, A. A. (1945). ערכן של כתבות צוער לכרונולוגיה. *Qedem*, 2: 92–8.

—— (1950). סוד העבור של השומרונים. *Melila*, 3–4: 328–47.

—— (1951/2). ספר מיוחד לעניני העבור. *Sinai*, 30: 118–37.

—— (1955). ברייתא דשמואל כתעודה לתולדות העיבור. *Melila*, 5: 119–32.

ALBANI, M. (1994). *Astronomie und Schöpfungsglaube: Untersuchungen zum astronomischen Henochbuch* (WMANT 68). Neukirchen–Vluyn (*n.v.*).

ALBECK, S. (1904). ספר ראב׳ן. Warsaw.

ALLONY, N. (ed.) (1969). האגרון. Jerusalem.

ALON, G. (1957). מחקרים בתולדות ישראל בימי בית שני ובתקופת המשנה והתלמוד, 2 vols. Tel-Aviv.

—— (1980). *The Jews in their Land in the Talmudic Age*, 2 vols. Jerusalem.

ANKORI, Z. (1959). *Karaites in Byzantium*. New York.

APTOWITZER, A. (1964–5). ספר ראבי׳ה, 2nd edn., 4 vols. (vol. iv with S. Y. Cohen and A. Prisman). Jerusalem.

ASSAF, S. (1942). תשובות הגאונים. Jerusalem.

ASSIS, M. (1978). תשובה על קביעתה של שנת ד׳א תתל׳ח ליצירה (1077-8 לס׳). *HUCA* 49: 1–27 (Hebrew section).

AUJAC, G. (1975). *Geminus: Introduction aux Phénomènes*. Paris.

BAILLET, M. (1982). *Qumran Grotte* 4 III (DJD 7). Oxford.

BAILLY, M. A. (1903). *Dictionnaire grec-français*, 4th edn. Paris.

BALDWIN BOWSKY, M. (1987). 'M. Tittius Sex. f. Aem., and the Jews of Berenice (Cyrenaica)'. *American Journal of Philology*, 108: 495–510.

BAR-KOKHBA, B. (1997). חג הפורים בימי הבית שני ומגילת אסתר ב׳אסיא׳. *Sinai*, 121: 37–85.

BARNES, T. D. (1981). *Constantine and Eusebius*. Cambridge, MA.

BARON, S. W. (1952). *A Social and Religious History of the Jews*, 2nd edn., 18 vols. Philadelphia.

BARRETT, A. A. (1989). *Caligula: The Corruption of Power*. London.

BARTENURA, R. OVADIA (1922). המסע לארץ ישראל בשנת רמ'ז-רמ'ח. Berlin.

BAUMGARTEN, J. M. (1962). 'The Calendar of the Book of Jubilees and the Bible'. *Tarbiz*, 32: 317–28; repr. id., *Studies in Qumran Law* (Leiden, 1977), 101–14.

—— (1986). '4Q503 (Daily Prayers) and the Lunar Calendar'. *RQ* 12: 399–407.

—— (1987). 'The Calendar of the Book of Jubilees and the Temple Scroll'. *VT* 37: 71–8.

BECKWITH, R. T. (1970). 'The Modern Attempt to Reconcile the Qumran Calendar with the True Solar Year'. *RQ* 7: 379–96.

—— (1992). 'The Essene Calendar and the Moon: A Reconsideration'. *RQ* 15: 457–66.

—— (1996). *Calendar and Chronology, Jewish and Christian*. Leiden.

BENOIT, P., MILIK, J. T., and VAUX, R. de (1961). *Les Grottes de Murabbaʿât* (DJD 2). Oxford.

BEN-ZVI, I. (1943). שתי כתובות-קברים יהודיות-ארמיות מסביבות צוער. *Bulletin of the Israel Exploration Society*, 10: 35–8.

BERLIN, N. Z. (*Netziv*) (1955). העמק שאלה, 3 vols. Jerusalem.

BEYER, K. (1994). *Die aramäischen Texte vom Toten Meer*, ii. Göttingen.

BICKERMAN, E. J. (1968). *Chronology of the Ancient World*. London.

—— (1983). 'The Calendars', in *Cambridge History of Iran*, iii/2. Cambridge, 784–90.

AL-BIRUNI (1879). *The Chronology of Ancient Nations*, trans. C. E. Sachau (London).

BOFFO, L. (1994). *Iscrizioni greche e latine per lo studio della Bibbia*. Brescia.

BORNSTEIN, H. Y. (1887). פרשת העיבור. *Ha-Kerem*, 1: 290–338.

—— (1904). ספר היובל לנ' סוקולוב, in מחלוקת רב סעדיה גאון ובן מאיר. Warsaw, 19–189.

—— (1908). פליטה מיני קדם, in D. N. Günzburg and I. Markon (eds.), ספר א'א הרכבי. St Petersburg, 63–104.

—— (1919). משפט הסמיכה וקורותיה. *Ha-Tequfa*, 4: 394–426.

—— (1920). סדרי זמנים והתפחותם בישראל. *Ha-Tequfa*, 6: 247–313.

—— (1921*a*). תאריכי ישראל (חלק א'). *Ha-Tequfa*, 8: 281–338.

—— (1921*b*). תאריכי ישראל (חלק ב'). *Ha-Tequfa*, 9: 202–64.

—— (1921*c*). חשבון שמיטין ויובלות. *Ha-Tequfa*, 11: 230–60.

—— (1922*a*). דברי ימי העיבור האחרונים (חלק א'). *Ha-Tequfa*, 14–15: 321–72.

—— (1922*b*). דברי ימי העיבור האחרונים (חלק ב'). *Ha-Tequfa*, 16: 228–92.

—— (1924). עיבורים ומחזורים. *Ha-Tequfa*, 20: 285–330.

—— (1927). חשבון תקופות ומזלות. Warsaw.

BOWEN, A. C., and GOLDSTEIN, B. R. (1988). 'Meton of Athens and Astronomy in the Late Fifth Century BC', in Leichty *et al.* (1988): 39–81.

—— (1994). 'Aristarchus, Thales, and Heraclitus on Solar Eclipses: An Astronomical Commentary on P.Oxy.53.3710 cols.2.33–3.19'. *Physis*, NS 31: 689–729.

BOWERSOCK, G. W. (1995). *Martyrdom and Rome*. Cambridge.

BRAUDE, W. G., and KAPSTEIN, I. J. (1975). *Pesikta de-Rab Kahana*. London.

BRIANT, P. (1996). *Histoire de l'Empire perse*. Paris.

BRIND'AMOUR, P. (1983). *Le Calendrier romain: Recherches chronologiques*. Ottawa.

BRODY, R. (1997). *The Geonim of Babylonia and the Shaping of Medieval Jewish Culture*. New Haven.

BROSHI, M., and QIMRON, E. (1989). שטר חוב עברי מימי בר כוכבא. *Eretz Israel*, 20: 256–61.

BUBER, S. (ed.) (1868). פסיקתא דרב כהנא. Lyck.

—— (1884). מדרש לקח טוב (פסיקתא זוטרתא), 4 vols. Vilna.

—— (1889). מדרש תהילים. Lvov.

—— (1899). איכה רבה. Vilna.

—— (1901). מדרש שכל טוב, 2 vols. Berlin.

BURSTEIN, A. (1955/6). לבעיית עיבורי השנה בחוץ לארץ. *Sinai*, 38: 32–46.

BUSCHMANN, G. (1994). *Martyrium Polycarpi: Eine formkritische Studie*. Berlin.

CAMELOT, P. T. (1951). *Ignace d'Antioche et Polycarpe de Smyrne* (Sources chrétiennes, 10). Paris.

CASSON, L. (1971). *Ships and Seamanship in the Ancient World*. Princeton.

—— (1974). *Travel in the Ancient World*. London.

CASSUTO, M. D. (= U.) (1943). על מה נחלקו רב סעדיה גאון ובן מאיר?, in Y. L. Fishman (Maimon) (ed.), רב סעדיה גאון. Jerusalem, 333–64.

—— (1945*a*). התאריכים שבכתובות צוער. *Qedem*, 2: 90–1.

—— (1945*b*). הכתובות העבריות של המאה התשיעית בוינוסה. *Qedem*, 2: 99–120.

CHARLES, R. H. (1913). *The Apocrypha and Pseudepigrapha of the Old Testament*, 2 vols. Oxford.

CHARLESWORTH, J. H. (ed.) (1983–5). *The Old Testament Pseudepigrapha*, 2 vols. New York.

CHAJES, Z. H. (1952). *The Student's Guide through the Talmud*, trans. J. Shachter. London.

CHIESA, B., and LOCKWOOD, W. (1984). *Yaʿqūb al-Qirqisānī on Jewish Sects and Christianity*. Frankfurt am Main.

COHEN, S. J. D. (1984). 'The Significance of Yavneh: Pharisees, Rabbis, and the End of Jewish Sectarianism'. *HUCA* 55: 27–53.

COLLINS, N. (1991). 'Ezekiel, the Author of the Exagoge: His Calendar and Home'. *JSJ* 22: 201–11.

COLSON, F. H. (1937). *Philo*, vii: *Decalogue and Special Laws* (Loeb Classical Library). London.

COTTON, H. M. (1995). 'The Archive of Salome Komaise Daughter of Levi: Another Archive from the "Cave of Letters"'. *ZPE* 105: 183–203.

—— and GREENFIELD, J. C. (1994). 'Babatha's Property and the Law of Succession in the Babatha Archive'. *ZPE* 104: 211–24.

—— and YARDENI, A. (1997). *Aramaic, Hebrew and Greek Documentary Texts from Nahal Hever and Other Sites* (DJD 27). Oxford.

—— COCKLE, W. E. H., and MILLAR, F. G. B. (1995). 'The Papyrology of the Roman Near East: A Survey'. *JRS* 85: 214–35.

COWLEY, A. E. (1923). *Aramaic Papyri of the Fifth Century B.C.* Oxford.

—— (1925). 'A Jewish Tomb-Stone'. *Palestine Exploration Fund Quarterly Statement*, 57: 207–10.

CRAWFORD, M. (1996). 'Italy and Rome from Sulla to Augustus', in A. K. Bowman *et al.* (eds.), *Cambridge Ancient History*, x: *The Augustan Empire*, 2nd edn. Cambridge, ch. 13a.

CROSS, F. L., and LIVINGSTONE, E. A. (1997). *Oxford Dictionary of the Christian Church*, 3rd edn. Oxford.

DAUNOY, F. (1925). 'La question pascale au concile de Nicée'. *Échos d'Orient*, 24: 424–44.

DAVIDSON, I. (1919). *Maḥzor Yannai*. New York.

DAVIES, P. R. (1983). 'Calendrical Change and Qumran Origins: an Assessment of VanderKam's Theory'. *Catholic Biblical Quarterly*, 45: 80–9.

DEKKERS, E. (1995). *Clavis Patrum Latinorum*, 3rd edn. Turnhout.

DEMAN, A. (1974). 'Notes de chronologie romaine'. *Historia*, 23: 271–8.

DENIS, A.-M. (1970). *Fragmenta Pseudepigraphorum quae supersunt Graeca*. Leiden.

DEPUYDT, L. (1997). *Civil Calendar and Lunar Calendar in Ancient Egypt*. Leuven.

DIEHL, E. (1927). *Inscriptiones Latinae Christianae Veteres*, ii. Berlin.

—— (1961). *Inscriptiones Latinae Christianae Veteres*, iii. Berlin.

DI LELLA, A. (1962). 'Qumran and the Geniza Fragments of Sirach'. *Catholic Biblical Quarterly*, 24: 245–67.

DINDORF, L. (1832). *Chronicon Paschale* (Corpus Scriptorum Historiae Byzantinae, 9/i). Bonn.

DOGGETT, L. E., and SCHAEFER, B. E. (1994). 'Lunar Crescent Visibility'. *Icarus*, 107: 388–403.

DOR, Z. M. (1971). ‏תורת ארץ ישראל בבבל‎. Tel-Aviv (*n.v.*).

DUCHESNE, L. (1880). 'La question de la Pâque au concile de Nicée'. *Revue des questions historiques*, 28: 5–42.

Duval, P.-M., and Pinault, G. (1986). *Recueil des inscriptions gauloises*, iii: *Les Calendriers*, Paris.

Edmonson, Munro S. (1988). *The Book of the Year: Middle American Calendrical Systems*. Salt Lake City.

Eisenman, R., and Wise, M. O. (1992). *The Dead Sea Scrolls Uncovered*. Rockport, MA.

Elizur, S. (1999). לקורות הגאונות במאה השמינית: הספד על ראש הישיבה בארץ ישראל. *Zion*, 64: 311–48.

Elkin, Z. (1996–7). הנוסח הקראי של 'ספר החילוקים בין בני ארץ-ישראל לבני בבל'. *Tarbiz*, 66: 101–11.

Epstein, A. (1901). 'La querelle au sujet du calendrier entre Ben-Meir et les académies babyloniennes'. *REJ* 42: 173–210.

Eshel, E., and Kloner, A. (1996). 'An Aramaic Ostracon of an Edomite Marriage Contract from Maresha, Dated 176 BCE'. *IEJ* 46: 1–22; translation of Hebrew article in *Tarbiz*, 63 (1994), 485–502.

Evans, J. (1999). 'The Material Culture of Greek Astronomy'. *JHA* 30: 237–307.

Fatoohi, L. J., Stephenson, F. R., and Al-Dargazelli, S. S. (1999). 'The Babylonian First Visibility of the Lunar Crescent: Data and Criterion'. *JHA* 30: 51–72.

Feldman, L. H. (1989–90). 'The Enigma of Horace's Thirtieth Sabbath'. *SCI* 10: 87–112.

Ferrar, W. J. (1920). *Eusebius: The Proof of the Gospel*. London.

Filipowski, Z. (ed.) (1851). ספר העיבור לר' אברהם בר חייא הנשיא. London; repr. 'פועל ה, 2nd edn., 3 vols. (Bnei-Braq, 1998), ii.

Fleischer, E. (1973). בירורים בבעיית ייעודם הליטורגי של פיוטי קידוש ירחים. *Tarbiz*, 42: 337–63.

—— (1983). לוח מועדי השנה בפיוט לר' אלעזר בירבי קיליר. *Tarbiz*, 52: 223–72.

—— (1984a). היוצרות בהתהוותם ובהתפתחותם. Jerusalem.

—— (1984b). תעודות ספרותיות לתולדות הגאונות בארץ ישראל. *Zion*, 49: 375–400.

—— (1984c). הערה להארה: בדבר שני ימים של ראש-השנה בארץ-ישראל. *Tarbiz*, 53: 293–5.

Floëri, F., and Nautin, P. (1957). *Homélies pascales: Une homélie anatolienne sur la date de Pâques en l'an 387* (Sources chrétiennes, 48). Paris.

Follet, S. (1976). *Athènes au IIᵉ et au IIIᵉ siècle: Études chronologiques et prosopographiques*. Paris.

Fossum, J. (1987). 'The Magharians: A Pre-Christian Jewish Sect and its Significance for the Study of Gnosticism and Christianity'. *Henoch*, 9: 303–44.

Fraenkel, A. H. (1945). הערה לכתובת ג' מצוער. *Qedem*, 2: 89.

Frank, H. (1938). 'Ambrosius und die Bußeraussöhnung in Mailand'. *Heilige Überlieferung (Festschrift I. Herwegen)*. Münster.

FRIEDLANDER, M. (1893). 'Life and Works of Saadia'. *JQR*, os 5: 177–99.

FRIEDMAN, M. A. (1980). *Jewish Marriage in Palestine*, 2 vols. Tel-Aviv and New York.

GAFNI, I. M. (1987). לחקר הכרונולוגיה התלמודית באיגרת רב שרירא גאון. *Zion*, 52: 1–24.

—— (1997). *Land, Centre and Diaspora. Jewish Constructs in Late Antiquity* (*Journal for the Study of the Pseudepigrapha*, Supplement Series, 21). Sheffield.

GANDZ, S. (1949–50). 'Studies in the Hebrew Calendar (2)'. *JQR*, ns 40: 251–77.

GANS, D. (1743). ספר נחמד ונעים. Jesnitz.

GELLER, M. (1997). 'The Last Wedge'. *Zeitschrift für Assyriologie und vorderasiatische Archäologie*, 87: 43–95.

GIL, M. (1992). *A History of Palestine, 634–1099*. Cambridge.

—— (1996). עיונים בתולדות יהודי עראק במאה העשירית. *Teʿudah: Studies in Judaica*, 10, Tel-Aviv University, 81–153.

GINZBERG, L. (1928–9). גנזי שעכטער, 2 vols. New York.

GINZEL, F. K. (1911). *Handbuch der mathematischen und technischen Chronologie*, 3 vols. Leipzig.

GLESSMER, U. (1996a). 'Horizontal Measuring in the Babylonian Astronomical Compendium MUL.APIN and in the Astronomical Book of 1En'. *Henoch*, 18: 259–82.

—— (1996b). 'The Otot-Texts (4Q319) and the Problem of Intercalations in the Context of the 364-Day Calendar', in H. J. Fabry, A. Lange, and H. Lichtenberger (eds.), *Qumranstudien: Vorträge und Beiträge der Teilnehmer des Qumranseminars auf dem internationalen Treffen der Society of Biblical Literature, Münster, 25–26 Juli 1993* (Schriften des Institutum Judaicum Delitzschianum, 4). Göttingen, 125–64.

—— (1999). 'Calendars in the Qumran Scrolls', in P. W. Flint and J. C. VanderKam (eds.), *The Dead Sea Scrolls after Fifty Years. A Comprehensive Assessment*. Leiden, ii. 213–78.

GOLB, N. (1960). 'Who were the Maġārīya?' *Journal of the American Oriental Society*, 80: 347–59.

GOLDBERG, D. (ed.) (1848). יסוד עולם לר' יצחק ישראלי, 2 vols. Berlin; repr. פועל ה', 2nd edn., 3 vols. (Bnei-Braq, 1998), ii.

GOLDSTEIN, B. R. (1967). *Ibn al-Muthannâ's Commentary on the Astronomical Tables of al-Khwârizmî*. New Haven.

GOODMAN, M. D. (1994). 'Sadducees and Essenes after 70 CE', in S. E. Porter, P. Joyce, and D. E. Orton (eds.), *Crossing the Boundaries: Essays in Biblical Interpretation in Honour of Michael D. Goulder*. Leiden, 347–56.

GRABBE, L. J. (1991). 'Maccabean Chronology: 167–164 or 168–165 BCE'. *Journal of Biblical Literature*, 110: 59–74.

GRAETZ, H. (1890–1909). *Geschichte der Juden*, 4th edn., 11 vols. Leipzig.

—— (1919). *Popular History of the Jews*, trans. A. B. Rhine, 6 vols. New York: Hebrew Publishing Co.

GRAF, D. (1994). 'The Persian Royal Road System'. *Achaemenid History*, 8: 167–89.

GROSSMAN, A. (1995). חכמי צרפת הראשונים. Jerusalem.

GRUMEL, V. (1958). *La Chronologie* (Traités d'études byzantines, 1). Paris.

—— (1960). 'Le problème de la date pascale au IIIe et IVe siècles'. *Revue des études byzantines*, 18: 163–78.

GRZYBEK, E. (1990). *Du calendrier macédonien au calendrier ptolémaïque: Problèmes de chronologie hellénistique*. Basel.

GUILLAUME, A. (1914–15). 'Further Documents on the Ben-Meir Controversy'. *JQR*, NS 5: 543–57.

—— (1955). *The Life of Muhammad: A Translation of Ishaq's Sirat Rasul Allah*. London.

GUTMAN, S., *et al.* (1981). 'Excavations in the Synagogue at Horvat Susiya', in Levine (1981) 123–8.

HADASSI, JUDAH (1836). אשכול הכופר. Eupatoria.

HAGEDORN, D., 'Zum ägyptischen Kalender unter Augustus', *ZPE* 100 (1994), 211–22.

HALEVY, I. (1901). דורות הראשונים, ii. Frankfurt am Main.

HANSEN, G. C. (1995). *Sokrates: Kirchengeschichte* (Die griechischen christlichen Schriftsteller der ersten drei Jahrhunderte, NF 1). Berlin.

HARKAVY, A. E. (1903). *Studien und Mittheilungen*, viii. St Petersburg.

—— (1984). 'Abū Yūsuf Ya'qūb al-Qirqisānī on the Jewish Sects', trans. W. Lockwood, in Chiesa and Lockwood (1984) 49–90.

HARKINS, P. (1979). *John Chrysostom: Discourses against Judaizing Christians* (Fathers of the Church, 68). Washington, DC.

HARTNER, W. (1979). 'The Young Avestan and Babylonian Calendars'. *JHA* 10: 1–22.

HARTOM, A. S. (1967). הספרים החיצונים: חזיונות, 2 vols. Tel-Aviv.

HAWKINS, J. B. H. (1869). 'Peter, Bishop of Alexandria', in *The Writings of Methodius etc.* (Ante-Nicene Christian Library, 14). Edinburgh, 269–332.

HAYWARD, R. (1991). 'Pirqe de Rabbi Eliezer and Targum Pseudo-Jonathan'. *JJS* 42: 215–46.

HEALEY, J. F. (1993). *The Nabataean Tomb Inscriptions of Mada'in Salih* (*Journal of Semitic Studies*, Supplement 1). Oxford.

HEIKEL, I. A. (1902). Eusebius Werke. Leipzig.

HENDEL, R. (1995). '4Q252 and the Flood Chronology of Genesis 7–8: A Text-Critical Solution'. *Dead Sea Discoveries*, 2: 72–9.

HERR, M. D. (1976). 'The Calendar', in S. Safrai and M. Stern (eds.), *The Jewish People in the First Century* (Compendia Rerum Iudaicarum ad Novum Testamentum, i/2). Assen, ch. 16.

292 *References*

—— (1979/80). עניני הלכה בארץ ישראל במאה הששית והשביעית לספירת הנוצרים. *Tarbiz*, 49: 62–80.

—— (1984). עוד על שני ימים של ראש השנה בארץ-ישראל. *Tarbiz*, 53: 142–3.

HESS, H. (1958). *The Canons of the Council of Sardica, AD 343*. Oxford.

HIRSCHLER, M. (1977). *Babylonian Talmud with Variant Readings*, ii: *Ketubot*. Jerusalem.

—— (1984). תוספות ישנים: ראש השנה. Jerusalem.

HIRSCHFELD, H. (1903–4). 'The Arabic Portion of the Cairo Genizah at Cambridge (4th Article)'. *JQR*, os 16: 290–9.

HOLL, K., rev. DÜMMER, J. (1980). *Epiphanius*, ii (Die griechischen christlichen Schriftsteller der ersten drei Jahrhunderte). Berlin (DDR).

HORBURY, W., and NOY, D. (1992). *Jewish Inscriptions of Graeco-Roman Egypt*. Cambridge.

HOROVITZ, C. M. (1972). פרקי דרבי אליעזר. Jerusalem.

HURWITZ, S. (1923). מחזור ויטרי. Nuremberg.

HYMAN, A. (1964). תולדות תנאים ואמוראים, 3 vols. Jerusalem.

IBN EZRA, R. ABRAHAM (1839). אגרת השבת, ed. S. D. Luzzatto. *Kerem Hemed*, 4:158–74.

—— (1874). ספר העיבור. Lyck; repr. פועל ה', 2nd edn., 3 vols. (Bnei-Braq, 1998), ii.

ISAIAH OF TERRANI (1966). פסקי הרי"ד, ii. (עירובין, פסחים, וכו'). Jerusalem.

ISSER, S. J. (1976). *The Dositheans*. Leiden.

JACOBSON, H. (1983). *The Exagoge of Ezekiel*. Cambridge.

JAFFE, Z. H. (1931). קורות חשבון העיבור, ed. A. A. Akavia. Jerusalem.

JAUBERT, A. (1953). 'Le calendrier des Jubilés et de la secte de Qumran: ses origines bibliques'. *VT* 3: 250–64.

—— (1957a). *La Date de la Cène*. Paris.

—— (1957b). 'Le calendrier des Jubilés et les jours liturgiques de la semaine'. *VT* 7: 35–61.

JONES, A. (1997). 'On the Reconstructed Macedonian and Egyptian Lunar Calendars'. *ZPE* 119: 157–66.

JONES, C. W. (1943). *Bedae Opera de Temporibus*. Cambridge, MA.

JUSTER, J. (1914). *Les Juifs dans l'Empire romain*, 2 vols. Paris.

KAPPLER, W., and HANHART, R. (1959). *Septuaginta*, ix/2: *Maccabaeorum Liber II*. Göttingen.

KARELITZ, A. Y. (1973). חזון איש, חלק אורח חיים. Bnei-Braq.

KASHER, M. M. (1949). תורה שלמה, xiii. New York.

KATSH, A. I. (1975). גנזי תלמוד בבלי, 2 vols. Jerusalem.

KATZ, J. (1979). 'Rabbinical Authority and Authorization in the Middle Ages', in I. Twersky (ed.), *Studies in Medieval Jewish History and Literature*. Cambridge, MA, 41–56.

KNIBB, M. (1978). *The Ethiopic Book of Enoch*, 2 vols. Oxford.

KRUSCH, B. (1880). *Studien zur christlich-mittelalterlichen Chronologie: Der 84jäh-rige Ostercyclus und seine Quellen*. Leipzig.

LAKE, K. (1913). *The Apostolic Fathers*, ii (Loeb Classical Library). London.

LANGERMANN, T. (1987). ‏אמתי נוסד הלוח העברי?‏. *Assufot*, 1: 159–68.

LARONDE, A. (1987). *Cyrène et la Libye hellénistique: Libykai Historiai, de l'époque républicaine au principat d'Auguste*. Paris.

LASKER, A. A., and LASKER, D. J. (1990/1). ‏תרמ׳ב חלקים: עוד על מחלוקת רב סעדיה גאון ובן מאיר‏. *Tarbiz*, 60: 119–28.

LEICHTY, E., ELLIS, M. de J., and GERARDI, P. (eds.) (1988), *A Scientific Humanist: Studies in Memory of Abraham Sachs* (Occasional Publications of the Samuel Noah Kramer Fund, 9). Philadelphia, Pa.

LEMAIRE, A. (1977). *Inscriptions hébraïques*, i: *Les Ostraca*. Paris.

LEVI, I. (1900). 'La lettre de Ben Méir'. *REJ* 40: 261–3.

—— ADLER, E., and BROYDE, J. (1900). 'Nouveaux fragments relatifs à Ben Méir'. *REJ* 41: 224–32.

LEVINE, L. I. (1975). *Caesarea under Roman Rule*. Leiden.

—— (ed.) (1981). *Ancient Synagogues Revealed*. Jerusalem.

—— (1989). *The Rabbinic Class of Roman Palestine in Late Antiquity*. New York and Jerusalem.

—— (1996). 'The Status of the Patriarch in the Third and Fourth Centuries: Sources and Methodology'. *JJS* 47: 1–32.

LEWIN, B. M. (ed.) (1920). ‏אגרת רב שרירא גאון‏. Frankfurt; repr. ‏הגאונים‏, vii (Bnei-Braq, 1987).

—— (1931). ‏אוצר הגאונים‏, iv: ‏יום טוב‏. Jerusalem.

—— (1932/3). ‏אוצר הגאונים‏, v: ‏ראש השנה‏. Jerusalem.

—— (1942). ‏אוצר חילוף מנהגים בין בני ארץ ישראל ובין בני בבל‏. Jerusalem; repr. ‏הגאונים‏, vii (Bnei-Braq, 1987).

LEWIS, D. M. (1977). *Sparta and Persia*. Leiden.

LEWIS, N. (1985–8). 'A Jewish Landowner in Provincia Arabia'. *SCI* 8–9: 132–7.

LIEBERMAN, S. (1929). ‏על הירושלמי‏. Jerusalem.

—— (1934a). ‏הירושלמי כפשוטו‏. Jerusalem.

—— (1934b). ‏תיקוני ירושלמי, חלק ו׳‏. *Tarbiz*, 5: 102–4; repr. ‏מחקרים בתורת ארץ ישראל‏. Jerusalem, 1991, 205–7.

—— (1946). 'Palestine in the 3rd and 4th Centuries'. *JQR*, NS 36: 329–70; repr. Lieberman (1974) 112–53.

—— (1956). ‏תוספתא כפשוטה‏, i. New York.

—— (1962). ‏תוספתא כפשוטה‏, v. New York.

—— (1963). 'How Much Greek in Jewish Palestine?', in A. Altmann (ed.), *Biblical and Other Studies*. Cambridge, MA, 123–41.

—— (1974). *Text and Studies*. New York.

—— (1992). שקיעין, 2nd edn. Jerusalem.

Lieu, J. (1997). *Image and Reality. The Jews in the World of the Christians in the Second Century*. Edinburgh.

Lim, T. (1992). 'The Chronology of the Flood Story in a Qumran Text (4Q252)'. *JJS* 43: 288–98.

—— (1993). 'Notes on 4Q252 fr. 1, cols. i–ii'. *JJS* 44: 121–6.

Lipkin, A. L. (ed.) (1902). ברייתא דשמואל הקטן. Pietrkov; repr. פועל ה', 2nd edn., 3 vols. (Bnei-Braq, 1998), i.

Loewinger, Y. (1986). *Al Hasheminit*. Tel-Aviv.

—— (1994). חיזוי הראייה של הירח החדש. *Teḥumin*, 14: 473–500.

—— (1995). 'Some Comments on the Article of Dr B. E. Schaefer'. *QJRAS* 36: 449–52.

—— (1996*a*). הקריטריון של הרמב'ם לראיית הירח החדש. *BaDaD – Be-Khol Derakhekha Daʿehu*, Journal of Torah and Scholarship, Bar-Ilan University Press, 3: 45–85.

—— (1996*b*). שלושת סוגי המולדות. *Sinai*, 118: 71–82.

—— (1998). הייתכן בירור אסטרונומי למועד ייסוד הלוח העברי? *Bar-Ilan University Weekly* (*Parashat wa-ʾEthanan* issue).

Lüderitz, G. (1983). *Corpus jüdischer Zeugnisse aus der Cyrenaika*, with appendix by J. M. Reynolds. Wiesbaden.

Luria, D. (1852). פרקי דרבי אליעזר. Warsaw.

Luzzatto, S. D. (1854), untitled letter, *Kerem Ḥemed* 8: 37. Berlin.

MacAdam, H. I. (1986). *Studies on the History of the Roman Province of Arabia* (BAR International Series, 295). Oxford.

MacMullen, R. (1982). 'The Epigraphic Habit in the Roman Empire'. *American Journal of Philology*, 103: 233–46.

Macran, H. S. (1902). *The Harmonics of Aristoxenus*. Oxford.

Magie, D. (1950). *Roman Rule in Asia Minor to the End of the 3rd Century after Christ*, 2 vols. Princeton, NJ.

Mahler, E. (1916). *Handbuch der jüdischen Chronologie*. Leipzig.

Malter, H. (1942). *Saadia Gaon: His Life and Works*. Philadelphia.

Mandelbaum, B. (1987). פסיקתא דרב כהנא, 2nd edn. New York.

Mann, J. (1920–2). *The Jews in Egypt and Palestine under the Fatimid Caliphs*, 2 vols. London.

—— (1925). 'Gaonic Studies'. *HUCA* Jubilee Volume, 223–62.

—— (1931–5). *Texts and Studies in Jewish History and Literature*, 2 vols. Philadelphia.

Marcus, R. (1953). *Philo, Supplement 2: Questions and Answers on Exodus* (Loeb Classical Library) London.

MARGALIOT, M. (1956). מדרש הגדול, ii. Jerusalem.

—— (1974). הלכות ארץ ישראל מן הגניזה. Jerusalem.

MARMORSTEIN, A. (1921). קידוש ירחים דרבי פנחס. *Ha-Tzofeh le-Ḥokhmat Yis-rael*, 5: 225–55.

—— (1928). תשובות הגאונים. Deva; repr. *Gaonica*, i (Bnei-Braq, 1985).

MARX, A. (1910–11). 'Studies in Gaonic History and Literature'. *JQR*, NS 1: 61–104.

MEEKS, W. A., and WILKEN, R. L. (1978). *Jews and Christians in Antioch in the First Four Centuries of the Common Era* (Sources for Biblical Study, 13). Missoula, MT.

MEEUS, J. (1991). *Astronomical Algorithms*. Richmond, VA.

MEIMARIS, Y. E., with KRITIKAKOU, K., and BOUGIA, P. (1992). *Chronological Systems in Roman-Byzantine Palestine and Arabia: The Evidence of Dated Greek Inscriptions* (Meletemata, 17). Athens.

MENAḤEM HA-MEIRI (1947). בית הבחירה, ed. A. Sofer. Jerusalem.

METZGER, D. (1994). פירושי רבנו חננאל: ראש השנה, סוכה. Jerusalem.

METZGER, M. (ed.) (1985). *Les Constitutions apostoliques* (Sources chrétiennes, 320). Paris.

MILIK, J. T. (1976). *The Books of Enoch: Aramaic Fragments of Qumran Cave 4*. Oxford.

MILLAR, F. G. B. (1992). 'The Jews of the Graeco-Roman Diaspora between Paganism and Christianity, AD 312–438', in J. Lieu, J. North, and T. Rajak (eds.), *The Jews among Pagans and Christians*. London, 97–123.

—— (1993). *The Roman Near East 31 BC–AD 337*. Cambridge.

MIRSKY, S. K. (ed.) (1964). שאילתות דרב אחאי גאון, iii. Jerusalem.

MOHRMANN, C. (1962). 'Le conflit pascal au IIᵉ siècle — note philologique'. *Vigiliae Christianae*, 16: 154–71.

MUNK, S. (1848). 'De la philosophie chez les Juifs'. *Archives israélites*, 9: 169–84, 325–36, 419–33.

—— (1881). *Philosophy and Philosophical Authors of the Jews*, trans. I. Kalisch. Cincinnati.

NAGY, R. M., MEYERS, C. L., MEYERS, E. M., and WEISS, Z. (1996). *Sepphoris in Galilee*. [Raleigh, NC].

NAVEH, J. (1978). על פסיפס ואבן. Tel-Aviv.

—— (1985). 'Another Jewish Aramaic Tombstone from Zoar'. *HUCA* 56: 103–16.

—— (1987). 'The Fifth Jewish Aramaic Tombstone from Zoar'. *Liber Annuus (Studium Biblicum Franciscanum)*, 37: 369–71 and pls. 53–4.

—— (1995). מצבות צוער. *Tarbiz*, 64: 477–97.

—— (1999). עוד על מצבות צוער. *Tarbiz*, 68: 581–6.

NEAMAN, P. (1972). אנציקלופדיה לגאוגרפיה תלמודית, i. Tel-Aviv.

NEGEV, A. (1971). 'A Nabatean Epitaph from Trans-Jordan'. *IEJ* 21: 50–2.

—— (1978). 'The Greek Inscriptions from 'Avdat (Oboda)'. *Liber Annuus (Studium Biblicum Franciscanum)*, 28: 87–126.

NEMOY, L. (1930). 'Al-Qirqisānī's Account of the Jewish Sects and Christianity'. *HUCA* 7: 317–97.

NEUGEBAUER, O. (1949). 'The Astronomy of Maimonides and its Sources'. *HUCA* 22: 321–63.

—— (1955). *Astronomical Cuneiform Texts*, 3 vols. Princeton.

—— (1979). *Ethiopic Astronomy and Computus* (Sitzungsberichte der Österreichischen Akademie der Wissenschaften, Philosophisch-historische Klasse, 347). Vienna.

—— (1985). Appendix A to M. Black, *The Book of Enoch or I Enoch*. Leiden, 386–419.

NEUSNER, J. (1965–70). *A History of the Jews of Babylonia*, 5 vols. Leiden.

NIESE, B. (ed.) (1894). *Flavii Iosephi Opera*, vi: *De Bello Iudaico*. Berlin.

NOLL, R. (1968). 'Eine verschollene Katakombeninschrift'. *Epigraphische Studien*, 5: 184–90.

NOY, D. (1993–5). *Jewish Inscriptions of Western Europe*, 2 vols. Cambridge.

OLSZOWY-SCHLANGER, J. (1998). *Karaite Marriage Documents from the Cairo Geniza*. Leiden.

OPPENHEIMER, A. (1995). נהרדעא ונציבין בתקופה הפרתית, in Z. A. Steinfeld (ed.), *Bar-Ilan Annual: Studies in Judaica and the Humanities*, 26–7. Ramat-Gan, 117–30.

—— (1996). גישה הסטורית מהי?. *Zion*, 61: 225–30.

PARDO, R. DAVID (1994). חסדי דוד, 10 vols. Jerusalem.

PARISOT, J. (ed.) (1894). *Patrologia Syriaca*, i. Paris.

PARKER, R. A. (1950). *Calendars of Ancient Egypt*. Chicago.

—— and DUBBERSTEIN, W. H. (1956). *Babylonian Chronology 626 BC–AD 75*, 3rd edn. Providence, RI.

PARMENTIER, L., and SCHEIDWEILER, F. (1954). *Theodoret: Kirchengeschichte* (Die griechischen christlichen Schriftsteller der ersten drei Jahrhunderte). Berlin.

PEDERSEN, O. (1974). *A Survey of the Almagest*. Odense.

PERL, G. (1971). 'Die römischen Provinzbeamten in Cyrenae und Creta'. *Klio*, 53: 369.

PETERSEN, V. M., and SCHMIDT, O. (1968). 'The Determination of the Longitude of the Apogee of the Orbit of the Sun according to Hipparchus and Ptolemy'. *Centaurus*, 12: 73–96.

PIERRE, M. J. (1989). *Aphraate le sage persan: Les Exposés* (Sources chrétiennes, 359). Paris.

PINSKER, S. (1860). לקוטי קדמוניות, 2 parts. Vienna.

POLITIS, K. D. (1998). 'Survey and Rescue Collections in the Ghawr As-Safi'. *Annual of the Department of Antiquities of Jordan*, 42: 627–34.

PORTEN, B. (1990). 'The Calendar of Aramaic Texts from Achaemenid and Ptolemaic Egypt', in S. Shaked and A. Netzer (eds.), *Irano-Judaica*, ii. Jerusalem, 13–32.

—— and YARDENI, A. (1986). *Textbook of Aramaic Documents from Ancient Egypt*, i. Jerusalem.

POWELS, S. (1977). *Der Kalender der Samaritaner*. Berlin.

—— (1989). 'The Samaritan calendar', in A. D. Crown, *The Samaritans*. Tübingen, ch. 11, 691–742.

POZNANSKI, S. A. (1905). 'Philon dans l'ancienne littérature judéo-arabe'. *REJ* 50: 10–31.

—— (1918). מיסדי כתות בישראל בתקופת הגאונים. *Reshummot* (Odessa), 1: 207–16.

PUCCI, M. (1981). מקור בלתי ידוע על ברית אפשרית בין הורקנוס הראשון לבין הפרתים. *Zion*, 46: 331–8.

RABINOVITZ, Z. M. (1972). ספר המעשים לבני ארץ ישראל: שרידים חדשים. *Tarbiz*, 41: 275–305.

—— (1976). גנזי מדרש. Tel-Aviv.

RAMSEY, A. M. (1925). 'The Speed of the Roman Imperial Post'. *JRS* 15: 60–74.

RAPAPORT, S. I. (*Shir*) (1914). ערך מילין. Warsaw (first published in Prague, 1852).

REYNOLDS, J. M. (1977). 'Inscriptions', in J. A. Lloyd (ed.) *Excavations at Sidi Khrebish, Benghazi (Berenike)*, i (*Libya Antiqua*, suppl. v/1). Tripoli, 233–54.

RICHARD, M. (1974). 'Le comput pascal par octaéteris'. *Le Muséon*, 87: 307–39; repr. in id., *Opera Minora* (Turnhout, 1976), i, no. 21.

ROBBINS, F. E. (1940). *Ptolemy: Tetrabiblos*, in W. G. Waddell, *Manetho* (Loeb Classical Library). London.

ROBERT, L. (1959). 'Les inscriptions grecques de Bulgarie'. *Revue de philologie*, 33: 165–236.

ROBERTSON, E. (1950). הטבלות האסטרונומיות והלוח של השומרונים. *Melila*, 3–4: 311–27.

ROSENTHAL, D. (1977). פרקא דאביי. *Tarbiz*, 46: 97–109.

ROUX, J., and ROUX, G. (1949). 'Un décret du politeuma des Juifs de Bérénikè en Cyrénaïque'. *Revue des études grecques*, 62: 281–96.

RUTGERS, L. V. (1995). *The Jews of Late Ancient Rome*. Leiden.

SACHS, A. J., and HUNGER, H. (1988–96). *Astronomical Diaries and Related Texts from Babylonia*, 3 vols. Vienna.

SAFRAI, S. (1965a). העליה לרגל בימי הבית השני. Tel-Aviv.

—— (1965b). המקומות לקידוש חדשים ולעיבור השנה בארץ לאחר החורבן. *Tarbiz*, 35: 27–38.

SAMUEL, A. E. (1962). *Ptolemaic Chronology*, Munich.

—— (1972). *Greek and Roman Chronology: Calendars and Years in Classical Antiquity*. Munich.

SANDERS, J. A. (1965). *The Psalm Scroll of Qumran Cave 11* (DJD 4). Oxford.

SAR-SHALOM, R. (1984). שערים ללוח העברי. Netanya.

—— (1988). מתי נוסד הלוח העברי?. *Sinai*, 102: 26–51.

—— (1992/3). מחלוקת רס׳ג ובן מאיר. *Sinai*, 111: 97–124.

SASSOON, S. D. (1950). הלכות פסוקות לרב יהודאי גאון. Jerusalem.

SCHAEFER, B. E. (1987). 'An Algorithm for Predicting the Visibility of the Lunar Crescent'. Paper delivered at the conference on 'The Lunar Calendar', Herndon, VA, 5–6 June 1987 (unpublished).

—— (1988). 'Visibility of the Lunar Crescent'. *QJRAS* 29: 511–23.

—— (1996). 'Lunar Crescent Visibility'. *QJRAS* 37: 759–68.

SCHÄFER, P. (1995). *The History of the Jews in Antiquity*, trans. D. Chowcat. [Luxembourg].

SCHECHTER, S. (1902). 'Geniza Specimens: Saadyana', 3 parts. *JQR*, os 14: 37–63, 197–249, and 449–516.

SCHIFFMAN, L. (1994). *Reclaiming the Dead Sea Scrolls*. Philadelphia.

SCHLOSSBERG, A. L. (1886). ספר הלכות פסוקות או הלכות ראו. Versailles.

SCHÜRER, E. (1898–1902). *Geschichte des jüdischen Volkes im Zeitalter Jesu Christi*, 3rd edn., 4 vols. Leipzig.

—— (1973–87). *The History of the Jewish People in the Age of Jesus Christ* (175 BC–AD 135), rev. and ed. G. Vermes and F. G. B. Millar (with M. Black (vols. i–ii) and M. Goodman (vols. iii/1–2)), 3 vols. in 4 parts. Edinburgh.

SCHWARTZ, D. R. (1997). 'Cassius' Chronology and Josephus' Vagueness'. *SCI* 16: 102–12.

SCHWARTZ, E. (1905). *Christliche und jüdische Ostertafeln* (Abhandlungen der Gesellschaft der Wissenschaften zu Göttingen, NF 8). Berlin.

—— and MOMMSEN, Th. (1908). *Eusebius' Werke*, 3 vols. Leipzig.

SEAGER, R. (1972). *Tiberius*. London.

SHAW, B. (1996). 'Seasons of Death: Aspects of Mortality in Imperial Rome'. *JRS* 86: 100–38.

SHINAN, A. (1985). 'The "Palestinian" Targums—Repetitions, Internal Unity, Contradictions'. *JJS* 36: 72–87.

SIJPESTEIJN, P. J. (1979). 'Some Remarks on Roman Dates in Greek Papyri'. *ZPE* 33: 229–440.

SILBER, Y. A. (1993). בירור הלכה, אורח חיים חלק ב׳. Bnei-Braq.

SIMON, M. (1986). *Verus Israel: A Study of the Relations between Christians and Jews in the Roman Empire (AD 135–425)*, trans. H. McKeating. London.

SIRAT, C., CAUDERLIER, P., DUKAN, M, and FRIEDMAN, M. A. (1986). *La Ketouba de Cologne: Un contrat de mariage juif à Antinoopolis* (Papyrologica Coloniensia, 12). Opladen.

SKEAT, T. C. (1954). *The Reigns of the Ptolemies*. Munich.

SLONIMSKY, H. S. (1852). יסודי העיבור, 1st edn. Warsaw.

SMELIK, K. A. D. (1991). *Writings from Ancient Israel*, trans. G. I. Davies. Edinburgh.

STARCKY, J. (1954). 'Un contrat nabatéen sur papyrus'. *Revue biblique*, 61: 161–81.

STEELE, J. M., and STEPHENSON, F. R. (1997). 'Lunar Eclipse Times Predicted by the Babylonians'. *JHA* 28: 119–31.

STEPHENSON, F. R. (1997). *Historical Eclipses and Earth's Rotation*. Cambridge.

—— and MORRISON, L. V. (1995). 'Long-Term Fluctuations in the Earth's rotation: 700 BC to AD 1990'. *Philosophical Transactions of the Royal Society of London*, 351A: 165–202.

STERN, E., *et al.* (1993). *The New Encyclopedia of Archaeological Excavations in the Holy Land*, 4 vols. Jerusalem.

STERN, M. (1974–84). *Greek and Latin Authors on Jews and Judaism*, 3 vols. Jerusalem.

STERN, S. (1994*a*). 'The Second Day of Yom Tov in Talmudic and Geonic Literature'. *Proceedings of the Eleventh World Congress of Jewish Studies* (1993), Jerusalem, vol. C.1, 49–55.

—— (1994*b*). 'Attribution and Authorship in the Babylonian Talmud'. *JJS* 45: 28–51.

—— (1994*c*). *Jewish Identity in Early Rabbinic Writings*. Leiden.

—— (1995). 'The Concept of Authorship in the Babylonian Talmud'. *JJS* 46: 183–95.

—— (1996). 'Fictitious Calendars: Early Rabbinic Notions of Time, Astronomy, and Reality'. *JQR* 87: 103–29.

—— (1997). 'The Origins of the Jewish Calendar'. *Le'ela*, 44: 2–5.

—— (1999). מצבות חדשות מצוער (אוסף מוסיוף). *Tarbiz*, 68: 177–85.

—— (2000*a*). 'The Babylonian Calendar at Elephantine'. *ZPE* 130: 159–71.

—— (2000*b*). 'Qumran Calendars: Theory and Practice', in T. Lim *et al.* (eds.), *The Dead Sea Scrolls in their Historical Context*, Edinburgh, 179–86.

STONE, M. (1988). 'Enoch, Aramaic Levi and Sectarian Origins'. *JSJ* 19: 159–70.

STRACK, H. L., and STEMBERGER, G. (1991). *Introduction to the Talmud and Midrash*. Edinburgh.

STROBEL, A. (1984). *Texte zur Geschichte des frühchristlichen Osterkalenders*. Münster.

SUKENIK, E. L. (1945). מצבות יהודיות מצוער. *Qedem*, 2: 83–8.

SUSSMAN, Y. (1990). ושוב לירושלמי נזיקין, in id. and D. Rosenthal, מחקרי תלמוד, i. Jerusalem, 55–133.

SWETE, H. B. (1899). *The Old Testament in Greek according to the Septuagint*, iii, 2nd edn. Cambridge.

TABORY, J. (1995). מועדי ישראל בתקופת המשנה והתלמוד. Jerusalem.

TALMON, S. (1951). 'Yom Hakippurim in the Habakkuk Scroll'. *Biblica*, 32: 549–63 (repr. Talmon 1989: 186–99).

—— (1958). 'The Calendar of the Covenanters of the Judean Desert', in C. Rabin and Y. Yadin (eds.), *Aspects of the Dead Sea Scrolls* (Scripta Hierosolymitana, 4): 162–99 (repr. Talmon 1989: 147–85).

—— (1986). *King, Cult and Calendar in Ancient Israel*. Jerusalem.

—— (1989). *The World of Qumran from Within*. Jerusalem and Leiden.

—— and KNOHL, I. (1995). 'A Calendrical Scroll from a Qumran Cave: Mismarot Ba, 4Q321', in D. P. Wright, D. N. Freedman, and A. Hurvitz (eds.), *Pomegranates and Golden Bells: Studies in Honor of Jacob Milgrom*. Winona Lake, IN, 267–301.

TELFER, W. (1943). 'The Codex Verona LX (58)'. *Harvard Theological Review*, 36: 169–246.

THORNTON, T. C. G. (1989a). 'Problematic Passovers—Difficulties for Diaspora Jews and Early Christians in Determining Passover Dates during the First Three Centuries AD'. *Papers Presented to the Tenth International Conference on Patristic Studies, Held in Oxford, 1987*, ed. E. A. Livingstone (*Studia Patristica*, 20). Leuven, 402–8.

—— (1989b). 'Jewish New Moon Festivals, Galatians 4:3–11 and Colossians 2:16'. *Journal of Theological Studies*, NS 40: 97–100.

TOBI, Y. (1981). המחלוקת על מחזור רמ'ז בתימן, in S. Morag and I. Ben-Ami (eds.), *Studies in Geniza and Sepharadi Heritage: Volume in Honour of S. D. Goitein*. Jerusalem: 193–228.

TOOMER, G. J. (1984). *Ptolemy's Almagest*. London.

—— (1988). 'Hipparchus and Babylonian Astronomy', in Leichty *et al.* (1988): 353–62.

TURNER, C. H. (1913). *Ecclesiae Occidentalis Monumenta Juris Antiquissima*, ii/2. Oxford.

—— (1939) *Ecclesiae Occidentalis Monumenta Juris Antiquissima*, i. Oxford.

VANDERKAM, J. C. (1981). '2 Maccabees, 6,7A, and Calendrical Change in Jerusalem'. *JSJ* 12: 52–74.

—— (1992). 'The Jubilees Fragments from Qumran Cave 4', in J. Trebolle Barrera and L. Vegas Montaner (eds.), *The Madrid Qumran Congress* (STDJ 11), 2 vols. Leiden, ii. 642–3.

VAUX, R. de (1950). 'A propos des manuscrits de la mer Morte'. *Revue biblique*, 57: 417–29.

VERMES, G. (1994). *The Dead Sea Scrolls in English*, 4th edn. London.

WACHOLDER, B. Z. (1973). 'The Calendar of Sabbatical Cycles during the Second Temple and the Early Rabbinic Period'. *HUCA* 44: 153–96.

—— (1983a). *The Dawn of Qumran*, Cincinnati.

—— (1983b). 'The Calendar of Sabbath Years during the Second Temple Era: A Response'. *HUCA* 54: 123–33.

—— and WACHOLDER, S. (1995). 'Patterns of Biblical Dates and Qumran's Calendar: The Fallacy of Jaubert's Hypothesis'. *HUCA* 66: 1–40.

—— and WEISBERG, D. B. (1971). 'Visibility of the New Moon in Cuneiform and Rabbinic Sources'. *HUCA* 42: 227–42.

WASSERSTEIN, A. (1989). 'A Marriage Contract from the Province of Arabia Nova: Notes on Papyrus P. Yadin 18'. *JQR* 80: 93–130.

—— (1991/2). 'Calendaric Implications of a Fourth-Century Jewish Inscription from Sicily'. *SCI* 11: 162–5.

WATT, W. MONTGOMERY, and McDONALD, M. V. (1988). *The History of Al-Tabari*, vi. Albany, NY.

WEISS, M. (1995). ניסן שיצאו בו ישראל ממצרים, in Z. A. Steinfeld (ed.), *Bar-Ilan Annual*, 26–7. Ramat-Gan, 185–201.

WELLES, C. B., FINK, R. O., and GILLIAM, J. F. (1959). *The Excavations at Dura-Europus, Final Report V, Part I: The Parchments and Papyri*. New Haven.

WELLESLEY, K. (1967). 'The *Dies Imperii* of Tiberius'. *JRS* 57: 23–30.

WERTHEIMER, S. A., and WERTHEIMER, A. J. (1953). בתי מדרשות, 2nd edn., 2 vols. Jerusalem.

WIESENBERG, E. (1961). Appendix to S. Gandz and H. Klein, *The Code of Maimonides, Book 3: The Book of Seasons*. New Haven, 557–602.

—— (1962). 'Elements of a Lunar Theory in the Mishna, Rosh Hashana 2:6, and the Talmudic Complements Thereto'. *HUCA* 33: 153–96.

WILKEN, R. (1983). *John Chrysostom and the Jews*. Berkeley and Los Angeles.

WILLIAMS, F. (1994). *The Panarion of Epiphanius of Salamis, Books II and III*. Leiden.

WINKELMANN, F. *Leben des Kaisers Konstantin* (Die griechischen christlichen Schrifsteller der ersten drei Jahrhunderte; rev. edn., Berlin (DDR), 1975).

WISE, M. O. (1994*a*). 'Second Thoughts on *duq* and the Qumran Synchronistic Calendars', in J. C. Reeves and J. Kampen (eds.), *Pursuing the Text (Journal for the Study of the Old Testament*, Supplement 184). Sheffield, 98–120.

—— (1994*b*). *Thunder in Gemini (Journal for the Study of the Pseudepigrapha Testament*, Supplement Series, 15). Sheffield.

WORP, K. A. (1991). 'Remarks on Weekdays in Late Antiquity Occurring in Documentary Sources'. *Tyche*, 6: 221–30.

WRIGHT, W. C. (1949–54). *The Works of the Emperor Julian*, 3 vols. (Loeb Classical Library). London.

YADIN, Y. (1962). 'Expedition to the Judaean Desert, 1961: Expedition D—The Cave of the Letters'. *IEJ* 12: 227–57.

—— (1965). *The Ben Sira Scroll from Masada*. Jerusalem.

—— (1983). *The Temple Scroll*, 4 vols. Jerusalem.

—— (1989). *The Documents from the Bar-Kokhba Period in the Cave of Letters: Greek Papyri*, ed. N. Lewis. Jerusalem.

YARDENI, A. (1990). 'New Jewish Aramaic Ostraka'. *IEJ* 40: 130–52.

YUDLOV, Y., and HAVLIN, S. (eds.) (1992). תורתן של גאונים, 7 vols. Jerusalem.

ZELZER, M. (1978), 'Zum Osterbrief des heiligen Ambrosius und zur römischen Osterfestberechnung des 4. Jahrhunderts', *Wiener Studien*, NF 52: 187–204.

—— (1982). *Sancti Ambrosi opera*, x (Corpus Scriptorum Ecclesiasticorum Latinorum, 82). Vienna.

ZERNOV, N. (1933). 'Eusebius and the Paschal Controversy at the End of the Second Century'. *Church Quarterly Review*, 116: 24–41.

ZUCKERMANN, B. (1866). *A Treatise on the Sabbatical Cycle and the Jubilee*, transl. A. Loewy. London.

Index